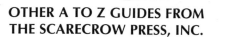
OTHER A TO Z GUIDES FROM
THE SCARECROW PRESS, INC.

1. *The A to Z of Buddhism* by Charles S. Prebish, 2001.
2. *The A to Z of Catholicism* by William J. Collinge, 2001.
3. *The A to Z of Hinduism* by Bruce M. Sullivan, 2001.
4. *The A to Z of Islam* by Ludwig W. Adamec, 2002.
5. *The A to Z of Slavery & Abolition* by Martin A. Klein, 2002.
6. *Terrorism: Assassins to Zealots* by Sean Kendall Anderson and Stephen Sloan, 2003.
7. *The A to Z of the Korean War* by Paul M. Edwards, 2005.
8. *The A to Z of the Cold War* by Joseph Smith and Simon Davis, 2005.
9. *The A to Z of the Vietnam War* by Edwin E. Moise, 2005.
10. *The A to Z of Science Fiction Literature* by Brian Stableford, 2005.
11. *The A to Z of the Holocaust* by Jack R. Fischel, 2005.
12. *The A to Z of Washington, D.C.* by Robert Benedetto, Jane Donovan, and Kathleen DuVall, 2005.
13. *The A to Z of Taoism* by Julian F. Pas, 2006.
14. *The A to Z of the Renaissance* by Charles G. Nauert, 2006.
15. *The A to Z of Shinto* by Stuart D. B. Picken, 2006.
16. *The A to Z of Byzantium* by John H. Rosser, 2006.
17. *The A to Z of the Civil War* by Terry L. Jones, 2006.
18. *The A to Z of the Friends (Quakers)* by Margery Post Abbott, Mary Ellen Chijioke, Pink Dandelion, and John William Oliver Jr., 2006
19. *The A to Z of Feminism* by Janet K. Boles and Diane Long Hoeveler, 2006.
20. *The A to Z of New Religious Movements* by George D. Chryssides, 2006.
21. *The A to Z of Multinational Peacekeeping* by Terry M. Mays, 2006.
22. *The A to Z of Lutheranism* by Günther Gassmann with Duane H. Larson and Mark W. Oldenburg, 2007.
23. *The A to Z of the French Revolution* by Paul R. Hanson, 2007.
24. *The A to Z of the Persian Gulf War 1990–1991* by Clayton R. Newell, 2007.
25. *The A to Z of Revolutionary America* by Terry M. Mays, 2007.
26. *The A to Z of the Olympic Movement* by Bill Mallon with Ian Buchanan, 2007.

The A to Z
of the Shakers

Stephen J. Paterwic

The A to Z Guide Series, No. 106

The Scarecrow Press, Inc.
Lanham • Toronto • Plymouth, UK
2009

Published by Scarecrow Press, Inc.
A wholly owned subsidiary of
The Rowman & Littlefield Publishing Group, Inc.
4501 Forbes Boulevard, Suite 200, Lanham, Maryland 20706
http://www.scarecrowpress.com

Estover Road, Plymouth PL6 7PY, United Kingdom

British Library Cataloguing in Publication Information Available

Library of Congress Cataloging-in-Publication Data

The hardback version of this book was cataloged by the Library of Congress as
follows:

Paterwic, Stephen.
  Historical dictionary of the Shakers / Stephen J. Paterwic.
    p. cm. — (Historical dictionaries of religions, philosophies, and religions ;
    no. 87)
  Includes bibliographical references.
    1. Shakers—History—Dictionaries. I. Title.
  BX9765.P38 2008
  289'.803—dc22   2008009185

  ISBN 978-0-8108-6893-9 (pbk. : alk. paper)
  ISBN 978-0-8108-7056-7 (ebook)

Printed in the United States of America

To the Shakers of the future. . . .
Mother's beautiful song will always be sung.

Contents

Editor's Foreword

With no more than 4,500 members at any one time, the Shakers are definitely the smallest group included in this series on religions, philosophies, and movements. Yet small causes can have disproportionately large effects, and that is certainly the case with the Shakers. Although very few remain, they are still known far and wide. Their position on many important issues—including communitarian lifestyle, communistic economy, self-reliance, the sanctity of labor, and gender relations—are worthy of closer study. Relatively few people have converted entirely to the Shaker worldview over the religion's roughly 235-year history in America, but the number who have been partially convinced or at least influenced by Shakerism is legion.

The A to Z of the Shakers describes the religion's beliefs and actions with entries that examine the lives of significant members; its history, structure, and organization; leadership and activities; ethical standards; and theology. Particularly notable are the synopses of all Shaker communities. The introduction and chronology provide an overview, which traces early hopes followed by painful retrenchment, showing how Shakerism functioned and what it contributed to its own members and others—finally explaining why it ultimately failed and has almost disappeared. A comprehensive bibliography provides a list of additional sources and locations of museums.

This completely new edition was written by Stephen J. Paterwic, who was drawn to Shakerism while still young and has spent decades learning about the religion, spending considerable time at various communities and getting to know a large number of Shakers. He has become one of their foremost authorities and has been passing his knowledge along to others. Mr. Paterwic has participated in Shaker seminars, forums, and major conferences, including one, at which he was the keynote speaker, to commemorate the Mount Lebanon Peace Convention. He has also been writing articles for the major specialized journals, including *The Shaker Quarterly*, *World of Shaker*, and *Shakers World*. This historical dictionary is therefore the result of a long and mutually beneficial relationship, one that will be both informative and of interest to others.

Jon Woronoff
Series Editor

Endorsement

We as a people have often been misunderstood, due in no small part to a lack of the "world's" understanding of our beliefs, language, and terminology. We feel that this dictionary accurately answers those many questions and queries as well as sets straight many erroneous statements and ideas that proliferate even today.

We pray that in reading this book you will truly gain a better understanding of our history, life, and beliefs. Therefore we are delighted to offer our endorsement to this important work and book.

Peace and blessings,
The Sabbathday Lake Shakers

Preface

My paternal grandfather bought his small farm in Somers, Connecticut, in 1919. This farm had been an "out family" of the Enfield, Connecticut, Shakers, and it was located on the eastern edge of the former Shaker property, just over the town/county line in Somers. That is why, though we were not Shakers, I always knew of them. My father would tell stories he had heard of the Shakers whenever we passed through their former community. This slight acquaintance, however, changed abruptly in March 1967, when I read an article on them that appeared in *Life* magazine. Since that day, I have never been able to get the Shakers out of my mind, and my desire to learn more about them has never stopped increasing.

My first contact with actual Shakers was in 1969 when I visited Canterbury. I had written Eldress Marguerite Frost that winter, and her reply encouraged me to drive up to Canterbury as soon as I was able. I will never forget the hours we spent in conversation, and I still envision the Shakers as a result of her guidance. One of the very first things she said to me, for example, was that one should always begin any study of the Shakers by reading *Shakerism: Its Meaning and Message*.

Although I had written to the Sabbathday Lake Shakers, I did not visit them until 1973. The moment I entered the Boys' Shop, which is the center for visitors, Brother Theodore "Ted" Johnson greeted me, and a lifelong friendship was begun. Brother Ted was an intelligent, sensitive, and insightful Shaker. He could take a detailed piece of Shaker history and totally define it in a few, well-chosen sentences. His vast depth of knowledge was incredible; I never saw him at a loss for words. My Shaker studies, started by Eldress Marguerite, were nurtured by Brother Ted. As I visited Sabbathday Lake, I also got to know Sister Mildred Barker and Sister Frances Carr. They freely shared their faith, and in Sister Frances I found my mother in Zion. After Brother Arnold Hadd joined the community in 1978, I had another friend. Not only could I share my love of the Shakers with him, but he and I both grew up in Springfield, Massachusetts. Though we did not know each other then, we have this common bond. He remains the one person I can really "talk Shaker to." Everything I have accomplished in my many decades of Shaker research I owe to the firm foundation I received from those who have lived the life.

From the encouragement of my father to my deep friendship with the Shakers of today, my life has been blessed by the gospel. The testimony that Mother Ann opened so many years ago in Manchester, England, is as relevant a response to living the Christlife as it ever was. No matter what one's religious beliefs may be, anyone reading this dictionary with a desire to understand Shakerism will be caught up in the work of the Shakers.

Chronology

1736 Ann Lee is born in Manchester, England.

1747 The Shakers as a distinct church begins.

1758 Ann Lee becomes an active member of the Wardley society, a group of religious enthusiasts led by James and Jane Wardley, former Quakers. Members of the Lee family are also part of this group; the name *shaking Quakers* or *Shakers* is used by a reporter from the *Manchester Mercury* to designate the Wardley society. The Shakers simply called themselves "The Church." The term Shaker hearkens back to the founders of the Quakers who, like the Shakers, were seized by the Spirit. Under the influence of the Holy Spirit they would whirl, dance, sing in unknown tongues, and prophesy.

1762 Ann Lee marries Abraham Standerin (Stanley) at Christ Church, Manchester.

1772–1773 Ann Lee and her companions are arrested on various occasions. It is during this time that she becomes known as Mother Ann, the leader of the society.

1774 Inspired by a vision, Ann Lee leaves England for America. Mother Ann, Abraham Stanley, William Lee, James Whittaker, John Hocknell, James Shepherd, James Partington, Mary Partington, and Nancy Lee depart from Liverpool on the *Mariah*. They land in New York City on 6 August 1774.

1776 The Shakers buy a tract of land outside of Albany, New York, as their permanent home. This place is called Niskeyuna.

1778 Eleanor Vedder becomes the first American convert.

1779 A large New Light Revival occurs at New Lebanon, New York.

1780 The Shaker gospel is opened to the world.

1781 Ann Lee is jailed from July to December.

1781–1783 Mother Ann and other Shaker leaders embark on a missionary tour throughout New York, Massachusetts, Rhode Island, and Connecticut.

1784 Father William Lee and Mother Ann die at Niskeyuna. Father James Whitaker assumes the leadership of the church.

1785–1799 The Shaker testimony is closed while the church is gathered into "gospel order."

1787 Father James Whittaker dies, and Father Joseph Meacham assumes the lead of the church. He establishes New Lebanon as the "center of union," or headquarters of the church. He begins to formally gather the believers into community.

1790 The first Shaker publication, *A Concise Statement*, written by Father Joseph Meacham, is published.

1790–1794 New Lebanon is fully established and leaders are sent out to gather Shakers in other locations. The original Shaker communities were gathered in this order: Watervliet/Niskeyuna, New York (1788); Hancock, Massachusetts (1790), and from there Enfield, Connecticut, and Tyringham, Massachusetts (1792); Harvard, Massachusetts (1791), and from there Shirley, Massachusetts (1793); Canterbury, New Hampshire (1792), and from there Enfield, New Hampshire (1793); and Alfred, Maine (1793), and from there Sabbathday Lake/New Gloucester, Maine (1794).

1796 Father Joseph Meacham dies. Mother Lucy Wright succeeds him as head of the church.

1799 A "Gathering Order" is established at New Lebanon and the Shaker Gospel is formally opened to the world once again.

1800 There are about 1,375 Shakers living in community.

1805 Mother Lucy sends John Meacham, Issacher Bates, and Benjamin Seth Youngs as missionaries to Ohio and Kentucky. "Western" Shakerism develops from this effort.

1806–1824 Seven Shaker communities are founded in Ohio, Kentucky, and Indiana: Union Village, Ohio (1805); Pleasant Hill, Kentucky (1805); Watervliet, Ohio (1806); West Union, Indiana (1807); South Union, Kentucky (1807); North Union, Ohio (1822); and White Water, Ohio (1822).

1808 The first major work on Shaker theology, *The Testimony of Christ's Second Appearing Containing a General Statement of All Things Pertaining to the Faith and Practice of the Church of God in This Latter-day*, is published by the Shakers.

1813 *Millennial Praises* is published.

1816 Rufus Bishop and Seth Y. Wells edit *Testimonies of the Life, Character, Revelations and Doctrines of Our Ever Blessed Mother Ann Lee, and the Elders with Her; through whom the Word of Eternal Life was Opened in this Day of Christ's Second Appearing: Collected from Living Witnesses, by Order of the Ministry, in Union with the Church. . . .*

1818 John Dunlavy publishes the *Manifesto, or A Declaration of the Doctrines and Practice of the Church of Christ*.

1819 There are about 3,500 Shakers.

1821 Mother Lucy Wright dies. She appoints Elder Ebenezer Bishop, Elder Rufus Bishop, Eldress Ruth Landon, and Eldress Asenath Clark to lead the church; The *Millennial Laws* are codified, expanded, and put into writing and circulated throughout the Shaker communities.

1823 Calvin Green and Seth Y. Wells publish *A Summary View of the Millennial Church, or United Society of Believers, Commonly Called Shakers. Comprising the Rise, Progress and Practical Order of Society, Together with General Principles of Their Faith and Testimony*.

1824 A large number of children are gathered into Shaker communities—a practice carried on through the 20th century.

1824 The second meetinghouse at New Lebanon is constructed.

1826 A Shaker community is gathered at Sodus, New York. In 1836, this society moved to Groveland, New York. This was the last major Shaker society formed.

1830 The Shaker societies at Alfred and New Gloucester, Maine, are placed under the New Hampshire Ministry. The Maine Ministry was not restored until 1859 as an independent body.

1830s Large numbers of young people leave the Shaker communities.

1837 Era of Manifestations, also known as the Era of Mother's Work, begins.

1840s Shakers reach their peak population of fewer than 4,500.

1842 Shaker communities receive spiritual names, and outdoor worship areas called feast grounds are laid out; Philemon Stewart of New Lebanon receives by inspiration *A Holy, Sacred and Divine Roll and Book; From the Lord God of Heaven, to the Inhabitants of Earth.* . . .

1845 The *Millennial Laws* are published. These orders, including those from 1821, 1860, and 1887, were for internal circulation exclusively.

1844–1846 Hundreds of Adventists join the Shakers.

1849 Paulina Bates of Watervliet receives by inspiration *The Divine Book of Holy and Eternal Wisdom, Revealing the Word of God; Out of Whose Mouth Goeth a Sharp Sword.*

1850s The Shaker seed industry reaches its peak.

1859 Rebecca Jackson holds meetings in Philadelphia and gathers a small community of African Americans and others.

1860 *Rules and Orders for the Church of Christ's Second Appearing/Established by the Ministry and Elders of the Church* is published.

1861 New Lebanon becomes Mount Lebanon when the government establishes a post office at the Shaker village there.

1861–1865 The Civil War severely disrupts Shaker economic life.

1870 The Ministry proposes that a special time be set aside to pray for more converts to Shakerism.

1870s The Shakers increase their missionary activities but in totally different venues from the past. They align with the Spiritualist movement and give public performances of their song and worship as well as sermons.

1871   A Shaker newspaper is founded at Watervliet, New York; Elder Frederick Evans of the Gathering Order of Mount Lebanon travels to England on a missionary tour.

1874   The Shakers number about 2,400.

1875   A fire destroys eight buildings at the First Order of the Church at Mount Lebanon; Tyringham closes—the first long-lived society to dissolve due to lack of membership.

1887   *Orders for the Church of Christ's Second Appearing: Established by the Ministry and Elders of the Church* is published.

1890   Elder Giles Avery, de facto head of Shakerism, dies. There had not been a real leader of Shakerism since 1821.

1892   Elder Frederick Evans, the most well-known Shaker of his age, dies.

1896   A Shaker society is founded at Narcoossee, Osceola County, Florida.

1898   Union Village, Ohio, Shakers attempt to establish a society at White Oak, Georgia.

1899   The Shaker newspaper ceases publication.

1900   The Shakers number about 800.

1904   Eldress Anna White and Sister Leila Taylor of the North Family of Mount Lebanon publish *Shakerism: Its Meaning and Message*, the last major Shaker history written by Shakers.

1905   The North Family of Mount Lebanon Shakers holds a national peace conference; Elder Henry Blinn of Canterbury, Elder John Whiteley of Shirley, and Elder Louis Basting of Hancock die. Elder Henry was the last male member of the New Hampshire Ministry and Elder John and Elder Louis were the last elders of their communities.

1916   White Water Shaker village, the last Shaker community in Ohio, closes.

1922   South Union, the last Shaker village in Kentucky, closes.

1925   The Shakers number about 250.

1927 The Maine Ministry, the last regional bishopric, is dissolved.

1929 The option of turning over to lawyers the managing of Shaker affairs is introduced. No community took up the option at first.

1930 The Church Family at Mount Lebanon is sold.

1939 Elder Irving Greenwood, the last male member of the Ministry, dies at Canterbury.

1947 Mount Lebanon, the last society in New York, closes. Leadership officially resides at Hancock, Massachusetts, under Eldress Frances Hall.

1950 The Shakers number 45. Three communities remain: Hancock, Massachusetts; Canterbury, New Hampshire; and Sabbathday Lake, Maine.

1957 After the death of Eldress Frances Hall, the Ministry is dissolved by the sole survivor of the Ministry, Eldress Emma King of Canterbury. A few months later she reconstitutes a Ministry that is Canterbury-based.

1959 Hancock, the last Shaker society in Massachusetts, closes. The Shaker Trust Fund is set up.

1960 Theodore Johnson comes to live at Sabbathday Lake.

1961 The Sabbathday Lake Shakers begin the publication of *The Shaker Quarterly*.

1963 Eldress Emma King, speaking for the reconstituted Ministry in a pastoral letter, declines to accept new members at Canterbury. She gives the Sabbathday Lake Shakers the freedom to accept new members.

1963 The meetinghouse is reopened at Sabbathday Lake and public meeting is held once again.

1971 The herb industry is revitalized at Sabbathday Lake.

1974 The bicentennial of the arrival of the Shakers in America is celebrated by a conference and worship service at Sabbathday Lake. An outdoor service conducted by non-Shakers is held at Canterbury.

1986   Brother Theodore Johnson dies suddenly at Sabbathday Lake.

1988   Eldress Gertrude Soule dies at Canterbury, and the Reconstituted Ministry is dissolved because Eldress Bertha Lindsay does not name a successor.

1990   Sister R. Mildred Barker, spiritual leader of the Sabbathday Lake Shakers since 1950, dies.

1992   Sister Ethel Hudson, the last Canterbury Shaker, dies.

2000   The Shakers at Sabbathday Lake number nine: four brothers and five sisters.

2007   Shakers at Sabbathday Lake obtain conservation and preservation easements to ensure that their lands will always remain open space.

Introduction

The Shakers, like many religious seekers throughout the ages, honor the revelation of God but cannot be bound up in an unchanging set of dogmas or creeds. Freeing themselves from domination by the state religion, Mother Ann Lee and her first followers in mid-18th-century England labored to encounter the godhead directly. They were blessed by spiritual gifts that showed them a way to live the heavenly life on Earth. The result of their efforts was the fashioning of a celibate communal life called the Christlife, wherein a person, after confessing all sin, through the indwelling of the Holy Spirit, can travel the path of regeneration into ever-increasing holiness. Pacifism, equality of the sexes, and withdrawal from the world are some of the ways the faith was put into practice.

Even at its largest, however, Shakerism claimed only about 4,500 members. From their perspective, then, especially as they have diminished, the Shakers have come to terms with the fact that they are not in fact "The Church" but only a part of it. They firmly believe that out of every generation a few souls are called to live a consecrated life. Moreover, it is the duty of the Shakers, no matter how few, to labor for the whole world. In this context, the Shakers can be seen as exemplars or signs for the larger Church of a true and deep spiritual unit not obscured by anything that diminishes growth in Christ. These hindrances, to name but a few, include preoccupation with the accumulation of personal wealth, the exclusion of women, love solely defined by sexual actions, reverence for past customs for their own sake, natural family ties, sinful habits, violence as a means to solve problems, and a preoccupation with anything not of the Spirit. Few can live this ideal, but all can see the efforts of the Shakers and try to glimpse the hand of the divine and know it is possible to live the Christlife on Earth. This is why the Shakers have been called the Millennial Church. They do not seek a kingdom to come. For them the kingdom has already been revealed, and they are living it.

When life in England became difficult, Mother Ann and her companions came to America, where the power and the confidence of the Shaker testimony touched the minds and hearts of thousands of Americans. In fewer than 30 years, Shaker societies were formed in New England, New York, Ohio, Kentucky, and Indiana. In the East, the momentum generated by the first converts was continued by their children. After 1800, however, the Shakers sought to attract families to their way of life, and for a generation their newly established Gathering Orders were full.

Still, the movement remained very small, and it never was able to attract suitable people to spread widely. The Shakers were tied to an agrarian way of life at a time when America was changing from a farming economy to one based on manufacturing. Even their industries based on the land, such as the seed business and the herb industry, could not compete with outside forces once capitalism took hold. Adaptations might have been made had the Shakers been able to maintain their population. Shaker authorities thought that adopting a large number of children without their parents might be the best way to ensure a steady number of workers and leaders. Instead of building up the societies, however, this custom weakened them since it led to instability and complacency.

As the crisis of membership became apparent after the Civil War, everything seemed to go wrong at once. Dishonest trustees, the loss of markets due to the opening up of the west, continued defections, disastrous fires, and doctrinal disputes caused the Shakers to collapse. The Ministry adopted a policy of trying to save what it could and individuals were left more and more to fashion a Shaker life of their own.

By the 20th century the survivors continued to decline, decade by decade, in spite of a number of stalwart members who did not want the way of life to end. Ironically, as the Shakers diminished, the objects made by them, especially furniture and oval boxes, became much sought after, causing one contemporary Shaker to remark that the world wants everything but the cross.

HISTORY

In 1904, Eldress Anna White in *Shakerism: Its Meaning and Message* asked the question "Why was Ann Lee so unlike all the other poor women of Manchester, her neighbors in Toad Lane?" Eldress Anna then went on to answer her own question: "Because she was called of God and obeyed the call, and thus became the Chosen, the Daughter of God . . ." (21). As Manchester industrialized and the masses began to live lives of greater degradation than ever before, there was a void of religious experience. When Ann Lee joined the small society led by James and Jane Wardley, she became caught up in a religious atmosphere in which she was free to encounter God. In ecstatic worship services marked by prophecy, she labored for a revelation of the divine. So intense were her efforts that she was granted a vision that was to be key to the source of humanity's sinfulness. She saw that the original sin was sexual intercourse and that sexual activity had no place in a godly life. Her testimony was so powerful that she became the leader of the Wardley society and was given the title Mother Ann. Her message captured the hearts of scores of followers, and Shakerism began.

It is important to realize that this does not imply that the Shakers see Mother Ann as divine. Her uniqueness was that she was the first one, in the providence of God, to receive the fullness of the Christ Spirit. In other words, what was begun by Jesus, a male, at the time of his baptism was completed in Ann Lee, a female. Instead of looking for a spectacular, cataclysmic end of the world, Christ entered into the world in Mother Ann's acceptance of the divine call. This second coming, moreover, is available to anyone who wants to live the life that Mother Ann taught. Thus the second coming is in the Shaker church. The cornerstones of this life are celibacy, confession, and community.

In addition to these radical views, so different from the accepted religious practices of the day, the small group that followed Mother's counsel expressed themselves in frenzied dance as part of their worship. This laboring for the gift of God made them even more suspect, and they were violently persecuted. The mob violence and the apparent indifference of officials to stop it caused Mother, guided by a vision, to decide to come to America in 1774.

Eventually land was purchased near Albany by member John Hocknell, and the Shakers prepared to welcome new converts who, Mother assured them, would come like doves. In 1780, a few people who had participated in the New Light "stir" in New Lebanon, New York, went to see Mother and her companions. They became Shakers as did those who had led the revival. Most prominent among these was Joseph

Meacham, who would become the first American to head the Shaker church. When these new converts returned to their homes, the result was the planting of pockets of Shakerism in New York and New England. To keep the faith alive, Mother and other Shaker leaders went on three major missionary tours. The violence directed against them no doubt shortened their lives, and both Mother Ann and her brother, Father William Lee, died in 1784. Under Father James Whittaker, her successor, Shakerism adjusted itself to Mother's death, and by the time Father Joseph Meacham became the leader in 1787, Shakers were ready to be gathered into permanent communities. Father Joseph's task was to gather the scattered Shakers, still living in individual families, into societies based on gospel order. By 1794, 10 years after Mother's death, 11 communities had been gathered in this way. In 1805, 10 years after this, Mother Lucy Wright, Father Joseph's successor, sent missionaries to Kentucky, Ohio, and Indiana. The result was six additional societies.

These missionary efforts greatly increased the number of Shakers. In 1803 there were about 1,375 believers. In 1810, the communities in the West alone numbered 1,280, while the societies in the East continued to grow as well. By 1823, two years after Mother Lucy's death, there were about 4,200 Shakers in all. In 1826, the last long-lived Shaker community was gathered at Sodus (later moved to Groveland), New York. By all accounts, Shakerism seemed to be moving forward. Industries, including the selling of seeds and herbs, were increasing each year. Every community had a number of mills for grain, lumber, and wool carding. Home farms and orchards produced an abundance of food products, and large herds of cows and cattle provided dairy products and meat to the communities.

As the believers settled down in the context of this prosperity, they followed the lead of many other Americans. The accumulation of material wealth and other distractions caused some to be less enthusiastic for spiritual matters. Indeed, it was proving difficult to keep up intense spiritual activity as time passed. Though the largest sources of converts had once been from religious revivals, Shaker missionary efforts seemed to slacken off in this area. A new policy of taking in as many children as possible, with the hope that they would grow up to be Shakers, began after Mother Lucy's death in 1821. Mother Lucy had strongly advised against taking in children without at least one parent. In time, the wisdom of this counsel would be proved many times over. As the 1830s progressed, the first wave of these children had grown to maturity and started leaving in large numbers. Those who had been teenagers when the communities in the East were gathered were now approaching 60 years of age. Though there was still a sufficient number of young and middle-aged members, many insightful Shakers wondered what the future would hold if the young continued to leave and indifference to religion continued to increase.

Visions and dreams had remained a part of Shaker life since the earliest years, and this guided a few to have confidence that Mother was still with them, but it was not until 1837, when many young women and girls started to receive messages from the Spirit world, that Shakerism seemed to revive. This time has been called the Era of Manifestations or the Era of Mother's Work. What began at the Watervliet, New York, society spread rapidly to all other Shaker communities. Religious fervor ran high as scores of men and women became instruments. They described visions and dreams that inspired songs, dances, art, and new rules. Each society was given a spiritual name and set up outdoor worship areas known as feast grounds. The Millennial Laws of 1845 were published, very different in tone and substance from the previous laws of 1821. They sought to regulate Shaker life into fairly narrow terms. As one modern Shaker, Brother Ted Johnson, remarked, these were a rear-guard effort that failed to produce a lasting result. Just as the Era of Manifestation started to wane, it was extended by the arrival of many Adventists into the Shaker communities after the great disappointments of 1845 and 1846.

In so many ways, the 1850s is the pivotal decade in the history of the Shakers. By then, the societies were so overloaded with preadults that it was not uncommon to have them make up over one-third of the membership. One society was half composed of individuals under 21 years of age. That decade also saw the start of a long series of financial scandals caused by dishonest or incompetent trustees. The traditional, male-dominated industries peaked at that time as well. In 1861, a new, much-modified set of Rules and Orders were published to guide Shaker life, but the long years of the Civil War disrupted trade routes and changed the tenor of society. It was clear to all that Shakerism was in crisis. The departure of the young, the death of the old stalwarts, the failure to attract sufficient numbers of capable adult converts, and the serious financial losses all contributed to a malaise reflected in "dead" worship services and great anxiety about the future.

For the handful of the young that decided to stay faithful and the many older members that remained, it became a question of finding a way to live the life in a fashion that had individual meaning in spite of a very apparent decline. During the 1870s organ music and new harmonies were introduced in worship while the exercises or dances faded out. Public meetings, a new Shaker newspaper, and increased missionary efforts were aimed to appeal to a gentle and genteel audience. Most of the Shakers were directing efforts to hold on to their societies. A few members, most notably those who lived at the North Family at Mount Lebanon, became very interested in reform movements. Well into the 20th century a great volume of literature was published that reflected a preoccupation with these various movements, including pacifism, women's rights, land redistribution, and diet and clothing reforms.

Nothing the Shakers did, however, was able to stop the erosion of membership. Every decade from the 1870s until the 1950s saw at least one Shaker community close, though the greatest number was dissolved between 1900 and 1922. By a combination of circumstances, Canterbury and Sabbathday Lake had managed to survive, although it seemed by 1950 that they too would hardly last out the century.

In the 1950s, a young man named Theodore E. Johnson, a Harvard graduate and Fulbright Scholar, read Shaker theology and decided to investigate the community. Living in Massachusetts, he went to Hancock where he was promptly directed to Sabbathday Lake. His arrival there came at a propitious time. More than half the community was composed of former Alfred Shakers. These sisters had been raised under the tutelage of Eldress Harriett Coolbroth. She instilled in them a deep love of the Shaker religion. When Alfred consolidated into Sabbathday Lake in 1931, the newcomers obediently followed the lead of their new home. At the same time, in spite of the leadership, they clung to many of the old ways and retained their faith. When Ted Johnson visited, he ignited a spark that had always been there. Gradually, working in cooperation with some of the sisters, most notably Sister R. Mildred Barker of Alfred and Sister Frances Carr of Sabbathday Lake (and also the youngest Shaker), Ted help revive the Shaker religion. These efforts really began after he joined the community in May 1960. The following year, the *Shaker Quarterly* was begun. It was the first Shaker publication since the *Manifesto* ceased in 1899. In 1963, Public Meeting was reintroduced and the Meeting House was used again for services. In addition, Brother Ted supervised the opening of a new herb industry.

Brother Ted was not the only person trying the life at that time. There seemed to be an awakening of the spirit. For the first time in decades, adult men and women were applying for membership at Sabbathday Lake and at Canterbury. However, Eldress Emma King of the Ministry and also eldress of the Church Family at Canterbury did not feel that adult converts made good Shakers. In a lengthy pastoral letter written in 1963, she cautioned the Sabbathday Lake Shakers against taking in such converts, but allowed them freedom to decide for themselves. In truth there was little she could have done otherwise since each Shaker family has its own covenant patterned after the same Church Order covenant. Article II, Section 4 of this covenant states that membership must be kept open. Any amendments made to the Church Order covenant would have to be read and approved by the entire covenanted membership. Shaker leadership, as the 20th century progressed, had become used to acting independently of the community, a group made up almost entirely of women who had grown up as Shakers from childhood and were well ingrained to be obedient no matter what the consequences. The Canterbury Shakers, under Eldress Emma and those who assumed the leadership after her, took no more members, and the last Shaker there died in 1992. At Sabbathday Lake children continued to be taken in through the 1950s and adults have always been given opportunities for membership. It is the only place today where the Shaker life is lived and where a visitor may attend Shaker religious services.

ORGANIZATION AND LEADERSHIP

The first leaders of the Shakers were Mother Ann Lee, Father William Lee, and Father James Whittaker. Born in England, they had come to America in 1774 and, with the temporal assistance of Father John Hocknell, were able to form a small community near Albany, New York, by the summer of 1776. In the spring of 1780, hundreds of revivalists from New Lebanon, New York, and their families had been attracted to Shakerism. For them, Mother Ann, Father William, and Father James were their first parents in the gospel. Of course, they could not have been successful and the church would not have lasted if strong American leaders had not been formed and chosen to assist them. Right from the beginning, Father Joseph Meacham and Mother Lucy Wright showed excellent leadership ability and much promise for the future.

During the summer of 1784, both Mother Ann and her brother Father William died. Traditional Shaker history has it that leadership smoothly passed to Father James Whittaker, who headed the church until his untimely death in 1787. Few documents survive from the period, however, and subsequent leaders may have destroyed evidence that might have shown that the time of Father James was far from peaceful. The period after the death of Mother Ann and the prominence of New Lebanon beginning in 1787 is a forgotten time in Shaker history. It appears that Father James was not content to have Shaker leadership reside in one place or have a center of union. He moved around, and if there were one location he favored, it may have been Enfield, Connecticut, where he chose to live before his death. In fact, he may have favored David Meacham of Enfield over his brother Father Joseph Meacham of New Lebanon. Whatever the nature of the power struggle may have been, after Father James' death in 1787, Father Joseph, assisted by Mother Lucy, took over leadership. When Father Joseph died in 1796, Mother Lucy became the head of the church and maintained her prominence, in spite of opposition, until her death in 1821. By that time, the church was fully organized into gospel order, a framework that exists with modifications to the present day.

Under Father Joseph Meacham, a cadre of potential leaders was gathered to live at the Meeting House at New Lebanon starting in 1785. After Father James Whittaker died in July 1787 and Father Joseph became the head of the church, the Shakers at New Lebanon began to gather into the first Shaker community following a pattern called gospel order that had been devised by Father Joseph. The society at New Lebanon became not only the first organized community but also the model for all other Shaker villages.

Starting in 1790 and completed by 1794, the 11 earliest Shaker communities were organized. All subsequent Shaker villages would follow this same plan. From the onset, this pattern was closely akin to a biological family. Shakers were invited to leave their individual families and gather into large Shaker families under spiritual leaders called elders. These elders consisted of two men and two women. Members and their elders in a particular Shaker family lived in one or two large communal dwelling houses. Most of these were, at first, existing buildings that had been adapted for communal use. Smaller units of leaders within the family consisted of a class of deacons. These men and women had charge of daily affairs and activities. For example, there was a kitchen deaconess, an orchard deacon, a farm deacon, and a family deaconess. The latter made sure that the sisters were properly provisioned for their work such as tailoring, housekeeping, and the like. A special branch had charge of all temporal matters. These were the Office deacons and deaconesses. Later called trustees, they were organized in the same foursquare leadership configuration, two men and two women, that characterized the elders' lot. They did not live with the family, however, but resided in the Office, a building specifically set up for trade and commerce with outsiders. A Shaker family was not considered fully organized and independent until it had its own set of Office deacons and deaconesses.

A number of Shaker families in close proximity made up a society, and a society or number of societies made up a bishopric. Each bishopric had a Ministry whose job was to supervise all the families, both spiritually and temporally. The members of the Ministry, two men and two women, lived in apartments located in the upper floors of the Meeting House. In later years, most communities built a separate Ministry Shop to house the Ministry when it was in residence. Other societies built larger Meeting Houses that provided spacious apartments and workplaces for the Ministry.

The first bishopric was that of New Lebanon. The Ministry of New Lebanon was often called the Lebanon Ministry and later, as Shaker circumstances changed, the Ministry of Mount Lebanon, the Central Ministry, and finally the Parent Ministry. The Lebanon Ministry had charge over the eight Shaker families that made up the society at New Lebanon and the four Shaker families that made up the Shaker community at Watervliet, New York. In 1859, this Ministry also took over the supervision of the two families at Groveland, New York, when the Ministry there was dissolved. The Lebanon Ministry also had the overall supervision of all Shaker families everywhere. Individual Ministries from the various Shaker bishoprics were expected to visit New Lebanon annually or send detailed reports of events. The Lebanon Ministry also made frequent tours, visiting all of the Shaker villages. Until the 1850s, there were 10 Shaker bishoprics: New Lebanon, Groveland, Hancock, Harvard, Canterbury, Alfred, North Union, Union Village, South Union, and Pleasant Hill.

Ministerial vacancies were filled by the surviving members of the Ministry. In this way, the Ministry was self-perpetuating. Most often ministerial vacancies were filled by those who had been elders in one of the major families in the bishopric. When a vacancy occurred in Shaker family leadership, the Ministry of the bishopric also chose someone to fill the position. Most Shakers never attained a position of leadership; however, some youths or adult converts were recognized for their potential and were given smaller jobs such as teacher, caretaker of the children, or helper in the Office. These jobs helped prepare them for more important positions. It is important to note that when the Ministry chose a candidate for a specific job, they consulted the elders, the trustees, or any other appropriate members before making a decision and then the proposed appointment was brought before the individual family for their approval. Such community approbation was eventually lost completely during the 20th century, the unintended consequence of having a membership made up almost entirely of adults who had been brought up from childhood by adults who, in turn, had been brought up from childhood in the society. In this context, most sisters living in Shaker communities came to give unconditional obedience to leadership. This was a great departure from earlier days.

Over time, Shaker families came to be called by different names and have specific functions. The family living nearest the Meeting House was called the First or Church Family in New York and New England. In Ohio and Kentucky, this family was known as the Center Family. All other Shaker families in the East were at first known by the name of the original landowner whose farm was now a Shaker family. Starting in 1799 and completed by 1810, all of the original Shaker villages were reorganized to accommodate a new type of Shaker family not originally envisioned by Father Joseph. This was a Gathering Order, also called a Novitiate Family, into which new members would be gathered. When Gathering Orders were started, they took over existing families and villages started calling all families, including the Gathering Order, by the compass direction they lay from the Church Family. For example, the Watervliet, New York, society was made up of the Church, North, West, and South Families. The Gathering Order was at the South Family. Here adults and children would join and later be assigned to one of the other families.

COMMUNITY LIFE

Shaker families ranged in size from 20 to 150 members. As a rule, the Church or Center Family was the largest. This family in most communities had at least 100 members. This number also included many children, often called the Children's Order. Other families also had children, though not as many as the Church. In the early years, members of the Church Family were considered to be the most fervent, and in the larger societies they did not even worship with Shakers from the other families. However, whether a person lived in the Church Family, the Gathering Order, or one of the other families, all were expected to work, from the youngest to the most aged, each according to ability.

It is difficult to depict a typical Shaker family. Since societies not only ranged in size from two to eleven families, Shaker communities adapted themselves to local circumstances. For example, some families were mill families, such as the North Family at Hancock, Massachusetts. They ran grist and sawmill operations. Others were almost entirely agricultural, and some had unique industries, such as the chair factory at the South Family of New Lebanon, New York. This does not mean, though, that they did not have much in common.

All Shakers lived by a regulated horarium. In the first decades, a conch shell was used to signal important times. Later, a bell was placed in a cupola on the roof of the dwelling. Though the Shakers lived celibate lives, men and women lived together in the same large dwelling houses. Most often hallways separated the retiring rooms of the sexes, but sometimes a certain portion of the house was designated for a particular group. Double stairways obviated the need for the sexes to pass each other while going from floor to floor. Shakers lived at least two, most often three or four, to a retiring room. At the rising bell, 4:30 in the winter and 5:30 in the summer, all were expected to take care of personal needs and go out to the shops or barns to start the daily chores before the bell summoned believers to breakfast. Before every meal, each sex gathered in separate waiting rooms adjacent to a communal dining room, usually located on the lowest floor of the house. At the signal, men and women entered the dining room through separate doors and sat in designated places at separate tables. Before eating and after eating, Shakers knelt and said a silent grace. Meals were also silent. There was some free time in the evenings, but most nights had various meetings. There were singing meetings to practice songs. The exercises and dances used in worship were also practiced. Some evenings were devoted to union meetings, during which a handful of brethren and sisters would sit in rows facing each other and converse over topics of interest. At least one other evening was a worship service. This was held in the large meeting room in the dwelling. Here Shakers also worshipped in the winter when society meeting was not possible because the Meeting House was too cold. There were also large meetings to discuss matters of concern, seasonal entertainments, and guest speakers from other Shaker villages or from the world.

Occasionally whole Shaker families would walk over to visit nearby Shaker families and they would have a song fest as they massed along the street. Depending on the season, there were picnics, ride-outs, and sleigh rides. Caretakers often gave children time for berrying or swimming. Sundays, however, were reserved for worship and quiet time. In the warmer weather, public meeting was held in the morning at the Meeting House. Each Shaker had an assigned place. Of course as the 19th century progressed, Shaker daily life became less structured and visitors and trips off Shaker property became common.

Children lived under the aegis of a caretaker, often in a separate building until the age of 14, when they went to live with the adult Shakers in the dwelling. Until after the Civil War, boys went to school in the winter and girls in the summer. When not in school, children were expected to work. Much of the farm work was done by the boys. Girls assisted in cooking, housekeeping, sewing, and knitting. Boys who had an aptitude for a specific occupation were encouraged to pursue such an interest. As a result, Shaker boys developed many skills besides expertise in farming, some of them becoming, for example, blacksmiths, teamsters, woodworkers, and tailors. All children living in a Shaker society, if they did not join with a parent, were indentured by a parent or guardian to a Shaker trustee. This agreement stipulated the length of time a child was to be cared for by the Shakers. Some indentures lasted until the child was 16 or 18, but most later ones stipulated age 21. At that time, a decision had to be made to stay or leave. In reality, most preadults left whenever they no longer wanted to live in the community. Some parents and relatives also tried to get children that had been indentured. Though law enforcement officials almost always sided with the parents, the courts upheld the Shakers if a lawsuit ensued.

The first Shakers were so full of zeal that when the communities were gathered into gospel order, informal oral covenants bound them together. Since no Shaker was allowed to receive compensation for any work done for the community, problems arose in the 1790s when people left the society. They sought back wages and shares of land and property that had been donated by them or their parents. To protect the society from lawsuits, a written covenant was drawn up in 1800. This was revised in 1814 and in 1830. Each revision made it more difficult for apostates to seek damages or back wages. All Shakers 21 years of age or older were expected to sign the covenant. A look at the surviving covenants shows that some signed the covenant much later and some, especially after 1890, never signed it at all. In any event, the covenant not only protected members from legal troubles, it also provided them with numerous protections. Everyone who had signed the covenant could live out their lives in a community and share the benefits of food, clothing, and shelter. Any reasonable need was provided as well as the best medical care.

Shaker communities always had large farms. In fact, the Shakers loved to buy land. Most Shaker societies owned in excess of 2,000 acres and some communities had over 5,000 acres. In addition, many communities owned extensive acreage in other states. For example, New Lebanon owned tens of thousands of acres in Virginia and Michigan. Canterbury had a large farm in western New York. Even small communities such as Harvard and Shirley had pasture land in New Hampshire. It is therefore impossible to know how much land a particular community had at any given time. Moreover, there is evidence that as trustees died, records of landholdings were forgotten and thousands of acres bought by the Shakers eventually passed out of their hands as abandoned property. Managing just the home farm and pasture land took tremendous human resources. As time went on this work fell to the boys and hired laborers.

Until the Civil War, Shaker societies also had numerous industries. With the possible exception of Watervliet, Ohio, every Shaker society had a seed industry. Most also prepared herbs for sale. At the Church Family at New Lebanon, both dried herbs and liquid extracts from herbs were sold. Besides industries, brethren were employed in shops making clothing, repairing or making furniture, and doing everything else needed to run a large community. Sisters rotated turns in the kitchen, dining room, laundry, and housekeeping. By 1900, the sisters were the principal wage earners from the sale of their large array of homemade fancy goods. This included the famous Shaker cloak and poplar ware.

Most Shakers worked until old age. Communal life has many opportunities for willing hands to work. When age and infirmity ended this phase of life for a believer, medical care was provided in the dwelling or in a special infirmary called the nurse shop. Until modern times, the presence of so many young girls and teenagers made it relatively easy to care for the aged. When communities no longer had young people, the infirm often have had to go into nursing homes in the world to receive adequate care.

DECLINE

The numerical high point of the Shakers occurred more than 160 years ago. Writing in 1890, Elder Louis Basting of the Church Family at Hancock, Massachusetts, tackled the question in his pamphlet *Christianity*: If the Shakers have such an ideal life, why were they declining? He said that it was not the concept that was wrong, but internal forces within Shakerism that were the trouble. He confidently looked forward to a time in the near future when there would be an influx of new members. Such optimism did not play out and Shakerism has continued to fade away.

Perhaps it is the nature of an ideal that it cannot last indefinitely. The most fervent flowering of the Shaker gospel certainly occurred with the generation of the first converts and this momentum lasted until the 1820s, about 50 years. In the East this meant a very strong first generation of adult converts who had received the faith at the time of the opening of the gospel. For the most part, their children proved to be faithful as well. In addition, from the 1790s until the early 1820s, large families joined the Shakers and these converts and their children also had a fairly high perseverance rate. These children came of age during the 1840s and made a third strong generation. By 1910 all of these men and women had died, and subsequent generations had not retained sufficient numbers to keep the communities viable. As a result, between 1909 and 1918, four of the ten surviving societies in the East closed.

In Ohio and Kentucky, Shakerism enjoyed just one very strong generation, those who were adults when the gospel opened there from 1805 to 1825. By the 1820s, serious internal disputes had caused large defections among the children of the founders as well as the younger Shakers. Though there were capable men and women who joined after the early years, few stayed faithful to death. As a result, between 1889 and 1912, five of the six Shaker villages in Ohio and Kentucky were closed.

SUMMARY

Until the 1820s, the Shakers were growing and founding new villages. After this, the addition of large numbers of children without their parents masked the fact that few suitable adults were joining. By the 1830s in the West, retrenchment was noticeable, especially at Union Village, once the largest of all Shaker societies. The decline was further masked by the decade of the 1840s when the Era of Manifestations preoccupied Shakerism. In fact, for a time, the renewed spirituality among the younger members looked promising. Yet by the 1850s, even in the East, the lack of adults, especially men, was having a negative effect on the societies.

It would be easy simply to say that Shaker leadership from the 1820s onward allowed missionary efforts to slacken and was content to fill up the communities with hundreds of children they hoped would join when they came of age. Though there is some truth in this, a larger view must be taken. Since the beginning, religious revivals had been the best opening to gain new members, and the leaders of the Gathering Orders were always on the lookout for places to go as missionaries. Perhaps the large-scale influx of children did cause a shift in missionary priorities, but the elders still looked for and followed up on any lead that would help them gain new followers. After the 1820s, however, there were no large-scale religious revivals to which the Shakers had access. The movement westward, urbanization, and growing industrialization had profound effects on the places where the Shakers had colonies. Subsequent immigration to these areas starting in the 1840s brought a large and overwhelming class of new people, with faith traditions very different from those among whom the Shakers had traditionally drawn converts. In addition, some Shaker trustees bought huge amounts of land and speculated in areas far beyond their expertise. Many rank and file Shakers also became caught up in the world. These factors and the wholesale addition of children without their parents weakened all of the societies.

Clinging to large farms in an industrial time, Shakerism took on romantic aspects. Looking back on a stronger past, some of the sisters, especially at Canterbury, took on genteel mannerisms that evoked a faded elegance. In any event, Shakerism seemed like an anachronism.

With the sale of former Shaker properties and wise conservation of existing resources, it would have seemed natural for the Shaker leaders to have developed some plan to ensure that surviving members were well cared for. This was not done on any consistent basis after the 1920s. The lack of an effective oversight of the remaining societies is but another of the many signs of the almost total collapse of Shakerism by then. Although the symbolic end of Mount Lebanon's prominence occurred in 1930 when the Church Family property was sold, leadership had eroded significantly since the deaths of Elder Joseph Holden in 1919 and Eldress Catherine Allen in 1922. At the same time, Canterbury assumed an important leadership role in terms of control of the Parent Ministry; yet this did not translate to actual pastoral supervision. Brother Arnold Hadd, a present-day Shaker at Sabbathday Lake, contends that Shakerdom was never 18 major villages, but consisted of the 60 families that made up these communities. He feels that the Shaker family unit was always the strongest cohesive element. Certainly this was true by the 1920s. Single families existed at Hancock, Alfred, Canterbury, Watervliet, and Sabbathday Lake. One small and three tiny families made up Mount Lebanon. The Parent Ministry let nature take its course at these places. They intervened to close Alfred and Watervliet when financial circumstances compelled them to do so, yet no systematic plan was devised to use the greater wealth of the Shaker church to benefit members although perhaps more than a million dollars in assets were held by the trustees at Hancock.

Ironically, as the Shakers diminished, the objects made by them, especially furniture and oval boxes, have become much sought after, causing one contemporary Shaker to remark that the world wants everything but the cross. The impetus for this new phase of Shaker history began in the early 20th century as Eldress Catherine Allen and Elder Alonzo Hollister began collecting objects and manuscripts to give to museums and historical societies. John Patterson MacLean of Ohio and Wallace Hugh Cathcart of the Western Reserve Historical Society in Cleveland were the first major collectors in this regard. MacLean's collection became part of the Library of Congress, and due to Cathcart's efforts, the Western Reserve Historical Society remains the largest depository of Shaker manuscripts. By the 1920s collecting things Shakers had made moved into the realm of furniture. Pioneers in this area were Edward and Faith Andrews of Massachusetts. For the last 75 years, Shaker artifacts of all kinds have become extremely collectible.

A few Shakers, wanting to keep an awareness of their history alive, started small museums. During the 1890s, Elder Henry Blinn of Canterbury collected artifacts and catalogued them. In 1918, not long after she moved to the North Family at Mount Lebanon, Eldress Josephine Jilson, formerly of Shirley and Harvard, set up a collection of her saved treasures that she showed to visitors. Similarly, in 1931 at Sabbathday Lake, a collection was put together for viewing in the Meeting House. The first large-scale Shaker museums, however, were created by non-Shakers. In 1921, Clara Endicott Sears opened a museum in what had once been the original Office building of the Church Family at Harvard. She had this building removed to her estate as part of a museum complex called Fruitlands. In 1950, collector John Williams of Old Chatham, New York, opened up an extensive museum of Shaker artifacts. Sears and Williams housed their museums in buildings on their own land. Abandoned Shaker villages were nearby, but were in private hands. This changed in 1960 when at Hancock, Massachusetts, and at Pleasant Hill, Kentucky, groups formed to buy and restore former Shaker villages. Today these Shaker sites are large, open villages offering numerous Shaker agricultural and craft activities. As circumstances have changed, South Union, Kentucky, and Enfield and Canterbury, New Hampshire, have become restored Shaker villages open for visitors. All of these sites have sparked renewed interest in the Shakers and this has led to new scholarship.

Meanwhile, the remaining Shakers are confident and secure in their faith, for "essential Shakerism can never die, for it holds within itself principles which the developed life of humanity demands to have embodied in practical daily living." (White and Taylor, *Shakerism*, 395)

The Dictionary

– A –

ADVENTISTS. Also referred to as Advents in some Shaker journals, the Adventists were followers of William Miller and joined the Shakers in large numbers after the disappointment of 1844 and 1845. Hundreds joined the Shakers, but their impact was especially great at **Union Village**, **White Water**, **Harvard**, and **Canterbury**. Most of the former Adventists were short-lived converts, but some of them stayed faithful to Shakerism and lived into the 20th century in a few communities. The greatest influence of the Adventists on the Shakers was the introduction of the concept of **spiritual marriage**.

ALETHIAN BELIEVERS. This is actually the official name of the Shakers. During the late 1890s, **Alonzo Hollister** petitioned the **Central Ministry** to have the title Alethian Believers used instead of Shakers. He felt that too many derogatory connotations were connected with the term Shaker and that it had come from those outside the faith. Alethia, which means spirit of truth, seemed to him a more accurate way to describe Shakers. The Ministry granted his request, but the use of Alethian Believers never caught on. Besides Hollister's *Mission of Alethian Believers, Called Shakers*, only two other Shaker publications use the title. *A Full Century of Communism. The History of the Alethians, Formerly Called Shakers* by **M. Catherine Allen** was published in 1897. The second edition of the work published in 1902, however, was *A Century of Communism; The History of the People Known as Shakers*. Trustee **Aurelia Mace** of **Sabbathday Lake** wrote a book called *The Alethia: Spirit of Truth* in 1899. The 1907 second edition of this work retains the same title.

1

ALFRED, MAINE (1793–1931). SPIRITUAL NAME: Holy Land. FEAST GROUND: Holy Hill of Zion. BISHOPRIC: Maine. FAMILIES: Church, Second, North. MAXIMUM POPULATION AND YEAR: 200 in 1823. INDUSTRIES: Woven cloth, seeds, herbs and herbal medicines, brooms, brushes, saw and grist mill, horsehair sieves, woodenware, spinning wheels, wagon wheels, oval carriers, and fancy goods. NOTABLE SHAKERS: **R. Mildred Barker**, **John Vance**, Elisha Pote, **Harriett Coolbroth**, **Henry Green**. UNIQUE FEATURES: In 1900, Alfred was a typical Shaker community—small numbers, mostly old and seemingly doomed to die out within the next 20 years. Between that time and 1920, through the efforts of Eldress Harriett Coolbroth, Eldress Mary Ann Walker, and their companions, a tremendous Shaker revival took place at Alfred. In 1920 almost the entire community consisted of young women—the vast majority of whom would stay faithful. Alfred was very poor, but rich in young Shakers who had a fervor not seen in other Shaker societies for decades. In every way, the fact that Shakerism survives to the present day was due to the strong faith that the Alfred Sisters brought to **Sabbathday Lake** when they moved there in 1931.

BRIEF HISTORY: Until 1820, the district of Maine was part of the Commonwealth of Massachusetts. Though there was a low population and plenty of empty land, Maine had been settled for more than 150 years. The waves of religious enthusiasm that affected those who had become dissatisfied with the standing order of Congregationalism in older parts of New England had their representation in Maine as well. In Alfred around 1780, the religious community was ripe with revivalism of all sorts. John Cotton had only recently moved to the town and was caught up in its enthusiasm. When the revivalism waned, he, like many others sought to go west in search of a better life. On his way, he traveled through **Canterbury, New Hampshire**, where some of his New Light Baptist friends lived. From there he got as far as **Enfield, New Hampshire**, where he came under the influence of James Jewett, a Shaker missionary. Filled with the Shaker testimony, Cotton returned to Alfred to open the gospel to his friends John and Sarah Barnes.

Cotton met with great success and soon hundreds were gathering to hear his testimony. In March 1793, the Shaker community at Alfred was organized under Father John Barnes, Brother Robert McFarland,

Mother Sarah Kendall, and Sister Lucy Prescott. Although the seat of the Maine Ministry, Alfred was always one of the smaller Shaker communities. In fact, it peaked very early in the 19th century. As time went on, economic conditions steadily worsened as numbers gradually diminished for most of the 19th century. In 1870, the community decided to sell out and move to Kansas. The entire village was put up for sale, but no buyer came forth. The Shakers then decided to reorganize their village and stay put. Sale of a lot of timberland gave them a financial boost, but later losses and the premature deaths of Frank Libby (1870–1899) and John Vance (1832–1896) left the community virtually without industries or sufficient men by 1900.

For many years, the relatively large number of sisters remaining in various Shaker communities had been making fancy goods to sell in the **Office** stores as well as at resorts during the summer. This trade became a mainstay of the Alfred community and Elder Henry Green made annual sales trips for decades. In addition, teams of sisters went out to the seaside and to the mountains to sell fancy goods. This industry kept Alfred afloat financially. Unfortunately, two fires destroyed their small fund of accumulated wealth and made it inevitable that the community would have to close. The first of these fires took place in 1901 and destroyed the **Church Family** dwelling, the **Meeting House**, and the Ministry shop. Valuable records and irreplaceable manuscripts were lost. Incredibly to most other Shakers, the Alfred society decided to build a replacement dwelling. Elsewhere, Shakers could barely fill one dwelling, and the **Central Ministry** gave the Alfred Shakers the option of dissolving their community. The Alfred Shakers refused to even think of going to live anywhere else and resolved to rebuild. At the time it seemed like folly since Alfred did not have many young members and few men. Much to the surprise of many, not only was a new dwelling built, but many young women became Shakers. Much of the credit for the latter goes to Eldress Harriett Coolbroth of the **Second Family**. Her deeply religious vision was one of hard work and a total giving of oneself in service to the community. Through her ministrations, R. Mildred Barker, Ethel Peacock, Della Haskell, the Philbrook sisters, and many other women became lifelong Shakers.

In 1912, a fire set by a girl only recently taken in by the Shakers destroyed the new dwelling at the Church. It was the construction of the third dwelling to replace the one lost in this fire that pushed the community over the financial edge. Even the presence of so many young and faithful Shakers could not make up for the lack of cash. Various ways were tried to make money, but these all fell short. In 1927, the Maine **Ministry** was abolished. No doubt the **Parent Ministry** wished to be in a position to sell Alfred if an acceptable price could be received. Finally, in 1931, during the early years of the Great Depression, the situation had become so desperate that the decision was made to close and consolidate with Sabbathday Lake. The decision was announced to the Alfred community on 14 February 1931. Preparation for the move began immediately, but lagged as Elder Henry Green was so ill that they decided to wait for his passing before moving; however, he rallied and the consolidation was completed on 28 May. After the move, an offer was made by the Roman Catholic Brothers of Christian Instruction. This French Canadian religious order was seeking a headquarters for its many grammar and high schools scattered throughout the parishes of New England.

Though Alfred may be no more, the light and the love of Shakerism that existed at Alfred lay dormant at Sabbathday Lake until it could find its freedom during the 1960s. Since that time, in cooperation with recent converts to Shakerism, much of the spirit of the old-time faith of the Shakers has been able to survive to the present day.

LAST SHAKER: Minnie Greene (1910–2001) was the last Alfred Shaker. She joined the community in 1921 with her younger sister Ellen. In 1931, she moved to the Sabbathday Lake society when the Alfred Shakers were consolidated with this community. Here she signed the covenant, and for decades worked in the sewing department and the candy-making industry. She also did the baking and helped out in the kitchen and with housekeeping. Sister Minnie was a very self-effacing and shy sister. In the 1990s her health needs prompted her removal to a nursing home. For the final few years of her life, she was constantly visited by community members. When she passed into Eternity, the last tangible link to the glorious Alfred Shakers was lost.

ALLEN, MINNIE CATHERINE (1851–1922). Catherine Allen came from a family of reformers. Her father John Allen, a clergyman, and her mother Ellen Lazarus had been members of Brook Farm. After that failed, her mother financed a similar community outside of Terre Haute, Indiana. Minnie was born there, in Patriot, Indiana, on 3 September 1851. This venture was not a success and they moved to the Modern Times Colony in Brentwood, Long Island, in 1857. In 1865, her mother decided to send her children, Minnie and a younger brother Ernest, to the Shakers to board. Accordingly, they arrived at the **North Family** of **Mount Lebanon** on 2 February 1865. At that same time, **Anna White** had just been made second **eldress** of the **family**. In this capacity she worked with the older girls and youngest sisters. Minnie Allen became the first girl Eldress Anna raised. They became best friends for the rest of their lives. Symbolic of her new life, Minnie adopted the exclusive use of her middle name Catherine within three weeks of living with the Shakers. Her mother never intended that her daughter should actually become a Shaker, and she was very angry when Catherine, unlike her brother, did not wish to return Brentwood.

She attended the Shaker district school for a brief time before being assigned to the various housekeeping tasks, including cooking and sewing. She was surrounded by leaders and members who were passionate reformers. As a consequence she wrote articles on Shaker life and history for the *Manifesto*. Some were later reprinted for a wider distribution. At home, she had charge of visitors. In any given year, over 1,000 people would visit the North Family. Some would stay to dinner. She also managed the Shaker store located at the **Office**. It seemed that she was perfect for this role. Leadership positions with the Shaker hierarchy seemed to be out of her range. That is why almost all Shakers were surprised when she was chosen to be a member of the **Central Ministry** in 1908. This was the first time a member from the ranks had gone directly into the **Ministry**.

Catherine had many talents to contribute. She was devoted and religious. In addition, her years in the store had given her a sense of business. She also knew how to be persistent. These traits served her well. Her tasks were not generally pastoral. Rather, she had the onerous burden of helping to close out communities that were no longer viable. This entailed months of traveling. Her companion in the Ministry, Eldress **Harriet Bullard** was 84 years old when Eldress Catherine took office. This meant that most of the work became her responsibility. When she turned 90, Eldress Harriet resigned and Catherine took her place as first eldress.

While she was busy closing out communities and shifting Shakers from one place to another, she reserved a large portion of her time for attempting to save Shaker records, manuscripts, and imprints. After Eldress Harriet retired for the evening, Eldress Catherine would stay up sorting through piles of forgotten papers. She made sure that libraries near former Shaker societies got a collection of items. Her greatest achievement in this regard, however, was her partnership with librarian Wallace Cathcart of the Western Reserve Historical Society in Cleveland, Ohio. Together they helped preserve 10,000 items of Shaker interest and, as a result, the Western Reserve has the largest holdings of Shaker manuscripts. Eldress Catherine's image appears on the nameplate of the Shaker material in this collection.

When she took office, she pictured helping to create a revitalized Shakerism based on the high ideals she had known at the North Family. She was discouraged that so many of the surviving Shakers seemed to have lost their zeal. Since Shakerism looked like it could not be resurrected, she helped transform the Ministry into a board of financial supervisors. Individuals and families could live the Shaker life as they saw fit, but the Ministry would make sure that valuable assets were not squandered. For example, when the survivors at **Union Village** wanted to donate their property for charitable use, the Central Ministry stood firm and stepped in to sell the lands and buildings for $325,000, an enormous sum at the time.

Eldress Catherine wanted to return to the North Family when her years of service were over. She did return, but not in the manner that she had envisioned. She died there in 1922 after seven months of severe suffering from cancer.

ANN LEE COTTAGE. During the early 20th century, the **North Family** of **Mount Lebanon** embarked on a few endeavors to attract capable adults to join the Shakers. Laura Langford, a friend of Eldress **Anna White**, proposed that the Shakers refit one of their many unused buildings as a summer home for visitors from the more refined class. She reasoned that if people saw Shaker life close-up, some would want to join. Trustee **Emma Neale** of the **Church Family** agreed to lend a building for this project. The building chosen was the original dwelling of the **Second Order** of the Church at Mount Lebanon. In July 1896, the Second Order, also known as the **Center**

Family, had merged into the **First Order**. Both the original dwelling and the one that replaced it had stood vacant since that time. Renovations, including modern bathrooms, were done so that the building, called Ann Lee Cottage, was ready to accept visitors for the 1904 season. In 1905, Church Family trustee Robert Valentine claimed that the cottage was needed for a dairy. That is why during the peace conference held on 31 August 1905, Ann Lee Cottage was not occupied by visitors, though refreshments were served there. In 1906, the cottage was opened again for visitors, but this proved unsatisfactory and the venture ended. It may seem that Eldress Anna had been naïve to think upper-class people would join the Shakers if only they had the chance to live with them. This may be a true judgment. However, trustee Emma Neale was no idealist. The Church Family was in tremendous debt, and she and the other few able-bodied sisters worked making fancy good and cloaks to pay off the money. Why would she agree to expensive renovations? The answer shows just how shrewd she was.

Sister Emma knew it was likely that the society at Mount Lebanon would have to close someday. Indeed, within 10 years, the property of the Church Family was put up for sale. She knew that those who would still be alive would someday need a nice smaller home if they wished to remain on the site. They could not hope to continue to live in the cavernous brick **dwelling house**. If the North Family wanted to finance the renovation and modernization of one of the best buildings, why should she object? In October 1930, the Church Family property of 300 acres was sold for $75,000. Trustees Emma Neale and her natural sister Sarah Neale, along with the three other surviving Church Family members, moved to Ann Lee Cottage. They lived there until the 1940s.

APOSTATE. Since almost no one is born a Shaker, membership is on a voluntary basis. Throughout Shaker history people have joined and left the community. An adult person who leaves the Shakers is called an apostate. Perhaps the most famous apostate was **Mary Marshall Dyer**. Her lifetime crusade against the Shakers of **Enfield, New Hampshire**, caused no end of problems for this community. In recent years many Shaker scholars have begun studying the writings of Shaker apostates. This has created a new genre within Shaker Studies called "Apostate Literature." The finest example of these is Elizabeth DeWolfe's careful and exhaustive study *Shaking the Faith*, which chronicles the story of Mary Marshall Dyer. DeWolfe uses the word apostate to define a person who left the Shakers *and* engaged in anti-Shaker activity afterward. This is a narrower description than the one presented here. Other common names for apostates include backsliders and turn-offs.

ASHTON, FLORIDA. *See* NARCOOSSEE, FLORIDA.

AVERY, GILES B. (1815–1890). If one single person could be chosen whose life epitomized that of the ideal Shaker leader, then that soul would be Giles Avery. From his youth to old age, he worked tirelessly for the cause of Shakerism. Much more often than not, he met with failure, but he persevered to the end.

Born on 3 November 1815 in Saybrook, Connecticut, his earliest years were spent in this charming town at the estuary of the Connecticut River. After his uncle **Richard Bushnell** joined the Shakers at **New Lebanon** in 1813, Avery's family was influenced to go there as well. His father Gilbert Avery had had two children, Gilbert and Julia Ann Avery, by a previous marriage. They went to live at the Shaker society at **Enfield, Connecticut**. Although Gilbert Jr. did eventually leave the Shakers for a numbers of years, he returned and died at Enfield in 1908, just a few days short of his 100th birthday.

When Avery was admitted to New Lebanon, he first lived at the **North Family** and then the **Lower Canaan Family**. In 1821, he had the good fortune to be sent to live at the **Second Order of the Church** at New Lebanon. This **family** had many fine leaders and a number of excellent role models, especially for young boys. His contemporaries were such notables as **Orren Haskins** and Calvin Reed. From his **caretaker** Benjamin Lyon, Avery was introduced to the art of woodworking, one of the many trades he carried with him throughout his life. Avery was also a prolific tailor, an occupation well suited to the life he would later lead as a member of the **Ministry**.

During the 1830s he served as the schoolteacher of the boys and boys' **caretaker**, a task that was burdensome to him. In September 1841, he became second **elder** of the Second Order and first elder in

November 1849. His enthusiasm and strong work ethic no doubt caught the eye of the Ministry, and when a vacancy opened in October 1859, Avery became second elder of the Ministry of New Lebanon. For over 31 years, he practically carried the entire burden of the Ministry. His senior, Daniel Boler, was a silent man quite content to spend his days at basket work. It was left to Avery to exhort, encourage, and do anything necessary to build up collapsing Shaker communities. Incredibly, Avery seems to have been happy to do whatever he could even though he was always the second elder.

In 1872, for example, dishonest trustee Edward Chase had left the East Family at New Lebanon financially ruined. A tremendous debt of over $25,000 had been contracted without the knowledge of the Ministry. It was Avery who tackled the arrangement of the debt payment and the eventual breakup of this family. This type of occurrence was not out of the ordinary. Virtually all of the last 30 years of his life were spent in crisis management.

He was a stalwart standard-bearer for Shakerism, but in spite of his efforts, the Shakers continued to decline. Worn out by his lifetime of service, he died on 27 December 1890. His partner in the Ministry, Daniel Boler, though 11 years older, outlived Avery by two years.

Many scholars who have studied the Shakers have credited Mother **Lucy Wright** with being the best leader the Shakers ever had. Her accomplishments were many, including the expansion of the **believers** into Ohio, Kentucky, and beyond. Yet it is easy to be a leader when there are plenty of youthful, obedient, and talented people who can be relied upon to do what is needed. Avery, always the second elder, had to do the work of many, and as the years went by, the pool of capable people available to assist him diminished considerably. That he did as well as he did for so long and continued to press for a renewal of Shaker fortunes until he died speaks exceedingly well of him. In every way, Avery was a strong force for good at a time when few cared.

In 1880, he was encouraged to publish his autobiography. He also wrote various circulars, sermons, and tracts, including *The New Creation* and *Spiritual Life*. He also updated the *Rules & Orders*, which still serve as the working bedrock of today's *Rules*. He was also working on a greatly revised **covenant** at the time of his passing.

– B –

BABBIT, ABIATHER (1761–1847). When **Mother Ann** died in 1784, she was succeeded by two very strong men, Father **James Whittaker** and Father **Joseph Meacham**. When Mother **Lucy Wright** came to dominate after 1796, many Shakers may have been surprised and some were openly resentful. When **Henry Clough** died, however, Abiather Babbit was appointed to be the only man in the **Ministry**. Except for the two years he was assisted by **Ebenezer Bishop**, Babbit served alone for 23 years. Very few people were in the Ministry so long, and none as silent and invisible as he was. He seems to have carried self-effacement to an extreme. This willingness to let Mother Lucy have all the power continued after her death. She appointed two men and two women to succeed her after her demise. Babbit was not one of these, and after her death he voluntarily moved to **Watervliet, New York**, to live. He died there in 1847.

The main problem with any discussion of Babbit is that we know so little about him. He must have possessed some remarkable traits for Mother Lucy to want him to serve in the Ministry all those years. However, when Mother Lucy died, he was old, and it is apparent that Mother Lucy wanted a young and vibrant Ministry to come and serve together for decades as she had done with her team. In addition, his complete obedience is seen from the church's point of view as a very positive attribute.

BACK ORDER. This was a group of people who had some faith in Shakerism, but could not go beyond the most rudimentary stages of membership. Sometimes serious financial obligations prevented full **union**. For others, family ties for them were too difficult to break. Still others were relatives of Shakers and wanted to live near them, but did not know whether they themselves wanted to be Shakers. All these situations could be accommodated in a Back Order if a community wished. In a few societies such people lived on adjacent farms. Only at **New Lebanon** was a Back Order more fully articulated. After 1821, the old Walker House or West House served the purpose of a Back Order for a number of years. The most notable family who lived in the Back Order was the Taylors. *See also* FAMILY; ORDER.

BARKER, R. MILDRED (1897–1990). Some Shakers seem to be larger-than-life figures who through their presence radiate the gospel. Mildred Barker was one of these rare souls. She was born in Providence, Rhode Island, on 3 February 1897. On 7 July 1903, her mother placed her with the **Alfred** Shakers, and Eldress Fanny Casey sent her to live at the **Second Family**. There she had the good fortune to come into contact with Eldress **Harriett Coolbroth**, in whom she found a true mother. Not long after she arrived, she was given the task of helping a very elderly sister named Paulina Springer. The two formed a deep friendship and Mildred loved doing chores for her. In addition, Sister Paulina taught Mildred the song, "Mother Has Come with Her Beautiful Song." Paulina claimed to have received the song from a bird. In 1905, as Sister Paulina was dying, she asked Mildred to promise her that she would become a Shaker. She promised and this promise always stayed with her throughout her life.

One of Eldress Harriett's favorite things to do with her charges was teach them the old Shaker songs. Mildred made it a point to learn as many of these as she could. In fact, she often claimed that it was the "vim and vigor" of the songs that attracted her to Shakerism. Eldress Harriett had a gift for attracting young people to stay as Shakers. When Mildred's mother came from Providence in 1911 to take her home, she declined to go. She had promised to be a Shaker when she was a young child, and she intended to spend her life making good on this promise.

In 1918, after the **Ministry** closed the Second Family, and she moved to the **Church Family**. When Alfred was sold in 1931, she had the heartbreaking task of leaving the happy home she had known for almost 30 years. At **Sabbathday Lake**, she became in charge of the young sisters. She organized a "Girls' Improvement Club" where they wrote poetry, did recitations, and studied the Bible. Sister Mildred herself had once belonged to a similar club at Alfred called the "Beacon Light Circle." Besides sewing and knitting for the store, she worked in the candy business for decades. She became an expert in hand-dipping chocolates.

In 1950, she was made a **trustee**. At the same time, the **Parent Ministry** selected **Gertrude Soule** as family **eldress**, so Sister Mildred by default became the spiritual leader of the community as well. When adult inquirers came to learn about becoming Shakers, they were welcomed by her. In close association with one of these young men, Brother **Theodore Johnson**, who entered in 1960, Sister Mildred led a revival of Shaker life at Sabbathday Lake. She helped found the *Shaker Quarterly* and was its business manager from 1961 until 1974. She was the force behind opening up **public meeting** once again in 1963. In addition, she wrote four books: *The Sabbathday Lake Shakers: An Introduction to the Shaker Heritage*; *Holy Land: A History of the Alfred Shakers*; *Poems and Prayers*; and *Revelation: A Shaker Viewpoint*. She also contributed articles and Home Notes for the *Shaker Quarterly* and traveled and lectured on Shakerism. Late in 1971, after Eldress Gertrude decided not to return to Sabbathday Lake, Sister Mildred was appointed second eldress by the Ministry. The following year, the community (not the Ministry) gave its approbation to her as their eldress.

The list of her awards include those received from the Catholic Art Association in 1965, the Maine Arts Commission in 1971, the National Endowment for the Arts in 1983, and the Woman's Career Center at Westbrook College in 1987. Furthermore, she spoke at numerous events and was never too busy to spend time with visitors.

As she neared the end of her life, she witnessed much ill feeling directed at her for simply wanting Shakerism to continue. Ironically, she outlived Brother Ted Johnson, the center of much of the controversy, by almost four years. When he died, she humbly remarked that he gave her far more than she ever gave him. It was this spirit of humility, backed by a strong will and a never-wavering faith in Shakerism, that caused her to be the greatest 20th-century Shaker. Certainly no person born since 1900 had more faith in **Mother Ann** and her gospel.

BARLOW, LILLIAN (1876–1942). Born in Mississippi, Lillian Barlow joined the **Second Family** at **Mount Lebanon** before 1886. Very few manuscript records have survived from this **family** so virtually nothing is known about her life before coming to Mount Lebanon. One aspect is certain, however: She was always a hard worker with little time for nonsense.

The Second Family had been one of the largest families at **New Lebanon** (called Mount Lebanon after 1861). By the time Lillian joined, the family had shrunk to fewer than 40 members, many of whom were children. Under the capable management of Elder Dewitt Clinton Brainard, the family specialized in many aspects of horticulture, especially the drying of sweet corn. Sister Lillian cultivated large gardens and canned vegetables for sale. When Elder Dewitt died in 1897, the family lacked any major industry. The family had just 20 members and some of the sisters under the direction of Clarissa Jacobs worked on cloaks and fancy goods. When Sister Clarissa died in 1905, the small family of a dozen, including children, seemed to be headed for extinction. Eldress Emily Smith was in her eighties and the family faced a future that was uncertain at best.

Since the Second Family was an important part of the main Shaker holdings at Mount Lebanon, the **Ministry** decided to try to save it. In 1908, after the **Shirley** community was consolidated into **Harvard**, Sister Margaret Eggleson was sent to live at the Second Family as **eldress**. Eggleson had originally come to Harvard from **Upper Canaan** in 1883. She had been sent there to help that struggling community. Once again her energy and talents were sent back to Mount Lebanon, this time to the Second Family. She had plans to revive the **chair industry** and involve the Second Family. Up until then, the chair business was centered at the South Family. This family had been a part of the Second Family until 1863 when it was split off. She replaced Emily Smith as eldress and, with Lillian Barlow of the Second Family and Eldress **Sarah Collins** of the South Family, a new business scheme was launched. By 1910, the chair business, which had once been housed in a large factory building, had diminished as the South Family declined. That year the South Family had just seven members, while the Second Family had 14. Without actually merging the two small families back together again, some members from each family would work on parts of the business. The large stone brethren's workshop at the Second Family was refitted to be a factory. Here Lillian Barlow and Elder **Ernest Pick** would make the chairs. Eldress Sarah Collins would then finish the chairs for sale at the South Family. This business received a tremendous boost in 1915 when Brother William H. Perkins moved from the **North Family** to the Second Family. He had newly arrived in the United States with the purpose of joining the Shakers at Mount Lebanon. He was a carpenter and loved woodworking. After a short while at the North Family, he requested to go to the Second Family. There he worked with

Sister Lillian in the chair factory. Together they formed a team that manufactured chairs for 20 years. They were known as the Mt. Lebanon Woodworking Company.

After the stone workshop burned in 1923, operations were moved to an adjacent wooden structure. Though Brother William died in 1934, Sister Lillian continued to make chairs at the Second Family until 1940. That year the property was sold. She moved to the North Family where she died in 1942. She was the last Shaker chair-maker.

BATES, ISSACHAR (1758–1837). He was born in Hingham, Massachusetts, on 29 January 1758. His parents, William Bates and Mercy Jay Bates, had 11 children, and they moved a number of times. In 1771, they settled in Petersham, Massachusetts. During the Revolutionary War, young Issachar had a one-year enlistment and witnessed some of the most famous battles in Massachusetts. He married Lovina Maynard in May 1778, and they had 11 children, nine of whom lived to be adults. Although he had been brought up a strict Presbyterian, he had many questions about religion. He was especially curious of signs that might appear in a comet or a storm. When the Shaker gospel was opened at Petersham, he was especially drawn to the words of Father **James Whittaker**, who was a powerful preacher. Still, he was unable to commit himself enough to join. Instead he farmed and tried his hand at trade and speculation. He lost money on these ventures and moved to Hartford, New York, in 1786.

His religious quest made him stop and wonder about his life. Though he attended the Baptist church, he still retained the crude language and behavior he had learned while he was a soldier. This contradiction weighed heavily upon him. While visiting his father, who by then also lived in New York State, he decided to stop to see the Shakers at **New Lebanon**. The seed of Shakerism had been in his soul for 18 years, since the time he first heard Father James speak in Petersham. The visit to the **North Family** brought him into contact with Elder Ebenezer Cooley, who encouraged him to become a Shaker. He confessed his sins in 1801. In March 1803, he moved his entire family to **Watervliet, New York**. Besides his wife, seven of his nine children joined. The two oldest sons, since they did not wish to be Shakers, were given their share of the inheritance. Two of his children, Issachar Bates Jr. and Betsey Bates, became well-known Shakers. Issachar Jr. was **elder** of the **Church Family** at Watervliet and Betsey Bates was in the **Ministry of New Lebanon**.

Along with **Benjamin Seth Youngs**, Brother Issachar traveled around New York and New England as Shaker missionaries. In late December 1804, Elder **Ebenezer Bishop** told him that he was going to be one of the three missionaries sent out to the Kentucky Revival. Accordingly, **John Meacham**, Benjamin S. Youngs, and Issachar Bates left New Lebanon at 3 a.m. for the West. They arrived at Paint Lick and Cane Ridge, Kentucky, at the beginning of March. On 19 March they crossed into Ohio. Three days later, they were at the home of **Malcolm Worley** at **Turtle Creek**. Here they were so warmly received that they felt this was the first real rest they had had since leaving New Lebanon. They had gone 1,233 miles in two months and 22 days. Malcolm Worley, a **New Light** preacher, had asked God for help and was promised he would receive it. When the Shakers came to Turtle Creek, Worley and his congregation were ready for them.

Between 1801, when he began to preach for the Shakers, and 1811, Brother Issachar traveled 38,000 miles, mostly by foot. He visited every place Shakers had gathered in Ohio, Kentucky, and Indiana. It is said that he heard the first confessions of 1,100 souls. He also made a trip back to New Lebanon in 1805 to get money to buy the land of Timothy Sewall in Turtle Creek. This property was needed as part of the future Shaker society of **Union Village, Ohio**. In 1812, Brother Issachar finally settled down to live at **Busro**, but not long after he got there, the entire society had to flee the onslaught of the ravages brought on by the War of 1812 and the unsettled conditions on the frontier. The Shakers from Busro were dispersed among Union Village, **South Union**, and **Pleasant Hill**. He stayed at Union Village until August 1814, when it was safe to return to Busro. He spent the next 10 years there.

On 24 October 1824, he was appointed to be elder of the small Shaker society at **Watervliet, Ohio**. Before he even arrived there, he had heard that this community had a reputation for challenging the leadership. Elder Issachar faced the problem head-on. He moved people around and tried to consolidate all power in himself. This led to many confrontations, especially with the leaders of the sisterhood. Moreover, bad influences from some of the Shakers at Pleasant Hill seemed to infiltrate the society. These ideas were open threats to Shaker order in that they demanded that power be shared. Elder Is-sachar would not give way. During this time he rearranged the families at Watervliet and built the **Meeting House**. After a decade of struggles, he was released from Watervliet and returned to New Lebanon. He died there in 1837, at the age of 79.

While at Watervliet, Ohio, he wrote a sketch of his life. This autobiography was published by Elder Henry Blinn in the *Manifesto* starting in August 1884 and running for eight subsequent issues. It was copied by scribes in a number of Shaker communities, and, in 1960, John S. Williams of Old Chatham published part of the sketch in a booklet.

BEAVER CREEK, OHIO. This was the original name for the **Watervliet, Ohio**, community.

BELIEVER(S). This is what the Shakers call themselves. Though they do refer to themselves as Shakers, the word believer is a term of endearment, and has never had the negative connotation that the word Shaker once did. Believer is used in various contexts. For example, it can be found in some Shaker songs and it is used to denote a convert's **Shaker Birthday**. The origin of the word believer is from the Shaker religion's official title, the **United Society of Believers (called Shakers)**.

BISHOP, EBENEZER (1768–1849). The largest single group to live at **New Lebanon** and convert to Shakerism was the Bishop family. When it is considered that the Bishops were intermarried with many of the other families there, a strong sense of the interconnectedness of early Shakerism emerges. This served as an excellent way to have community cohesion. The leaders were most often relatives of some sort. For Ebenezer Bishop this must have been a source of great comfort.

Born in Stamford, Connecticut, on 7 October 1768, he came into the church at New Lebanon during the first in-gathering in 1788. In 1805, he was appointed to the **New Lebanon Ministry**. Mother **Lucy Wright** wanted him in the **Ministry** to test him and see if he was capable of leading. He proved to be so and was given charge of the first **Gathering Order**—a tremendous responsibility. In 1807, he left the

Ministry to go to the **North Family** as **elder**. The creation of this fledgling family was the latest Shaker innovation on how to integrate converts into their society. In those early years, converts were mostly married couples with children. Strong leadership was needed and good role models essential for those young in the faith.

Mother Lucy observed his excellent abilities and during her final illness named him to be first elder in the New Lebanon Ministry after her demise. For the next 28 years, Bishop led the Shaker faith. Although he shared power with his associates, he was a dominant force in policymaking. He died on 9 October 1849.

BISHOP, JOB (1760–1831). Of all the large family groups at **New Lebanon** when the gospel was first opened, the Bishop family was the most extensive. Moreover, the scores of Bishops were also interrelated to all of the other families. This created a strong network that made for a stable community. It also meant that many leadership positions went to members of the same family. **Ebenezer Bishop** and **Rufus Bishop** served for decades in the **Ministry** of New Lebanon. Their older brother Job was the founder of the Shaker societies at **Canterbury** and **Enfield, New Hampshire**.

Job Bishop was born on 29 September 1760 at Stamford, Connecticut. During the 1780s, he was part of the young cadre of men and women chosen by Father **Joseph Meacham** to be the future leaders of the Shakers. In 1787, he gathered to the church at New Lebanon when it was started. In February 1792, along with Edward Lougee, Hannah Goodrich, and Anna Burdick, he went to Canterbury to be the **Lead**. He gathered that community as well as the one at Enfield, New Hampshire. Father Job was the last to die of the original leaders sent out by Father Joseph.

BISHOP, RUFUS (1774–1852). Born on 16 July 1774 in Montague, Massachusetts, Rufus Bishop was a younger brother of **Job** and **Ebenezer Bishop**. As a part of the large Bishop clan, he grew up among some of the most important figures of early Shakerism. Following in the leadership path of his brothers, he was appointed second **elder** of the **First Order of the Church** at **New Lebanon** in 1808. This First Order was the most important Shaker **family**. Its members were supposed to be of the highest caliber, the best of the best Shakers. To be chosen as second elder of this family was a great responsibility. In this capacity he had charge of the younger brethren and kept the family journal.

His successes brought him to the attention of Mother **Lucy Wright**, who named him to be second elder in the **Ministry** after she died. In 1849, when his brother **Ebenezer Bishop** died, he became first in the Ministry. He died on 2 August 1852, at the Shaker community of **White Water, Ohio**, while on one of the Ministry's periodic visits. His unexpected death brought forth a flood of affectionate testimonies from the brethren and sisters he served for so long.

BISHOPRIC. All of Shakerdom was divided into communities grouped in governing units called bishoprics. Each bishopric had a **Ministry** that resided in a primary community of the bishopric. Generally this society gave the bishopric its name. The most influential bishopric was the one containing the Shaker communities of **New Lebanon** and **Watervliet, New York**. This was the New Lebanon Bishopric (1787–1946). The other Shaker bishoprics were (primary community is in italic): **Hancock** (1790–1893), *Hancock* and Tyringham, Mass., and Enfield, Conn.; **Harvard** (1791–1918), *Harvard* and Shirley, Mass.; **Canterbury** (1792–1918), *Canterbury* and Enfield, New Hampshire; and **Alfred** (1793–1927), *Alfred* and Sabbathday Lake. From 1830 to 1859 Alfred and Sabbathday Lake retained their Ministry but were placed under the Canterbury Ministry for supervision rather than New Lebanon; **Groveland** (1836–1859), *Groveland* (after 1859, Groveland became part of the New Lebanon bishopric); **Union Village** (1805–1910), *Union Village*, Watervliet, and **White Water** (after 1889, Union Village had charge of all the societies in Ohio and Kentucky); **North Union** (1826–1862) (in 1862 the Ministry at North Union was dissolved and the society came under the supervision of Union Village); and **Pleasant Hill** (1808–1889). Both Pleasant Hill and South Union had their own **South Union** ministries. These were combined in 1868 with South Union as the primary community. In 1889, they came under the supervision of Union Village.

BLINN, HENRY CLAY (1824–1905). For those who might seek to know what **Canterbury, New Hampshire**, was like in the 19th century, the life and career of Elder Henry Blinn is the key to this un-understanding. He was born on 16 July 1824 in Providence, Rhode Island. His father, James M. Blinn, was the captain of a merchant ship. His mother was Sarah Warner of Connecticut. His father died while Henry was a boy. This forced him to go out to work. His first job was at the age of 12 at the tailoring firm of Beets and Lockwood. The next year he was apprenticed to Edward P. Knowles, a jeweler. Since the port city of Providence was visited frequently by Shaker **trustees** and other Shakers engaged in trade, young Henry came into contact with Nathan Willard of Canterbury. His brother William Willard was a trustee. Henry and Nathan Willard formed a friendship and he decided to try living with the Shakers. Accordingly, he was admitted to the **Church Family** on 9 September 1838. In 1841, he became **caretaker** of the boys. He greatly enjoyed this job and also taught in the school. It was with deep regret that he had to give up the care of the boys in 1849 to go into the print shop. His work there was brief and he was sent back to have the care of the boys until 1852 when he was appointed second **elder** under Robert Fowle. Three months later, he was placed in the **Ministry** as second to Elder **Abraham Perkins**. While in the Ministry, he did tailoring and dentistry. In November 1859, he became first elder of the Church Family. In those days the family had 128 members. He was in charge of the 55 men, and in 1865 took charge also of the **public meeting** which opened every year in May and ran every Sabbath until October. Public meeting at Canterbury closed for good in 1889.

During the 1870s, the Canterbury society gradually took over all aspects of the *Manifesto*, the Shakers' monthly newspaper. From 1882 until the paper closed in 1899, all of the work was done at Canterbury. This occupied much of Elder Henry's time, but it served as a vehicle for his interest in Shaker history and religion. He wrote many articles for publication in the paper as well as books and booklets. He also had an intense interest in music and published hymnals collecting Shaker songs. As a young man he mapped the village. In addition, he collected items for a Shaker museum and wrote many unpublished pieces on Shaker history and theology. His talents even included beekeeping.

In 1880, Elder Henry was appointed to go into the Ministry in place of Elder Abraham Perkins. When Alexander Cochrane defected in 1890, Blinn went back to being first elder of the Church Family. The next year he became a trustee, and in 1893, went into the Ministry once again. These appointments were made late in his life when his health had begun to fail. They were necessary, however, because so many men had left or died that there were too few remaining to hold down the necessary jobs. He was frail and feeble during the final years of his life. This did not prevent him from trying to meet and greet the younger members. He was fond of telling them stories about the old days and about those who had lived at Canterbury when he was young. He died on 1 April 1905. In all he served 61 years as a spiritual leader and two years as a temporal leader.

When Elder Henry's life is considered in total, it can be noted that as the 19th century changed and different social conditions presented themselves, he adapted Shaker life to meet these challenges. For example, he styled himself as a refined gentleman and encouraged politeness and gentility in others. He published a work on good manners and demanded that the Shakers with whom he lived follow a life based on rules of etiquette. Certainly his encouragement of choral singing and instrumental music in worship helped transform meetings. The marches and dances faded away. After 1889, all services were held in the **dwelling house** chapel, which someday would house a pipe organ. This refined tradition at Canterbury would come to flower at its highest point under Elder **Arthur Bruce**. Besides singing and playing musical instruments, the sisters were also encouraged to take elocution lessons. The world might be changing around them but Canterbury would remain an island of refinement. This caused Elder Henry and subsequent leaders to find it difficult to relate to what was happening in the real world. More seriously, it also set them apart from their more earthy fellow Shakers, especially those in poorer communities.

BOLER, DANIEL (1804–1892). Daniel Boler served in the **Ministry** longer than anyone else, yet, like **Abiather Babbit**, he remains almost unknown. Although he was the first **elder** of the **Ministry of New Lebanon** until 1892, well after photography became common, no pictures of him are known to exist. In fact, for the 40 years he served in the Ministry, he seems to have done very little except work on basketmaking.

He was born on 2 May 1804 in Jasper Springs, Kentucky. During the opening years of the Shaker gospel in the West, his father William joined the Shakers at **South Union, Kentucky**. In 1814, his father took him to **New Lebanon** to put him out of reach of his mother, who did not wish to be a Shaker. Apparently, this worked because no mention of her is made again. The Bolers first lived at the **North Family**, but in November of that year, Daniel was sent to live at the **First Order of the Church**. For his entire life he was associated with this, the most prominent **family** within Shakerdom.

When he was growing up at the First Order, his associates were the Hinkley brothers, the Sizers, and the Crosmans, among others. Most of these boys went on to fill important positions in the family as elders, physicians, or **deacons**. In this context, it was natural that Boler be chosen for some leadership role. That he became the second elder of the family in 1833 was a sign that he was seen to have deep spiritual gifts. Standing in association with him as first elder was David Meacham, a brother of Father **Joseph Meacham**. On the female side was future Ministry eldress Betsey Bates. This was a high-powered team.

Due to his prominence as an **instrument** during the **Era of Manifestations**, **Philemon Stewart** took his place in 1841, but this was short lived, and Boler was back in 1842. For the next 50 years he held the highest positions within Shakerism, becoming first elder of the First Order in 1844, second elder of the New Lebanon Ministry in 1852, and finally serving as first Elder in the Ministry from 1858 until 1892.

The years he spent in the Ministry witnessed the beginnings of a decline in membership that grew worse every year. For example, in 1852, the First and **Second Orders** of the Church at New Lebanon had over 200 members. In 1892, there were only 84. This drastic reduction was more than reflected by similar declines all over Shakerdom. It would seem that any leader of an organization in such a serious situation would be a leader who would try to come up with a plan to stem the tide of decline. Boler seems to have been silent on all major issues affecting the Shakers. From 1852 until 1858, he was second in the Ministry and **Amos Stewart** was the dominant force. After 1858, the second in the Ministry, **Giles Avery**, ran everything. While Avery was laboring with people who were thinking of leaving, coming up with new industries, traveling from one corner of the Shaker world to the next, etc., Boler was collecting basket stuff for the sisters and weaving baskets. All important decisions seem to have been made by Avery. The single exception were the many actions he took on behalf of the **Groveland** Shakers. In fact, if someone did not know that Boler was actually the first minister, this could never have been guessed using the evidence of his actions. For all of this, however, he remained a beloved leader, and the Shakers spoke highly of him.

When he died in 1892, the Ministry was about to change in ways earlier Shakers could not have envisioned. Whatever opportunity the Shakers may have had for making innovative changes that might have helped build up the religion were not realized under the many decades of Boler's tenure. Elder Daniel did the best he could, and his associate Avery had no desire to be first, but was content in his role within the Ministry. It is obvious that they worked well as a team. Furthermore, there is no internal evidence that Elder Daniel was incompetent, and not a bad thing was ever said about him, save by Philemon Stewart who wanted to be in the Ministry. This is an important consideration, given the length of his eldership.

BOYS AND THE BOYS' SHOP. After 1824, the Shakers started to take in a large number of children. In each **family** where there were sufficient boys, a young Shaker **brother** was appointed as **caretaker** and teacher. If the family was large enough, a separate building to house these boys was built. It was in such a Boys' Shop that the boys and the caretaker lived. The boys also had a common room and a place to learn trades. Their primary responsibility in each community was to carry on the farming. They did the milking, ran the gardens, and carried wood. In the larger Shaker societies, where there were scores of boys, various families had caretakers for the boys, and for most of the 19th century, these boys only attended the Shaker school during the winter terms. Until the 1870s they were taught by brothers.

Very few of the boys raised by the Shakers ever joined the society upon reaching adulthood. As a result, by the 1880s, as the number of Shaker men declined to very low levels, there was a noticeable decline in the number of boys taken in. By 1900, few societies took boys at all, and most Shaker boys were in the Maine communities or at **Canterbury**. For almost all of the 20th century, **Sabbathday Lake** was the only Shaker society to have boys. The last boy left Sabbathday Lake in the early 1960s.

BRETHREN. Formerly this was used as the plural of **brother** when referring to more than one Shaker man. It is not in common use today.

BROTHER. This is the title that precedes the name of every Shaker male of legal age. The exception to this is the term **elder**, used to designate those of that rank. For most of Shaker history the plural of brother was **brethren**. In modern times, the word "brothers" is most commonly used to denote more than one Shaker man. This is the case whether speaking of contemporary events or those from the past.

BRUCE, ARTHUR (1858–1938). He was born on 22 December 1858 in Springfield, Massachusetts. His father, Rufus N. Bruce, was a machinist. His mother was Pamella Keet Bruce. On 3 November 1874, he was admitted to the **Church Family** of **Enfield, Connecticut**. He worked with the dairy herd and helped at gardening until he left in 1877. The next year he came back, and he signed the covenant in 1880. He left again in 1884. His wanderings took him to the societies at **Shirley** and **Canterbury**. It has been suggested that he was searching for the best Shaker home. Back at Enfield, his ambitions would not have been realized as long as Elder **George Wilcox** was in charge. Perhaps he found Shirley so small that it really had no viable future. At Canterbury he would have the benefit of living in a large, prosperous society. He joined the **North Family** or **Gathering Order** at Canterbury on 10 October 1885.

On 17 June 1886, he moved to the Church Family. Although he did not know it at the time, Canterbury was about to undergo a crisis in leadership among the men. In 1890, the second elder of the Church Family, Alexander Cochrane, suddenly left the community. During the 1890s, Nicholas and William Briggs left. They had been Shakers over 40 years and had held important leadership roles. That decade Benjamin Smith and James Kaime died. They too had been **elders** and **trustees**. Finally, Elder **Henry Blinn**, the most important leader, was becoming feeble. This great vacuum in the leadership accounted for the rapid rise of Arthur Bruce who was the only young man remaining.

When he first came into the Church Family, he was made the teacher of the boys. On 8 May 1889, he was appointed a trustee. From that point onward he was busy in all aspects of the cattle and dairy business. He was also away on trade. In 1899, he was made elder of the Church Family. Though he retained this later title his whole life, he was much more of a trustee than an elder. His interest in anything spiritual seems to have been very low, and his contribution to Shaker meetings was principally musical. He styled himself a great singer and organized groups of **sisters** to entertain visitors and travel about giving concerts.

As greater Shakerism collapsed, he was called upon by the Ministry to assume financial control over villages that were about to close. This took him away from the community still further and greatly increased his responsibilities. For example, in 1912, trustee **James Fennessey** of **Union Village, Ohio**, resigned after a dispute with the **Ministry**. Elder Arthur had to assume the management of the large property at Union Village while it was being sold. To help him, he sent out a number of young sisters to care for the remaining Union Village Shakers. In like manner he managed property at **Harvard**, Shirley, and **Enfield, New Hampshire**. On 8 May 1919, after the death of Elder **Joseph Holden**, he was appointed to be second elder in the **Parent Ministry**. When Elder **Walter Shepherd** of **Mount Lebanon** died in 1933, he became first in the Ministry. He died of pneumonia while recuperating from eye surgery at Phillips' House, Boston, on 18 April 1938.

Perhaps from a temporal viewpoint, Elder Arthur's life was a success. He headed the largest family in Shakerdom for almost 40 years and everyone was materially provided for in an acceptable fashion. Yet many aspects of his life were far below the ideal of a Shaker **brother**. There are many reasons for this judgment. The most important was that he rarely attended Shaker religious services during the last decades of his life. When he visited **Sabbathday Lake**, for example, the Shakers there canceled meeting because he did not wish to attend, or he would leave early to avoid meeting. He made no pretense about his priorities. In lieu of Sabbath meeting he would go to the racetrack. In addition, for a number of years he maintained an apartment in Concord, New Hampshire. Here he entertained visitors in ways that would not have been tolerated by the founders of Shakerism. Furthermore, in all things, along with his associate Eldress **Emma B. King**, he was autocratic. People had to gain his favor by flattery, and if he took a dislike to someone, nothing would make him take an interest in that person again. Always having his own way was his method of operation. This might have worked well in business transactions, but it was harmful for community life. There have always been **apostates** from Shakerism. In Elder Arthur the apostate stayed a Shaker and was a member of the Parent Ministry. Nothing shows the deterioration of Shakerism in the 20th century more than this.

BRUNSWICK, GEORGIA. In February 1898, the **Union Village, Ohio**, Shakers under the direction of Elder **Joseph Slingerland** purchased over 10,000 acres of land near Brunswick, Georgia. This property consisted of the former Altama and Hopeton plantations. Their intention was to start a new colony and perhaps move all of the Ohio and Kentucky Shakers to coastal Georgia. Two of the seven founding members, Julia Foley and William Ayer, left and got married the following April. Consequently, the Shakers returned to Union Village to briefly regroup before buying more land at **White Oak** the following October. White Oak is 20 miles south of Brunswick.

BULLARD, HARRIET (1824–1916). Many Shaker women possessed remarkable skills that were freely shared with the community. Few, however, lived as long and contributed so abundantly as did Harriet Bullard.

Born on 18 November 1824 in Pike, Wyoming County, New York, she came to the Shakers when she was 13 years old with her older sister Marcia Bullard and her aunt Caroline Webber. Her father and her brothers tried to force them to leave the community, but, it seems, divine intervention prevented it. Bullard was first gathered at the **North Family** of **New Lebanon**. When her father showed up to claim his daughters, they had already fled to the East Family, which was situated in a remote mountainous area. On their way they got lost and an old man appeared and showed them the way. The Shakers took this person to be an angel spirit.

This encounter with the angelic happened as the Shakers were experiencing the period in their history known as the **Era of Manifestations**. Both Bullard girls were active **instruments** in the work of this spiritualistic time, as were many of their age. Their testimonies as instruments and later their firm faith made both of them likely candidates for leadership.

In 1850, Harriet was appointed second **eldress** at the North Family. In this capacity she labored with young **sisters**. Since she had the talents needed for success in a **Gathering Order**, she was sent to the South Family at **Watervliet** in 1865 to be second eldress. The South Family was the Gathering Order for Watervliet, and there was a great need of new life. Bullard brought with her a number of enthusiastic and faithful sisters from New Lebanon. In 1881, she was elevated to be second in the **Ministry**, standing in association with Eliza Ann Taylor. Ten years later she became first in the Ministry, a position she held until she was 90 years old, when she resigned.

As a member of the Ministry, it was her task to attempt to keep Shaker communities strong and vital for as long as possible. This meant consolidations and closing communities. She had the sad task, after visiting what was left of some places, of recommending that they be closed. In addition, she tried to shift capable Shakers from less promising societies to good farms that existed at other Shaker communities. For example, it was through her exhortation that the **Groveland** society closed and its members removed to the North Family at Watervliet. In the same way, the **Upper Canaan Family** was sent to the superb farm at the North Family, **Enfield, Connecticut**.

Bullard gave without reserve and her judgments were known to be fair and unbiased with no hidden agendas. Even in the face of the extinction of Shaker life in most communities, she remained reluctant for artifacts or documents to be sent to museums and libraries for preservation. She believed these items belonged in Shaker communities.

BURNETT, MICAJAH (1791–1879). Of all the Shaker sites, **Pleasant Hill** retains the highest percentage of truly spectacular buildings. These structures were possible due to the genius of Micajah Burnett. He was born on 13 May 1791 in Patrick County, Virginia. By the mid-1790s his family had settled in Wayne County, Kentucky. In 1808, not long after the Shaker testimony was opened, his parents converted. They moved to Pleasant Hill with their children: Micajah, Charity, Andrew, and Zachiah.

Brother Micajah lived a long life as a Shaker and had a major influence on the physical development of Pleasant Hill. For example, when he was just 22 years old, he changed the original layout of the village. The **Center Family dwelling house**, along with a cluster of other buildings, was on a north-south axis. He reoriented the main road so it would run east-west. He then supervised and designed the construction of the three dwelling houses of the **Church Order** on this road. The East Family dwelling was constructed in 1817, followed by the West Family in 1821. Both of these were large brick buildings. The truly magnificent Center Family dwelling was begun in 1824 and completed 10 years later. Made of white limestone, this building is in the shape of a T. The front section is 55 by 60 feet while the ell is 34 by 85 feet. In the meantime, the large clapboard **Meeting House**, 60 by 44 feet, was completed in 1820. As memorable as these structures are, however, it was the construction of the **Trustees' Office** in 1839–1840 that guaranteed him lasting note. Its most famous features are the twin spiral staircases that rise three stories and seem unsupported.

The dwelling houses, the Meeting House, and the Trustees' Office were not Brother Micajah's only architectural work. During the 1830s he directed the building of the first public waterworks west of the Alleghenies. Part of this project, the Water House, was finished in 1831 and houses a cypress tank that holds 4,400 gallons of water. As a result, every shop, dwelling, and barn had running water. Brother Micajah's expertise in these matters was shared with the **South Union** Shakers when they wished to build a waterworks system.

Another important job Brother Micajah had was that of trustee. He peddled Shaker goods to markets all over the Mississippi Valley as far as New Orleans. Some of these products were garden seeds, brooms, medicinal herbs, raw silk, and preserves. To facilitate access to the Kentucky River, he managed the construction of the road to Shaker landing. During these years he also oversaw the construction of the West Family Wash House, the West Family Sisters' Shop, the East Family Brethren's Shop, and the post office. In 1872, due to old age, he was released as a trustee. He died on 10 January 1879.

What is remarkable about the work of Brother Micajah: twin spiral staircases, interior arched doorways, the balanced fenestration, engaged columns, paneled wainscoting, and transoms of borrowed light—to list a few features—were conceived by him without help from formal architectural training. He read the best works on architecture that he could find and then came up with his own design to integrate Shaker standards (Thomas, "Micajah Burnett and the buildings at Pleasant Hill," *Shaker Tradition and Design*, 50–56). The Shakers had many very talented members, but no one left more tangible evidence of this than Micajah Burnett.

BUSHNELL, RICHARD (1791–1873). Though he is almost entirely forgotten today, Bushnell had a major impact on Shaker history. His life spans the years of the greatest vitality to the darkest days after the Civil War. He was born on 19 November 1791 in Saybrook, Connecticut. As a young man he worked in New York City. When he was 21 years old, he decided to seek his fortune in the West. En route, he found himself in the town of **New Lebanon, New York**. He could see the scores of large buildings of the nearby Shaker village. When he investigated, he was so enamored of the life that he converted. In addition, he returned to Saybrook and, through his laborings, converted most of his family. He gathered his four sisters (Sally, Patience, and Patty "Martha" Bushnell and Sophia Bushnell Avery), a brother-in-law (Gilbert Avery), his brother Charles, two nieces (Eliza and Julia Ann Avery), and two nephews (Gilbert Avery and **Giles Avery**). Every one of these people remained faithful and contributed decades of service to the cause. His nephew, Gilbert Avery, did not die until 1908, 95 years after Bushnell's conversion. Another nephew, Giles Avery, would eventually become a member of the **Ministry of New Lebanon**. His brother Charles was a **trustee** at the **North Family** for over 20 years while his sister Sally was first sister at **Lower Canaan** and later second **eldress** at the North Family. If nothing else, his conversion helped gather stalwart people who seemed to fit perfectly into Shaker life and worked tirelessly for its continuance.

Under the usual circumstances, after his training at the North Family, Bushnell would have been sent to one of the other **families** at New Lebanon to live. Since he proved to be a gatherer of souls, however, he was appointed second elder at the North Family in 1827. Five years later he became the first elder. In this position, he was responsible for preaching at the **public meeting** on Sundays. In conjunction with his brother Charles, who was a trustee of the family, a large amount of money was saved. This cash would later be used to transform the property of the North Family under the eldership of **Frederick Evans**. The tremendous stone barn, innumerable out-buildings, orchards, and many other improvements were possible un-der the decades of Bushnell prudence.

In 1858, he was appointed to be part of the Ministry of New Lebanon. For a full year his lack of confidence in himself prevented him from actually working as minister. He asked to be released from this burden in 1859, and his nephew Giles Avery was appointed to fill his place. He returned to the North Family as a regular member. In the meantime the eldership at the North had been filled by Frederick Evans, who became the best-known Shaker of the 19th century.

Bushnell died in 1873 and memory of him has faded, yet he was able to gather many bright souls for the Shakers, and his financial re-straint allowed others the chance to create a model farm at the North. Finally, his appointment to the Ministry, although a disaster, allowed Frederick Evans to succeed him as elder and gave Bushnell's nephew, Giles Avery, the chance to be in the Ministry. Both Evans and Avery were extremely influential Shakers in the decades that fol-lowed.

BUSRO, INDIANA. Until 1816, this was the name of the only Shaker village founded in Indiana. *See* WEST UNION, INDIANA.

– C –

CANAAN, NEW YORK. This town, located in Columbia County, New York, and bordering on Massachusetts, had two Shaker **families**, known as the **Upper Canaan** and **Lower Canaan** families. At the time of the opening of the Shaker gospel in America in 1780, **New Lebanon** was a section of the town of Canaan. The north part of Canaan was not set off as the separate town of New Lebanon until 1818.

CANTERBURY, NEW HAMPSHIRE (1792–1992). SPIRITUAL NAME: Holy Ground. FEAST GROUND: Pleasant Grove. BISHOPRIC: Canterbury. FAMILIES: Church, Second (also known as the Middle Family or "the Branch"), North (**Gathering Order**), West (part of the North

Family). MAXIMUM POPULATION AND YEAR: 260 in 1840. INDUSTRIES: brooms, seeds, large washing machines, mangles, sarsaparilla syrup, checkerberry oil, sweaters, woolen socks, fancy goods. NOTABLE SHAKERS: **Job Bishop, Henry Clough, David Parker, Henry Clay Blinn, Arthur Bruce, Irving Greenwood, Dorothy Durgin, Dorthea Cochrane, Emma Belle King, Mary Whitcher, Cora Helena Sarle,** Josephine Wilson, **Marguerite Frost, Bertha Lindsay.** UNIQUE FEATURES: While New Lebanon dominated 19th-century Shakerism, Canterbury became the leading society of Shakerism after 1900. In 1957, a new **Ministry** was reconstituted there by Eldress Emma King, and this **Parent Ministry** officially ran the Shaker religion until 1988. Also, so many young women had decided to remain Shakers under Eldresses Dorothy Durgin and Dorthea Cochran that the society was destined to be long-lived, and there were Shakers at Canterbury until 1992. This made Canterbury the second-to-last Shaker community. Finally, Canterbury is one of the most beautiful of all Shaker sites. The **Church Family**, a large cluster of frame buildings, sits eloquently on a hill and is an impressive sight as the property is approached from the town of Canterbury.

BRIEF HISTORY: In 1781, a **New Light** Baptist revival took place in New Hampshire. One of the most prominent men in the town of Canterbury, Esquire Clough, had a son Henry who became a New Light preacher. The next year, a peddler named Benjamin Thompson who knew of **Mother Ann** at **Niskeyuna,** told the New Lights at Canterbury about her. They sent representatives to **Harvard** to learn more, and later two Shaker missionaries, Ebenezer Cooley and Israel Chauncy, were sent to them from Mother Ann. In 1787, Henry Clough moved to the Meeting House at New Lebanon to join the leaders of the Shaker church. At Canterbury Benjamin and Mary Whitcher became Shakers and their 100-acre farm formed the basis of the Church Family. The society was gathered 10 years later in February 1792, and by 1803 there were 159 believers in three families. The **Second Family** was organized in 1800 on land once owned by the Wiggins family. It merged into the Church Family in 1871. A few members still lived there to care for the buildings and it became known as "the branch." The North Family was founded on the Sanborn farm in 1801. In 1894, it moved into "the branch" and remained there until 1917 when it too was merged into the Church Family.

Under David Parker, principal trustee from 1848 until 1867, Canterbury reached its highest point in prosperity. Since the land at Canterbury was not very fertile, a parcel of 250 acres of land was bought in 1850 at Mt. Morris near **Groveland**. The society at **Enfield, New Hampshire**, and Canterbury were joint owners of this property until 1864 when Canterbury bought out Enfield's share. This excellent land was used to raise wheat and broom corn. It was sold in 1882. Also under David Parker, the home grounds were beautified.

In May 1855 on each side of the main road sugar maples were set out, from the Office to the Second Family. Henry Blinn planted the ones on the south side and Benjamin H. Smith planted those on the north side. Each was named after and cared for by a little girl in the society. The sugar maples in the lane in front of the **Meeting House** were planted in 1860. The next year, Canterbury got its own post office. From 1861 until 1888 the address was Shaker Village, New Hampshire. On 10 January 1888 it was changed to East Canterbury. This remained until the post office was closed on 14 June 1939.

Typical of most other Shaker places, membership seems to have peaked in the 1840s and leveled off at about 240 until after 1860. By 1870, there were 177 and it seemed the decline would continue to be steep. In 1875, however, a transforming event occurred that would keep Canterbury from this fate. In fact, it would assure that Canterbury would be one of the last Shaker societies to close. This was the transfer of the Shaker newspaper from **Mount Lebanon** to Canterbury in 1876. As all aspects of this paper, the *Manifesto,* gradually passed to Canterbury, it replaced Mount Lebanon as the public face of Shakerism. A great surge in applications for membership continued until after 1900. Although very few of these inquirers actually joined, and still fewer of these stayed as lifelong Shakers, enough were added to stem the rapid decline that was devastating other communities. For example, during the first five months of 1893, 70 letters from inquirers were received. Other Shaker communities such as **Pleasant Hill** even petitioned Canterbury to send Shakers to them.

Another reason for their success in keeping their population high was that Church Family **Eldress** Dorothy Durgin and her successor Dorthea Cochran were deeply religious women who attracted a bevy of young girls to remain in the community when they grew up. Durgin became second eldress in 1853 and in 1857 was made first eldress. Except for one year in the Ministry, she served the Church as eldress for 46 years. Cochran became first eldress after Durgin's death in 1898 and held the position until her untimely demise in 1912. For 60 years, then, Canterbury had excellent female leadership with the gift to inspire others. As late as 1920, there were 40 sisters between the ages of 21 and 40. Only at the **Alfred, Maine**, Shakers was there a higher percentage of young sisters.

In 1902, Canterbury surpassed Mount Lebanon as the largest Shaker society, and it held that distinction until 1931 when the Alfred community was consolidated into **Sabbathday Lake**. From 1918 until 1966, Emma B. King was the first eldress at Canterbury, and so much of what happened to the community can be attributed to her outlook in conjunction with that of Elder Arthur Bruce. There was a shift away from many of the traditional practices that had marked the believers from the beginning. Regular worship services, the yearly **fast day**, and Shaker religious education gave way to Shakers listening to religious services on the radio or holding a number of small private meetings conducted by the various cliques that existed in the community. Sometimes, no services were held at all. In fact, the last child adopted by the Shakers recalls that no religious instruction was ever given to her on Shakerism.

The great momentum that characterized the community from the 1880s until the 1910s was lost. By 1929, the decision had been made to take no more children. The girls who were teenagers were encouraged to leave since the sisters did not believe there was a future for Shakerism. By 1950, 16 women remained, the last remnant of the young girls who had chosen to stay 40 years previous. In 1971, the Shaker property was transferred to Shaker Village, Inc., a nonprofit educational institution.

LAST SHAKER: Ethel Mary Hudson (1896–1992) was born in Salem, Massachusetts, and joined the Second Family at Canterbury in 1907. It was there that she came under the influence of Sister Alice Howland (1884–1973) who became her lifelong mentor and best friend. In 1917, when the Second Family closed, Sister Ethel moved to the Church Family where she lived the remaining 75 years of her life. One of her many talents was as a pastry chef, and the community's first television set was won as a first prize for her pastry. Sister Ethel was full of life and delighted in gently provoking some of the more staid Shakers, especially Eldress Emma King. She made flip remarks, climbed trees, and always had a witty saying or a play on words at hand.

CARETAKER. This is the title given to a person who has charge of either the boys or the girls under 14 years of age in a Shaker community. Often a young Shaker was chosen to fill this duty as a test to see whether he/she had potential for future leadership. Depending upon circumstances, a caretaker could also be an older Shaker who was suitable as a role model. Often this caretaker was also the teacher. *See also* BOYS AND THE BOYS' SHOP; GIRLS AND THE GIRLS' SHOP.

CARR, FRANCES E. (1927–). In deference to the fact that Sister Frances is a present-day Shaker, a certain degree of privacy must be maintained. In her book *Growing Up Shaker*, she speaks about her life and tells her story in the best way. Anyone wishing to know the particulars can easily obtain the facts from this publication. Only the most general outline of her life is given here.

She was born on 13 March 1927 in Lewiston, Maine. She was the youngest of a large family, many of whom had been placed with the Shakers at Sabbathday Lake. She and her younger sister joined them in 1937. She attended the Shaker school and was allowed to move into the dwelling house and live a couple of years before it was customary. Her mentor as a teenager was Sister **R. Mildred Barker**, who had charge of the older girls. Although she helped out at various jobs and took her turn at duties, her greatest fondness was for kitchen work. In the well-appointed kitchen and bake room, she helped prepare meals in the company of many well-known community members. Her descriptions of these experiences and some of her favorite recipes are found in her book *Shaker Your Plate: Of Shaker Cooks and Cooking*.

In 1948 she signed the covenant. During the 1950s she worked in the candy industry in addition to her work in the kitchen. As her youthful companions left the Shakers one by one, it may have caused her to speculate about the community's future. In 1960, new hope was born when **Theodore E. Johnson** joined the community. Many men and women have tried the life since then. In addition, she was able to benefit from the renewal of Shaker spiritual life under Sister

Mildred and Brother Ted. The three of them gave presentations and were the real force behind the push to add new life to the society. Furthermore, she contributed many articles to the *Shaker Quarterly*. As a consequence, she was one of those who suffered when those forces in the greater Shaker world decided that they should determine the fate of Sabbathday Lake rather than let the Shakers there have a voice. While much of the persecution of Brother Ted was done by ignoring him or speaking behind his back, Sister Frances had to suffer direct insults from non-Shakers. It takes a great deal of fortitude to persevere in the face of such open hostility.

In 1989, she was appointed to serve as **trustee** with Sister Mildred Barker. The following year, with the death of Sister Mildred, she became the **eldress** of the community. Although this is her official title, in keeping with the traditions of such Sabbathday Lake stalwarts as Brother **Delmer Wilson**, who did not use the title of elder after his appointment, and Sister R. Mildred Barker, she has chosen not to use the title of eldress. Today she continues to lead the community along with Brother **Arnold Hadd**. She still works in the kitchen and her generous hospitality is known to all. Her sermons on the Sabbath are much anticipated, for they offer a glimpse of the long spiritual tradition of the Shakers.

CELIBACY. Of all the practices the Shakers believe in, this is the one most often mentioned by detractors or the first one named by people who may know nothing else about them. **Ann Lee** was favored with visions throughout her life. In England on one occasion, while imprisoned, she saw Adam and Eve having sexual intercourse. It was revealed to her that this was the sin that caused them to be cast out of Paradise. When Lee brought this revelation back to the group, she was proclaimed as **Mother Ann**.

The subsequent way of life that Mother Ann taught is known as the **Christlife**. Fundamental to any living of the Shaker life is a deep-seated belief in celibacy. Even during the latter years of the 19th century when the decline in numbers tempted a few Shakers to question the practice, the commitment of the Shakers to celibacy never wavered. In addition to the revelation of Mother Ann, Shakers refer to the New Testament passages that seem to favor a celibate life: Matthew 19:10–12, Mark 12:24–27, Luke 20:34–40, and 1 Corinthians 7:8–35. For the believer, rather than travel a life of generation, they travel a life of regeneration. That is, they live a life that shines with the fullness of the Christ as lived by **Jesus** and Mother Ann. The Shakers have always recognized that it is a calling from God and not meant for all, but only those chosen to live the life.

CENTER FAMILY. In the Shaker societies of Ohio and Kentucky, the **family** that included the **Meeting House** was called the Center Family. The exception was the society at **White Water, Ohio**. The Meeting House there was at the **North Family**. After the Civil War, the Shaker society at **Mount Lebanon, New York**, designated its **Second Order of the Church** as the Center Family. This family was responsible for the herbal extract industry. This Center Family was broken up in July 1896.

While some people at the **Enfield, Connecticut**, Shaker community called their 1876 brick dwelling the Center House, the family remained the **Church Family**. Various authors and the index of the Western Reserve Historical Society incorrectly use the title Center Family in connection with Enfield. This was due to one incorrect label on the outside cover of an Enfield journal when it was collected for preservation.

CENTER OF UNION. This phrase describes how Shakers saw the society at **New Lebanon**, New York. It was considered the model society and the **Ministry** there had the final say in spiritual matters. Shaker **covenants** use this phrase to describe the importance of New Lebanon. It is important to note, however, that the immediate duties of the **New Lebanon Ministry** extended only to the societies of New Lebanon and **Watervliet** until 1859 when **Groveland** was added. In 1893, the severe decline in membership caused the addition of the former Hancock bishopric as well. From this point onward this **Central Ministry** had direct involvement in almost all of the societies.

In the time of **Mother Ann Lee**, Watervliet was the home base of the English Shakers. After Mother died in 1784, Father **James Whittaker**, who succeeded her, did not seem to favor one place over another. Although Father James traveled to all the centers of union he chose to die at **Enfield, Connecticut**, for reasons we cannot state, but it seems that he threw his support to David Meacham and not **Joseph**

Meacham. There is no indication that Father James and Father Joseph ever got along. It was under Father Joseph Meacham that New Lebanon, New York, became the center of union. *See also* BISHOPRIC.

CENTRAL MINISTRY. This continues to be the most popular name used when describing the **Ministry** that had ultimate spiritual control of Shakerdom from 1787 until 1988. The origin of this name dates back to the summer of 1893, when the **Hancock Bishopric** was dissolved. The **Mount Lebanon Ministry** took charge of the two remaining societies in this bishopric. In terms of Shaker geography, this constituted a large centrally located bishopric, consisting of four societies: **Watervliet** and **New Lebanon** in New York and Hancock, Massachusetts, and **Enfield, Connecticut**. To the east and north were six Shaker societies in three bishoprics. To the west and south were five Shaker societies in one bishopric. Thus this centrally located bishopric was headed by a Ministry that became known as the Central Ministry.

Subsequent Shaker history has reinforced this idea of a Central Ministry. From the 1890s onward, the role of the Ministry came to be much more temporal than spiritual. For example, when a place was on the verge of closing, members of the Ministry moved there or at least had themselves appointed **trustees**. This enabled them to sell the property and make financial arrangements with the survivors. The tremendous temporal power and mostly residual spiritual power gave the Central Ministry a power that it never had had before.

The popularity of the term Central Ministry also comes from the fact that Eldress **Anna White** and Sister **Leila Taylor** used this term in their book *Shakerism: Its Meaning and Message*. Published in 1904, it is the last major history of the Shakers written by Shakers. The next history of the Shakers, *The Shaker Adventure* by Marguerite Fellows Melcher, published in 1940, uses the term Central Ministry as well. Even today, few people know that this is not quite an accurate way to describe the Ministry for most of its history.

One negative and misleading result of using the term Central Ministry is that observers of Shaker history have been tempted to compare **Mount Lebanon** with the Vatican. There can be little comparison between the two. First, when the Central Ministry began to have its greatest temporal power, not all of its members even lived there. Leadership was split between the women who stayed at Mount Lebanon and the men who had moved to Hancock. Second, though it was self-appointed, for the majority of its history the Ministry governed by consultation and consensus. For example, although they did choose their own successors, the appointment was not ratified unless they had the approbation of the membership.

CHAIR INDUSTRY. The most readily identifiable of all the types of Shaker furniture are chairs. The principal reason for this is that from the 1780s until the 1940s, thousands of Shaker chairs were made and sold by the **New Lebanon** Shakers. Furthermore, the success of the Shaker chair industry caused many outside furniture makers to copy Shaker styles. This has further expanded the prevalence of Shaker chairs or Shaker-like Shaker chairs in the marketplace.

The first Shaker chairs were made for community use. As the population of the communities expanded, there was a great need for all types of seating. Shaker craftsmen took the ordinary slat-back chair and modified it to reflect simplicity, lightness, and usefulness. Although all Shaker-made chairs have a distinctive look, by the 1840s there were 10 identifiable styles. These variations can be traced to the individual communities where they were produced. Charles R. Muller and Timothy D. Rieman, in their work *The Shaker Chair*, identify unique styles that can be attributed to: **Watervliet** and New Lebanon, New York; **Enfield** and **Canterbury, New Hampshire**; **Harvard, Massachusetts**; **Enfield, Connecticut**; Maine, Ohio, and **South Union** and **Pleasant Hill, Kentucky**. There are a number of indicators of these types, but perhaps the easiest to use is the pommel or finial. For example, chairs from Enfield, New Hampshire, with their elongated elliptical pommels, are said by some collectors to be the most desirable. After the 1850s the decline of the villages ended a great need for chairs. Since chairs produced for use in particular communities are relatively scarce, they are more sought after by collectors than chairs the Shakers made specifically for sale to the **world**.

Though most communities made chairs, only Harvard, Massachusetts and New Lebanon, New York, actually sold chairs to the world as a large-scale industry. Harvard was located in the northern central part of Massachusetts, where large quantities of furniture, especially chairs, have always been produced. The chair industry at Harvard, however, was short lived, only lasting from the 1820s until the 1850s. In contrast, the chair industry at New Lebanon expanded tremendously during the 1850s and continued to grow into the 1880s. Thereafter it held its own into the 1930s.

Records indicate that the first chairs for sale by New Lebanon were sold by the **Church Family** in 1789. Since no other **family** had a set of **Office deacons** or **trustees** at that time, these chairs may not have been actually made in the family. They might well have been manufactured elsewhere and sold by the officials at the Church. If the chairs were not made in the Church Family, they were made by those Shakers living on the hill east of the Church. These biological families included members of the Talcott, Spires, and Hawkins clans. The hill was also known as the brickyard since bricks were manufactured there.

In 1824 all Shakers living on the hill became a distinct family known as the East Family. There are strong connections between individuals who grew up or lived on the hill and involvement in the later manufacture of chairs. For example, Benjamin Lyon (1780–1870) was originally a resident of the hill and transferred to the Church Family in 1806. He made chairs at the Church until at least 1817. The most important, however, was Daniel J. Hawkins (1781–1873) who joined the Shakers at the hill in 1792 and later served as second **elder** of the East Family, a trustee at the **Second Family**, and first elder at the South Family. Every place he went developed a chair industry. Indeed, when the **Canaan Shakers** began making chairs they were living at the West House, property owned by the Second Family where Hawkins was a trustee. It is important to realize that what later became the East and South Families were originally a part of the Second Family. This large family also had a branch at the West House, which never became an independent family. The influence of the Second Family in one way or another extended over at least half of all Shakers at New Lebanon. When records indicate chairs made at the Second Family, the reference is more accurately interpreted as referring to the South House where an industry was being concentrated by 1850. In the 1850s, when it was decided to make the South House an independent family, Daniel J. Hawkins was chosen as its first elder.

Development of the industry was rapid. At least 200 chairs were made in 1850 and two years later George O'Donnell of the Second Family patented a tilter device for chairs. In 1863, the South Family was set off as totally independent from the Second Family and Daniel J. Hawkins and **Robert Wagan** were appointed elders. The first chair broadside was published in 1867 and earliest bound catalog in 1874. Eight more catalogs were issued before 1880. Since the South Family never had more than 40 members, outside labor was employed in the manufacture of chairs. Under Elder Robert Wagan, a new factory was built in 1872. Chairs were sized from 0 to 7. This number was stamped into the back of the top slat. In addition, a decal identifying the chair as of true Shaker manufacture was applied to one of the inside runners of rocking chairs. Various seats and covering could also be ordered.

This profitable business, known as the R. M. Wagan Company, continued after Elder Robert Wagan's untimely death in 1883. He was succeeded by William Anderson (1841–1930). By 1900, the industry was fading due to the drastic decline of the number of Shakers at the South Family. In 1908, Margaret Eggleson arrived from the Harvard Shakers and took charge of the Second Family. Her vision was to revive the chair industry by bringing the Second Family back into close association with the business. Under her plan, **Lillian Barlow** and **Ernest Pick** would make chairs at the Second Family, then the chairs would be sent to the South Family to be finished and sold by Eldress **Sarah Collins** and her associates. A large unused stone shop at the Second Family was made into the chair factory. When William Perkins (1854–1934) joined the Second Family in 1915, his background as a woodworker was of tremendous help. In fact, he and Lillian Barlow formed the Mount Lebanon Woodworking Company. They manufactured chairs together for almost 20 years, in spite of a fire that destroyed the stone shop in 1923. By 1935, Eldress Sarah Collins was living alone at the South Family, and it was decided to have her move to the Second Family with Sister Lillian Barlow. Chairs in limited numbers were still being produced, finished, and sold until 1940, when the Second Family property was sold. At that time Eldress Sarah and Sister Lillian moved to the **North Family**. After Sister Lillian died in 1942, no more chairs were made at New Lebanon. *See also* FURNITURE.

CHILDREN'S ORDER. This remains an ambiguous term at best. After 1824, the Shakers accepted a large number of children. So many children were taken in at the **New Lebanon, New York**, society that it was decided to begin a Children's Order as a juvenile branch of the **Church Family**. In this they were reviving the Children's Order set up by Father **Joseph Meacham** during the early years when many children had come into the community with their parents. Until the 1860s the Church Family at New Lebanon was considered a cut above the rest of Shakerism. Its members worshipped separately from the other Shakers and it was expected that these Church Family members be role models as ideal Shakers. It was thought that if children were brought up at the Church Family in association with the best Shakers, they would become strong Shakers themselves. These children would have lived a life of **celibacy** right from birth and thus would be natural Shakers. From the 1820s until the 1850s, the Shakers remained optimistic that the presence of numerous children would prove to be of benefit. During that time, hundreds of young people were taken in, but with few lasting gains. Also, the Children's Order at the Church was never fully implemented and was created and dissolved a number of times.

Other families at New Lebanon had children; some had many children, relative to their population as a whole. Shakers in these other families and other societies may have referred to their children as part of a Children's Order, but such an order was not articulated as such. It is proper to say that the term Children's Order refers to children living in a Shaker community and being cared for by an adult assigned to this task rather than to think of a special, highly structured organization that was responsible for children. *See also* BOYS AND THE BOYS' SHOP; CARETAKER; GIRLS AND THE GIRLS' SHOP.

CHRISTLIFE. For the Shaker, the second coming of Christ has already occurred. It was not heralded by cataclysmic events that signaled the end of the world. Rather, it came in the life and testimony of **Mother Ann Lee**. She was not the Christ, but merely the first to receive the fullness of the Christ Spirit and follow this new path of salvation. The life she espoused is the perpetual second coming of the Christ and is open to all who believe. As a result, each Shaker strives to be another Christ. This is embodied in a life lived in community.

This Christlife is what Shakerism is all about. The person who would be a Shaker must confess all sin and become obedient to the **elders**. In this context, there is potential for unlimited spiritual growth as the individual participates in the work of the Christ. *See also* JESUS OF NAZARETH.

CHURCH FAMILY. In the Shaker societies of New England and New York, the **family** that included the **Meeting House** was called the Church Family. The single exception to this was at **Groveland**, which did not have a Church Family. The East Family of that society had the Meeting House. In Ohio and Kentucky this family was designated as the **Center Family**. The exception to this was **White Water, Ohio**. The Meeting House in that community was at the North Family.

CHURCH ORDER. Also at times called the Senior Order, this is the level of membership that all Shakers who have signed the Church Order **covenant** belong to. This Church Order, or simply the Church, is "a collective body of Christians separated from the world, and enjoying in their united capacity, one common interest" (Green and Wells, *A Summary View of the Millennial Church*, 590). All Shakers who are not in the **Gathering Order** are in the Church Order; moreover, in the course of Shaker history, such Shakers did not necessarily live in the **Church Family**. Church Order Shakers lived in every family in a Shaker society that was not specifically designated as a Gathering Order. These were branches of the Church Family. There was even some overlap when Church Order Shakers were sent to live at one of the gathering families. Moreover, Gathering Order Shakers also lived at the Church Family, especially in the later years. *See also* COVENANT; FIRST ORDER OF THE CHURCH; JUNIOR ORDER; SECOND ORDER OF THE CHURCH.

CLARK, ASENATH (1780–1857). One of the prominent landowning families at **New Lebanon** during the opening of the Shaker gospel was the Clark family. Although from this important family, Asenath Clark seems to have been very self-effacing. She was born in Granby, Massachusetts, on 15 January 1780. She joined the church at the time of the first in-gathering. Not much is known of her early life, and she seems to have been one of the hundreds of young women of the second generation of Shakers who remained faithful. Promise of her future leadership potential must have been evident because in 1815 she was appointed a **family deaconess** in the **First Order of the Church**. As such, she provided for the needs of the family. She purchased supplies such as foodstuffs and matches and provided rugs, mats, and the general needs of the brothers and sisters and their rooms. This was a demanding job that had neither outward show nor power. Her successful completion of this duty caused her to be chosen by Mother **Lucy Wright** as second **eldress** in the **Ministry**.

CLOSING OF THE COVENANT. No idea has done more damage to the Shakers than this erroneous one. By its very nature the **covenant** cannot be closed. There are a number of reasons for this. First, there is not just one covenant. Each independent Shaker **family** had a covenant or more than one as families tended to deal with all sorts of degrees such as **novitiates**, articles of agreement, and **Church Order**. In addition, in order to close a covenant, a family would have to decide this for themselves. This action would be rather curious, however, since Article II Section 4 of the Church Covenant states, "the door must be kept open for the admission of new members into the Church." Subsequent revisions of this covenant, which originated from the **Ministry** as a model for all other Church Order covenants have retained this passage (Hadd, "Agreeable to Our Understanding: The Shaker Covenant," 87, 109).

It is supremely ironic that this trouble about the covenant should be connected with the relatively recent question of whether the Shakers should admit new members. By the late 1950s, the Shakers had been suffering for one hundred years from the lack of suitable adult converts. Much to the surprise of some surviving Shakers, around 1960 a few adults petitioned **Canterbury** and **Sabbathday Lake** for admission. By then all of the members in the two surviving communities had been brought up as children in the society. It was difficult for the leadership to believe that adults, especially adult men, would want to be Shakers.

In a pastoral letter written to the Sabbathday Lake Shakers, Eldress **Emma King** of Canterbury and head of the **Parent Ministry** strongly advised against the admission of adults, but she left the decision entirely up to them. (Emma B. King, letter to Eldress Gertrude M. Soule, 30 April 1963, The United Society of Shakers, Sabbathday Lake, Maine). Nonetheless, when the Sabbathday Lake Shakers offered membership to likely candidates, a terrible realignment began in the greater world of Shaker. Every antique dealer, every scholar, and every worker at a Shaker museum seemed to have a viewpoint. Since the Parent Ministry resided at Canterbury and the Shakers there were not accepting new members, most followers of things Shaker sided with Canterbury. That the covenant was somehow closed began to become a truth. The favorite dates given are 1957 and 1965. Some scholars use both, though none cite an official Shaker record as a source for this claim. No document from the archives of the Parent Ministry states a closure of the covenant.

CLOTHING. Mother Ann Lee and her contemporaries did not wear distinctive clothing. Wearing apparel that was ostentatious or ornate might have called for a rebuke, but no guidelines were given that specified dress. As time passed, however, the Shakers kept the style of clothing that had been popular in the 1790s. This is similar to how some of the distinctive clothing once worn by Roman Catholic nuns developed. In the case of nuns, peasant garb from a particular locale continued to be worn long after it was fashionable.

In general, "the sisters' dress style, established shortly after the turn of the 19th century, was a one-piece dress with a long and generally full skirt. The bodice was always completely covered by a white collar and a large neckerchief, or scarf, pinned so that a triangular point or points fell just below the waist. In the latter years of the 19th and in the 20th century, a separate shoulder cape or 'bertha' replaced the kerchief" (Gordon, *Shaker Textile Arts*, 150).

Until 1895, sisters were required to wear a cap of clear muslin or net. This fitted over the hair which was worn pulled straight back off the face. When out in the elements, a bonnet made of straw, cloth, or palm leaf was worn over the cap. Washing and preparing the cap for wear became increasingly difficult as membership aged. In addition, many sisters no longer wished to wear the cap so late in 1895, the **Central Ministry** sent a circular letter requiring all sisters over 30 to wear the cap only in worship. Those younger than that were not expected to wear the cap anymore. Three communities resisted the change: **Canterbury, New Hampshire**, and both of the Maine societies. Eventually **Sabbathday Lake** and some of the sisters at **Alfred** gave up the cap. Only at Canterbury was the cap worn universally until almost the end. Not long after the caps were no longer worn, many Shaker sisters adopted fashions from the **world**. Twentieth-century photographs show sisters from the same community dressed in various styles from the traditional Shaker garb with a cap to contemporary clothing with no cap. Again, only at Canterbury did all of the sisters always wear the Shaker habit. At Sabbathday Lake the custom of wearing contemporary clothes had never been strong, and through the influence of the Alfred Shakers who moved there in 1931, sisters there continued to wear the habit until the 1970s. Today, the distinctive clothing is worn on official occasions, at worship, and while working in the store.

Even for those who chose to wear traditional clothing, there was never complete uniformity in the dress of Shaker sisters. Climate, regional style, the availability of fabric, and finances all influenced clothing style. The length of the dresses also fluctuated. Most wore floor-length or very long dresses until well into the 20th century. Finally, there were virtually no restrictions on color or fabric prints.

"Shaker men wore the same articles of clothing as men of the world—white shirt, vest, jacket, coat, and trousers or pantaloons—but their styles were old fashion and 'peculiar'" (Gordon, *Shaker Textile Arts*, 151). They often wore hats made of various materials such as fur, straw, or wool. As the number of Shaker tailors diminished, Shaker men began to buy ready-made clothing from the world. By 1900, the few Shaker men dressed in clothing that reflected contemporary tastes. Today Shaker men, when dressing for special occasions or worship, wear collarless long-sleeved shirts, dark pants, and vests. Otherwise Shaker men wear regular work clothes, casual garb, or even sport coats as situations demand.

CLOUGH, HENRY (1754–1798). He was born in **Canterbury, New Hampshire**, 6 February 1754. He belonged to one of the first families to convert to Shakerism. His fervor caught the attention of Father **Joseph Meacham**, and Clough was invited to live at the **Meeting House** at **New Lebanon** with other young people of promise. From 1787 until his death in 1798, he served in the male part of the **New**

Lebanon Ministry. In this capacity he was associated with not only Father Joseph Meacham, but also Mother **Lucy Wright**, the most powerful woman in Shakerdom. Elder Henry was the strongest supporter of Mother Lucy and her preeminence in the **Ministry**. If not for him, Mother Lucy Wright would have never risen to the position of power that she did. Father Joseph said that no one knew his mind as Henry did. He was a capable, forceful leader. His early death was a tragedy for the church.

COCHRANE, DOROTHEA T. (1844–1912). She was born in Duntalker, Scotland, in 1844. In 1857, she arrived at **Canterbury** with her four siblings. She became second **eldress** of the **Church Family** in 1879 and succeeded Eldress **Dorothy Durgin** as first eldress in 1898. Having been nurtured by Eldress Dorothy, Eldress Dorothea had a gift with the young girls. She was especially fond of **Bertha Lindsay**, to whom she referred as her "golden child." Under her leadership, the last large group of young **sisters** was gathered under her loving ministration. Her death in 1912 marked the end of Canterbury eldresses who could attract and retain the young.

COHOON, HANNAH (1788–1864). During the **Era of Manifestations**, the heavens seemed to open upon Shaker villages. Thousands of Spirit visitors came to the **believers**, most with messages of comfort or warning. As the later stages of this revival waned, a number of Spirit or gift drawings were received. Although Shakers at other villages, most notably **New Lebanon**, received such artistic gifts, the drawings that have come to be associated with this era are paired with **Hancock** and are primarily the work of two sisters, Polly Collins and Hannah Cohoon. Certainly those of Cohoon are the most famous since they include the Shaker tree of life, a symbol that has become emblematic of all things Shaker.

The most well-known Shaker artist, Hannah Cohoon, did not become a Shaker until she was 29 years old. Born in Williamstown, Massachusetts, in 1788, she was the third and youngest daughter of Noah and Huldah Harrison. On 15 March 1817, she and her two children, Harrison and Mariah, joined the Hancock Shakers. Very little is known about her life as a believer. She signed the **covenant** in 1823 and the Sacred Roll in 1843. It appears that she lived her entire

Shaker life at the **Church Family**. She died 7 January 1864, a time when the whole nation was preoccupied with the Civil War. If her signed drawings had not been "discovered" in the 1930s, she would have remained as anonymous as thousands of other 19th-century Shakers.

Well-known music historian and folklorist Daniel Patterson characterizes the reason why her work is special. Calling this "a deeper reason for her success," he states that Hannah Cohoon finds "a subtle, slightly off balance placement of leaves and fruits," that creates for the viewer "the illusion that her tree rustles with a living spirit. This is the mystery that we call art" (Patterson, *Gift Drawing and Gift Song*, 50). Her works that have survived are: "Tree of Light or Blazing Tree," 9 October 1845; "A Bower of Mulberry Trees," 13 September 1854; "The Tree of Life," 4 October 1854; and "Basket of Apples," 29 June 1856.

COLLINS, (MARY JANE) SARAH (1855–1947). For many years, Shakers at the South House of the **Second Family** of **New Lebanon** wanted to be set off on their own as an independent **family**. The **Ministry** decided to acquiesce to this in 1858. On 30 December of that year, Daniel J. Hawkins of the Second Family was appointed to be the first **elder** of a partially independent South Family. Elder Daniel, who was 79 years old, agreed to take the position if he could also get a number of children to raise. Slowly the Second Family ceded control over buildings and land, but though elders were put into place, temporal affairs were managed by the **trustees** of the Second Family until 1863, when the South Family became totally independent. True to his promise, in 1863 Elder Daniel traveled to Boston to get children.

Mary Jane Collins was born 1 May 1855 in Boston. Her mother Catherine Collins died while she was a child. Her father enlisted in the Civil War and was killed. She was at one of the orphanages Elder Daniel visited, and he chose her along with others to accompany him to the South Family. When she arrived, her name was changed by Sister Polly Lewis to avoid confusion with another girl from Boston who had the same first names. Sarah was chosen because Sister Polly thought that she resembled an aunt of hers with that name.

The principal industry at the South Family was the production of chairs for sale. Since Elder Daniel was 83 when the family was set off, a much younger man, **Robert Wagan**, age 30, from the Second Family was put in as second elder. Under Elder Robert's supervision, the **chair industry** expanded until a large factory had to be built to accommodate the trade. The first task Sarah Collins was asked to perform was wrapping finished chairs for shipment. From here she went on to taping and finishing chairs. One interesting diversion she never forgot was a visit Tom Thumb and his wife made to the South Family in 1868. In addition to chairs, the family also made blankets used in the circus. Since the main road from Pittsfield to Albany passed directly in front of the buildings, circuses would travel by and elephants and other tame animals would drink from the ponds along the Shakers' street.

As idyllic as **Mount Lebanon** may have seemed on the surface, however, serious problems were never far away. In 1875 Mount Lebanon suffered two major fires in February at the **First Order** of the Church. This helped further destabilize the entire community. For many years, almost all of the young left as soon as they could. That year after the fires, Sarah Collins, age 20, had decided she too would leave. She packed her belongings and had secured a job in New York City through a friend. Deaconess Polly Lewis pleaded with her to stay. Sarah was moved by "Aunt Polly's" appeal. She had been raised by her and thought of her as her mother. In addition, the Shakers needed her help, especially in the chair factory. Polly promised that Sarah would be made an **eldress** if she stayed. After much inner turmoil she decided not to leave. The Ministry appointed her second eldress in September 1875. Although from this point onward Eldress Sarah Collins has been closely identified with the chair industry at the South Family, in truth, this business—officially R. M. Wagan and Company—had diminished by 1900. During the early years of the 20th century, she was engaged in the fancy goods industry. In 1908, after the death of Eldress Ann Charles, she became first eldress of the South Family. Seemingly unfazed by the decline in membership, she still led the small family in meeting and played the organ for the service. She also wrote prayers.

Starting in 1908, the chair industry was revived in a partnership with the Second Family. Chair-making moved from the factory at the South Family to the large stone workshop at the Second Family. Sister **Lillian Barlow**, Elder **Ernest Pick**, and Brother William Perkins made the chairs which were then shipped to the South Family where they were finished by Eldress Sarah Collins. Photos from the 20th century show Eldress Sarah taping chairs. After a fire destroyed the stone shop in 1923, an adjacent building at the Second Family was refitted for use. In 1935, Eldress Sarah was 80 years old and the sole remaining Shaker at the South Family. That year she moved into the Second Family where Sister Lillian Barlow lived. In 1940 the Second Family was closed and its three survivors moved to the **North Family**. Sister Lillian died in 1942 and no more chairs were made after that date. However, Eldress Sarah, for a short while longer, continued to work on fancy goods and made repairs on chairs. In October 1947 she moved to **Hancock** when the North Family was closed. She died a month later.

CONFESSION. This is also called opening the mind. Before one can be a Shaker, it is necessary privately to confess one's sins to the designated person in the community. This is one of the **elders** or eldresses. By making this confession, a person is freed from sin and can embark on a new life in Christ. Shakers are encouraged to confess whenever necessary, but always at least once a year during the **Fast Day**.

COOLBROTH, HARRIETT NEWELL (1864–1953). She was born in Scarborough, Maine, on 30 April 1864. Her parents were Joseph and Harriet Bragdon Coolbroth. In 1875, after their death, she and her two brothers were admitted to the **Alfred** Shakers. Elder **John Vance** placed her at the **Second Family** under the care of the saintly Eldress Francella Blake. Eldress Francella was an exceptionally talented woman and shared her love of the gospel with young Harriett. Though Eldress Francella died in 1879, Harriett often remarked that one of the greatest treasures of her life was the time she spent under her care. Eldress Eliza Smith, another deeply religious and devoted leader, took Eldress Francella's place. Under the guidance of Eldress Eliza, Harriett grew to maturity and embraced Shakerism with energy and enthusiasm.

Harriett became the **eldress** at the Second Family when Eldress Eliza's health declined. In every way she was the spiritual leader of this small family. While changes raged in other Shaker places, an emphasis on hard work and traditional Shaker dress and mannerisms remained the norm at the Second Family. She also taught her girls as many of the old Shaker **songs** as they could absorb. As a result, many of these songs have been preserved and are still sung today.

Contemporary Shakers, some of whom knew her well, have remarked that she had a gift with young people. Borrowing the idea from **Canterbury**, she organized a club called the "Beacon Lights," which met once a week. She served as the president and at their meetings each member had to offer an original presentation. Under her tutelage a large number of young girls were formed into Shaker sisters who remained faithful for life. Since many of these young Shakers were under her care in the early 20th century, Alfred was one of just two Shaker communities to have a high percentage of youthful members by 1920. Ironically, as rich as Alfred was in spiritual resources, it was poor in temporal matters. The Second Family closed in 1917 and the next year its members were absorbed into the **Church Family**. Eldress Harriet then became first eldress. Since her associate Elder **Henry Green** was in bad health, she virtually ran the whole place.

In spite of strong appeals, the **Parent Ministry's** decision to close Alfred was a heartbreaking ordeal for Eldress Harriett. In 1931, she led the 20 survivors from Alfred to live at **Sabbathday Lake**. Eldress **Prudence Stickney** was the leader at Sabbathday Lake, but Eldress Harriett retained a strong spiritual influence over the former Alfred Shakers until the 1940s. The final five years of her life she was an invalid. She died 2 September 1953. Her influence is still felt at Sabbathday Lake. *See also* ALFRED; BARKER, R. MILDRED; JOHNSON, THEODORE ELLIOTT.

COVENANT. This is the legal document or agreement made between an individual Shaker and the church. It offers the Shaker a home for life with all of the temporal and spiritual benefits. In turn it states the conditions by which this is granted. The covenant also explains the duties of the various leaders of a community: **Ministry**, **elders**, **trustees**, **deacons**, etc.

It is difficult to make any other general statements concerning the covenant. Covenants evolved over time to reflect the changes that were taking place within Shakerism. The first covenants were oral, but these did not prove adequate as more people joined and then left. Those who had lived in a community often sought to be remunerated for their time. The first covenants were then written down and revised to offer greater protection to the Shakers. The earliest written covenants date from 1795, but major revisions were made at **New Lebanon** in 1801, 1814, and 1830. Other societies took these revisions and rewrote their covenants so that changes in most covenants are dated close to these years. Almost every individual Shaker **family** had its own covenant and its language reflected whether the family was of the **Church Order** or the **Gathering Order**.

When an adult joins the Shakers he/she signs a **probationary covenant**. This protects the Shakers from lawsuits to reclaim wages. At the present time, a person must live with the Shakers five years before being allowed to sign the Church Order covenant. Signing is done privately with a Shaker trustee as a witness. *See also* CLOSING OF THE COVENANT.

– D –

DAMON, THOMAS (1819–1880). He was born in Johnston, Rhode Island, on 26 December 1819. His parents were Arthur and Olive Damon. At that time, the **Enfield, Connecticut**, Shakers had been doing a great deal of missionary work in nearby Rhode Island and scores of converts joined the society from there. People with names such as Burlingame, Wilcox, and Damon would have an impact until well into the 20th century. Indeed, the last of the Rhode Islanders, Elder **George Wilcox**, did not die until 1910, literally on the eve of Enfield's dissolution.

Thomas Damon joined the Enfield Shakers with his family in 1827. He first gathered at the West Family and in 1834 moved to the **Church Family**. He was sent back to the West in 1836 and then back a final time to the Church in 1839. From this point onward, his life became one of prominence as he slowly ascended the ranks and took on more responsibilities. In 1841, he signed the **covenant**, and that next year he became **caretaker** of the boys. A special **boys' shop** had been erected to house the large population of boys that the society had taken in. Brother Thomas was their guide and teacher. In addition to these time-consuming duties, he continued to develop and refine the cabinetmaking skill he had learned from older members of the community. Perhaps indicative of the future he would have, he helped prepare Enfield's **feast grounds**, the Mount of Olives. In 1843, he lettered the marble **fountain stone** that stood in the most pivotal spot in this sacred place. This setting up of outdoor worship areas and the use of mystical names was a major aspect of the last part of the **Era of Manifestations**. Only those considered to be the most worthy were given the type of tasks that he performed. His involvement in the manifestations, his skill as a cabinetmaker, and his tutelage of the boys pointed to a future as the **elder** of the Church Family.

Though thoroughly involved with life at Enfield, his destiny as a Shaker, however, was to be played out in a larger field, the **bishopric Ministry** at **Hancock**. On Christmas Day, 1845, he was consulted about joining the Ministry to stand second to Elder **Grove Wright**. The Church Family reluctantly agreed to sacrifice him for the greater good of the bishopric, and consequently he became second in the Ministry on 1 January 1846. In this job he traveled among the three communities of the bishopric, Enfield, **Tyringham**, and Hancock. Yet most of his time was spent at Hancock. He held this position until 7 October 1860 when he became first in the Ministry. During these years the Shakers reached the peak of their strength and his tenure spanned the years from the Era of Manifestations to the time of apparent decline. He died in 1880 at the age of 60. This was early enough so that he did not see the communities that had been under his care become moribund. Nevertheless he had the sad task of closing the first major society, Tyringham, in 1875.

When he went into the Ministry, many of those who had been children of **Mother's First Born** were still alive. In fact, he did not live in the **Meeting House** at Hancock until 1 June 1848, the day that Mother **Dana Goodrich** died. Since all members of the Shakers had to be gainfully employed, including the Ministry, he used his considerable mechanical skills to help out where needed, but his energies were most spent manufacturing table swifts for winding yarn, a business begun by his associate Elder Grove Wright. For over 30 years he made thousands of these devices. A good number of them survive today as a testimony to his craftsmanship.

As a Shaker minister, he was ever optimistic and had a real enthusiasm for the work of the gospel. His diaries and correspondence reveal that at times he was frustrated by the condition of the Shaker religion, but he never wavered in his commitment. For various reasons, Enfield, Connecticut, held a special place in the heart of some Shakers. For example, Father **James Whittaker** went there to die in 1787. In like fashion, Elder Thomas returned to Enfield shortly before his demise. He is buried among the believers on the hill opposite the Meeting House. After Damon's death, the Hancock bishopric lacked a vigorous male leader, and it was just a matter of time, a dozen years or so, before its Ministry was dissolved.

DANCE. *See* EXERCISES.

DARROW, DAVID (1750–1825). The strength of early Shakerism was the network of large families that joined during the 1780s and 1790s. The Darrow family was one of these groups. Originally from Connecticut, they lived in **New Lebanon** during the time of the **opening of the gospel**.

David Darrow was born on 21 June 1750 in Norwalk, Connecticut. After the **New Light** revival faded, he converted to Shakerism along with his wife Prudence. They had four known children: Selah or Cecilia, Betsey, Lucy, and Ruth. All of them died Shakers, and, in fact, Betsey, Lucy, and Ruth were **eldresses**. David Darrow joined the Church at New Lebanon when it was gathered in 1787, and his family's land became the nucleus of the **Church Family**. In 1792, he was appointed the first elder of the **First Family of the Church**. This was a tremendous honor. Elder David led the most important **family** of Shakerdom, the group that was supposed to be the most advanced. High standards of behavior and a deep religious faith were demanded of all those who lived in the Church Family. Therefore, it was only natural that Mother **Lucy Wright** would send Elder David out to Ohio to be the **Lead** in 1805. He had been successful in setting up **gospel order** at New Lebanon. His task in the West would be to pull together the scattered and diverse groups—people who had never known **Mother Ann** or the **First Parents**.

nally she asked her father for permission to join the Shakers. She was just 14 years old, and her father cautioned against the move, but in the end, allowed her to choose for herself. She joined and spent the next 62 years giving everything she had to the community. Her entire Shaker life was spent at the **North Family**, New Lebanon.

In 1838, she became second eldress and in 1850 became first eldress. She held this position for the remainder of her life. One of her many strengths was that she could not abide evildoing and was not afraid to confront someone whom she felt was not living up to Shaker ideals. First in association with Elder **Richard Bushnell**, and later with Elder **Frederick Evans**, she helped propel the North Family into being the best known of all Shaker families. One avenue that helped accomplish this was publication. Not content to conduct missionary tours to cities, the elders of the North Family published tracts, sermons, books, poems, and songs. In 1873, they took over the Shaker newspaper as well. As a symbol of their egalitarian views, the monthly, the *Shaker*, was renamed the *Shaker and Shakeress*. Doolittle contributed many articles for it over the years and for a while ran a department for submission of articles by female Shakers or any sympathetic woman. In 1880, she published an autobiography. Among her other works were the broadsides "Conflict between Right and Wrong" and "A Shakeress on American Institutions." Her tracts include "Thoughts Concerning Deity" and "War Positively Unchristian."

Evans and Doolittle were considered to be liberal Shakers and so their tenure running the paper only lasted until 1875. After this, Doolittle continued her efforts on behalf of reform, especially women's rights and pacifism. She died on 31 December 1886. Her final words, "It is the gift of God," sum up her lifetime of service to the religion she loved.

DUMONT, WILLIAM (1851–1930). By the 1870s few capable adult men were joining the Shakers. An exception to this was William Dumont. Born 15 August 1851 in Rockland, Maine, William was among the seven children of Irish immigrant John Dumont (originally McDermot) and Hannah Curtiss. He was orphaned when he was three years old and sent to live with an uncle in Ossipee, New Hampshire. A year later he became a cabin boy on a ship out of Portsmouth, New Hampshire, and most of his youth was spent at sea. One of his sisters married a man who lived near the **Sabbathday Lake** Shakers. While visiting this sister, he came in contact with the **believers**. Elder Joseph Brackett and Brother Granville Merrill worked to draw him into the community. What made the decision to join the Shakers especially difficult was that he had been promised the position of captain on a vessel. In the end, William chose to become a Shaker and joined on 20 November 1870.

It would seem that he never regretted his decision nor did he ever look back at his former life. Rapidly he rose in the ranks. In 1872, he had charge of the horses. Two years later he managed the large farm. By 1878 he was second **elder** of the Church and in 1880 was made first elder. While retaining the eldership of the Church, he became first **trustee** in 1884 and, in 1896, first in the Maine **Ministry**. Due to the serious shortage of men, he filled the position of family elder, first trustee, and minister all at the same time. This would not have been possible if he did not have Eldress **Elizabeth Noyes** as his associate. In every way they were the perfect team, and together they led Sabbathday Lake for most of the 50 years of its greatest prosperity, 1880–1926.

Since the large majority of the community was made up of women, Elder William wisely became involved with their industries and helped them whenever he could. For example, he supplied poplar shavings and turkey feathers for their fancy goods trade. In addition to his duties as an elder and trustee, he ran the farm and orchards. One of his greatest achievements was to help raise money to build the large brick dwelling that was completed in 1884. He seemed to be able to do all things well. Unlike so many other Shaker men, he had success in attracting many males into the church. Between 1880 and 1930, he gathered 87 men and boys into the Shakers.

As long as he was physically able, he worked to build up not only Sabbathday Lake but also **Alfred**. During the 1920s his health gradually declined, and he died 7 April 1930, aged 78.

DUNLAVY (DUNLEVY), JOHN (1769–1826). Born in Virginia, John Dunlavy was a Presbyterian minister at the time of the great Kentucky Revival. He cared for settlements at Eagle Creek, Straight Creek, and Red Oak Church in Ohio. The intensity of the revival in 1801 spilled over into Ohio at Eagle Creek, the first place in that state to be affected. When Shaker missionaries arrived in 1805, Dunlavy was the first of his congregation to convert.

The arrival of the Shakers at Eagle Creek was not by chance. Dunlavy was married to **Richard McNemar**'s sister Cassia. McNemar, a convert to Shakerism at **Turtle Creek (Union Village)** had also been a Presbyterian minister and a close associate of Dunlavy's. A small number of Shakers gathered around land purchased by Dunlavy. Other members of his family, including siblings, also became Shakers. Believers also could be found at various other nearby locations, including Straight Creek and White Oak. Shaker leadership from Union Village made valiant efforts to advance these groups toward a permanent embrace of Shakerism and gather them into **order** in one place. By 1810, it was evident that this might never be accomplished, and Shakers from that section of southwestern Ohio were encouraged to remove to **Busro** in Indiana. Accordingly, in March 1811, 80 people moved to Busro and 70 to Union Village (Boice, Covington, and Spence, *Maps of the Shaker West*, 25–33). John Dunlavy went to Union Village and later to **Pleasant Hill**. In 1818, while at Pleasant Hill, he wrote one of the major works on Shaker theology, the *Manifesto, or a Declaration of the Doctrines and Practice of the Church of Christ.* He died at **West Union, Indiana**, on 16 September 1826.

DURGIN, DOROTHY ANN (1825–1898). It is not too much to say that the reason so many young women stayed as Shakers at **Canterbury** was due to the loving care of Eldress Dorothy Durgin. In addition, her influence reached into the administration of Eldress **Dorothea Cochrane** who succeeded her. Thus, from 1857 until 1912, the female leaders of the Canterbury Shakers were people who had the necessary qualities to reach the young. The number of young women who joined was great and the society endured as long as it did because of this.

She was born on 23 November 1825 in Sanbornton, New Hampshire. Her father was William Durgin and her mother was Dorothy Dearborn Sanborn. When she was eight, her mother died, and she was adopted by her uncle and aunt, Asa and Abigail Bean. Her uncle had known of the Shakers and on 13 July 1834, along with her brother Henry, she was admitted to the Canterbury Shakers. Though this was intended to be a visit, she remained there for life. One of the aspects of her life that made her a good Shaker was that she was very religious. Her mother had also been religious and, during Dorothy's early childhood, had held prayer meetings in their house. For Dorothy, prayer was the key to all problems, and this confidence helped her face all issues throughout her life.

From 1846 until 1852, she became a teacher in the Shaker school. Her associate in this work was **Henry Blinn**. In 1852, she was made second **eldress** under Marcia Hastings. In this capacity she had the responsibility of working with the older girls and the youngest **sisters**. Most of these had been her students, so her loving care of them continued. Five years later she was appointed first eldress of the **Church Family**. Except for one year, which she spent in the **Ministry** (1860–61), for the remainder of her life she was first eldress. In all she was a **family** eldress for 46 years. Her competence and the stability of the leadership at Canterbury were great strengths that benefited the community.

In so many ways Dorothy was the ideal Shaker sister. She was focused on the home and nothing could deter her from building it up in any way she could. All facets of domestic life caught her attention. She encouraged the sisters to be industrious, and she provided care and comfort to all. In addition, she had the gift of **song**. Over 500 pages of hymns are attributed to her. Once again, however, her greatest gift was the ability to attract and retain the young. She died of cancer 24 August 1898. Her funeral on 26 August was the occasion of numerous tributes to her years of service.

DWELLING HOUSE. The principal building housing a **family** of Shakers is called a dwelling house or dwelling. The earliest dwellings were modified farmhouses that had been owned by the first converts. In time large gambrel-roofed structures were built in some of the earliest communities. All of these were replaced or altered by large clapboard, gable-ended structures. These dwellings housed from a dozen to one hundred members. Not all Shakers lived in the dwelling house, however. Some lived at the **Office**, the place where business was transacted. Others lived in the **Infirmary** or in the **Girls' Shop** or **Boys' Shop**. A few others lived in the shop where they worked. Finally, the **Ministry** lived in its own shop or in the apartments above the **Meeting House**.

Most Shaker dwellings in the East built before 1850 were made of wood, though the large brick dwelling at **Hancock**, the South Family at **Shirley**, and the massive stone dwelling at **Enfield, New Hampshire**, are notable exceptions. In the Shaker West, Ohio, and Kentucky, wooden dwellings were the exception. This simply shows the use of native materials in each instance.

Though the layout of a dwelling could differ, a typical Shaker dwelling had a dining room and kitchen on the lowest level. Waiting rooms, storage rooms, and cellars were here as well. Above this on the floor that opened onto the street was a meeting room that could be used for worship. All along passageways on this floor and above were rooms that housed the Shakers or served as common areas, such as music rooms and offices. The retiring rooms were segregated into male or female areas. In most dwellings the rooms of the brethren and sisters were separated by a hallway. At the top of the dwellings were spacious attics, lit by borrowed light from skylights or glass transoms. A bell on the roof was used to summon Shakers to meals or give alarm. Before bells came into common use, conch shells, trumpets, or triangles were used.

Shakers took great pride in their dwellings, and the prosperity of a society could be judged by the condition of its dwelling, as visitors to Shaker communities often note. For many years, the dwelling of the richer societies remained in the vanguard of innovations for comfortable living. For example, by 1870, the North Family at **Mount Lebanon** had central heating from radiators. As soon as electricity and telephones were available, most Shakers dwellings had them as well.

DYER, CALEB MARSHALL (1800–1863). *See* ENFIELD, NEW HAMPSHIRE.

DYER, MARY MARSHALL (1780–1867). Of the thousands of people who have left the Shakers over the years, the most famous is Mary Dyer. For 52 years she conducted an anti-Shaker campaign that included several books. She also lectured and preached against the Shakers for decades. In the end, she never got her children back, her principal intent, but she achieved a fame that no other Shaker **apostate** has even approached.

She was born in Northumberland, New Hampshire, on 7 August 1780. Her parents were Caleb Marshall and Zeruiah Harriman Marshall. In 1799, she married Joseph Dyer, a widower, and settled in Stratford, New Hampshire. They had five children: **Caleb**, Betsey, Orville, Jerrub, and Joseph. In 1805, they moved to Stewartstown, New Hampshire, where they farmed and formed part of a tight-knit rural community. At times her husband served as town clerk and selectman.

Since the region where they lived was on the edge of settlement, organized religion did not have a hold on the scattered households. Religious activity in the form of revivals was common, but permanent churches were few. In 1809, Mary and her husband were baptized as Freewill Baptists. This did not end their religious quest. In fact, they were open to preachers who would come by the area. One of these, Lemuel Crooker, had a copy of the 1810 edition of *The Testimony of Christ's Second Appearing*. This work was the catalyst that eventually led the Dyers to embrace Shakerism. They visited the Shakers at **Enfield, New Hampshire**, and later received visits by the Shakers. The Dyers were at the center of the region's enthusiasm for the Shakers. At one point 30 people around Stewartstown were interested in converting.

In 1812, Betsey and Orville Dyer were brought to live at Enfield. By the end of January 1813, the other three children were gathered and Mary and her husband joined in November 1813. They lived at the North Family, which was the **Gathering Order** at Enfield. The next year they signed the **probationary covenant** and **indentured** their children. As the family gradually progressed deeper into Shaker practices, all of her family except her youngest child and her husband were moved to different **families**. The loss of contact with her children was a heavy cross for her, and the longer she lived as a Shaker, the more dissatisfied she felt. She was ambitious and wanted to preach. In addition, she had independent ideas that did not fit Shaker doctrine. She found herself constricted by not being allowed to debate and discuss theology. Soon she found that there was no room for open defiance and personal interpretation of rules or practices.

As long as she had the prospect of having some control of her children, Mary Dyer uneasily acquiesced to life at Enfield. When it became clear that she would never again have any real say in the upbringing of her children, she decided to leave the society. When she informed her husband of her intention, she expected him to honor a pledge he had made three years earlier that if she ever left, she could take some of the children with her. Joseph Dyer refused to allow her to have any of their children. This set her heart against the Shakers and, though she was no longer living as a Shaker by the end of January 1815, she remained connected with them for the rest of her life through her anti-Shaker activities.

When Mary Dyer left the society, her immediate home was nearby Hanover, New Hampshire. Here she formed a network of supporters that helped launch her lifelong crusade. Her published works include: *A Brief Statement of the Sufferings of Mary Dyer* (1818); *A Portraiture of Shakerism* (1822); *Reply to the Shakers' Statements* (1824); *The Rise and Progress of the Serpent from the Garden of Eden, to the Present Day* (1847); and *Shakerism Exposed: Being an Account of the Persecution Suffered by the Author at the Hand of the Shakers of Lebanon and Canterbury* (1855). As noted, she frequently lectured about the evils of Shakerism and how her life had been ruined by them.

As time passed, general dislike of the Shakers waned and Mary Dyer might have seemed an anachronism as the Civil War loomed and America continued to change. One small satisfaction for her was that her son Jerrub left the Shakers in the early 1850s. If, however, she expected to have a home with him, she was to be disappointed. He left New Hampshire and did not return until 1861.

The definitive work on her life and anti-Shaker campaign is *Shaking the Faith* by Elizabeth DeWolfe.

– E –

EADES (EADS), HARVEY LAUDERDALE (1807–1892). Throughout his entire life Harvey Eades was fond of saying that he was born a Shaker, and that he always believed.

His claim was true since his parents, Samuel and Sally Eades, converted before his birth on 28 April 1807. He was placed in the **Children's Order** at **South Union** before he was even a year old.

Though his entry into the Shakers may have been unique, his early life as a young man growing up in the society was not. He was prepared to work at various trades. He was a teamster, gardener, shoemaker, schoolteacher, bookbinder, tailor, and carpenter. When he was 29 he was appointed second in the **Ministry** at South Union. He served under Father **Benjamin Seth Youngs**. In 1844 he was transferred to the **Center Family** at **Union Village** and eventually became the elder of the **Gathering Order** at Union Village. In 1862, he was reappointed to the Ministry of South Union and, in 1868, was made first in the new Ministry formed when those of South Union and **Pleasant Hill** were combined into one. This Ministry was dissolved in 1889.

Elder Harvey had always been a zealous Shaker, yet he came from a religious tradition and climate very different from the one that existed at **Mount Lebanon, New York**, where the Shaker leadership lived. In time, this put him in serious conflict with some of the Shaker **elders** there. Perhaps the most vivid of these involved his feud with Elder **Frederick Evans**. Ever since the Shaker newspaper had started in 1871, it had espoused viewpoints that were from the perspective of **Watervliet** and Mount Lebanon, New York. All Shakers were encouraged to read the paper, contribute articles, and pay for the cost of production. Yet at the same time, not all Shaker opinions were valued equally. This difference in opinion boiled over into a tense discussion that followed the publication of an article by Elder Frederick in the December 1874 issue of the *Shaker and Shakeress*. In it Elder Frederick asserts that Jesus was a sinner before he was anointed the chosen one. This was too much for Elder Harvey and after garnering some support in the West, he journeyed to see the Ministry at Mount Lebanon. He arrived shortly after the great fires of February 1875. Literally the heart of Shakerism, the **First Order of the Church** at Mount Lebanon, was destroyed. Amid the charred ruins, Elder Harvey pleaded his case that spiritually the Shakers were dead as well. When the Ministry eventually reprimanded Elder Frederick for his views, he resigned as editor.

Over the course of his lifetime, Elder Harvey wrote many works. His most widely known are *Shaker Sermons: Scripto-rational*, which went through five printings between 1879 and 1889, and *Discourses on Religion, Science, and Education*. Some of the latter were reprints from the Shaker newspaper and others were reprints from his Shaker sermons. He also wrote a book on tailoring and collected and wrote songs.

His autobiography, never published but existing in manuscript form, gives many vivid details about life at South Union. He also kept a journal that shows the tensions as well as the joy of living in a communal society. As he aged, it was heartbreaking for him to see the decline of Shakerism. Nothing he did seemed to help stem the downward trend. His efforts as **trustee** were particularly disastrous, causing a loss of over $80,000 over the years. He died 13 February 1892.

ELDER AND ELDRESS. Each Shaker **family** was under the spiritual direction of a set or lot of elders. Generally this was a team of two men and two women. Their duties were to lead the worship and provide spiritual guidance in all forms. Until 1862, the title first elder and first eldress were reserved for the first in the **Ministry**. The seconds in the Ministry were only referred to as **brother** or **sister**. The title of elder brother and elder sister were used for those in charge of a family until that time. After this the more familiar reference to any elder as either first or second came into common use. Most often the first elder and first eldress were older, tried-and-true Shakers. The second elder and second eldress were younger and had the charge of youth from the time they left the **caretakers** at age 14 until they reached adulthood.

ENFIELD, CONNECTICUT (1792–1917). SPIRITUAL NAME: City of Union. FEAST GROUND: Mount of Olives. BISHOPRIC: Hancock. FAMILIES: Church (**First Family**), North Family (**Second Family**), East Family (part of the North Family), South Family (**Gathering Order**), West Family (Gathering Order). MAXIMUM POPULATION AND YEAR: 215 in 1850. INDUSTRIES: seeds, herbs, fancy goods, cattle, dairy products, poultry, eggs. NOTABLE SHAKERS: Father **Joseph Meacham**, **John Meacham**, David Meacham, Jefferson White, Omar Pease, **Thomas Damon**, **George Wilcox**, **Thomas Fisher**, **Walter Shepherd**, Gilbert Avery, Caroline Tate, Sophia Copley, Maria Lyman, Miriam Offord. UNIQUE FEATURES: Of all of the original Shaker societies, Enfield had the best land. Unlike the hilly Berkshires and Taconics or rocky northern New England, Enfield was in the Connecticut River Valley and benefited from excellent land near abundant water. Other Shaker places claim to have originated the seed industry, but the Enfield Shakers always maintained that they were the first, in 1802, to engage in the trade. Whether this is true or not, the society, under the skilled direction of **trustee** Jefferson White, developed extensive seed routes in the South prior to the Civil War. His death in 1859 and the Civil War not long after brought this industry to a halt almost at once. Finally, this society had a number of exceedingly impressive buildings. One was the Sisters' Shop built in 1872 at the North Family. It was so commodious that when the **Upper Canaan Shakers** moved there in 1897, they took over this building as their **dwelling house** rather than use the old and run-down North Family dwelling. Another structure of note was the 1876 brick dwelling at the **Church Family**. It was constructed in anticipation of the arrival of the Shakers from **Tyringham**.

BRIEF HISTORY: Father Joseph Meacham was born in Enfield, but moved to **New Lebanon, New York**, where he was a Baptist minister. After his conversion, his father and brother David, who were still living at Enfield, joined the Shakers, along with most of the town's Baptists. These religionists lived in the extreme northeast corner of the town and in the bordering town of Somers, Connecticut. The Meacham property became the Church Family, while Lot Pease's farm was gathered into the South Family. The North or Second Family was at the Allen farm. Since Father Joseph was from Enfield, much of his large, extended family eventually moved to New Lebanon. In spite of this, so many people joined at Enfield that by 1803 there were 146 members. This made the society the third largest; only New Lebanon and **Canterbury** were larger. Moreover, the perseverance rate among the large families that joined was high. For example, of the 48 Church Family Shakers in 1792, 90 percent remained with the Shakers for their entire lives. When it is considered that well over half of this family consisted of young adults from age 20 to 31, this high rate of faithfulness gave the Enfield Shakers a pool of talent and leadership that served the community well for the next 50 years. By that time, their inspiration had attracted another strong generation.

With the wholesale addition of children starting in the 1820s, Enfield maintained a large population. Indeed, not until the 1850s did the community begin to fail to keep sufficient young members. After this, the departure of most of the children and an aging membership caused the decline to be rapid. It occurred at the same time that the seed industry collapsed. This did not diminish the zeal for building, however, and large structures such as the North Family Sisters' Shop and the 1876 brick dwelling at the Church were erected long after there was any need for them. In 1875, the society was enriched by the addition of 12 Shakers from Tyringham, which had broken up. In 1897, the entire **Upper Canaan, New York**, Shaker family moved to the North Family at Enfield. Outwardly, as late as 1900 Enfield seemed to be doing well. It still had 87 members, making it the fourth largest Shaker society. Serious internal problems, deaths, and the failure to retain enough young people caused the population to plummet to only 24 in 1910. Late in 1914, the property was sold to a tobacco syndicate. The last four Shakers left there in October 1917. Elder Walter Shepherd and Daniel Orcutt went to the **North Family** at **Mount Lebanon**. Eldress Caroline Tate and Lucy Bowers went to the South Family at **Watervliet, New York**.

LAST SHAKER: Adeline Patterson (1882–1968). She joined as a youth at the North Family and moved to the Church at Mount Lebanon, when the North closed in 1913. In 1921 she was transferred to the Church at Hancock, where she survived the closing of the community in 1960. After Hancock, she went into a nursing home in Concord, New Hampshire, because her health did not permit her to join nearby Canterbury. She is buried at Canterbury.

ENFIELD, NEW HAMPSHIRE (1793–1923). SPIRITUAL NAME: Chosen Vale. FEAST GROUND: Mount Assurance. BISHOPRIC: Canterbury. FAMILIES: Church, South (**Second Family**), North (**Gathering Order**). MAXIMUM POPULATION AND YEAR: 297 in 1840. INDUSTRIES: seeds, spinning wheels, buckets, tubs, brooms, dry measures, roots, herbs, maple syrup, applesauce, shirts, and medicines. NOTABLE SHAKERS: **Moses Johnson**, **Caleb Dyer**, **Abraham Perkins**, John Cummings, Fannie Fallon, Rosetta Cummings. UNIQUE FEATURES: The **Church Family** dwelling, made of granite, is the largest Shaker **dwelling house** ever constructed. Known as the **great stone dwelling**, it measures 100 feet in length and 58 in width with four full stories above the full basement. The cupola housing the bell is 100 feet above the ground. The society also sits directly on a large body of water known as Lake Mascoma. The Shakers had a half-mile-long bridge built in 1849 at the narrows of the lake to connect them to the new railroad line. This **Shaker Bridge** was destroyed in the great hurricane of 1938 but was replaced by the state of New Hampshire.

BRIEF HISTORY: Israel Chauncy and Ebenezer Cooley had been sent by **Mother Ann** to preach at **Canterbury** to the **New Lights** of that district. Later, on 1 September 1782, these missionaries arrived at Enfield, New Hampshire, at the home of New Light Baptist James Jewett. Just as at Canterbury, so many people became Shakers that it was decided to organize a society there in 1793. Accordingly, a **Meeting House** was raised in May, and a dwelling house built the following year. By 1803, Enfield had 132 members, and this number climbed to almost 300 in 1840. Much of the prosperity was due to Caleb Dyer. He became an assistant **trustee** of the Church Family in 1821 when he was 21 years old. In 1838, he became senior trustee and held this position until his murder in 1863. For over 40 years his excellent financial abilities and management skills transformed the community. The great stone dwelling, the massive cow barn at the Church Family, and the large stone machine shop resulted from his direction.

Starting in the 1850s he used Shaker money to speculate on a number of businesses in North Enfield, including a tannery, a blacksmith shop, a bedstead factory, a gristmill, and even a boarding house. These were not run by the Shakers but leased out. Going against Shaker rules, he loaned vast sums of money to Shaker Mills Company, which made flannel from the herds of Merino sheep owned by the community. It is likely that he was allowed to do these things because his brother Orville was **elder** at the Church Family. Had Caleb lived to a ripe old age, the subsequent history of the community might have been different. Unfortunately, he was shot by a drunken man who arrived at the Shakers and had demanded to see his two girls who had been indentured to them. Soon after his unexpected death, the new owners of the Shaker Mills Company realized that Dyer had kept few records and managed things alone. They put in falsified claims for money owed to them, though in reality it was the reverse. The Shakers failed to hire competent lawyers and the court trials dragged on for 20 years and cost the Shakers $20,000. The society never recovered from the loss of Dyer and from the money drained away in a needless lawsuit.

In 1880 there were 144 Shakers, down almost 55 percent since the death of Caleb Dyer. By 1900, this had been reduced to 68. In 1918, members from Enfield were shifted to Canterbury. A small group stayed until the summer of 1923 when they too went to live at Canterbury. In 1927, the **Ministry** at **Mount Lebanon** sold the property for $25,000 to the Missionaries of Our Lady of LaSalette, a Roman Catholic order of priests and brothers.

LAST SHAKER: Flora Appleton (1881–1962). She was born in Boston, Massachusetts, and in 1885 went to live with the Enfield, New Hampshire, Shakers along with her natural sisters Margaret and Abigail. When preparations were being made to close Enfield, she joined the Canterbury Shakers in 1918. Her best-known skill was that of weaving poplar wood for the fancy goods trade. In more than 40 years she wove over three miles of poplar web for baskets. She also did housekeeping and made hundreds of potholders. She is buried at Canterbury.

ERA OF MANIFESTATIONS. Also known as the Era of Mother's Work, this important time serves as a dividing line in Shaker history. Before the era, the momentum set forth by **Mother Ann** and her companions was continued by the generation of **Mother's First Born** children. After the era, new Shaker leaders had to deal with complex issues brought about by changes both within Shakerism as well as in the outside world. No single moment or event marks this division, but the Era of Manifestations lasted so long that by the time it faded, a clear distinction can be made.

The traditional view is that the Era of Manifestations suddenly began on 16 August 1837 when young girls at the Second and South Families at **Watervliet, New York**, began to go into trances and have visions. A closer look, however, reveals that a gradual awakening to things of the Spirit had been going on for some time and, in fact, visions and dreams had always been a part of Shaker religious history. What makes the Era of Manifestations special is its extreme intensity, its quick and pervasive spread among the communities, its longevity, and the volume of its messages, **songs**, **dances**, and artwork.

By the 1830s large numbers of the first wave of children who had reached maturity and had been taken in without their parents were leaving the Shakers. This, combined with a growing lack of religious enthusiasm by older **believers**, worried Shaker leadership. A few members were encouraged by the occasional vision or dream that Mother Ann had not forgotten her children, but it was not until 1835 that much widespread attention was redirected into thinking about Mother Ann and the first Shakers. That year the **Ministry** decided to move her remains and that of some of the earliest Shakers to the newer graveyard at Watervliet. Mother Lucy's grave was also moved. Though the removals were done in May, the anticipation of this unleashed a real zeal that was evident in the singing during the commemoration of her birth on 1 March. Religious fervor in worship started to replace the lethargy of the previous years. More visions took place over the next year, and at Watervliet, in particular, the spiritual enthusiasm seemed to be running high. Back at **New Lebanon**, on 7 August, before the trances and visions of the young women and girls at Watervliet, one of the **Church Family** brethren saw an army of spirits led by Mother Ann marching south.

The trances and visions that occurred at the Second and South Families of Watervliet in mid-August 1837 marked the commencement of a tide of such events that quickly spread to every Shaker society and family. Prophesying, shaking, bowing, and singing in unknown tongues became the norm at religious meetings. This outpouring of visions led to thousands of songs, new dances, and inspired art. The men and women who received the messages were known as **instruments**, and their role was valued by the Ministry which supported the work.

Fearing ridicule and misunderstanding, the Ministry closed **public meeting** between 1842 and 1845. Starting in 1842, by inspiration, outdoor **feast grounds** for worship were laid out and each Shaker society received a **spiritual name**. That year, **Philemon Stewart**, the principal male instrument at New Lebanon, received *A Holy, Sacred and Divine Roll and Book; From the Lord God of Heaven, to the Inhabitants of Earth. . . .* This was published by the Shakers in 1843 and distributed not only among themselves but also to various rulers around the world. Meanwhile, the "Holy Laws of Zion," which had been received from the heavenly parents, influenced a revision of Shaker rules and resulted in the **Millennial Laws of 1845**.

After 1844, much of the impetus for the continuing support of the manifestations came from the influx of hundreds of **Adventists** into the Shakers after the disappointments of 1844 and 1845. In 1849, one last inspired book was published, *The Divine Book of Holy and Eternal Wisdom, Revealing the Word of God; Out of Whose Mouth Goeth a Sharp Sword,* by Paulina Bates of Watervliet. By this time, however, the era had largely ended, though visions and inspired art and song continued for years afterward.

In retrospect, some have seen the events of the Era of Manifestations taken collectively as a time of extremes that only hastened Shaker decline. They may also be seen, however, as the somewhat logical progression of long-held Shaker beliefs that came to the fore just as Shaker society seemed to need them. *See also* FEAST GROUNDS; GIFT; HANNAH COHOON; PHILEMON STEWART; SPIRITUAL NAMES OF THE COMMUNITIES.

ERA OF MOTHER'S WORK. *See* ERA OF MANIFESTATIONS.

EVANS, FREDERICK WILLIAM (1808–1893). Elder Frederick Evans is easily the most well-known Shaker. So much was he in the public eye that many do not realize even today that he was never a member of the **Ministry**. That his influence was international in scope has led to the assumption that he was in charge of the Shakers, but for his entire Shaker life he was a member of the **North Family** of **New Lebanon**. This was the principal **family** of the **Gathering Order**.

He was born on 9 June 1808 in Leominster, England. His father, George Evans, was of a lower social class than his mother, Sarah White. This caused endless friction between the two families, and when his mother died, he did not see his father or older brother for eight years. The experiences of upper-class life he gained while living with his mother's family left a lasting negative impression that influenced his work later in his life.

In 1820, Frederick's father and brother took him to America. They settled in New York, and he and his brother became involved in issues of land reform and the separation of church and state. They published three newspapers: the *Workingman's Advocate*, the *Daily*

Sentinel, and *Young America*. On 3 June 1830, he called at the North Family, New Lebanon, New York. He expected to be attacked for his views. Instead he found a religious society that used reason and logic to support each of its beliefs. This appealed to him because he was a self-proclaimed materialist. Indeed, he was not a believer in a personal God or anything else he could not experience first hand. This made him a contrast to the majority of seekers who came to the Shakers in that era. It seemed unlikely that he would become anything more than one of the hundreds who visited the North House each year. As it turned out, however, he would spend the remaining 63 years of his life at the North Family.

In the normal course of events, he should have eventually been sent to one of the other families at New Lebanon after his training at the North Family was completed. One of the many reasons this never happened was that the North Family was largely agricultural. As a gathering family, it did not engage in large-scale industries. These required a stable work force. Instead the family had a large farm. Brother Frederick was extremely interested in all aspects of farming. His years as a child on the estate of his maternal relatives had made him very familiar with agricultural operations. He was fascinated by the needs of individual plants, and the home farm and orchards of the North Family were the perfect places for him to experiment.

In addition, on 4 October 1838 he was appointed second **elder** of the family. He assisted Elder **Richard Bushnell**. In 1858 Elder Richard went into the Ministry, and Elder Frederick took his place as first in the family. Elder Richard and his natural brother Charles, who was the family's principal **trustee**, were very prudent when it came to all aspects of finance. For well over 25 years they had saved a large amount of money. Elder Frederick used his new position to use this cash to totally transform the farm and grounds of the North Family. Almost immediately, one of the largest stone barns ever constructed was built. It measured 55 by 196 feet and had five floors. In many ways it resembled one of the enormous stone mills that industrialists were constructing along the waterways of New England to house textile production. The comparison is apt because the barn housed the best in agricultural technology. Twenty other buildings were constructed, remodeled, or moved, and hundreds of fruit trees were planted. Physically, Elder Frederick had made his mark, all in five years.

He also had a wider significance on Shaker life in general. When he became first elder at the North Family he gained immediate control of the three gathering families at New Lebanon and indirect control of all the other families, since most adult converts in those days passed through the Gathering Order. As the principal speaker at **public meeting**, his voice reached thousands of outsiders who worshipped with the Shakers each year.

Though he published works as early as 1853, Elder Frederick's great volume of printed material began to appear in the 1870s. The vehicle that accomplished this at first was the Shaker newspaper, the *Manifesto*. On 3 December 1872, Elder Frederick and his associate Eldress **Antoinette Doolittle** took charge of this paper when the **Watervliet, New York**, Shakers could no longer publish it alone. As editors, they shaped the message sent out to the world and to the other Shaker communities.

This message was one of hopeful reform in matters of diet, health, clothing, burial practices, government, farming, temperance, land ownership, woman's rights, working conditions, pacifism, and religious beliefs. When Shaker conservatives attacked Elder Frederick's ideas, the North Family gave up editing the Shaker newspaper. Individual members of the family, but above all Elder Frederick, began writing hundreds of tracts, pamphlets, books, poems, and songs on these topics. Some of these were also published in the *Manifesto*. Elder Frederick also wrote articles for the secular press, especially the dailies in New York City. America was changing, and he was determined to show that the Shakers understood the world.

As elder of the Gathering Order in Shakerdom's largest and most important community, Elder Frederick faced great pressure by the 1870s from the fact that few capable adults had joined the Shakers in over 20 years. He and many members of the North Family went on missionary tours. This took them to friendly Protestant churches, big city lecture halls, and meetings of reform-minded individuals. Elder Frederick also went twice to England to try to gather souls. He presented Shaker beliefs from a rational, logical viewpoint. For him, liberalism and Shakerism were the same. As Shakerism passed through cycles of growth and decline, external forms were no longer as important as they once had been. This kind of thinking had an impact on Shaker daily life. Eventually, for example, the Shaker restriction on growing beards was lifted, and in the mid 1890s **sisters** no longer had to wear a lace cape. By the early 20th century, many sisters had even begun to wear secular dress.

Elder Frederick had always enjoyed a large correspondence, even exchanging letters with Leo Tolstoi. The last 10 years of his life were especially active in this regard. As he aged, Elder Frederick required the help of the sisters, who used a typewriter to write the replies he dictated. On Thanksgiving 1892, he was released as elder. He died 6 March 1893. His funeral attracted hundreds, and included testimonials, poems, letters, and songs. These were published in a memorial book.

Over his decades at the helm of the important North Family, Elder Frederick had cultivated not only the gardens, but also an atmosphere that ensured that the work he believed in would continue. His successors, **Anna White**, **Catherine Allen**, **Daniel Offord**, and others took his vision well into the 20th century.

E. W. These are the initials of Eleazar Wright, the name given to **Richard McNemar** by Mother **Lucy Wright** in 1811. After she heard him speak about his faith, she renamed him Eleazar Right, because he had the right knowledge of Shakerism. Eleazer means "the help of God." He asked to be allowed to add a "W" to the last name so that his name was the same as Mother Lucy's. He used the name Eleazer Wright or the initials "E. W." for the rest of his life.

EXERCISES. This is the proper name for the dances the Shakers performed during worship. In the earliest years of the movement, the Shakers did not follow a pattern in their exercises. They let the Spirit individually direct them. Under Father **Joseph Meacham**, however, laboring exercises were developed. These at first were performed using vocables (words composed from various sounds and letters without regard to meaning) in place of words. Sung words and many variations of the exercises occurred, and during the 1820s, **marches** were introduced to accommodate those requiring a less strenuous dance. Exercise steps were performed in a skip, often in more than one direction. In contrast, marches were done by pacing forward. The **Era of Manifestations** saw the introduction of more exercises.

One of the most fascination aspects of Shakerism to outsiders was that they danced at meeting. Though to visitors, the songs, exercises, and marches seemed spontaneous, the Shakers practiced them during the week. Moreover, **elders** directed the routines but tried to do it unobtrusively. Sometimes there were also marks on the floor which showed where certain singers should stand and form lines.

Organ music was introduced into the communities during the 1870s. This and an aging membership caused a decline in the use of exercises and marches at worship. Some simple marches, however, were still done into the 20th century in a few of the communities. At **Alfred**, for example, some of the **motion songs** and the dances were done until the society closed in 1931. One of the former Alfred Shakers even had the whirling gift at meeting at **Sabbathday Lake** during the 1940s. Today the Shakers may do some of the simpler exercises at private worship. In public many of the motion songs are still sung.

– F –

FAMILY. This is the name given to a group of Shakers living together in community. The word family is not used to denote a biological relationship, though many early Shakers lived in family groups with blood relatives. The first Shaker family to be gathered was the **Church Family** of **New Lebanon, New York**, in 1787. The last Shaker family to be gathered was at **White Oak, Georgia**, in 1902. Families ranged from just over a dozen members to almost 150 people. The largest single Shaker family was the Second Family at New Lebanon, New York, which had 165 members in 1835. It should be noted, however, that some of these lived at the South House, which was a branch. The Church Family at New Lebanon, collectively, had many more members than 165. Yet, the Church Family at New Lebanon was split into two totally separate parts called **orders**. According to the U.S. Census, the **First Order of the Church** had almost 130 members in 1860. The **Second Order of the Church** had just under 85 members that year. The latter became known as the **Center Family** after the 1860s.

When Shaker communities were first organized, those thought to be the most fervent and promising were gathered to the Church Family. This included young unmarried adults as well as zealous early converts whose land may have been used to form the family. So many people belonged to this group that at many of the early villages, including **Watervliet, New York**, and **Hancock, Massachusetts**, **First** and **Second Families** of the Church were created to accommodate the overflow. New Lebanon was so large that it had three such families. These first, second, and third families were also known as the First, Second, and Third Orders of the Church. All other Shakers were gathered to farms and property owned by prominent Shaker converts. These Shakers belonged to what was called the **Order of Families** and the name of the Shaker family was often the same as the name of the original landowner. For example, those Shakers living at the farm west of the Church families at Hancock were called John Talcott's Family.

Shaker organization continued to evolve, and when **Gathering Orders** were created during the first decade of the 19th century, all of the villages were reorganized. One of the families that had been part of the Order of Families was taken for a gathering family. At Hancock, for example, the Williams Family became the gathering family. The other non-Church families were eventually organized into separate units using the direction they were by compass from the Church Family. At Hancock, for example, John Talcott's Family became the West Family and the Williams Family the East Family. If a society was large enough, such as at Watervliet and Hancock, its Church or First Family was considered one family divided into two orders, the First and Second Orders of the Church. At New Lebanon, the original First Family became the First Order of the Church. The Second Family was broken up and its members divided between the First Order and the Third Family which then became the Second Order of the Church. In 1814, all other families at New Lebanon were part of a newly created Second Family. This Second Family of the Church gathered all of the small individual families into a united interest with branches at the East House (later the East Family) and at the South House (later the South Family).

FARRINGTON, RUTH (1763–1821). Many of the important Shaker leaders from the generation of **Mother's First Born** are largely overlooked today. This certainly can be said of Ruth Farrington. She was born on 27 April 1763 in Somers, Connecticut. Her parents, Nathan and Mehitabel, were members of **Joseph Meacham**'s Baptist church in nearby Enfield. The Farringtons, along with some of the Meachams, eventually settled in **New Lebanon, New York**. They were part of the **New Light** Revival in 1779 that precipitated the opening of the Shaker gospel. When she passed through New Lebanon, **Mother Ann** visited Nathan Farrington's home, the site of one of the most violent mob attacks against the Shakers. The house was not finished, and a group of armed men broke through the side, but were prevented from reaching Mother Ann because a group of **brethren** blocked them. Mother Ann was on an upper floor of the place. All of this must have made a deep impression on Ruth, who was a teenager at the time.

The **Church Family** at New Lebanon began to gather in 1787, and Ruth joined in 1788. When the **First Family of the Church** was organized by Father Joseph, Ruth Farrington and **David Darrow** were its first **elders**. This First Family was made up of young adults of superior faith, and it was considered to be the upper echelon or strongest part of the Church. Farrington and Darrow were children of the original converts and took on the onerous task of guiding the Church through its infancy. In light of their success, it is not surprising that both of them were sent out to Ohio to organize the Church at **Union Village**.

Eldress Ruth and a few sisters went to Ohio in 1806. They were the first Shaker women sent to the West by Mother **Lucy Wright**. They made a tremendous impression on the new converts, who were anxious to meet them. Their deportment, their devoutness, and the brightness of their countenances caused **Richard McNemar**, one of the important early western Shakers, to describe these women as "angels in human form" (E. Wright [pseudo.], *A Review of the Most Important Events Relating to the Rise and Progress of the United Society of Believers in the West*, 35–36). Using her years of experience at New Lebanon, Eldress Ruth helped to establish **Church Order** in the West. In 1812, along with other western Shaker leaders, she received the title of "Mother." Her willingness to embrace every trial and squarely face her duties made her a formidable leader. Many of the Shakers sent West eventually returned to New Lebanon. This was not the case with Mother Ruth. She died of dropsy on 26 October 1821 at Union Village. Her loss was a keen one for a society still evolving.

Had she lived another dozen years, perhaps she could have lessened the great number of young people who left the society in the 1820s. Like Mother Lucy Wright, whose birth and death dates are almost the same as Mother Ruth's, she filled the role as a **First Parent**. She laid the foundation, but did not live to see it come to fruition.

FAST DAY. Around Christmas each year, ideally during Advent, the **Ministry** traveled to the various communities within the **bishopric** to conduct a "general opening" or fast day. The rules governing the Shakers were read at meeting and all retired to their rooms to think and pray about theirs sins and the status of their souls. During the course of the day, every person was called individually to the **elder**'s room to confess privately. The elders went to confession to the Ministry.

There would be very little food provided during the day. The intent of this special day was so that everyone could feel reborn with the Christ on Christmas and allow the new year to begin in a more spiritual manner. This practice continues at **Sabbathday Lake**, where it has been carried out continuously since the beginning.

FEAST GROUNDS. These were the sacred places set up in 1842 for outdoor worship. They have been called holy hills, but this is inaccurate since some were not hills at all, but level pieces of land such as the feast grounds at **Pleasant Hill, Kentucky**. The use of holy hill to describe the feast grounds no doubt comes from the fact that the Shakers often chose the highest piece of ground on their property for these outdoor worship sites. In many of the eastern communities these would have been places on hills, yet so many communities, even in the East, did not have very high hills.

Feast grounds were used twice annually, in May and in September, for only a few years. The practice started in 1842 and was all but abandoned by 1852. The physical remains of these feast grounds, however, remained for years since the Shakers did not just clear an open area for worship. They fenced in the area and erected a **fountain stone** that was also fenced in. A small shelter was also built for the comfort of worshippers in case of rain. Even today there is ample physical evidence to reconstruct what some feast grounds looked like.

Though feast grounds were not all exactly the same, Shakers believed that they were laid out under the direction of the spirits. Specially chosen **instruments**, guided by angel spirits, searched out a place for the feast grounds. Once a spot was chosen it was leveled off and prepared so that as many as 500 worshipers could **march** and **dance**. Those unpolluted by sins were invited to wash themselves in the spiritual fountain that the fountain stone symbolized.

Such outdoor worship services must have helped break the monotony of daily life in a highly regulated community. Accounts of Shakers marching to the feast grounds are colorful. Some communities such as **Hancock** even had their own special song used only on that occasion. Believers also coordinated the times they went to the feast grounds. For example, on 14 May 1843, the Hancock Shakers and the **New Lebanon** Shakers were at their respective feast grounds at the same time. Since these hills were not too distant, the New Lebanon Shakers shouted a greeting and were answered by four shouts and four bows from the Hancock **believers**. These feast grounds had **spiritual names**. From these descriptive names it is easy to know whether the spot was a hill or a plain.

Community	Feast Ground
Alfred, Maine	Holy Hill of Zion
Canterbury, New Hampshire	Pleasant Grove
Enfield, Connecticut	Mount of Olives
Enfield, New Hampshire	Mount Assurance
Groveland, New York	Holy Ground
Hancock, Massachusetts	Mount Sinai
Harvard, Massachusetts	Holy Hill of Zion
New Lebanon, New York	Holy Mount
North Union, Ohio	Jehovah's Beautiful Square
Pleasant Hill, Kentucky	Holy Sinai's Plain
Sabbathday Lake, Maine	Mount Hermon
Shirley, Massachusetts	Holy Hill of Peace
South Union, Kentucky	Holy Ground
Tyringham, Massachusetts	Mount Horeb
Union Village, Ohio	Jehovah's Chosen Square
Watervliet, New York	Center Square
Watervliet, Ohio	Holy Circle
White Water, Ohio	Chosen Square

See also ERA OF MANIFESTATIONS.

FENNESSEY, JAMES H. (1854–1928). He was born in Cincinnati, Ohio, in 1854. When he was 28 years old he joined the Shakers at **Union Village, Ohio.** When he came into the society, it was already in rapid decline. In addition, the community was heavily in debt. Little did anyone realize it at the time, but he would someday be the one to save Union Village from ruin.

From the moment he arrived, his talents were recognized. In 1887, he became farm **deacon.** Since the Shakers could not work the extensive land themselves due to the lack of able-bodied brethren, he supervised the rental of it to small farmers. By 1895, almost the entire farm had been rented out. This not only kept the land in use, it assured a steady income that was desperately needed. In 1898, he was appointed a **trustee.** A man as capable as Brother James must have been aware of the large-scale financial mismanagement by **Elder Joseph Slingerland.** It was not until he became a trustee, however, that he could do anything about it.

In theory, the $316,000 realized from the sale of **North Union** in 1892 should have been sufficient to meet Union Village's accumulated indebtedness of the 1870s and 1880s. However, Elder Joseph Slingerland squandered tens of thousands of dollars on property improvements in the early 1890s. These included miles of expensive fencing and the total renovation of the **Trustees' Office** at the **Center Family.** He also bought a hotel in St. Paul, Minnesota, a cemetery in Memphis, Tennessee, and a building in Chicago. All of this was before the property was bought in Georgia. About $500,000 was spent, and Shaker property, most notably the entire society of **Watervliet, Ohio,** was mortgaged to finance this thoughtless speculation.

Trustee James Fennessey tackled the problem of this enormous debt by going after the source of the trouble. He filed suit against Elder Joseph Slingerland and Eldress Elizabeth Downing of the **Ministry.** In 1902, Slingerland and Downing were removed from office and Brother James methodically cleared up the debt. His expert management allowed the community to be virtually free of debt by 1908. Perhaps for the first time in almost four decades, Union Village was in good financial shape. In spite of these heroic efforts, however, few people had joined the community and only 24 Shakers lived there in

1910. It was clear that it would soon pass out of Shaker hands. Brother James wanted the property donated for charitable use by a church or the state. He clashed with the **Central Ministry** over this issue. His attempts to block control of the Central Ministry created very hard feelings. Many of the Union Village Shakers wanted to dispose of their home as they thought proper. Court battles resulted and once again the Shaker **covenant** was upheld. The legitimate and ultimate authority was found to lie with the Central Ministry. The property was sold in 1912.

Under the terms of the sale, the surviving Shakers were allowed to live at **Marble Hall** until 1923. They were cared for by young sisters sent from **Canterbury**. In 1920, the Shakers were asked if they would leave early since the buyers of Union Village needed the space. Three Union Village sisters were still alive, and they moved east when the Canterbury sisters returned home. Brother James left the Shakers in 1920 rather than move to Canterbury, the home of his great nemesis Elder **Arthur Bruce** of the Central Ministry. So great was the ill feeling from the events in 1912 that those who died at Union Village after the property was sold did not want to be buried with the community. They purchased a separate plot in nearby Lebanon and are buried there. Though he was no longer in the community, James H. Fennessey was buried in this plot when he died in 1928.

FIRST FAMILY OF THE CHURCH. Originally this designated the **First Order** or most zealous part of the **Church Family** in the larger early Shaker communities. After 1811, when the terms **Second Order** and **Second Family** were no longer synonymous, the First Family of the Church meant the entire Church Family. In the larger societies this might include two divisions, a First and Second Order. *See also* FAMILY.

FIRST ORDER OF THE CHURCH. Also known as the **First Family**, originally this was the name of the group of Shakers who were considered the most fervent and gathered into the Church Family of the larger early Shaker societies: **New Lebanon**, **Watervliet**, and **Hancock**. These communities also had **Second Families** called the

Second Order of the Church, and New Lebanon was so large it had a Third Family of the Church called the Third Order of the Church. As Shaker life evolved, Hancock's First Order and Second Order merged when the great brick **dwelling house** was constructed in 1830 to accommodate all members of the Church Family. A separate Second Family of the Church at Hancock was formed that was never connected to the Second Order there. Watervliet's First Order became simply the Church Family and its Second Order of the Church eventually became the North Family. The Watervliet society likewise formed a Second Family of the Church that was also called the West Family. As at Hancock, this Second Family was not part of the Second Order. In 1811, at New Lebanon the three orders of the Church were consolidated into two. The First Family or First Order remained intact. The Second Family was broken up and its members were split between the First and Third Families. The Third Family site then became known as the Second Order of the Church. The Church was then one family in two orders. A nearby Shaker family was given the title Second Family of the Church. This group had charge of all other Shaker families that had been under the general name **Order of Families**. In time these branches of the Second Family of the Church would become the East Family and the South Family. *See also* CHURCH ORDER; FAMILY.

FIRST PARENTS. The first generation of Shakers, those who had been converted by Mother Ann and her companions, were known as **Mother's First Born**. No subsequent group of Shakers ever surpassed the collective fervor that this group displayed during their long lives. If they deserve highest praise, however, it is due to the leaders that guided them. These first ministers had exceptional skill and were chosen by Father **Joseph Meacham** to organize the communities. The men and women who were the first **bishopric** ministers are considered the First Parents of the societies they gathered into **gospel order**. Each had the title of Father or Mother. When they died, this honorary appellation did not continue with their successors. Today when Shakers refer to the First Parents they are speaking of **Mother Ann Lee**, Father **William Lee**, and Father **James Whittaker**. In the following list, the primary community is in italics:

First Parents	Bishopric
Joseph Meacham and Lucy Wright	*New Lebanon* and Watervliet, New York
Calvin Harlow and Sarah Harrison	*Hancock*, Tyringham, Mass., and Enfield, Conn.
Eleazar Rand and Hannah Kendal	*Harvard* and Shirley, Mass.
Job Bishop and Hannah Goodrich	*Canterbury* and Enfield, New Hampshire
John Barnes and Sarah Kendal	*Alfred* and Sabbathday Lake, Maine
Jeremiah Talcott and Polly Lawrence	Groveland
David Darrow and Ruth Farrington	*Union Village* and Watervliet, Ohio
Ashbel Kitchell and Lois Spinning	North Union
Benjamin Youngs and Molly Goodrich	South Union
John Meacham and Lucy Smith	Pleasant Hill

FISHER, THOMAS (1822–1902). Nothing is known of the early life of Thomas Fisher, except that he was born in Scotland and was a widower. He was about 50 when he joined the Shakers at **Enfield, Connecticut**, and apparently lived at the **Church Family** from the mid-1870s until his death by pneumonia in 1902. He signed the Church Family **covenant** on Christmas Day 1878 and is listed as a carpenter there in the 1880 federal census. These facts alone would not make him a Shaker worthy of more than a passing comment. For Shaker **furniture** aficionados, however, he is an important figure. He made and signed furniture that shows a heavy Victorian influence. Many of his oak pieces are at **Canterbury**. He also decorated some furniture and boxes using light and dark woods next to each other to make a contrast. Quite a number of objects, especially small items that show this contrast, are attributed to him.

FOUNTAIN STONE. During the **Era of Manifestations**, 1837–1850s, the Shakers set up outdoor worship areas called **feast grounds**. These places had a fountain stone, marking the spot where the waters flowed from heaven directly to earth. This spiritual water washed away sin and made the believer clean. Thus worshippers washed in this water and were renewed. These stones were often made of marble and had lettering that gave warning to those who would defile the feast grounds or touch the stone while they were in sin.

The stone at **Enfield, Connecticut**, was marble, four and a half feet high and two and a half feet wide. It was lettered by Brother **Thomas Damon**. It is not possible to know if this was typical because only one fountain stone is known to survive. This is the stone from **Groveland, New York**. Pieces of stones are extant, but most were broken up or buried after the feast grounds were no longer used. Incredibly, some remained abandoned and undefaced for over 50 years before the Shakers had them buried in preparation for selling the property. Most of those who might have known where these stones were buried are dead, but the location of some of the stones is still known by some. Amateur efforts to locate the stones have been unsuccessful.

FRIENDS OF THE HOLY SPIRIT. In the late 1960s many who could not join the Shakers at **Sabbathday Lake** formed a religious association with them. These people would be remembered by the Shakers in prayer each morning and during religious meetings. In some ways this group, called the "Friends of the Holy Spirit," resembles the third order of Roman Catholic religious orders. It also recalls the tradition of Shaker **out families**. Since its inception, the "Friends of the Holy Spirit" has been an important source of support for the Shakers. Members have the assurance that they are in some way helping with the work of the gospel.

FRIENDS OF THE SHAKERS. On 6 August 1974, the **Sabbathday Lake** Shakers held a large, scholarly conference to commemorate the 200th anniversary of the arrival of **Mother Ann** in America. The participants in the conference decided it would be beneficial if every year a group of friends of the community met to show support. The community needed financial and emotional support since those were the years of the greatest persecution of the Sabbathday Lake Shakers by non-Shakers who disapproved of the revival of Shaker life there. Starting in 1975, Friends' Weekend has become an annual event at Sabbathday Lake. It is held on the first weekend after 6 August and usually draws between 100 and 125 people. An elected board runs the program which features speakers, craft demonstrations, singing, a cookout, and Shaker worship. After expenses are subtracted, the remaining dues from the 600 members are given to the Shakers. Though the actual number of Shakers may be few, their network of friends is large.

FROST, LILLIBRIDGE (LILY) MARGUERITE (1892–1971). Capable people continued to join the Shakers at **Canterbury** through the years when Eldress **Dorothea Cochrane** led the **Church Family**. All of these came into the society as young girls. Marguerite Frost was one of these people. Born in Marblehead, Massachusetts, in 1892, she was brought to the Shakers in 1903. When she arrived at the center of the town of Canterbury, no vehicle was available for transport to the Shaker village, a few miles distant, so she and her sisters walked. When they came to Canterbury, the society had over 100 members and was the largest Shaker community. The Frost sisters were among the many girls in the village and, under the tutelage of the **sisters**, they learned the domestic arts. They also attended the Shaker school and took part in the many cultural activities that were an integral part of growing up at Canterbury.

Marguerite loved studying, especially comparative religion. When she was 25 she was appointed assistant teacher and **caretaker** of the girls. She eventually became the teacher of the school until it closed in 1938. Her specialty was teaching the high school subjects. It was the custom at Christmas for each sister to write down three things she wanted. In the late 1920s it had been decided to take in no more girls to raise, but for Christmas 1929, Sister Marguerite asked for a little girl to bring up as all three of her requests. As a result, Elberta Kirkpatrick was admitted as the last child to be raised at Canterbury. Kirkpatrick has very fond memories of Sister Marguerite and cherishes the days she spent in school under her care.

In 1931, in addition to her school duties, Sister Marguerite became the community's nurse. She also enjoyed music and played the harmonica in the Shaker's Tenuvius band. In addition she sang, played the saxophone, and collected **songs**. Some of these were **motion songs**, which she performed. In 1965 she went into the **Ministry** and was appointed second **eldress** of the Church Family. The next year,

Eldress **Emma King** died. She had been first eldress. No successor was appointed by the Ministry, and Eldress Marguerite held that title of first eldress unofficially until the summer of 1970 when Sister **Bertha Lindsay** assumed the position, again unofficially, as the Ministry never appointed anyone to succeed Eldress Emma, who was, as a result, the last eldress of the Church at Canterbury.

On 26 February 1971, Eldress Marguerite died after a long battle with Parkinson's disease. Her long life serves as a beautiful example of how a person could still live as a Shaker, adhering to the highest standards, in spite of what must have been many disappointments.

FURNITURE. As the Shakers began to gather into community in the late 1780s, many members brought furniture with them. At the same time, **brethren** skilled in cabinetry supplied the society's need for furniture. For the most part, they continued to make objects in the style most prevalent where they lived. For example, "While Queen Anne, Chippendale, and early Federal style were popular during the founding and early growth of the Eastern societies in the 18th century, Hepplewhite, Sheraton, and Empire designs prevailed in the West during the 19th century, when the Ohio and Kentucky communities were established" (Rieman and Burks, *The Complete Book of Shaker Furniture*, 50). In addition, furniture makers from rural areas tended to make pieces "more basic, pared-down interpretations of up-scale fashions—and these were, for the most part, the craftsmen who brought their talent and taste in to the Shaker population when they converted" (Rieman and Burks, 45). Community cabinetmakers also worked within the Shaker principles of utility and simplicity. The results were built-ins, desks, tables, **chairs**, candle stands, benches, and sewing desks reflecting aspects of contemporary furniture styles but distinctly Shaker in look.

From the 1820s until the 1850s, relatively stable populations and a system of apprenticeship allowed for the evolution and perfection of this distinct Shaker furniture. Objects made during this time are often referred to as "classic." In contrast, after 1850, the massive exodus of the young obviated the need for large amounts of community furniture. Craftsmen continued to make and repair furniture, but new furniture was often made to satisfy the need of the **sisters'** rapidly expanding fancy goods trade. Older cabinetmakers, such as **Orren**

Haskins of **Mount Lebanon**, for example, adapted their output by making sewing desks for the sisters. Also, as the 20th century approached, if furniture was made at all in a community, it was due to the lingering presence of a single **brother** who had the skills learned as a young boy brought up from childhood as a Shaker. **Henry Green** of **Alfred**, **Delmer Wilson** of **Sabbathday Lake**, and Franklin Youngs (1845–1935) of **Enfield, New Hampshire**, were taught by older brethren, but their pieces reflect Victorian and other contemporary influences. Furthermore, since it was the sisters who helped keep the societies solvent by their fancy goods trade, Green, Wilson, and Youngs also made sewing desks and worktables for them.

Finally two other late cabinetmakers, **Thomas Fisher** of **Enfield, Connecticut**, and William Perkins (1853–1934) of Mount Lebanon, joined the Shakers as middle-aged adults. Both were from the British Isles and brought with them a more ornate style of furniture making. Their work should not be seen as decadent, however, but the natural progression of Shaker craftsmanship over time.

After the early 1940s, little, if any, furniture has been made by the Shakers. This may be about to change. A young Shaker sister, Sasha Tovani, presently living at Sabbathday Lake, has a great interest in woodworking. She has already made numerous oval boxes and small wooden objects for sale in their store. As her skills expand into cabinetry, another page in the evolution of Shaker furniture may yet be written. *See also* CHAIR INDUSTRY.

– G –

GATHERING ORDER. When Father **Joseph Meacham** organized the communities into **gospel order**, he did not provide for the admission of any converts. This is not surprising since from 1784 to 1800, the Shaker testimony to the world had been closed. In fact, few from the **world** were interested. The Shakers were left with a remnant following **Mother Ann's** death, and they were working hard to keep these people together. Also, the missionaries felt no gift to preach and could not gather new souls. Consequently, all energies were spent organizing the first communities. By 1800, however, it became clear that a mechanism must be set up to allow interested adults to join.

Late in 1799, a house at the **Church Family** of **New Lebanon** was set up to receive any adults who might like to be Shakers. This became known as the **Young Believer's Order**, as opposed to those who had come in at the first great in-gathering during the time the communities were first organized. Those first Shakers were **Mother's First Born** children and their families. In 1800 a portion of the Church property was set up as a separate family for young believers called the **North Family**. This was the first Shaker Gathering or **Novitiate Order**. Interested adults could come to this place and be given the necessary information. If they decided to stay they would be formed as Shakers and later sent to one of the other families in the society that might need new members.

At first it was not thought that each society would have a Gathering Order. For example, the North Family was supposed to serve the societies at **Hancock** and **Watervliet** as well. Because of the large numbers of people joining the Shakers, it was not long before it was clear that each Shaker society should have its own Gathering Order. During the first decade of the 19th century, every Shaker village was reorganized to make room for a gathering family. For example, at **Enfield, Connecticut**, those living at the South Family were removed to other Shaker families so that this might be the Gathering Order. In time, as the number of admissions to the Shakers grew, branches of the Gathering Order were started at other families. Again, at Enfield, Connecticut, the West Family was set up to house the overflow from the South Family. At New Lebanon, two branches of the North Family were made in the nearby town of **Canaan**. Such expansion showed the power of the Shakers to attract members beyond Mother's First Born and their descendents.

The Gathering Order has also been referred to as the **Junior Order**. It is best to avoid this term since the Gathering Order usually had quite an array of people, each at different stages of development. Some were ready to make a commitment to Shakerism and seriously try the life. These were Junior Order Shakers. Others were entangled with families or financial obligations to the world or had weak faith. These lived in **out families**, or branches of the Gathering Order. The most loosely associated members were part of the **Back Order**, which was most fully articulated at New Lebanon during the early decades of the 19th century. *See also* BACK ORDER.

GENERAL OPENING. *See* FAST DAY.

GIFT. Gift is used by **believers** to denote anything and everything that comes from God. This noun is found throughout Shaker literature and is even in the title of the most well-known Shaker song, "Simple Gifts." Though used in many contexts, gift always brings to mind the ever-present God. The Shakers also used the word gift to mean any blessing or spiritual virtue. Calling something a gift helped infuse the mundane moment with the divine. For example, when an **elder** said that he had the gift that a certain **brother** should do a task, it was no longer just one man making a request of another. The implication was that the elder was carrying out God's plan and that the person he was speaking to was a part of this. That this type of speaking and writing in Shakerism was common is not surprising. The living of the **Christlife** meant that at every moment there were opportunities for spiritual advancement. The *Testimonies* are replete with **Mother Ann** exhorting her followers to "labor for a Gift of God."

GIFT SONG. Shakerism is a religion that has always held Spirit communication in high regard. Throughout Shaker history, thousands of **songs** have been "received" from the Spirit world. Such songs are known as gift songs. Many of these songs have been associated with the **Era of Manifestations**, though inspired songs have always been a part of Shaker worship.

GIRLS AND THE GIRLS' SHOP. The first girls in Shaker communities were the daughters of the early converts. These girls had a fair perseverance rate and after 1824 may have inspired the Shakers to decide to take in large numbers of girls. By the 1830s, Shaker communities were filled with scores of girls. Most of these had been dropped off by single parents or were orphans. The Shakers even sought girls from town and city poorhouses. By the 1850s and 1860s these girls made up a high percentage of the communities. In some places their numbers approached between a third and a half of all females.

To house these girls and make sure they were cared for properly, Girls' Shops were built in any Shaker family that had a sufficient number of girls. Here a young **sister** took the care of all girls under 14. This **caretaker** also often taught the Shaker school. For much of the 19th century, Shaker girls only attended school during the summer terms.

Those societies that lasted the longest were the ones that had the best caretakers and other sisters who encouraged the girls. As a result most of the Shaker societies continued to take in girls until well into the 20th century. **Hancock** had girls until 1940, as did **Canterbury**. **Sabbathday Lake** had girls until the late 1960s.

GOODRICH, CASSANDANA (1769–1848). To a large extent, the second generation of Shaker leaders was made up of the children of **Mother's First Born**. Though the first large number of **apostates** came from them, the majority remained faithful until death. They were able to keep the momentum of Shakerism in the East going forward until the middle of the 19th century. As long as they lived, Shaker communities could not easily stray from the pattern set down by the founders. Cassandana Goodrich was one of the most prominent of this second generation.

She was born on 8 September 1769 in **Hancock**. Her father, Daniel Goodrich, was the earliest settler of the town, and his farmstead later became the **Church Family**. In 1793 she was called out of the ranks of the Church Family to be first **sister** in the **Ministry** of the **bishopric**. Three years later she replaced Mother **Sarah Harrison** as first sister in the Ministry. Eldress Cassandana held this position until her death in 1848. Thus for 55 years she was able to provide the constant, stable leadership needed for a religious society.

Her duties were varied. As a member of the Ministry she was obliged to make periodic visits to the societies at **Tyringham** and **Enfield**. She labored with the sisters to guide them and provide counsel. She was especially keen to discourage gossip since she viewed the Shaker life as a holy calling that would be weakened by an imprudent tongue. On the Sabbath, whatever community she happened to be in, she presided over the Church Family meeting. Even advanced age did not daunt her enthusiasm. For example, when the **Era of Manifestations** gripped Shakerdom, she was over 70 years old. This did not deter her from helping to go on the expedition that found and laid out the outdoor **feast grounds** at Hancock. In fact, in spite of blindness and feebleness, she refused to resign her position and continued to visit Tyringham and Enfield as long as her strength held. When she died, a direct link with the earliest years of Shakerism was broken. An eyewitness to her death recalled that **Mother Ann** herself came into the room and took Eldress Cassandana's spirit in her arms to Heaven. She was succeeded in the Ministry by Sally Brewster who took the name of Cassandana to honor her predecessor. In this way the name of Cassandana lived on in the community until 1883, when Brewster died. Such was the influence of Cassandana Goodrich of the **royal family of Shakerism.**

GORHAM, MAINE (1807–1819). In 1784, a number of prominent farmers converted to Shakerism. Many of these joined the **Alfred** society when it was gathered in 1793. Those remaining in Gorham, Maine, still retained faith, but they no longer lived the Shaker life. Efforts were made by the Alfred Shakers to care for the souls of these Gorham believers, but it was not until 1807 that the decision was made to organize Gorham into a **family.** The **elders** and most of the members of Alfred's North Family went to Gorham to help establish it. At its largest, there were 60 Shakers at Gorham, and their zeal was so great that they even tried to organize a group of interested converts at Tuftonborough, New Hampshire, on the shores of Lake Winnepesaukee. Because of the lack of timber and the prevalence of disease, it was decided to close Gorham and move its members to **Poland Hill**, to begin a **Gathering Order** for the **New Gloucester (Sabbathday Lake)** Shakers. This was unusual, as the founders had all come from the North Family at Alfred. The lack of numbers at Sabbathday Lake made it impossible to set out a Gathering Order, so the Maine **Ministry** decided to move Gorham to Sabbathday Lake rather than return them to Alfred.

Although the time during the **Era of Manifestations**, when the Shaker communities received spiritual names, did not occur until the 1840s, Gorham was known as Union Branch. This name was bestowed on the Gorham community over 30 years after it closed. In 1850 when a group from **Canterbury**, including the Ministry, along with the **Lebanon Ministry** and the Maine Ministry, were going from Alfred to Sabbathday Lake, they passed by the old community at Gorham. Elder **Abraham Perkins** was inspired to call the former community Union Branch.

The last Gorham Shaker was also the last of the Tuftonboro Shakers: Anna Hurd (1792–1884). She moved to Gorham in 1808 and then to the family at Poland in 1819. She came to the **Church Family** at

New Gloucester to cook at the office and care for the sick in 1837. She was there 10 years before moving back to Poland. In 1853, she again came to the Church to work at the **Office**. Two years later she was appointed first **Office deaconess**. She died at the age of 92 after only a three-day illness.

GOSPEL ORDER. This was Father **Joseph Meacham**'s organizational plan for gathering and maintaining Shaker communities. In the system of gospel order, scattered Shakers were gathered into a central location, generally large farms owned by early converts. The group nearest the **Meeting House** was called the **Church Family** or, in the Shaker societies in Ohio and Kentucky, the **Center Family**. If the society was large enough this family was called the **First Family** or **First Order of the Church** and another group called the **Second Order of the Church** was formed. Other family groups were formed as needed to accommodate the remaining population. Each family was headed by two **elders** and two eldresses. These were the spiritual leaders of the family. Temporal matters for each family were handled by **Office deacons**, generally two men and two women. Until the 1890s, the male Office deacons were the **trustees**. After that time, due to a great declension in the number of men, women began to act as trustees. Other positions of trust were the **deacons** and **family** deaconesses. These men and women helped run the day-to-day matters that affected a particular family.

Shaker societies were grouped in **bishoprics** and these were headed by a team of elders and eldresses known as the **Ministry**. First of all the Ministries was the **New Lebanon Ministry**. Later names for this Ministry were the **Central Ministry** and the **Parent Ministry**.

The system of gospel order still organizes Shaker life today.

GREAT STONE DWELLING. This is the massive white granite **dwelling house** that was built for the **Church Family** at **Enfield, New Hampshire**. Begun in 1837 and completed in 1841, it measures 100 feet long by 58 feet in width. It has 200 windows, each with 20 panes of glass. There are four stories above a full basement, and the bell in the cupola is 100 feet above the ground. Ami Burnham Young, an architect from Lebanon, New Hampshire, designed the structure, which cost about $50,000. It was framed under the direction of Luther Kingsley, a master mason from Boston, and eight assistants. (Hess, *The Enfield (N.H.) Shakers; A Brief History*, 22–23). It replaced the original 1794 dwelling that had been enlarged four times but was still too small for the family, which numbered 150. The great Stone Dwelling was the largest dwelling ever built by the Shakers and, when it was completed, was one of the largest buildings north of Concord, New Hampshire.

GREEN, CALVIN (1780–1869). For a number of reasons, people writing about the Shakers today do not bother to use the works of Calvin Green. This is a serious oversight. **Elder** Calvin was not only a Shaker from the beginning of the movement, he lived through the years of its greatest flowering and witnessed the start of its decline. In addition, he was a major Shaker theologian and chronicler of Shaker history. When Eldress **Anna White** and Sister **Leila Taylor** wrote *Shakerism: Its Meaning and Message* in 1904, they borrowed heavily from Elder Calvin. Since the work has no footnotes, this influence is not acknowledged.

A few Shakers were born after their parents converted. In the case of Calvin Green, his unmarried mother Thankful Barce (1759–1839) joined the Shakers three months before he was born on 10 October 1780 at **Hancock, Massachusetts**. His father, Joseph Green, a shoemaker, lived at **Harvard** and **Shirley** before joining the Church at **New Lebanon** in 1788. He became first elder of the **Second Order** in 1803 and occupied this position until he left the Shakers in 1814.

Calvin Green was always thankful that he had been born a Shaker, and he thought it auspicious that he had been born only a few months after the **opening of the gospel**. In addition, about a year before his birth, his mother had a dream in which she saw **Mother Ann** leading a flock of white sheep. In his infancy, Mother Ann had taken him from his mother's arms and blessed him. Later Father **John Hocknell** took him by the hand and led him about. Father **James Whittaker** called Calvin his boy and made him a coat and a jacket. Furthermore, he was named after Calvin Harlow, the first in the **Ministry** at Hancock. These events all foretold a bright future for him with the Shakers. While under his mother's care, he lived in various places at New Lebanon and Hancock. In 1790, he was admitted to the Church and lived with the youth in a special house. Since the **believers** were not as prosperous as they later would be, he lived a life of hard work and privation. He chances at schooling were limited so he read as much as he could. Though many young people left during the 1790s, all the remaining youth stayed faithful for their whole lives. These were the associates of Calvin, and he grew into maturity surrounded by those who would one day be great burden-bearers. For example, one of his older companions, **Rufus Bishop**, would some day be in the Ministry for over three decades.

Calvin was a good singer and had labored to learn the music so he was given a singing class to teach. His next major assignment was to write the letters that had to be sent to the Shaker missionaries in Ohio and Kentucky. In March 1807, he was sent to live at the **North Family**. Elder Calvin became the preacher at public meeting and a missionary. In those days, the **Gathering Order** at New Lebanon also had the care of young believers at **Watervliet**, Hancock, and **Tyringham**. Eventually these societies developed their own gathering families and Elder Calvin helped them set these up according to the pattern at the North Family. In addition, he gathered many souls from Bennington, Vermont; Cheshire and **Savoy, Massachusetts**; Old Saybrook, Connecticut; and Valley Forge, Pennsylvania. In fact, a young boy born at Cheshire in 1821 was named after him. Calvin Green Reed later would become an elder at **Groveland** and an elder in the Church at New Lebanon. These were the most active and productive days of Shaker missionary activity at New Lebanon. When he returned to the **Church Family** in 1832, those that came after him were happy to rely on the wholesale adoption of children to fill up the ranks. In time, this shift from active missionary work among families to a hope that children brought up by the believers would become Shakers would have disastrous results.

While at the North Family, Elder Calvin helped edit the second edition of *The Testimony of Christ's Second Appearing* in 1810. Along with **Seth Y. Wells**, he authored *A Summary View of the Millennial Church* in 1823 and in 1830 they both published *A Brief Exposition of the Established Principles and Regulations of the United Society Called Shakers*. This latter work went through eight reprintings during the 19th century. In addition, his memoirs provide a minute account of happenings at the North Family and later at the Church Family.

When he returned to the **First Order of the Church** in 1832, he was happy to become a common member once again. Brother Calvin took his Shaker life very seriously and constantly held himself to a rigorous standard. He was dismayed at some developments as the days of Mother **Lucy Wright** dimmed for most Shakers. For example, he was vigorously opposed to the dropping of the parental titles of "Mother" and "Father" for those who serve first in the Ministry. Moreover, he thought that the shift from using the term **deacon** to the term **trustee** was unjustifiable and reflected a worldly influence and an abandonment of the religious nature of the society. As mentioned earlier, he was against the adoption of children without their parents. His status as a standard-bearer brought both praise and envy. When the **Era of Manifestations** started, Calvin Green was not convinced that they were genuine. **Philemon Stewart**, who was the principal male **instrument** at the Church, purposely humbled Calvin Green at meeting. To Philemon's ambitious mind, if he could bring down Calvin Green, he could pave the way for himself to have the most influence on the development of the Shaker religion. Calvin eventually allowed himself to be publicly chastised and became obedient.

When the fervor of the visionists subsided and the career of Philemon Stewart went into decline, Calvin was elderly. This did not prevent him from trying to build up Shakerism. In 1861, when he was 81 years old, he was sent to Groveland to be the spiritual leader. By that time, the Groveland Ministry had been dissolved. He stayed there two years and returned to the First Order at New Lebanon. His final formal tasks had to do with supervising the Shaker school. He died 4 October 1869. The rapid decline of membership, the ascendancy of Elder **Frederick Evans** as Shaker spokesman, and a changing America all combined to make Calvin Green seem an anachronism. His pure Shaker ideals, based on his experience among the founders, would later find a voice at **Sabbathday Lake** during the 1960s.

GREEN, GEORGE HENRY (1844–1931). Elder Henry was born in St. John, New Brunswick, Canada, on 1 May 1844. When he was five years old his family moved to Portland, Maine. In 1858, he came to live at the Shaker society at **Alfred, Maine**. As a youth he became skilled at cabinetmaking and learned the other trades practiced in the community: milling, lumbering, and farming. When he was 18, he was placed in charge of the boys—a task he disliked. In fact, for most of his life, he wanted little to do with the boys who lived at Alfred. His tenure as **caretaker** of the boys was brief, for the next year he became second **elder** of the Church.

For over 65 years Green served as an elder at Alfred, but he is best known for two occupations: furniture making and salesman of the **sisters'** products. He made tables, sewing desks, washstands, and secretaries, and worked on building repair. Other times of the year he went to the shore and mountains to peddle the fancy goods and other items made by the sisters for sale. After the 1890s, these goods were the real moneymakers for the community and helped keep it afloat financially. For well over 50 years, Elder Henry sold goods and never had one accident. He was dubbed "the Old Man of the Mountains" by his non-Shaker friends.

By 1926, due to his deteriorating physical and mental health, the sisters had taken over most of his duties. When the community closed in 1931, he was not aware that he had moved to **Sabbathday Lake**. He died 5 September 1931.

GREENWOOD, (ELMER) IRVING (1876–1938). He was born on 16 October 1876 in Providence, Rhode Island. His parents were William G. Greenwood and Annie Holbrook Greenwood. On 18 September 1886 he was admitted to the **Church Family** at **Canterbury**. He attended the Shaker school as a child and helped out on the farm, especially with the extensive dairy operations. His genius, however, did not lie in farming. He possessed natural engineering skills which he used to benefit the community. For example, in 1910, he wired the village for electricity. He also built a power plant. Whether it was water pipes or machinery, Brother Irving seemed to be ready with a solution. During his many decades of life at the village he constantly made improvements. Even today his handiwork is evident everywhere from the walkways to the porches. The persistent image many have of Brother Irving is a photo that shows him relaxing and listening to a radio that he rigged up while his beloved dog Dewey rests at his side.

Due to the shortage of men, during the last 20 years of his life he had to take on added responsibilities that removed him from his favorite occupations. On 6 May 1918 he was made a **trustee**. By this time he was the chauffer of Elder **Arthur Bruce**, who was also Canterbury's principal trustee. Elder Arthur was often away on business and eventually, when he became a member of the **Parent Ministry**, he relied on Brother Irving to help him. After the death of Elder **Walter Shepherd** of **Mount Lebanon** in 1933, Brother Irving became second brother in the Parent Ministry. When Elder Arthur died in 1938, he was made first in the Ministry. He did not hold this position very long, for in June 1939, he suffered a stroke and died a few days later on 19 June. Since he had not appointed a successor or named an associate, he was the last male to serve in the Parent Ministry. The Ministry sisters reorganized the order and included women only.

GROSVENOR, ROXALANA (1813–1895). She was born in Dana, Massachusetts, on 1 March 1813. Her parents were Ebenezer and Mary Grosvenor. On 6 May 1819 her family joined the **Harvard** Shakers. At first they were sent to live at the East Family, a branch of the **Gathering Order**. In 1822 she moved to the **Church Family** where she attended school. She was appointed second **eldress** of the Church Family in 1837. She had held this position 10 years when she was made second in the **Ministry**. In 1851 she went to **Shirley** to be first eldress of the Church Family. Ten years later she came back to live at the Church Family in Harvard.

Externally, up until the 1860s she may have seemed quite typical. Starting in her early adulthood, she had served the society in various capacities of trust and care. In fact, by this time, she had come to believe in the doctrine of **spiritual marriage** and other modifications of Shaker beliefs. The Shaker Ministry was quite opposed to such views and she and her sister Mary Fidelia Grosvenor left the community on 25 July 1865. Her brother Lorenzo also left. While their parents had died in the faith after many years of service, the Grosvenor children had proved difficult. Their older brother Augustus Grosvenor died the previous year. As elder of the North Family of Harvard, he had built a large **dwelling house** that far exceeded the needs of this modest sized family. The resulting debt drove him out of office, and he died in disgrace "of a broken heart" at the East Family in 1864. He was only 57 years old.

The official reason given that Roxalana and Mary Fidelia Grosvenor left the community was that they wished to study mesmerism. This was only partially true. Seeing how Shaker life was diminishing, they wanted **believers** to try the idea of spiritual marriage. A number of Harvard Shakers also left during this time for the same reason. What makes Roxalana and her sister so interesting is that after they moved to Boston, they continued to dress as Shakers and considered themselves such. In 1873, they published "The Shakers' covenant with a brief outline of Shaker history." They also sued to receive compensation for the decades they had spent in the community. They lost the court case, which was heard in 1875. The controversy they caused further weakened an already struggling community. Roxalana, Mary Fidelia, and Lorenzo never lost touch with the Shakers, though Shaker leaders were not sympathetic to them. When Lorenzo died, the Harvard Shakers sent a delegation to sing at his funeral held at the Tremont Temple. Roxalana died in Somerville, Massachusetts, in 1895.

GROVELAND, NEW YORK (1836–1892). SPIRTUAL NAME: Union Branch. FEAST GROUND: Holy Ground. BISHOPRIC: Groveland until 1859 when it came under the jurisdiction of New Lebanon. FAMILIES: East (**Church Order**), West (**Gathering Order**). MAXIMUM POPULATION AND YEAR: 148 in 1836. INDUSTRIES: brooms, dried apples, dried sweet corn, fancy goods. NOTABLE SHAKERS: **Ella Winship**, **Jennie Wells**, Lydia Dole, Hamilton DeGraw, Alexander Work, Polly Lee. UNIQUE FEATURES: Groveland was the only Shaker community moved from another location. In addition, the only **fountain stone** that has been found and on display is from Groveland. Also the Church Order at Groveland was not called the **Church Family** but the East Family. Finally, the community served as a stopping-off point when Shakers went from the East to the West or vice versa. It was never a completely eastern society, but also had little in common with the West.

BRIEF HISTORY: Though they started moving from **Sodus** in 1836, it was not until June 1838 that all of the former Shakers from Sodus were relocated. The 1,700-acre farm in Groveland had been owned by Dr. Fitzhugh, and it contained a brick house, a sawmill, and other structures. By 1836, Joseph Pelham, a native of Wayne County, had replaced John Lockwood as second **elder**. The transition to local leadership was completed within the next couple of years, and Groveland took its place as a Shaker community. The move to Groveland proved to be beneficial. The land was very fertile and a number of the eastern societies, most notably **Canterbury, New Hampshire**, bought land in the immediate area to grow broom corn.

The problem of retaining and attracting suitable membership plagued the society as it did all other Shaker places. By 1859, the **Ministry** at Groveland was discontinued. So few capable leaders or even members could be found that **New Lebanon** and **Watervliet** sent Shakers to fill key positions. In 1857, there were 130 members. This diminished to only 57 in 1874 and 41 in 1880. In 1883, the West Family closed. Meanwhile, a large debt had accumulated. At the same time, the large farm at the North Family, Watervliet, had fine buildings but only a few Shakers. The leading elder there was dying, and Eldress **Harriet Bullard** of the **Central Ministry** proposed that the Groveland community close and move to Watervliet. This would make them closer to the other Shakers, solve their financial plight, and settle Shakers on a very desirable place that would be lost otherwise. In 1892, the 34 Groveland Shakers made the move to the North Family, Watervliet. In 1894, the state of New York paid the Shakers $115,000 for 1,800 acres of land and buildings. The site became a home for epileptics known as Craig Colony.

LAST SHAKER: Jennie Wells (1878–1956). When Groveland closed in 1892, she moved with the community to the North Family at Watervliet. When this closed in 1919, she moved to the South Family, Watervliet. In 1930, she was sent to the **North Family**, New Lebanon, to care for the elderly Shakers there. In 1947, when New Lebanon closed she moved to the nearby Church Family at **Hancock, Massachusetts**, where she died.

– H –

HADD, ARNOLD (1956–). He was born 8 October 1956 in Springfield, Massachusetts. His connection with the Shakers began in his childhood. His father's mother knew former Shaker Ricardo Belden who was living next door to her in Springfield with another former member of the Enfield community. Brother Ricardo grew up a Shaker at **Enfield, Connecticut**, but left in 1910. Before rejoining the Shakers at **Hancock** in 1926, he lived in a couple of places. One of these sites was the city of Springfield, which is almost adjacent to Enfield.

Brother Arnold contacted **Sabbathday Lake** in 1972. He corresponded with them for several years and first visited in 1974. He was admitted to the **Church Family** of Sabbathday Lake on 19 January 1978. He assisted the late Brother **Theodore Johnson** until his death in 1986. He carries on the family's garden, does some printing, tends to the farm animals (cattle, sheep, and pigs), makes items for sale, and oversees the gift shop. In 1988 he signed the **covenant** and was made a **trustee** in 1990. In keeping with the tradition of Sabbathday Lake begun by Brother **Delmer Wilson**, he does not use the title of **elder**.

Most Shaker leaders of the past never studied too much Shaker history. The pressing needs of the community forced them to be involved with day-to-day events. Brother Arnold, in spite of his many roles, has always made time to become an expert on the theology and history of the community. This is due to his training under Brother Ted. No one knows more about the Shakers than he does. In this way he is a noble successor to his mentor Brother Theodore Johnson. Brother Arnold is fond of Elders **Alonzo Hollister**, **Calvin Green**, and **William Dumont**. He embodies the best characteristics of each of these three great Shakers.

HALL, MARY FRANCES (1876–1957). She was born on 19 June 1876 in North Adams, Massachusetts, and joined the **Hancock** Shakers on 18 November 1884. She grew up at the **Second Family** and also lived at the East Family. As a young woman she assisted **Elder Joseph Holden** since he suffered from very bad eyesight. The business expertise she gained from this provided her with valuable experience that she later would put to good use. When the East Family closed in 1911, she moved in to the large white **Trustees' Office**, and this was her home for the remainder of her life. When Elder Joseph died in 1919, she took his place as a **trustee** of Hancock. By all accounts, she was a very capable trustee. She was so skilled at managing both the affairs of Hancock and those of the **Ministry** under Elder Joseph that, after his death, his successors in the **Parent Ministry** felt it necessary to issue a caution that she was no longer to transact business in the name of the Ministry, but rather only had authority in matters relating to Hancock. No doubt Elders **Arthur Bruce** and **Walter Shepherd** of the Ministry felt threatened since they liked to be in charge. Bankers and those who have studied financial records from the time, however, believe Sister Frances would have done a far superior job had she been given the opportunity.

The power that had been denied her gradually came her way, and she became part of the **Parent Ministry** in 1936. In 1938, she was made a trustee of the remaining Shaker property at **Watervliet, New York**. This was in preparation for selling the place. By then, both Elder Arthur and Elder Walter were dead. In 1943, she was appointed trustee of **New Lebanon** in place of **Emma** and **Sarah Neale**. When Eldress Rosetta Stephens of New Lebanon resigned from the Parent Ministry in 1946, Eldress Frances Hall took her place as first **sister** in the Ministry. All of this gave her the ability to close New Lebanon in 1947. In 1950, the seat of the Ministry was moved from the defunct New Lebanon to Pittsfield, not Hancock where the majority of the community lived. The Hancock's Trustees' Office, Eldress Frances' home, is actually right over the city line in Pittsfield.

On 10 March 1957, when she could not be reached by phone, hired workers broke in to the Trustees' Office and found that Eldress Frances had died in her sleep. A member of the community remarked at the time, "She died as she lived, alone." After her death, Eldress **Emma King** of **Canterbury** lost no time in consolidating power. The Shaker **covenant** was amended to move the seat of the Ministry from Pittsfield to Canterbury. At this time, the secretiveness and power of Eldress Frances provided a final and, some might say, most significant surprise. As Eldress Emma went through her effects, she discovered bankbooks, a stock portfolio, and real estate holdings that indicated significant wealth. These funds were from the sale of former communities as well as Hancock's own accounts. The result was the setting up of the **Shaker Central Trust Fund** in 1959.

Some have wondered why the Hancock society lasted so long. After the early years of Shakerism, it was relatively small and had little to do with the major events of Shaker history during the 19th century. Hancock survived because of its tradition of excellent trustees. This rich society did not have to close, though it had small numbers. With the ascendancy of Eldress Frances Hall, Hancock's place as a long-lasting community was assured. As much as it was financially solvent, however, the membership was not aware of it and lived a very plain life in the brick dwelling.

HAMLIN, CHILDS (1760–1790). He is typical of the fervor of the first generation of Shakers. He was born in Alford, Berkshire County, Massachusetts, on 23 January 1760. His large family converted at the time of the **opening of the gospel** in 1780. These included his mother Joanna, and his siblings Samuel, Joanna Jr., Electa, Cynthia, and **Thankful**. At that time the society had not yet been gathered, but Childs Hamlin, because of his strong faith, became a close companion of Father **Joseph Meacham**. He traveled with him and assisted in spiritual labors. In 1785, Childs lived in the newly constructed **Meeting House** at **New Lebanon**. Here the spiritual powerhouse of the religion resided, and the young men and women there were being trained to assume roles of leadership when the scattered groups of **believers** would be gathered into permanent communities. Childs died on 4 May 1790 at the age of 30. He did not live to see the gathering of any of the societies except New Lebanon and **Watervliet**.

HAMLIN, THANKFUL (1768–1793). Just as Father **Joseph Meacham** gathered young men of promise around himself, so too did Mother **Lucy Wright** gather young women of potential. One of these was Thankful Hamlin. Born in Alford, Berkshire County, Massachusetts, on 21 April 1768, Thankful Hamlin joined the Shakers with her family during the **opening of the gospel**. Like her brother **Childs Hamlin**, Thankful was being groomed for Shaker leadership when she died on 16 April 1793.

HAMPTON, OLIVER C. (1817–1901). He was born on 2 April 1817. His parents, Charles D. and Julia Carey were originally from Pennsylvania. In 1822, the entire family, including Oliver and his siblings Emily, Eliza, and [Henry?] joined the Shakers at **Union Village**. He seems to have been a man of many talents, and during his long life as a Shaker he taught school, made brooms and shoes, did tailoring, and helped in the seed and woolen industries. He also was a talented musician and wrote hymns. In addition, he introduced new musical practices and bought musical instruments.

During the **Era of Manifestations**, he and his sister Eliza were among the **instruments** at Union Village. These visions formed the subject for his music. Since he preached at **public meeting**, he must also have been the **elder** of the **Gathering Order**. His years in the

Gathering Order prompted him to reach out to the **world** to try to attract more people to the rapidly diminishing ranks at Union Village. Starting in 1869 and continuing until shortly before his death in 1901, Elder Oliver published a number of pamphlets, broadsides, and poems. These were religious in scope and designed to provide the reader with a glimpse of Shaker theology. He also wrote a long memorial poem honoring Elder William Reynolds. Of great historical significance are his journals and his history of Union Village. This typed history was given to John P. MacLean before he wrote his article on Union Village in 1902.

In 1881, Elder Oliver was made second in the **Ministry**. He retained this position until 1898. Though not in the Ministry after that date, he continued to preach until his death. The Union Village Shakers made a costly and futile attempt to establish a colony at **White Oak, Georgia**, in 1898. Late in 1900 he decided to make a short visit there. Earlier reports had been favorable about the place. Not long after he arrived there he took sick and died on 29 March 1901. There is an oral tradition that says two Shakers are buried on the property in Georgia, but Elder Oliver is the only name that is documented.

HANCOCK, MASSACHUSETTS (1790–1960). SPIRITUAL NAME: City of Peace. FEAST GROUND: Mount Sinai. BISHOPRIC: Hancock. FAMILIES: Church (**First and Second Order**), **Second Family**, North Family, West Family, East Family (**Gathering Order**), South Family (Gathering Order). MAXIMUM POPULATION AND YEAR: 247 in 1829. INDUSTRIES: seeds; dried sweet corn; brooms; hats; grist, saw, and fulling mills; table swifts; fancy goods; iron mine; dairy products. NOTABLE SHAKERS: William Deming, **Grove Wright, Cassandana Goodrich, Hannah Cohoon, Ira Lawson**, Caroline and Sophia Helfrich, **Mary Frances Hall**, Fannie Estabrook, Louis Basting. UNIQUE FEATURES: What would have surprised 19th-century Shakers was Hancock's longevity as a community. Though prominent in the earliest years of Shakerism, after western Shakerism developed in 1805, Hancock was just one medium-sized community among many. When Charles Nordhoff, the famous chronicler of American communal life, visited the Shaker societies in 1874, he did not even think Hancock was worth a visit (Nordhoff, *The Communistic Societies of the United States*, 195). However, its extremely strong financial position under trustee Ira Lawson, Elder **Joseph Holden**'s move there in 1893, and the relatively large number of young **sisters** who joined around 1900, caused Hancock to endure past almost all other Shaker societies. In 1813, *Millennial Praises*, one of the first Shaker books and the first Shaker hymnal, was printed at Hancock. The most imposing external aspect of Hancock is the **round stone barn** built in 1826.

BRIEF HISTORY: The Berkshire county region was the last place in Massachusetts to be settled. Some of the pioneer settlers, the Demings, the Goodriches, the Talcotts, the Osbornes, the Rathbones, and many others lived in the Pittsfield/Hancock area adjacent to New York State. They became heavily involved in the large religious revival that inflamed the border country of Massachusetts and New York in 1779. When this "stir" petered out, a number of men, including Baptist preacher Valentine Rathbun of Pittsfield, went to **Niskeyuna** to see **Mother Ann**. His congregation, which met at his house, was composed of families from Hancock. In June 1780, a Shaker meeting was held at his barn. Already fueled by expectancy from the recent revival, settlers in the area were influenced by their religious leaders who converted to Shakerism. In like manner, Daniel, David, Nathan, and Hezekiah Goodrich became Shakers, as did John Deming, Hezekiah Hammond, John Talcott, and Ebenezer Cooley. These men brought their wives and families, and, of course, their lands, some very valuable and prosperous holdings.

On 30 August 1786 the foundation of the **Meeting House** was laid, and in 1790, Calvin Harlow and **Sarah Harrison** became the **First Parents** of Hancock. For assistants they had Jeremiah Goodrich, Rueben Harrison, and Hannah Goodrich. The Hancock Church was officially gathered on 14 January 1791 on the farm once owned by Daniel and Ann Goodrich. The property of John Deming became the Second Family in 1791, and the Talcott farm became the West Family in 1792. Finishing out the first round of expansion was the creation of the East Family in 1793. By 1803, Hancock numbered 142, making it the fifth largest Shaker society. Not for another 120 years, however, would Hancock be such an important Shaker center.

The Hancock **bishopric** was the second to be formed, and it included the communities at **Tyringham** and **Enfield, Connecticut**. Over the years scores of Shakers were transferred within this bishopric. In fact, some of Hancock's most important leaders actually were from other communities. For example, Grove Wright, originally brought to Hancock, actually grew up at Tyringham and lived there until he went into the **Ministry**, and **Thomas Damon** was from Enfield, Connecticut. Perhaps the best example, however, of Hancock as a living part of a larger whole was its full participation in the **Era of Manifestations**, also called the Era of Mother's Work. This religious revival began in 1837 at **Watervliet, New York**, and it spread rapidly to all of the societies. Under divine inspiration, the Hancock bishopric named its three societies the Cities of Peace, Love, and Union. Their feast grounds were Mount Sinai, Mount Horeb, and the Mount of Olives. This uniformity shows how closely these places were linked and how much control the Ministry exercised. Yet, as interesting as the Spirit messages and outdoor worship services were, it is the production of the **gift** drawings that are the best-known reminder of Hancock's participation in the Era of Manifestations. The famous Shaker "Tree of Life" by Sister Hannah Cohoon is but one of a score of famous drawings of blazing trees, angels, mulberry bowers, etc., produced by her and fellow Hancock sister Polly Collins. No other community produced as many of these large drawings, or at least none that have survived in such quantities.

In contrast to the tremendous energy unleashed during the Era of Mother's Work, the decades that followed seem to be a slow descent downward in both numbers and spirit. During the 1840s, the time of the Manifestations, Hancock had about 215 members. By 1876, there were just 115. This was reduced to a mere 43 in 1900. Fortunately, though Hancock had almost no adult men, those they had were very capable. Trustee Ira R. Lawson (1834–1905), for example, was perhaps the best **trustee** any Shaker village ever had. His wise stewardship of almost 50 years left Hancock with a strong and secure financial base. This continued under the formidable trustee Frances Hall. As other places were closing, Hancock could afford to stay open, and it received Shakers from some of the other communities. This included the last survivors from New Lebanon in 1947. When Hall died in 1957, the Ministry, now located at **Canterbury, New Hampshire**, made plans to sell the property. The society was closed in 1960 and a large museum occupies the site of the former Church, North, and West Families.

LAST SHAKER: Fannie Marie Estabrook (1870–1960). She joined the community in 1881 and became a trustee in 1919 upon the death of Joseph Holden. Ten years later she became the last eldress at Hancock. Her sister was Emma Fidella Estabrook (1874–1911). Adeline Patterson (1882–1968), although she spent most of her life at other communities, was the last Shaker to die who had actually lived at Hancock.

HARRISON, SARAH (1740–1796). Sarah Harrison was part of one of the prominent and prosperous farmer families of **Hancock, Massachusetts**. Such families formed the core of the early Shaker converts in that town. Born 23 August 1740, Sarah spent time at the **Meeting House** at **New Lebanon** before being sent out as a **First Parent** to gather into **gospel order**. From 1791 until her death on 19 September 1796, she was known as "Mother Sarah."

HARVARD, MASSACHUSETTS (1792–1918). SPIRITUAL NAME: Lovely Vineyard. FEAST GROUND: Holy Hill of Zion. BISHOPRIC: Harvard. FAMILIES: Church (**First Family**), North (**Second Family**), South (**Gathering Order**), East (Gathering Order). MAXIMUM POPULATION AND YEAR: 173 in 1820. INDUSTRIES: brooms, pressed herbs, seeds, fancy goods. NOTABLE SHAKERS: Grove Blanchard, Elijah Myrick, Simon Atherton, William Leonard, Augustus Grosvenor, **Roxalana Grosvenor**, Tabitha Babbitt, Olive Hatch, Hannah Kendal, Annie Walker. UNIQUE FEATURES: The **Square House** located at the **Church Family** predated the arrival of the Shakers. It was the home of **Shadrack Ireland** (?–1780) and his followers. It became the headquarters of **Mother Ann** during her extended stays in the area. Also, tradition has it that Harvard was the place Mother Ann saw in the vision that prompted her to take her followers to America. Supposedly, she liked Harvard the best of all the places she lived. Finally, the Shaker cemetery at Harvard is one of the few that still retains the individual grave markers. In this case almost all of them are cast-iron "**lollipop markers.**" Shakers at **Mount Lebanon** and possibly **White Water, Ohio**, also used this style of marker, but only at Harvard do they remain.

BRIEF HISTORY: The encounter with Mother Ann at **Niskeyuna** in 1780 resulted in scores of new converts. When these new Shakers returned to their homes in the various parts of New England, they asked to be visited by Mother and her companions. In May 1781, Mother

Ann, Father **William Lee**, and Father **James Whittaker** left on their first missionary tour of New England. One of their principal destinations was Harvard. They arrived there in late June and stayed at the home of Zaccheus Stephens in the Still River section of town. This was on the border of Lancaster. They then stayed at Isaac Willard's house, where the Harvard Shakers' South Family would eventually be. Willard had been an enthusiastic member of a small sect headed by Shadrack Ireland. Shadrack had died the previous year, and his remaining followers were disillusioned and became ready converts to Shakerism. The Square House, which could be seen from Willard's place, had been Ireland's home. Mother established the Square House as the headquarters for Shaker missionary efforts. These efforts led to serious persecutions. All three times Mother was at Harvard, she encountered firm opposition. Some of this ire was vented on her followers. To this day, a marble marker and cairn stand as a tribute to the spot where Father James Whittaker was whipped by a mob. Visiting Shakers still place a small rock at this "**whipping stone**."

Persecution of a religious group rarely has the desired effect and, by 1792, Harvard was gathered as a permanent community. Though it had a glorious early history associated with Mother Ann and the first leaders, Harvard never grew to be very large. By 1803, there were 103 Shakers. This number gradually increased until the early 1820s when 175 may have been reached. For the next 30 years, Harvard had about 170 Shakers but many were children, and there were relatively few men. This lack of suitable numbers of adult men affected Harvard decades before it became the norm in other societies. This can be seen in 1808, when no one was chosen to replace Father Eleazer Rand who had died. Such was the scarcity of men that Elder John Warner had to act alone until 1818 when, on the day of his 21st birthday, Grove Blanchard was appointed second to the Harvard **Ministry**. Nordhoff notes the imbalance in the ratio of men to women when he visits Harvard in 1874 (Nordhoff, *The Communistic Societies of the United States*, 192). That year, adult men numbered just 17, or less than 23 percent of all adults in the community. In fact, however, though there were many more adult women, most of them were aged. For example, the Church Family only had three adult women under 55 years of age in June 1880. In addition, children accounted for almost 25 percent of the 90 Shakers in 1874. It seemed that Harvard would not be too long in following **Tyringham** as one of the next Shaker societies to close. The **Ministry of Mount Lebanon** decided that Harvard, with its rich associations to early Shakerism and its prosperous farm and herb industry, could not be allowed to close. Starting in 1880, a dozen Shakers were sent from Mount Lebanon to live at Harvard. Most of these came from the **Lower Canaan Family**, which dissolved in 1884. These Shakers occupied crucial leadership positions in both of the remaining families and allowed Harvard to survive into the 20th century. By 1898, half of the adult **sisters** at Harvard were originally from Canaan.

In 1909, the three surviving sisters from **Shirley** joined the society, and the remaining eight years were full of tension and inevitability. In April 1918, the property was sold to Fisk Warren for $60,000. By June, the surviving members had moved to Mount Lebanon.

LAST SHAKER: Sarah Sullivan Maynard (1878–1953) joined Harvard in 1899. When the community closed in 1918, she moved to the **North Family** at Mount Lebanon. In 1947, all of the Shakers at Lebanon were moved to **Hancock**. "Little Sadie," as she was called, died there in 1953. She is buried at Hancock.

HASKINS, ORREN (1815–1892). Shaker **brother** Orren Haskins possessed an impressive array of talents. He was a skilled **furniture** maker, a useful carpenter, a general handyman, an **instrument** during the **Era of Manifestations**, a **caretaker** of the boys, and an experienced teamster.

He was born on 3 December 1815 in **Savoy, Massachusetts**. His parents were Nathan and Betsey Cornell Haskins. When he was a young child, his extended family became caught up in the work of Shakerism. For a time, they formed a small Shaker community at **Savoy**. Due to a prolonged drought and other economic problems, they were gathered into the Shaker communities of **Watervliet** and **New Lebanon, New York**. In fact, the **Upper Canaan Family** was set up to accommodate the influx expected from Savoy. On 10 October 1821, Orren, his parents, and brother Horace were admitted to the Upper Canaan Shakers. This was the beginning of his lifelong Shaker commitment. Two years later, he was sent to live at the **Second Order of the Church**. That **family** was interested in building up a large class of boys and Orren was one of the first of these. His caretakers were Benjamin Lyon and **Amos Stewart**. Later **Philemon Stewart** would have charge of him. He attended the Shaker school which was run on the Lancastrian system.

After he left school at the age of 15, he served the community by doing whatever job they needed to have done, especially carpentry and furniture making. He also went out on seed routes, teamed horses for the **Ministry**, and did gardening. In 1848, he moved to the **First Order** and 10 year later, when the scarcity of men became acute, he became caretaker of the boys. In 1862, he became the teamster for the First Order and held this position until 1875, when he was appointed a family **deacon**. This responsibility was compounded almost immediately when a month later eight buildings were lost by fire, including the **dwelling house**. It was his duty to help provide for the family, and all of his time was spent helping to reconstruct Shaker life amid the mass destruction. He retired as a deacon in 1882 when he took over the hens. During his final years, he still lent his talents to all who called upon him. After his death his workroom in the brethrens' brick shop remained intact until the 1930s.

Although Brother Orren was an important **Church Family** member, he is best remembered today as a furniture maker. His talents were nurtured by his caretakers. Both of these men were important woodworkers. He was so skilled that he moved to the First Order in 1848 to take the place of their principal carpenter who left. Whenever he could for the remainder of his life, he made furniture and tools and did repairs. As the number of men declined, he turned his attention to helping the **sisters** in the fancy goods trade. His biggest contributions to these efforts were the sewing desks he made. In addition, he fashioned smaller objects for their convenience. Since he signed his pieces with the stamp "OH," his work is readily identifiable.

HOCKNELL, JOHN (1722–1799). Born in Cheshire, England, he was originally a Methodist and later joined the religious group headed by James and Jane Wardley. He was a man of means, and tradition holds that he paid the passage for **Mother Ann** and her followers to come to America in 1774. That next year he leased the land at **Niskeyuna**, which became the Shakers' first permanent home in America. Later he returned to England and brought over more Shakers, including his family. During the earliest years of Shakerism, he used his temporal wealth to help establish the Church. His wife

Hannah Hocknell (1723–1797) and his daughter Mary Hocknell (1759–1825) died as Shakers at **Watervliet, New York**. His son Richard Hocknell eventually left the society to marry Nancy Lee, Mother Ann's niece.

HOLDEN, JOSEPH (1836–1919). He was born on 18 September 1836 in Shelburne Falls, Massachusetts. With his mother Olive, he entered the **New Lebanon** Shakers from Hawley, Massachusetts, in 1839. Eventually, Joseph was sent to live at the **Second Order of the Church**. Unlike most other Shaker **families**, the Second Order had good success with boys. Upon reaching adulthood, a number of very talented men decided to remain Shakers for life. Besides Joseph Holden, a few of these were **Giles Avery, Alonzo Hollister, Orren Haskins**, and Calvin Reed. While future Shaker leaders at other places came from the ranks of "shop men," Holden had been a farmer for his entire life. His bearing and his looks showed this. He was a family **deacon** in charge of the farm for 20 years but had never been an **elder** before being appointed to the **Ministry** in February 1891.

Elder Joseph's whole life in the Ministry would be taken up with crisis management. When he took office, his associate, **Daniel Boler**, was 87 years old and had been in the Ministry almost 40 years. At that same time, the nearby **Hancock bishopric** was experiencing problems because it had very few men, and no one who could serve as a member of its Ministry. Daniel Boler died in 1892, and Elder Joseph moved to Hancock. No one was appointed to stand as second with him. For the first time since the time of Father **Joseph Meacham**, there was just a single man in the Ministry, and that person did not even reside at New Lebanon. By the 1890s, the New Lebanon and the Hancock bishoprics were depleted in numbers. Consequently, in the summer of 1893, the Hancock Ministry was dissolved. Elder Joseph and his two female associates, **Harriet Bullard** and Augusta Stone, formed the **Central Ministry**, having direct oversight over **Watervliet** and **Mount Lebanon, New York**; Hancock, Massachusetts; and **Enfield, Connecticut**. The **sisters** were to live at Mount Lebanon, while Elder Joseph would stay at Hancock.

Elder Joseph's removal to Hancock showed that he did not intend to isolate himself at Mount Lebanon. He got right into the business of running the bishopric. Those who lived at Hancock remarked that he was always on the go. In the warm months he got up early and mowed the lawns. He tried to supervise the farm, but ministerial duties prevented this. To ease his burdens and learn something of finances, he appointed trustee **Ira Lawson** of Hancock as his associate in the Central Ministry in 1899. In 1901, he was appointed **trustee** of **Harvard** and **Shirley**. Most of his time was spent at Shirley until it was sold. Meanwhile he traveled around the remaining Shaker villages to help in any way he could. At most places he saw first hand how diminished Shaker life had become. Elder Ira died in 1905 and it was not until 1911 that Elder **Walter Shepherd** of Enfield, Connecticut, was chosen to be Elder Joseph's associate. This assistance helped ease Holden's tremendous burdens since first Ministry Eldress Harriet was almost 90 years old, and her associate **M. Catherine Allen** was preoccupied with preserving Shaker manuscripts and artifacts. Elder Joseph and Elder Walter sold off and consolidated some of the massive Shaker landholdings as villages dissolved one by one. Ten of the original 18 Shaker communities were closed while he was in office. To complicate matters, Elder Joseph had very poor eyesight and underwent a successful operation to help him see better. He relied upon a young sister named **Frances Hall** of Hancock to help him. This exposure to Shaker business would help her assume important financial matters at Hancock after Holden died in 1919. Elder Joseph was the only member of the Ministry to live all of his term at Hancock. His successor Elder Walter chose to live at Mount Lebanon and his associate, chosen after Elder Joseph died, was Elder **Arthur Bruce** of **Canterbury**.

HOLLISTER, ALONZO GILES (1830–1911). By the time **Elder** Alonzo Hollister died, his home at **Mount Lebanon** has been reduced to a mere shadow of what it had once been. Although he kept up a correspondence, he was often alone and had few visitors. His funeral did not attract outside notice, and he faded from view. Unknown to many outsiders was the fact that he was a great Shaker theologian and scholar. Until the end of his life he wrote on every scrap of paper, blank pages of hymnals, and notebooks. Collectively, these form a tremendous mass of insights into the Shaker religion and Shaker life in general. Historians trying to reconstruct what was happening in Shaker communities too often overlook his scribbled notes that are found here and there. These are generally the only places where important facts are recorded. Since right after he died Shakerism collapsed at Mount Lebanon, he still remains fairly unknown.

He was born on 24 May 1830 in Adams, Massachusetts. He and his large family joined the **New Lebanon** Shakers in 1838. From that time until 1896, he lived at the **Second Order of the Church**. He had the excellent fortune to come under the care of a young **brother** named **Giles Avery**. Here he grew up helping in the gardens, doing haying and any other necessary chores. He signed the **covenant** on 27 November 1851. Though this was his formal acceptance of Shakerism, Brother Alonzo was already a committed member. He had been a part of the **Era of Manifestations** and the impressions and influence of this time never left him.

The business of the **Church Family** was herbs. These were sold in dried and liquid form. He worked in the former until an accident claimed the fingers of his left hand in 1859. After this he worked almost exclusively making liquid extracts. He became an expert at this and continued to work at the extract works until he died. In fact, in 1875, he moved into the extract laboratory. That year an arsonist had destroyed the large building that housed the dried herb business. Brother Alonzo was determined that this fate would not befall the extract buildings. In 1891, he was made second elder of the Second Order. Even after the family closed five years later, he lived in the laboratory until he suffered a bad fall in 1906. Though he continued to run the business, he lived in the brick dwelling of the Church Family. He was appointed elder of the Church in 1911. He died seven months later and was not replaced. Thus he was the last elder of the Church at Mount Lebanon.

Elder Alonzo's legacy as a writer is that he resisted the temptation to dilute Shakerism by trying to appeal to the secular world. He did not think Shaker theology could change. His published and unpublished works show an unwavering faith in the religion as passed down from the **First Parents**. This orthodoxy stood in opposition to Elder **Frederick Evans**, and other Shaker leaders who went along with him. They clashed over issues such as the Bible and spiritualism. As Elder Frederick was writing and publishing scores of books, tracts, pamphlets, and newspaper articles, Brother Alonzo on a smaller scale was writing and publishing his own material. Moreover,

Brother Alonzo outlived Elder Frederick by almost 20 years, so much of his published writing appears later. This did not mean that it gained a wider appeal: Elder Frederick had captured the public's imagination, and the few remaining Shakers were too busy trying to keep their community going to get involved with theology. In this way, his valuable insights showing the continuity of Shakerism were virtually ignored.

From 1903 until his death, he corresponded with and helped John Patterson MacClean (1848–1939) of Ohio preserve Shaker manuscripts. Eldress **Catherine Allen** attended Elder Alonzo during his final illness. She was able to fulfill his requests about the disposition of his writings. His most famous work is the three-volume *Pearly Gate* Shaker catechism. Since the theology of **Calvin Green** was the basis of everything he wrote, Elder Alonzo gives him full credit with Green's name of the *Pearly Gate Bible Lessons*.

HOLY HILLS. This is the popular name for the outdoor worship sites that the Shakers set up in 1842. *See* FEAST GROUNDS.

HOLY MOTHER WISDOM. This aspect of the divine was used throughout the **Era of Manifestations**. It reflects the Shaker belief in the feminine characteristics of God. Her messages were set as guidance.

– I –

INDENTURES. The first children to form a part of Shaker communities were those whose parents had received the faith from **Mother Ann** or one of her companions. No thought at the time was given to situations in which the Shakers might not have legal control of the children they raised. The parents and relatives of these first children were in the community, and they supported it with fervor.

As time passed, the success of these first children in remaining faithful may have encouraged the Shakers to take in more children in the hope that they would stay for life. Mother **Lucy Wright**, **Elder Calvin Green**, and others cautioned against the practice of taking in children if their parents did not come into the community as well. As long as she lived, relatively few children were admitted. After Mother Lucy's death in 1821, the Shakers began to take in large numbers of children. Some were orphans whose relatives were happy to give them to the Shakers to raise. Others were dropped off by single parents. The Shakers even visited the poorhouses of cities and towns to get children to bring up. This practice destabilized the communities because children were always coming and going. The net gain in numbers to the Shakers was low, especially among the boys. The more serious effect of taking in children was that at first there was no legal way for the Shakers to prove that they had legal custody of the children. This problem was quickly solved by using indentures.

Indentures were agreements between the **trustee**, who legally represented all the Shakers, and the parent or guardian of the child. The Shakers agreed to raise the child and provide him/her with training in a particular trade as well as schooling. In turn, the child agreed to stay in the community until a certain age and obey the rules. Some indentures were handwritten and some were printed forms that only had to be filled in. The age when a child could leave varied from 16 to 21, depending upon circumstances. If a child ran away, the terms of the indenture were broken. Indentures also proved an effective way for the Shakers to prove in court that they had legal custody. Some parents or relatives tried to kidnap children against their will or sought monetary compensation for the work children did in the community. Using indentures was a way for the Shakers to defend themselves in these matters. *See also* CHILDREN'S ORDER.

INFIRMARY. *See* NURSE SHOP.

INSTRUMENT. Shakerism has always had a strong spiritualistic connection. Consequently, Shaker history is filled with examples of Spirit communications. These have taken various forms, most notably visions, **songs**, prayers, messages, and inspired art. An instrument is anyone who receives such communication. Instruments have most often received Spirit communications in dreams, while praying, or when at communal worship. Though there have always been such communications, the most famous period is known as the **Era of Manifestations**, also called the Era of Mother's Work. Really in two distinct parts, it began in 1837 and was finished by the early 1850s.

IRELAND, SHADRACK (17?–1780). His colorful life predates the arrival of the Shakers at **Harvard**, Massachusetts but made it possible for the Shakers to be so successful in gaining converts there. Ireland was from Charlestown, Massachusetts, where he had a wife and six children. He had been a pipemaker and a wood-joiner, but was so affected by the preaching of George Whitefield that he became a **New Light** minister. He believed in perfectionism and the millennium, and abandoned his family to move to Harvard. There he developed a small group of adherents and, since he also believed in celibacy, took on a soul mate, Abigail Lougee. His followers built him the **Square House** in 1769 and for the next 10 years he preached his doctrines to them. This congregation included future Shakers Isaac Willard, Zaccheus Stephens, Abijah Worster, Abel Jewett, and Jonathan Cooper. In the summer of 1780, he died, and when he did not return to the body as promised, he was buried secretly in a nearby cornfield. This left at least a score of disillusioned followers who were ripe to hear about Shakerism. The Shaker testimony had just opened that previous May and many came to **Niskeyuna** to see **Mother Ann** and her companions. Through Zaccheus Stephens and others, Mother Ann came to Harvard on her first missionary tour in 1781, and she had her followers buy the Square House as the base of operations for their missionary efforts.

– J –

JACKSON, REBECCA COX (1795–1871). Many people do not realize that the Shakers had some African American members for most of their history. The most important of these was Rebecca Cox Jackson or, as she was called by her followers, Mother Rebecca Jackson. Born in 1795, Jackson's early life is unknown. She was not a slave, and by the age of 10 was living in Philadelphia. It has not been determined when she married Samuel S. Jackson, and there is a strong likelihood that they had no children. Her religious conversion happened during a thunderstorm in 1830, and after that time she became a visionary. In 1831 one of these visions prompted her to turn away from sexual relations. She mortified her body and preached that **celibacy** was part of a holy life. These views set her in conflict with her brother Joseph, who was a well-known minister of the AME Church of Philadelphia.

In spite of his opposition, she preached to all who would listen and, in 1836, visited the Shakers for the first time. That was also the year she met Rebecca Perot, who would be her lifetime companion. Jackson continued to preach and, in 1843, while staying with a group of Perfectionists near Albany, she decided to become a Shaker. She did not join the community, however, until 1847. She and Rebecca Perot lived together at the South Family at **Watervliet** until 1851. At that time she felt called to go out once again into the **world** and preach. Family **Eldress** Paulina Bates opposed this, but Jackson and Perot left anyway. They felt compelled to follow God through an inner voice that was leading them in this direction. In 1857, they returned to the Shakers, convinced that now God was speaking to them through the leaders of the community. Eldress Paulina, a visionary herself, communicated that it was the wish of **Mother Ann** that Jackson return to Philadelphia and start a community there.

Accordingly, the first Shaker meeting was held there on 30 April 1859. In time as many as a dozen women and a few men lived in a racially integrated community. Mother Rebecca died in 1871 and her successor Rebecca Perot changed her last name to Jackson. She died in 1901 at Watervliet. *See also* PHILADELPHIA, PENNSYLVANIA.

JESUS OF NAZARETH. According to Shakers, Jesus of Nazareth was the first Shaker. He was not divine, but a man, born of the Virgin Mary. From birth, he had heavenly gifts, which developed as he grew to adulthood. His life of virgin purity, lived in a community of disciples, was the model for the Shakers. At the time of his baptism by John the Baptist, the fullness of the Christ Spirit came upon him. From this point onward, God was manifested through him. Unfortunately, the world rejected his gifts and crucified him. This act of being crucified, however, did nothing to save the world. Shakers reject the doctrine of the vicarious atonement; that is, the idea that God sent His Son into the world to save it by dying. Rather, it was his life of complete obedience to God's will unto death that is to be emulated. On this point alone, Shaker theology would be considered unorthodox by other Christians. In a related fashion, the Shakers also reject the concept of the **Trinity**. To them this is a man-made idea that has no basis in Scripture.

The ministry that was cut short by the death of Jesus, a man chosen by God, would be revived in its final form by the life founded by **Ann Lee**, a woman chosen by God.

JOHNSON, MOSES (1752–1842). He was born 1 March 1752 and was part of the scores of zealous men and women who joined the Shakers at **Enfield, New Hampshire**. In 1785, he arrived at **New Lebanon** where the **Meeting House** was being built. He was given charge of framing the structure and helped build it. The model of the Meeting House at New Lebanon was used with minor modifications for subsequent buildings in all of the 11 other original Shaker communities. He died at the South Family at Enfield, New Hampshire, on 25 March 1842. *See also* MEETING HOUSE.

JOHNSON, THEODORE ELLIOT (1930–1986). Of all the Shakers who lived in the 20th century, no one was more loved or feared than **Brother** Ted Johnson. He was a Shaker for a little less than 27 years, but his impact still continues to be felt.

He was born 9 September 1930 in Boston, Massachusetts, the only child of Elmer Carl and Ruth Collins Johnson. Ted graduated cum laude from Colby College. He was a Fulbright Scholar and studied at the Sorbonne and at the University of Strasbourg. In addition, he received a master's degree from Harvard Divinity School. During the 1950s he studied Shaker theology and became convinced of the truth of its testimony. Since he lived in Massachusetts, he paid a call on the **Hancock** Shakers to seek more information about the present-day community. He was directed by Brother Ricardo Belden to contact **Sabbathday Lake** since in his opinion that was the only place where Shakerism was still being lived.

He joined the Sabbathday Lake Shakers on 28 May 1960. For the remainder of his life he gave himself over to all aspects of the work of Shakerism. Many of his activities centered around making the Shakers accessible to contemporary audiences. His first task was to become the first director of the library. Brother Ted loved books and was a trained librarian. In 1961, he founded the *Shaker Quarterly* and became its first editor. This was the first Shaker publication since the **Manifesto** ceased in 1899. He felt it was time for the **believers** to be heard in the **world** once more. After Brother **Delmer Wilson** died in 1961, he took charge of meeting on Sunday. In 1963, he was made director of the museum. That year he also encouraged the community to open Sunday meeting to the public and use the **Meeting House**. This building had been closed since the late 1880s and had been used for storage.

Around the time Brother Ted entered Sabbathday Lake, other men and women were applying for admission there and at **Canterbury**. This was an unexpected phenomenon. For well over 100 years, the Shakers had suffered from a lack of suitable adult converts. All of a sudden, it seemed a few adults were willing to join just as the communities were fading out. When Eldress **Emma King** of Canterbury reconstituted the **Parent Ministry** in 1957, she did so to be able to sell Hancock and deal with the surprising amount of money, property, and stocks that had been in possession of the late trustee Eldress **Frances Hall**. The new **Ministry** was not intended to be pastoral in any sense. Moreover, for the 50 years that she had been a leader at Canterbury, she had come to the firm belief that only children brought up in the society would make good Shakers. Eldress Emma and her associate until the early 1930s, Elder **Arthur Bruce**, did not believe in governing by consensus. No disagreement with them was tolerated. People who did not conform were asked to leave. Furthermore, the many decades of children having been raised by those who had come in themselves as children had produced adult Shakers who obeyed no matter what the **eldress** said. This was a dramatic change from Shakerism as it had existed as late as the 1890s.

In 1963, in a carefully worded pastoral letter, her first and only one, Eldress Emma stated that Canterbury would not accept adults and enumerated many reasons for this decision. Having warned Sabbathday Lake, she felt it was now up to them to decide for themselves. She absolved herself of blame should these new adults cause problems. It must have been a tremendous shock to her when the Sabbathday Lake Shakers, citing the **covenant**, allowed the new members to stay and welcomed more. Brother Ted became the center of this controversy.

For those who wanted to see the Shakers continue, Brother Ted was a living symbol that **Mother Ann** had not forgotten her children and had raised up new believers just when all seemed lost. Even those who did not wish to become Shakers joined the community for worship and considered themselves **"Friends of the Holy Spirit**."

For those who wanted Shakerism to end, the work of Brother Ted was to be feared. Some wished to write the final chapter of Shakerism after their own ideas. Others wanted to get their hands on valuable Shaker objects at Sabbathday Lake. For many, a young and vibrant Shakerism was too much to contemplate. Also, there was a not-so-subtle superiority complex at Canterbury. It did not seem right that Sabbathday Lake should outlast Canterbury. Finally, there was the matter of Brother Ted's personality. He was no lightweight intellectual but a devoted scholar of immense memory and knowledge. Certainly he knew more of the essence of Shaker theology and traditions than anyone since Elder **Alonzo Hollister**. Far from shrinking from a confrontation, Brother Ted was ready and willing to give answers.

Rather than being talked to, Brother Ted was talked about. Historians writing about the Shakers ignored his insights and pretended he did not exist as they turned out their work. He was ridiculed and the object of false accusations. Money from the **Shaker Central Trust Fund** was cut from the Sabbathday Lake Shakers in the early 1970s since they kept their new members. The untruth that the covenant had been closed was accepted, though no one could come up with a citation for it. All the while Brother Ted endured and fostered in many hearts a love for Shakerism that enriched their lives. He revived the herb industry, reintroduced animals on the farm, sought to protect the land for future generations, reorganized the library and museum, introduced Bible study in the community, and through his efforts reached out to many other intentional communities, many of them Roman Catholic. In 1974, he ran the bicentennial conference commemorating the 200th anniversary of Mother Ann's arrival in America. He preached, wrote, and taught high school to bring in money for the community.

The years of slights and pressures wore upon him, yet his death was totally unexpected. He died in his sleep during the early morning of 20 April 1986. His passing sent shock waves throughout the world of Shaker. Over 250 people attended his funeral and 300 others sent cards to the community. His life had been an inspiration and a blessing to so many. For the Shakers it was a sign of hope. The work he began still lives on in the daily life of the Sabbathday Lake Shakers.

JUNIOR ORDER. This is an ambiguous term used to designate a stage certain people belonged to while members of the **Gathering Order**. Basically there are two types of Shakers: Those who have signed the **Church Order** covenant; and those who belong to one of the stages of the Gathering Order and have signed **probationary** or **novitiate covenants** or articles of agreement. During the first half of the 19th century, Church Order Shakers were sometimes called members of the Senior Order. This has led to great confusion because belonging to the Church or Senior Order did *not* mean that they had to belong to the **Church Family**. It also meant that not everyone who lived in the Church Family was in the Church or Senior Order. Although the Church Family was supposed to be reserved for the most fervent Shakers, Church Order Shakers lived in the other families as well. Covenants for these families were Church Order covenants. For example, at **Hancock, Massachusetts**, the Church Order consisted of the Church, North, West, and **Second Families**. The Gathering Order was composed of the East and South Families. Within the Gathering Order there were stages of development. Some had few or no obligations to discharge to the outside world and were serious about trying the life. At Hancock's peak, these people joined the East Family. This was the Junior Order. Others had families or serious financial obligations that prevented them from full **union**. These were gathered at the South Family. In addition, some members of the Gathering Order had weak faith or such outside entanglements that they could not be full members and were situated on nearby farms owned by the Shakers. At **New Lebanon** this was called the **Back Order**.

The Shakers never had a clear-cut answer or meaning of the term Junior Order, and it is to be wondered how widespread or universal the terminology was. *See also* OUT FAMILY.

"J. W." STONE. Angry mobs accosted the early Shaker leaders wherever they went. In September 1783, a particularly violent group attacked **Mother Ann** and her companions as they journeyed through **New Lebanon**. The man responsible for the worst of the violence, Thomas Law, seized Father **James Whittaker** and attempted to throw him headfirst against a large rock by the side of the road. Whittaker's fall was broken by the intervention of one of the **brethren**. Nonetheless, Whittaker broke three ribs in the fall. To commemorate

Whittaker's deliverance from harm, the initials J. W. were carved into the rock.

This stone still exists by the side of the old road that used to pass through the Shaker village. The roadbed had been abandoned for well over 100 years and is scarcely passable. In addition, weather has exfoliated much of the carving. Consequently the stone is very difficult to find.

– K –

KING, EMMA BELLE (1873–1966). Over its long history, **Canterbury** had very few women who held the position of first **eldress** of the **Church Family**. Nineteenth-century eldresses Mary Hatch and **Dorothy Durgin** had long terms of office, but the longest of them all was Eldress Emma Belle King who served from 1918 until 1966. Her tenure saw the community dwindle from 60 in 1920 to six in 1966.

She was born on 5 June 1873 in Johnston, Rhode Island. On 26 September 1878 she was placed with the Canterbury Shakers at the Church Family. When she entered, Canterbury was experiencing a surge in membership that would peak in the 1880s. **Public meeting** was crowded and inquirers were frequent. Since the society published the *Manifesto,* the official Shaker newspaper, Canterbury became the best-known society. Many young girls lived there, and they became her companions. Among these were Rebecca Hathaway, Blanche Gardner, Lizzie Horton, and Sadie Pinneo. Starting in 1891 she taught in the Shaker school. She assisted Sister Jessie Evans and eventually took over from her. She was a schoolteacher until 1912. On 25 December 1913 she became associate eldress standing with Eldress Mary A. Wilson. Later Jennie H. Fish became first eldress for a brief time and, in 1918, the **Parent Ministry** appointed Emma B. King as first eldress in her stead. In 1920 she officially took over all duties and had Lillian Phelps as her second. They served together for over 45 years. During this time not one girl brought up in the society stayed upon reaching adulthood. In the late 1920s, she decided, against the wishes of others in the community, that no more children would be taken.

On 12 February 1946, she replaced Rosetta Stephens as a member of the Parent Ministry. Later that year she became a trustee of

Canterbury. In 1957 with the death of Eldress **Frances Hall**, she became first in the Parent Ministry. One of her first acts was to dissolve the **Ministry**. She made the announcement at **Sabbathday Lake** while visiting there on 31 March 1957. Less than two months later, however, she decided to reconstitute the Ministry. Her idea was to appoint two Canterbury **sisters**, Ida Crook and Ada Elam, to stand with her. Together they could close out **Hancock** and deal with the unexpected money in bankbooks, stocks, and land left by Eldress Frances Hall. Her strategy to concentrate all power at Canterbury was begun when the official seat of the Ministry was moved from Pittsfield to Canterbury. Acquiescing to the inevitable, she chose Eldress **Gertrude Soule** of Sabbathday Lake as a member of the Ministry, but to assure that Sister Ada Elam of Canterbury would be the next one chosen, she had it officially recorded that Sister Ada would fill the next vacancy when it should occur. This promise was never fulfilled, because Sister Ada died of cancer in 1962.

Although a trust agreement was drawn up in 1957, it was rejected by the Ministry. In 1959, with the help of lawyers, she set up an irrevocable trust called the **Shaker Central Trust Fund**. This was the depository of the money and stock portfolio that had been in possession of Eldress Frances Hall. It held the accumulated wealth of Hancock and the money remaining from the sale of Shaker properties over the years. The money would be used to support the surviving Shakers and be used for educational purposes. New Shakers would have access to support from the Shaker Trust when they had lived in the community for five years. While she was dealing with these issues, Eldress Emma had to cope with a surprising development. A number of adult men and women began to petition both Sabbathday Lake and Canterbury for admission.

Once again her will prevailed in all things. She decided in opposition to a few of the Canterbury sisters that no adults would be taken into that society. Her opinion was that only children brought up in the society made good Shakers. Since Canterbury had decided against taking children in the late 1920s, it was doomed to die out. She anticipated this and thought that they should "go down gloriously" and not try to resurrect themselves at this late date in their history. She also was extremely suspicious that new members would join just to have access to money from the trust fund. She counseled the Shakers at Sabbathday Lake to follow the same course as she had decided for Canterbury.

The Shakers at Sabbathday Lake continued to accept new members, and Eldress Emma died in 1966 before the controversy over this would blossom into a severe strain in relations between the two communities. Somewhere along the line, the rumor developed that Eldress Emma had closed the covenant. Not only would this have been impossible for her to do, since each Shaker family had its own covenant (Canterbury had lost their Church Family covenant years before anyway), the two dates given, 1957 and 1965 contradict each other. Also there would have been no reason for the closing of the covenant in 1957, nor could she likely have done it in 1965. Her health had failed to such a great degree that **Marguerite Frost** was appointed as associate eldress of the Church Family at Canterbury in 1965. Ministerial meetings even had to be held in Eldress Emma's bedroom since she was not ambulatory. Since the reconstituted Ministry did not appoint a successor, Eldress Emma King was the last Church Family eldress at Canterbury. Eldress Marguerite took over from Eldress Emma in 1966, but she was never made first eldress by the reconstituted Ministry though she herself was a Ministry member and could have done so quite easily.

For a variety of reasons Eldress Emma has been made to take the blame for closing the covenant. When the history of Canterbury is written, the story behind these intentions will hopefully be made public. On the opposite side, there has been a great tendency of those writing about Eldress Emma to justify every autocratic move she made by appealing to intentions she may not have had in real life. Once again, a close examination of manuscript material will reveal a person far more interesting than has heretofore been depicted.

– L –

LABORING SONGS. These are songs meant to accompany the worship exercises or dances. The first of these were introduced by Father **Joseph Meacham** in the 1780s. They were wordless tunes using vocables. Starting in 1811, the laboring songs became worded and were used until the **exercises** and **marches** used in worship were discontinued during the 1870s.

LANDON, POLLY RUTH (1775–1850). Mother **Lucy Wright** led the Shakers from 1796 until her death in 1821. During that time, no man in the **Ministry** had much power. Two of the three women who served under Mother Lucy also lived very short lives. It would seem that Mother Lucy was destined to be alone. This situation changed in 1804 when Polly Landon was appointed to the Ministry. Born in New York City on 3 August 1775, Landon joined the Church with her parents during the time of **Mother Ann**. She was appointed second **eldress** in the Ministry in 1804 and at that time took the name of her predecessor Ruth Hammond. Hammond was a well-liked leader whose career was cut short by ill health. She died in 1805 at the age of 40. For the next 17 years, Landon worked closely with Mother Lucy. These years saw a tremendous growth in Shakerism and the Wright-Landon team seemed to be the perfect fit for dealing with managing everything. In 1821, after Wright died, Landon became first eldress in the Ministry. Her loving presence endeared her so much to the Shakers that she was called the "venerable" Ruth Landon by some. She died on 30 May 1850.

LAWRENCE, POLLY (1792–1826). She was born in the town of **New Lebanon, New York**, on 24 July 1792. She was admitted to the **North Family** of the New Lebanon Shakers in 1804. These were the earliest years of this new **Gathering Order**, and it was an exciting time. **Calvin Green**, **Ebenezer Bishop**, and a host of important Shakers lived in the family. In addition, preparations were being made to send missionaries out to Ohio and Kentucky.

Before becoming a Shaker, she had attended the common school in New Lebanon. Her teacher had been a young woman named Esther Bennet. Eventually Esther Bennet married Miles Doolittle. Esther Doolittle often spoke of Polly Lawrence and the Shakers to her children. This inspired her young daughter **Antoinette Doolittle** to seek out the Shakers to see for herself if she might like to join them. When she visited the Shakers for the first time, she asked for Polly Lawrence. In this way, even as a child, Polly had been a gatherer of souls. Antoinette Doolittle would later be an important **eldress** at the North Family.

In 1815, Polly was made second eldress of the North Family. In 1821, she moved to the **Church Family** but returned a year later to the North as a **deaconess**. In May 1826, she was sent to **Sodus, New York**, to be first ministry eldress. This was a brand new community still at the beginning of being gathered. It was envisioned by the Shaker leadership that she would be the eldress to see the society through its initial years. This was not to be. Almost upon arrival, she got the inspiration that she would not have a long time to live. This gave her an inner strength and beauty. During this time she composed the **song** "The Rolling Deep." This is one of the oldest songs still sung by the Shakers of today. Her premonitions proved correct. She was seized with a violent illness and died 30 July 1826. She was only 34 years old.

LAWSON, IRA REMINGTON (1834–1905). He was the youngest of seven children born to Ira Lawson and his wife Amy H. Remington. Ira was born 25 April 1834 in Union, Connecticut. His mother died when he was one year old, and if Ira's life had followed the pattern of the day, he and his older siblings might have been placed with the Shakers at this time. This did not happen, however, and Ira freely joined the Shakers on his own when he was 18. His family had been active members of the Presbyterian Church. This strong religious background would serve him well as a Shaker. Although Lawson had tremendous faith, it was not for religious matters that he would be known, but in the management of farms and land for profit.

When he joined the **Hancock** Shakers in 1851, he was assigned to live at the West Family. His first assignment was as manager of the family farm. He did so well that in 1857 he was made second **elder**. His skill with money was noticed by Elder **Thomas Damon** of the Hancock **Ministry**. In 1862 he was sent to live at the **Church Family** and become one of the **trustees**. In 1860, this family had 77 members; 29 percent of these, or 22 people, were over 65 years old. Another 34 percent, or 26, were youth under 20 years of age. Thus, almost two-thirds of the family was either very young or advanced in years. That year the family had $1,112 in savings and active seed routes that extended into New Jersey and New York as well as New England. By 1862, however, the family had a debt of $2,000. Lawson was placed in the trusteeship to deal with this financial crisis.

One of the first things he did was go out on the seed routes to check them. He traveled over 3,000 miles in this effort. When the seed business declined, he shifted operations to building up the farm. For a time, the drying and selling of sweet corn was carried on, but his greatest success was buying cattle and fattening them up for resale in Pittsfield. Besides the farm and dairy operations, income came from a wide variety of fancy goods made by the **sisters**. These items were sold at the **Office** stores maintained by the different Shaker families. At the same time, of the 3,000 acres owned by the society, 500 was in direct cultivation mostly by hired laborers and the rest was woodland, pasture, or mountain.

In the years between his appointment as trustee in 1862 and 1900, over $75,000 was spent in making internal improvements on buildings, grounds, and equipment. Another $75,000 was invested in high-grade securities such as Boston and Albany Railroad and Bell Telephone stocks. Money made more money for the society, and by the 1890s Lawson had a special long-distance telephone line installed in the office so that he could buy and sell his stocks and make any other necessary financial communications. The iron mine on the property brought in a good income for him as well.

He left the Shakers to elope in 1871. The next day, however, with the marriage unconsummated and his heart filled with remorse, he came back to Hancock for another **privilege**. In spite of this temporary lapse, he remained highly regarded, and in 1899 he was appointed a member of the **Central Ministry**. Many Shaker villages were closing at that time and consolidating resources. Lawson's expert financial sense helped manage this larger network of communities. Tragically for the Shakers, he died suddenly in 1905 of pneumonia. By then, some of his financial genius had been shared with his associate in the Ministry Elder **Joseph Holden**. Since Elder Joseph had poor eyesight, a young sister named **Frances Hall** acted as his secretary. In time she came to handle a good deal of the finances. Sister Frances Hall, later an eldress of the Ministry, did not die until 1957. Hancock, always a rich community since Ira Lawson became a trustee, was in no danger of closing in spite of its small membership until after the passing of Eldress Frances.

LEAD. The Shakers always use this word as a noun prefaced by the definite article "the" to refer to the **Ministry**. For example, a Shaker may write that it is necessary to follow the Lead. Sometime during the middle years of the 20th century, non-Shakers began using the word as an adjective to describe the Ministry. The result is the made-up term "Lead Ministry." Subsequent scholars have repeated the use until it is quite embedded into writing on the Shakers. The result is a redundancy that remains an inaccurate way to describe the Ministry. Using the term "Lead Ministry" to the Shaker would be akin to saying "Ministry Ministry."

LEBANON MINISTRY. This was the popular name for the **Ministry of New Lebanon**. It enjoyed a common use from the 1780s until the 1890s. *See also* MINISTRY OF NEW LEBANON.

LEE, MOTHER ANN (1736–1784). Shakerism is a way of life. Each and every Shaker must take the unique circumstances of his/her life and travel the path of faith. The triumphs, the hardships, and the ever-deepening love of God that mark an individual's journey in the **Christlife** might closely mirror Mother's life or they may not. Nonetheless, since **Mother Ann** was the first to receive the fullness of the in-dwelling of the Christ Spirit that is accessible to anyone who would live by the gospel, her life is worth noting. Mother herself could not write and her companions did not record their experiences of her in her lifetime. Over 30 years after her death, the story and history of Mother's life was written down and, no doubt, edited by the **Ministry**. In addition to official versions of her life, individual Shakers have reflected on her and added more information. Finally, "monastic memory" has always existed in Shaker communities. Older Shakers passed along stories about Mother Ann to younger Shakers, who one day would do the same. Today at **Sabbathday Lake**, the remaining Shakers often speak of Mother as if she were still physically present and they have their own memories of her.

Ann Lee (originally Lees) was born on 29 February 1736, the second of the eight children of John Lees, a blacksmith, and his wife. They lived in Toad Lane, **Manchester, England**. On 1 June 1742 Ann was baptized in the Anglican faith at Christ Church. By the time she was born, Manchester and the surrounding area had already been transformed into an industrial center. Large-scale textile production and related trades were the dominant businesses, and it is not surprising that Ann Lee went to work in the mills when she was eight years old. The meager income she earned was needed by her family, and following the common practice of the time, she never learned to read or write. Instead she cut velvet, prepared looms, and sheared fur 12 hours a day. In contrast to this bleak life, Ann remained a deeply religious girl. She was sensitive about her own sinfulness and wanted to learn how to live a pure life. The answers she sought did not come from the Anglican church. In 1758, while she was employed as a cook in the local hospital, an asylum for the insane, she began to attend meetings led by James and Jane Wardley.

The Wardleys, former Quakers, were tailors and were from Bolton-on-the-Moors. Though they had separated from the Friends in 1747, they retained the belief in pacifism. They added the practice of ecstatic worship that had characterized the Camisards of France. Also, they held that the coming of Christ would be in the form of a woman. The Wardleys' society became known for its lively worship services, which included dancing, shouting, singing and shaking. They were called shaking Quakers or just Shakers. Ann and other members of her family became active members.

In spite of her reluctance, Ann married Abraham Standerin or Stanley on 5 January 1762. They had four children. Three of them died while still infants. One child, a daughter named Elizabeth, lived a few years and died in 1766. These personal tragedies and her already heightened sense of sin made her an even more fervent member of the Wardley group. So powerful was her testimony that even her husband joined. Gradually, she assumed the leadership. At the same time, severe persecution resulted. Their crimes were generally profaning the Sabbath by their worship and disturbing the peace. They were imprisoned a number of times. In 1770, while in prison, Ann had a vision and a manifestation of the divine. She observed Adam and Eve in the Garden of Eden. The details of the first sin were revealed to her. Since she saw that sexual intercourse was the sin that drove humanity out of Paradise, **celibacy** became an essential part of living the Christlife.

From this point onward, Ann was known as Mother Ann and served as the focal point of the movement. The intensity of the testimony increased and accusations of heresy and fanaticism followed an incident in July 1773, when Mother Ann and her father disturbed the morning service at Christ Church. More jail sentences and persecution did not slow growth. Stories abound about her miraculous deliverance from physical harm from individual and mob attacks. For example, when authorities tried to starve her to death in prison, **James Whittaker**, a young man whom she had brought up, saved her by providing her with liquids through a pipe whose stem was inserted into the cell.

Her fame grew among her band, and she was regarded as the first to receive the fullness of the Spirit of Christ. Instead of the second coming of Christ being heralded by fanfare and notoriety, it had happened in relative obscurity. A lowly, illiterate woman had been chosen by God to reveal a way of life that would be the Heaven on Earth so long sought after. Yet this life could not flourish in England, and guided by a vision and financed by **John Hocknell**, one of her followers, Mother Ann decided to immigrate to America. On 19 May 1774 Mother Ann Lee, Abraham Stanley, **William Lee**, James Whittaker, Mary Partington, James Shepherd, John Hocknell, and Nancy Lee left England for New York. After a perilous trip that almost ended in disaster, they arrived in America on 6 August 1774.

For the first year, Mother lived with her husband with the Cunningham family of Queen Street. She did laundry work while he found a job as a blacksmith. When he fell ill, she nursed him back to health. He decided that he had had enough of the celibate life and threatened to go off with a prostitute if she continued to refuse to have sexual relations with him. She did not acquiesce to his demands, and he left her. His fate is not known. Without her husband, she was reduced to extreme poverty and this was, perhaps, the lowest point in her life. Meanwhile, John Hocknell had secured a piece of land at **Niskeyuna**, northwest of Albany. He left for England to bring back his family and raise money by selling his property. In 1776, the group moved to Niskeyuna, later known as **Watervliet, New York**.

As they cleared the land, planted crops, and built cabins, they anticipated the arrival of converts. In March 1780, Rueben Wright and Talmadge Bishop visited them. They had heard about the Shakers and came to investigate. Pleased at what they found, they returned to **New Lebanon, New York**, and shared the information with the leaders of the revival that had just ended there. **Joseph Meacham** and Samuel Johnson, the principal ministers, also interviewed Mother Ann and were so favorably impressed that they became Shakers. Their congregations joined as well. Families and friends learned of the faith, and Shakerism found its way into many places in New York and New England. Severe persecutions also resulted. Suspected as a spy for the British, Mother and some of her followers were arrested. From August until December 1780, she was imprisoned, first in Albany and later in Poughkeepsie.

Hoping to strengthen the faith of her new converts, in May 1781, she and five companions—William Lee, James Whittaker, Samuel Fitch, Margaret Leland, and Mary Partington—embarked on a long missionary tour. Abuse and mob violence awaited them at every turn. Using the **Square House** at **Harvard, Massachusetts**, as a sort of headquarters, they evangelized the region northwest of Boston and central Massachusetts. They also visited Rhode Island and Connecticut. Exhausted by her labors, Mother Ann returned to Niskeyuna on 4 September 1783. During the final year of her life she labored with the many people who came to see her. Her brother, Father William Lee, died in July 1784 and she followed him on 8 September 1784. Both of them died prematurely from the extreme violence they had suffered over the course of the long missionary tour. As she was dying, she had a vision of Father William returning for her in a chariot to take her to Heaven.

As thousands of Shakers have proudly asserted, what distinguished Mother Ann from the other women who lived at Manchester was that when God spoke to her, she unreservedly followed the call. Her life is the pattern others might think about as they make their own way through the Christlife.

LEE, WILLIAM (1740–1784). Father William was the natural brother of **Mother Ann Lee**. He was born in **Manchester, England**, and was a soldier. He later followed the trade of his father and became a blacksmith. He was married and at first did not accept his sister's religious ideas. By the time she left for America, however, he was a staunch Shaker. He arrived in New York City with her and helped set up their first permanent home at **Niskeyuna (Watervliet)**, New York, accompanied her on her long missionary tours, and was brutally treated by the mobs that persecuted the Shakers. He died prematurely as a result of his injuries. He was the first English Shaker to die in America. He died on 2 July 1784.

LETTERAL NOTATION. Before 1870, the Shakers used various notation systems in place of standard notation for their music. The most well known are the various types of letteral notation. The earliest form used capital letters and was introduced in 1824 by Abraham Whitney (1785–1882) of **Shirley, Massachusetts**. He claimed that **Mother Ann Lee** had revealed it to him. By 1835, small letteral notation had been developed by Russell Haskell (1801–1884) of **Enfield, Connecticut**. Linear and cursive letteral notation found in some hymnals are further modifications (Patterson, *The Shaker Spiritual*, 44–47).

LINDSAY, GOLDIE INA RUBY (1897–1990). She was born in New Braintree, Massachusetts, on 28 July 1897. Her family, however, was originally from Laconia, New Hampshire, and they returned there not long after she was born. When her parents died, she was placed with the **Canterbury** Shakers in 1905. Since Bertha Lillian Phelps, one of the **sisters**, had a major influence on her life, and eventually became her best friend, she adopted the name Bertha. This did not cause confusion because Phelps did not use her first name and was always called Sister Lillian.

Bertha Lindsay worked in many of the domestic departments at Canterbury, but her greatest love was the kitchen. Over her long Shaker life she worked on various aspects of food preparation and associated with many other Shaker cooks. In addition, she incorporated new recipes and gained experience with all kinds of foods. Her stories and recipes were collected and published in 1987 in a cookbook called *Seasoned with Grace: My Generation of Shaker Cooking*. This book not only has information on Shaker foods, it contains fascinating biographies of the Shakers that Sister Bertha knew. Also, the pictures give an interesting glimpse at the social history of Canterbury.

In 1944 she was given charge of the fancy work. This trade was a major source of income for the community, and she ran the operations until the industry closed in 1958. In 1965, she became a **trustee** of Canterbury and in 1967 was chosen by **Eldress Marguerite Frost** to be a member of the reconstituted **Parent Ministry**. Due to the infirmity of Eldress Marguerite, in the summer of 1970, Eldress Bertha assumed the position held by Frost of second eldress. Eldress Bertha, however, was never actually appointed as a **family** eldress. After the death of Eldress **Emma B. King** in 1966, no successor was chosen to fill the position of eldress, so that after the death of Eldress Marguerite in 1971, Canterbury had no family eldresses.

From the 1950s onward, Sister Bertha closely collaborated with Charles "Bud" Thompson to preserve Shaker objects. Together they worked to set up the museum that offered guided tours of some of the buildings. As a trustee and member of the Parent Ministry, Eldress Bertha was helpful in conveying the deed of the property to Shaker Village, Inc., a nonprofit educational institution in 1971. During the final years of her life, she became blind. This did not prevent her from greeting visitors and doing everything possible to further study and preservation of Canterbury. She died 3 October 1990, and her ashes were buried in a special spot she had chosen. Those who worked with her and developed friendships with her over the years have many good memories of her. She had a positive influence on those whose lives she touched.

LOLLIPOP MARKERS. These cast-iron markers in the shape of a large lollipop were used in the Shaker cemetery at **Harvard** as well as in the Church and **North Family** Cemetery at **New Lebanon**. Oral tradition has it that these markers were also used at **White Water, Ohio**, and designated the graves there until the scrap metal drives of World War II. This use of the marker in the West opens speculation that this type of marker may have been used in more places than Harvard, New Lebanon, and White Water.

LOMAS, GEORGE ALBERT (1840–1889). He was born in New York City in 1840. When he was 10 years old, along with his sister Isabella and brother Melville, he was admitted to the South Family at **Watervliet, New York**. The next year he was sent to live at the **Second Order of the Church**. During a time when almost all the boys brought up by the Shakers left as soon as they could, he stayed and became a very enthusiastic member. During the early 1860s he taught in the boys' school and in 1868 started speaking at **public meeting**. That was also the year he became second **elder** at the South Family.

As an elder in the **novitiate** family, it was his duty to help gather souls. In addition to his public speaking, in 1871 he started a monthly newspaper called the *Shaker.* Elder George was the first editor of this publication which eventually became known as the *Manifesto*. A fire and a shortage of help at Watervliet caused the paper to be transferred to Elder **Frederick Evans** and Eldress **Antoinette Doolittle** of the **North Family** at **Mount Lebanon**. In 1876, Elder George became editor again and still worked on the paper until it was finally transferred totally to the **Canterbury** Shakers during the 1880s. In the meantime, he became first elder at the South Family in 1875, succeeding Elder Issachar Bates Jr. who had died.

Besides contributing articles to the Shaker newspaper, he wrote hymns and anthems and acted as a singing teacher for the society. He also wrote many articles for periodicals and various pamphlets. These include: *Plain Talks upon Practical Religion, What Shall I Do To Be a Shaker?, The Life of Christ Is the End of the World, Decay of Shaker Institutions,* and *A Man Approved of God.*

It is not clear why the **Ministry of Mount Lebanon** seems never to have had much to do with him. He is either ignored in their journals or spoken of lightly. In 1875, he became second elder at the North Family. This was a demotion and meant that he no longer preached at the public meeting. He continued, however, to publish his views. In 1889 he died suddenly of heart disease. Over 300 people from outside the Shakers attended his funeral, but not the **Ministry**, who merely noted his passing in a journal. It would appear that even had he not died prematurely, he was not in favor and would never have risen to a position greater than that of second elder at a very small family at Watervliet.

LOWER CANAAN FAMILY (1814–1884). So many people were seeking admission to **New Lebanon** that in the spring of 1814, Mother **Lucy Wright** decided to set up a branch of the **Gathering Order** one half mile below the **Second Family**, near its carding mill. A house was taken down from the mountain east of the Church and moved to the site. Immediately, it was occupied by new converts from Rhode Island. Two years later a small **family** was organized under James Farnham and Phebe Smith. It was known as the Upper Family or the family by the carding machine. In 1823, a small farm known as the Madison Farm was purchased in the nearby town of **Canaan, New York**. This is the beginning of the Lower Family in Canaan.

From the start this family had problems with leadership. It also had many difficulties trying to sustain itself. As a Gathering Order, there was a constant turnover in the membership, making any industry difficult to carry on. For various short periods, there was an herb business, broom industry, chair making, syrup business, and mat making. The small family never had more than 42 members, and generally averaged about 30, two-thirds being females. In addition, they even struggled with farming. The lack of suitable converts, especially men, caused this family to close in 1884. It was the first of the eight **Mount Lebanon** families to dissolve. The property was sold for an industrial school for boys. Perhaps anticipating the closure, Marcia Bullard, a very capable sister, was sent to live with the **Harvard, Massachusetts**, Shakers in 1880. After the family closed, Louisa Green and three others were also sent to Harvard. Their talents helped keep the society going until well into the 20th century. In this manner, although the Lower Canaan Shakers dissolved in 1884, their direct influence at Harvard lasted over 30 more years.

– M –

MACE, AURELIA GAY (1835–1910). The Shaker society at **Sabbathday Lake** was never large, yet it had perhaps the largest number of capable leaders proportional to its size. One of the greatest of these was **Sister** Aurelia Mace. Her father was Marquis de Lafayette Mace and her mother Sarah Norton. Fayette Mace was a restless seeker after true religion, and on one of these quests, he decided to bring his family to live at the Shakers. Accordingly, he and his wife and eight children were admitted to the Sabbathday Lake community. Typical of new converts, his enthusiasm hardly knew any bounds. In 1838, he published *Familiar Dialogues on Shakerism; in which the Principles of the United Society are Illustrated and Defended*. Mace was an ordained Universalist minister and a close ally of Adin Ballou, whom the *Dialogues* are about. Also typical of those who start out so fervently is that he eventually became dissatisfied and left the community. His wife and four of his daughters remained faithful, however.

His youngest child was Aurelia Mace. Over her lifetime she served the community in many ways. First, she was the teacher in the Shaker exclaimed that he had the "right" knowledge of Shakerism. He asked her permission if he might add a "w" to right. She consented and he then shared her last name. His new first name, Eleazar, was very similar to her husband's name, Elizur. From this point onward he used this name or the initials **E. W.**

The next time he visited the East was in 1829. This visit was at the request of the **Ministry of New Lebanon**. They asked for his advice about conditions at Union Village. After Father **David Darrow** died in 1825, many of the children of the first converts, including McNemar's son Richard, left the community. In addition, there were financial troubles caused by dishonest **trustees**. Father David's successor, Solomon King, was not strong enough to lead such a large community. When asked if he would lead the society, McNemar declined since he thought that his work was for all of western Shakerism. He did not wish to be tied to one place. Instead, he was sent to live at Watervliet, Ohio, and became the **elder** 1 April 1832.

His years at Watervliet were busy trying to lead a community that had become polarized by the previous elder, **Issachar Bates**. His most lasting achievements, however, had to do with publishing. Besides a songbook, histories, and poems, McNemar began the first Shaker periodical, *The Western Review*. It began in 1834 and only lasted a couple of years. Nonetheless, Watervliet was an important center of Shaker publications while he lived there. On 18 December 1835 he was released as elder at Watervliet and returned to Union Village. It might be assumed that this stalwart who had given his family, his property, his congregation, his considerable talents, and his adult life to the Shakers would be retiring to enjoy a few years of peace at the village he helped found. Little did he realize that he was about to enter the most difficult phase of his life.

Elder Solomon King returned East in October 1835 and chose David Meacham to succeed him. Elder David lost no time in reorganizing and dealing with difficult members, yet he was replaced by **Freegift Wells** of **Watervliet, New York**. The Ministry of New Lebanon had never appointed Elder David and only allowed him to work in the interim until they could name a successor. Elder Freegift arrived on 27 April 1836. He was narrow and strict in his views. Outside publications were banned so that Shakers had no access to newspapers. He introduced diet reforms and placed many restrictions on

school from 1853 until 1880. At the same time, from 1860–1868, she also served as second **eldress** of the **Church Family**. From 1869 until 1880 she held this position again. As second eldress, it was her duty to work with the older girls and youngest sisters. The right person in this important job made the difference between youthful members staying or leaving. She lavished her attention on her charges, and nine of her girls became Shakers. She called them her "gems of priceless worth." When the young Lizzie Noyes joined in 1873, Sister Aurelia made her the 10th gem. This cadre of capable sisters in such a small community gave the society incredible strength.

Since she had been a teacher for so long, Aurelia was aware that the community needed a modern schoolhouse. It was her strong desire and persistence that led to the construction of the new schoolhouse in 1880. This building is now the Shaker library. In 1890, she served in the **Office**, most of the time as a **trustee**, until her death in 1910. As a trustee, she was interested in the temporal welfare of her home. She marketed old products such as Shaker Lemon Syrup and renewed the fir balsam pillow business. In addition she made frequent sales trips to the nearby Poland Spring House.

As an Office sister she also greeted visitors. Over the years, she developed many friendships which formed part of her large correspondence. She also did public speaking and was never afraid to undertake missionary work if she thought it would do some good. As a result of her many years of writing articles for newspapers and her keen sense of the Shaker religion, she published a book in 1899. It used in its title the new name for the Shakers that had been approved by the **Central Ministry**. The book was called *The Aletheia: Spirit of Truth.* It proved so popular that it was republished in 1907. One of the letters it contains is from Leo Tolstoi. He corresponded with her as well as with Elder **Alonzo Hollister**, Elder **Frederick Evans**, and Sister Asenath Stickney of **Canterbury**.

From 1888 until 1909 Aurelia kept the Church Family journal. Over these 25 years she eloquently shared her insights about her community and Shakerism as a whole. Her deep appreciation for the life and her enthusiasm are evident. After her death, the community published a memorial book filled with tributes to one who had done so much in so many ways to build up **Zion**. *See also* ALETHIAN BELIEVERS.

MCNEMAR, RICHARD (1770–1839). Shaker expansion in the West would not have occurred as it did without the conversion of Richard McNemar. The impetus that resulted from gaining this well-known preacher and almost his entire congregation lasted 20 years.

He was born on 20 November 1770 in the Tuscarora Valley of Cumberland, Pennsylvania. Even as a youth he exhibited a great love of knowledge. At the age of 15 he began teaching school, a profession he would follow until he became a full-time Presbyterian minister in 1797. In the meantime he also wove cloth and farmed land in western Pennsylvania. In 1791 he moved to Kentucky and studied Latin along with another young man named **Malcolm Worley.** Later while living in Cane Ridge, he married Jane "Jenny" Luckie on 8 April 1793. They had seven children: Benjamin (1794–1818), James (1796–1875), Vincy (1797–1878), Elisha (1799–1824), Nancy (1800–1860), Betsey (1803–1812), and Richard (1805–left the Shakers 1828).

In 1797 Richard was given his license to preach and received a church of his own at Cabin Creek, Kentucky. Up until that time he helped out preaching or taught school. The next year he was ordained a minister in the Presbyterian Church. His sermons were powerful and emotional but seemed to stray from traditional church doctrine. Some of the members of his congregation became unsettled and in 1800 three of them charged him with heresy. Not long after this, the Kentucky Revival began in the spring of 1801. McNemar became the leading preacher of this revival which affected the lives of thousands. The enthusiasm did not abate for years and news of this remarkable event made its way east. The Shakers heard of this extraordinary outpouring of the Spirit and bided their time for the right moment to send missionaries of their own. In the meantime, McNemar took over the congregation at **Turtle Creek,** four miles west of Lebanon, Ohio. As earlier, his sermons continued to arouse suspicions about his orthodoxy. To resolve these controversies, on 10 December 1803, he and five other ministers formed their own presbytery, called the **Springfield Presbytery.** Six months later on 28 June 1804 they no longer were contented to remain under the pretense of being Presbyterians and dissolved the presbytery. They became known as **New Lights,** schismatics, revivalists, or Christians.

When the Shaker missionaries arrived at Turtle Creek in March 1805, they found McNemar's congregation and many others that had been influenced by the revival fairly well prepared for Shakerism. For example, in 1804, dancing as worship had become part of the revival. Moreover, certain aspects of the revival emphasized the second coming of Christ, community of goods, and a high sense of moral integrity. All of these were conducive to Shaker doctrine. These similarities, however, did not mean that McNemar was without his reservations. He prayed deeply that he was not being deluded. While working in his garden, he had a vision showing a woman in the clouds waving her arm as if in summons. This vision and other events in his life, such as the difficult birth of his son Richard, contributed to his decision to become a Shaker. He converted on 24 April 1805.

His property became the home of the **Gathering Order** when the community at Turtle Creek was gathered into the Shaker society of **Union Village**. For the next 25 years, he worked wherever the **Ministry** needed him. These tasks included helping on a mission to the Indians in 1807; organizing the Shakers at **Beaver Creek** into the society at **Watervliet, Ohio**; the conversion of **John Dunlavy** at Eagle and Straight Creek; the establishment of **North Union** and **White Water**; attending to legal matters at **Pleasant Hill** and **South Union, Kentucky**, and taking over the eldership at **Busro** when John Dunlavy died. In this last position he helped the community break up and move to other Shaker sites. Clearly he was an expert in managing affairs.

Besides this troubleshooting, McNemar also answered attacks from apostates and hostile religious leaders. Some of these answers were published in poems and books that he authored and printed. He also wrote about the history of religion. His first work, published in 1807, was *The Kentucky Revival*. That next year he helped share his ideas with the authors of *The Testimony of Christ's Second Appearing*. He also wrote **songs** and some of these were published at **Hancock** in 1813 in *Millennial Praises*. Incredibly, he also had the time to make various types of **furniture**, including almost 1,500 chairs.

His first trip to the East was in 1811. After meeting with Mother **Lucy Wright** and telling her about his experiences, she renamed him Eleazar Right. The name Eleazar means "the help of God." She exclaimed that he had the "right" knowledge of Shakerism. He asked her permission if he might add a "w" to right. She consented and he then shared her last name. His new first name, Eleazar, was very similar to her husband's name, Elizur. From this point onward he used this name or the initials **E. W.**

The next time he visited the East was in 1829. This visit was at the request of the **Ministry of New Lebanon**. They asked for his advice about conditions at Union Village. After Father **David Darrow** died in 1825, many of the children of the first converts, including McNemar's son Richard, left the community. In addition, there were financial troubles caused by dishonest **trustees**. Father David's successor, Solomon King, was not strong enough to lead such a large community. When asked if he would lead the society, McNemar declined since he thought that his work was for all of western Shakerism. He did not wish to be tied to one place. Instead, he was sent to live at Watervliet, Ohio, and became the **elder** 1 April 1832.

His years at Watervliet were busy trying to lead a community that had become polarized by the previous elder, **Issachar Bates**. His most lasting achievements, however, had to do with publishing. Besides a songbook, histories, and poems, McNemar began the first Shaker periodical, *The Western Review*. It began in 1834 and only lasted a couple of years. Nonetheless, Watervliet was an important center of Shaker publications while he lived there. On 18 December 1835 he was released as elder at Watervliet and returned to Union Village. It might be assumed that this stalwart who had given his family, his property, his congregation, his considerable talents, and his adult life to the Shakers would be retiring to enjoy a few years of peace at the village he helped found. Little did he realize that he was about to enter the most difficult phase of his life.

Elder Solomon King returned East in October 1835 and chose David Meacham to succeed him. Elder David lost no time in reorganizing and dealing with difficult members, yet he was replaced by **Freegift Wells** of **Watervliet, New York**. The Ministry of New Lebanon had never appointed Elder David and only allowed him to work in the interim until they could name a successor. Elder Freegift arrived on 27 April 1836. He was narrow and strict in his views. Outside publications were banned so that Shakers had no access to newspapers. He introduced diet reforms and placed many restrictions on activities. Elder Freegift saw all of the older Shaker leaders as a threat to his power, including Richard McNemar, who had just returned there from Watervliet. He envied McNemar, who had up until this time worked at large for the Ministry. Elder Freegift confined McNemar to working as a common member at home. McNemar meekly agreed to do what he was told, though he expressed his dismay in his diary. The atmosphere of distrust did not lessen because of McNemar's obedience.

When the **Era of Manifestations** broke out at Union Village in 1838, Elder Freegift used one of the **instruments** named Margaret O'Brien to accuse McNemar of being an unworthy Shaker. She rebuked him openly in meeting. McNemar submitted once again, though he did not go along with the manifestations. Also, a young man named Randolf West imitated McNemar's handwriting and left messages around the village criticizing Elder Freegift. In June 1839, once again at meeting, Margaret O'Brien claimed to receive a communication from God that three elderly Shakers, including Richard McNemar and **Malcolm Worley**, had been made idols by the community so they must leave.

Accordingly McNemar was dropped off in Lebanon, Ohio, with his printing press. He went to the home of Judge Francis Dunlavy to live and wrote to New Lebanon. He made a final trip to **New Lebanon, New York**, to clear his name. Elder **Rufus Bishop** of the Ministry of New Lebanon asked the principal instrument of the community what was the divine will in the matter. She stated that McNemar and the others were innocent and should be reinstated. The Ministry then drafted a letter warning elders in all the communities to exercise a closer supervision of instruments. Margaret O'Brien left Union Village as a consequence, and McNemar returned in triumph. He addressed the crowds of jubilant Shakers at the next meeting and told them that he had no ill feeling toward Elder Freegift; they openly reconciled. Still, the turmoil, the heat, and the long journey had ruined his health and he died on 15 September 1839, not long after returning home. Later Randolph West admitted his malefaction and hung himself.

MANCHESTER, ENGLAND. This was the birthplace of **Mother Ann**. She was married there and lived in this place until she left for America in 1774.

MANIFESTO. This is the best-known name of the Shaker newspaper that ran from 1871 to 1899. Actually, the *Manifesto* was the name of the paper only during the final 17 years of its existence.

By the 1830s formal Shaker missionary work had ceased. The communities were confident that raising large numbers of children would be the best way to fill their ranks. By the 1850s it was clear that this policy had not worked. As a result, Shaker missionaries were once again sent out in the **world**. These missionaries came from the **elders'** lot and leading members of the **gathering families**. The **Gathering Orders** of the **Mount Lebanon bishopric**, the South Family of **Watervliet**, and the **North Family** of **Mount Lebanon** had enjoyed a long collaboration. Not satisfied that they were reaching a wide enough audience, they decided to start a newspaper. Under the impetus of the first editor, Elder **George Albert Lomas**, a monthly newspaper called the *Shaker* was launched at Watervliet in 1871. All Shakers were encouraged to write for the paper, but it was dominated by contributors from the Watervliet and Mount Lebanon communities.

The paper served many purposes. It not only discussed Shaker religious beliefs, it provided a glimpse into Shaker life in the various societies. Death notices, Shaker history, agricultural and housekeeping practices, music, poetry, editorials, and advertisements were only some of the features of the paper. In 1889, the "Home Notes" section started and various communities selected correspondents who regularly sent in newsworthy items about what was going on. This aspect of the paper has become extremely important, since for many of the less documented societies, this is one of the primary methods used to obtain information on what was occurring in these places.

After two years, due to a fire and lack of sufficient help, the editorial leadership of the paper was turned over to Elder **Frederick Evans** and Eldress **Antoinette Doolittle** of the North Family at Mount Lebanon. Though Elder George remained the publisher, and it was printed in Albany, the paper came under the strong influence of the North Family. For example, the name of the paper was changed to the *Shaker and Shakeress* and the editorials reflected Elder Frederick's views. Since he was far more liberal than most Shakers, this inevitably led to a serious confrontation with more conservative leaders such as Elder **Harvey Eades** of **South Union**. As a result of many problems caused by having Evans as an editor, Elder George assumed the role in 1876 and the name of the paper was changed back to the *Shaker*. The large-quarto format was also changed to a smaller form. It is important to note that this is when the **Canterbury** Shakers began to have more influence in the paper. Though still printed in Albany, Nicholas A. Briggs of Canterbury became the publisher.

In 1878, again the name of the paper was changed to *The Shaker Manifesto*. The size of the paper was reduced to octavo. In 1882, Elder **Henry C. Blinn** of Canterbury became the editor, and the **sisters** of that community set the type. The actual printing was done in Concord, New Hampshire. By 1887, all aspects of the paper's production were done at Canterbury. This continued until the paper ceased in 1899. By then, Shaker fortunes had reached such a low point that the paper could no longer be produced.

MARBLE HALL. This name originated in the 1930s and was given to the remodeled **Trustees' Office** at the **Center Family** of **Union Village, Ohio**. **Trustee Joseph Slingerland** had the old office, which dated from 1810, extravagantly done over in 1891–1892 by outside contractors. The changes included marble floors, a slate roof, Victorian-style towers, fireplaces, and porches.

MARCHES. These were first created during the 1820s to accommodate members, especially the elderly, who could no longer perform the livelier **dance** steps. In contrast to dance steps which required skipping, marches were spirited pacing steps done in a continuous forward manner. *See also* EXERCISES.

MEACHAM, JOHN (1770–1854). Born 8 March 1770 at Claverack, Columbia County, New York, he was the oldest child of Father **Joseph Meacham**. He was admitted to the Church at **New Lebanon** in 1788 at the first gathering. In 1800 he was sent to lead the organization of the first **Gathering Order** among believers. This **family** was known as the **North Family**. He remained there until January 1805 when he was sent as one of the three Shaker missionaries to the West.

Issachar Bates, **Benjamin S. Youngs**, and John Meacham arrived at **Turtle Creek, Ohio**, in March 1805. Immediately, they were able to reap the benefits of the Kentucky Revival. While at Turtle Creek,

John Meacham helped Benjamin S. Youngs write *The Testimony of Christ's Second Appearing*. In 1808, he was appointed to the newly established **Ministry** of **Pleasant Hill, Kentucky**. Following the practice in the East, in 1812 the founding Ministry of each community in the West was given parental titles. His tenure at Pleasant Hill resulted in the creation of a large and physically beautiful village. With his encouragement and support, in 1818 **John Dunlavy** published the *Manifesto*, the second major theological work on Shakerism to be published in the West. At the same time, however, the Ministry at Pleasant Hill did not have the ability to cope with members who were critical and dissatisfied. In particular, Mother Lucy Smith was deficient in leadership qualities. The deteriorating conditions also affected Father John. He was recalled to New Lebanon and returned there in May 1818.

Until his death on 26 December 1855, he lived a quiet life. He had no confidence in his ability to lead and never again held any position of care. Yet his years of service at the North Family and in Ohio and Kentucky caused him to be held in esteem. His passing was noted with regret.

MEACHAM, JOSEPH (1742–1796). Of all who were converted to Shakerism at the opening of the gospel in 1780, no one was of more importance than Joseph Meacham. Born on 22 February 1742 in **Enfield, Connecticut**, Meacham was the son of a Baptist minister and the grandson of a Congregationalist minister. By the time the **New Light** Revival electrified the border area of New York State and Massachusetts in 1779, Joseph Meacham was the head of a Baptist church in **New Lebanon**. He was a major leader of the revival and his congregation was fully involved. In the early months of 1780, as the fervor of the revival diminished, he and his followers were eager for a way to continue their spiritual advancement. After visiting with **Mother Ann** and her handful of followers at **Watervliet, New York**, Meacham was convinced that at last he had found what he had been yearning for. Not only was he converted, but also his large family and most of his congregation were converted.

From the time of his conversion onward, Meacham was a tireless worker for the advancement of Shakerism. Although he was not the first American convert, he is regarded as "Mother's First Born Son in

America." Almost at once, he became a leader of missionaries, and he labored long and hard to gather converts. Toward the end of her life Mother Ann predicted that Joseph Meacham would be the one to gather the church together into permanent homes. In 1787, he succeeded Father **James Whittaker** to become the primary Shaker leader. He was given the name Father Joseph and used his considerable spiritual gifts to organize the first Shaker communities into full **gospel order**. By the time of his death on 16 August 1796, the 11 original Shaker communities had been firmly established.

In every way, Father Joseph was an important link between the original English Shakers and the thousands of American converts. He was able to be that bridge so necessary if a religion from one place is to be successfully transplanted in a different country. The pattern of leadership and life he set in place is still in existence today. Such has been his lasting influence.

MEETING HOUSE. No fledgling Shaker society could be firmly gathered until a **Meeting House** was erected for the worship of God. In fact, **Enfield, Connecticut**, **New Lebanon** and **Watervliet, New York**, and **Alfred, Maine**, had Meeting Houses before they were gathered. In addition, a few centers of union that did not become communities, like Turner's Falls and Ashfield, Massachusetts, also had Meeting Houses.

Shakers today spell Meeting House as two words, each with a capital letter. There is some precedence for this in Shaker history, and in deference to them this is the spelling used here. Throughout time, however, Meeting House has had various spellings.

Moses Johnson, an early convert, is given credit for the design and supervision of 11 early Shaker Meeting Houses of very similar appearance. These were at Watervliet and New Lebanon, New York; **Hancock**, **Tyringham**, **Harvard**, and **Shirley, Massachusetts**; Enfield, Connecticut; **Canterbury** and **Enfield, New Hampshire**; and Alfred and **Sabbathday Lake, Maine**. Actually, when Johnson arrived at New Lebanon the building was already in progress and research shows that he only assisted in building the Meeting Houses at New Lebanon and Watervliet, New York, and Canterbury and Enfield, New Hampshire. Nonetheless, all eleven of these buildings are commonly called "Moses Johnson Meeting Houses."

These early buildings were white clapboard and had gambrel roofs. The first floor had a room suitable for Shaker worship. Here believers could **dance** and **march** in a large space designed with no support column to get in the way. Along the edges of the room were built-in benches and pegboards. The apartments on the upper floors served as a home to the **Ministry**. Each sex shared two rooms, a bedroom, and a study. The study was where they would consult and entertain the members of the community. They might do light work in the Meeting House such as sewing, but the majority of their work was done in their shops.

In time six of these Moses Johnson Meeting Houses were replaced or altered with gable roofs. The most noteworthy of the replacements was the great Meeting House at New Lebanon. Built in 1824, it is a massive structure with a distinctive boiler roof.

In most societies, the Meeting House was located at the **Church Family**. In Ohio and Kentucky this place was called the **Center Family**. There were exceptions, however. In **Groveland**, the Meeting House was located at the East Family. In **White Water, Ohio**, the Meeting House was at the North Family. At **Watervliet, Ohio**, the Meeting House was at the Center Family, but this had once been the South Family.

Initially, Shaker Meeting Houses were used year round. When the public began to flock to Shaker meeting, the Shakers seem to have developed a public season, only using the buildings during the warmest months of the year. For the remainder of the time, **families** worshiped in the meeting rooms located in their **dwelling houses**. Gradually, the Meeting Houses were used less as the Shaker population declined, the number of capable Shaker preachers diminished, and the public lost interest. Though an oral tradition has it that the Hancock Meeting House was used as late as 1928, by 1900 few, if any, Shaker Meeting Houses were still in use. Shaker families used their meeting rooms for worship from this point onward. The single exception to this has been at Sabbathday Lake. Anxious to open the Shaker gospel to the **world** once again, they reopened their Meeting House for public worship in 1963. Their beautiful, pristine Moses Johnson building had been closed and used for storage for 76 years. *See also* CHURCH FAMILY; CENTER FAMILY.

MILLENNIAL CHURCH. The Shakers in the early 19th century often referred to themselves as the Millennial Church. They used this description because they saw themselves as the living embodiment of the second coming, which had already occurred. Non-Shakers, especially in recent times, have mistakenly characterized the Shakers as having millennial expectations and imply that the name Millennial Church means that the Shakers lived gathered together to await the second coming. This is a serious misinterpretation of what the Shakers intended the term to mean.

MILLENNIAL LAWS OF 1821. These are more properly called Rules and Orders. They were established by **Mother Ann** and enhanced by Father **James Whittaker**, Father **Joseph Meacham**, and Mother **Lucy Wright**. Father Joseph was emphatic that the rules needed to be simple enough for everyone to memorize them. He did not want them written down as they would be carried to the **world**. In addition, Shaker leaders feared a rigidity that would inhibit the free work of the Spirit. After Mother Lucy Wright died in 1821, her successors published the first set of Rules and Orders. These were the Millennial Laws of 1821. They were in effect until 1845. *See also* MILLENNIAL LAWS OF 1845.

MILLENNIAL LAWS OF 1845. Starting in 1837, Shakerism became greatly affected by the **Era of Manifestations**. Among the thousands of messages that were received, many were about how the Shakers should conduct themselves. In 1840, the "Holy Laws of Zion" were received and given to the **Ministry**. These laws were from the departed spirit of Father **Joseph Meacham** and other **First Parents**. The Ministry used such messages to revise the **Millennial Laws of 1821**. The resulting Millennial Laws of 1845 was a collection of extreme and restrictive rules. They never found much favor outside of the immediate **New Lebanon bishopric**, and almost immediately they were modified even there. By 1860, a new set of much revised and more relaxed laws, the Rules and Orders of 1860, replaced the 1845 directives. Unfortunately, a combination of circumstances caused the Millennial Laws of 1845 to remain in the public eye and be used by most authors when writing about the Shakers.

Edward Deming Andrews was one of the first, and certainly the best-known, non-Shakers to write about **believers**. In 1953, Andrews published these 1845 laws at the end of his general history, *The People Called Shakers*. The result has been that these laws have developed a life of their own in many subsequent writings. Brother **Theodore Johnson** of **Sabbathday Lake** tried to point out the incorrectness of using these laws to characterize all of Shaker history. His efforts have remained unsuccessful. There is something about that set of rules that fascinates a public eager to hear extreme stories about the Shakers. In addition, it also shows the need for more in-depth research in the field of Shaker studies.

MINER, CLYMENA (1832–1916). Eldress Clymena Miner is well known because she lived long enough to survive the closing of three Shaker communities. She was a very friendly person so that visitors were drawn to her. When John P. MacLean (1848–1939) was writing his various histories of the western Shakers in the early 20th century, he used her as an important source of information. As a result, she achieved a fame in later life that she did not have when young.

She was born 1 December 1832 in Painesville, Ohio. In 1838, together with her parents and three older siblings, she joined the **North Union** Shakers. Her father, Lewis Miner, left the Shakers in a short while, but the rest of the family stayed lifelong Shakers. In fact, her older brother Simon S. Miner was an elder and leader for many decades. By the time she was 20, Clymena was a **deaconess** at the Mill Family. In 1860 she became second eldress of the Middle (**Center) Family**. When the society was dissolved in 1889, she and her brother were the leading elders of the Middle Family. They led the group of 20 former North Union Shakers who moved to the North Family at **Watervliet, Ohio**. In 1900, the Watervliet community closed, and she and the remaining North Union Shakers lived at the North Family, **Union Village**. She had charge of this family until it merged with the Center Family. When Union Village was sold in 1912, all of the surviving Shakers lived at **Marble Hall**, the former Center Family's **Trustees' Office**. They were cared for by groups of young sisters sent from **Canterbury**. There are a number of pictures taken of Eldress Clymena with these sisters. Her generation of western Shakers has faded from history without much notice. Eldress Clymena was an exception to this. She died midway between the closing of Union Village and the removal of the last three sisters to Canterbury in 1920. She is buried in Lebanon, Ohio.

MINISTRY. This refers to the men and women ultimately responsible for Shaker spiritual leadership. The Ministry, two men and two women, most often had religious charge of a number of Shaker communities grouped in a **bishopric**. For long periods of time, however, due to their geographical isolation, **Groveland**, **North Union**, **South Union**, and **Pleasant Hill** each had its own individual Ministry. Also known as the **Lead**, these ministers lived most of the year in a community that often gave the bishopric its name. Periodically they would travel and spend extended amounts of time at the other communities of the bishopric. For example, the Hancock bishopric was composed of the Shaker societies at **Hancock** and **Tyringham, Massachusetts**, and **Enfield, Connecticut**. Members of the Lead or Ministry had a higher role of spiritual and temporal direction than did those who made up the **elders** or **eldresses** of a particular **family**. The "**center of union**," or primary religious authority, was the **Ministry of New Lebanon**, New York.

"As faithful ambassadors of Christ, they are invested with wisdom and authority, by the revelation of God, to guide, teach and direct the church on earth, in its spiritual travel, and to counsel and advise in other matters of importance, whether spiritual or temporal" (Green and Wells, *A Summary View of the Millennial Church*, 66–67).

It was also the duty of the Ministry to appoint elders, **trustees**, and **deacons**. Until the 20th century, these family leaders only were appointed after consultation and approbation of the membership.

MINISTRY OF NEW LEBANON (1787–1946). This was the primary religious authority in Shakerism. The origins of this **Ministry** or **Lead** can be traced to Father **Joseph Meacham**. **Mother Ann's** base of operation for her missionary efforts had been at **Watervliet, New York**. She died in 1784 and was succeeded by Father **James Whittaker**. Although a **Meeting House** was built in **New Lebanon** in 1785, this place was not the **center of union** in Father James' day. Whittaker seems to have avoided New Lebanon, residing at Watervliet or on constant visits to other Shaker places, and finally making it apparent that he was going to **Enfield, Connecticut**, to die. This may show that he actually favored David Meacham of Enfield, rather than Joseph Meacham, to succeed him.

The shift to New Lebanon from Watervliet occurred when Father Joseph Meacham succeeded Father James in 1787. Meacham was from New Lebanon and a large number of very influential converts, former members of Meacham's church, lived there. It was only natural that the center of union should be where Father Joseph had the greatest influence. He was assisted by many young and middle-aged men and women of great talent. These he chose, a special core group, and they lived at the Meeting House with him. His efforts were aimed at making a united and permanent church. The leaders formed from this group were first called the **Lebanon Ministry**. This name survived in popular use for over a hundred years. More properly, the name for this ministerial group was the Ministry of New Lebanon or just the New Lebanon Ministry. They had the spiritual charge of the Shaker societies at New Lebanon and Watervliet, New York. In 1859, they assumed responsibility for the Shaker society at **Groveland, New York**. After 1861, the Shaker village in the town of New Lebanon became known as **Mount Lebanon, New York**. Subsequently the New Lebanon Ministry came to be known as the **Ministry of Mount Lebanon**.

In 1893, the Hancock Ministry was dissolved and the Ministry of Mount Lebanon took charge of the remaining societies in this **bishopric**. In terms of Shaker geography, the Ministry of Mount Lebanon now had all of the centrally located communities: Watervliet, and Mount Lebanon, New York; **Hancock, Massachusetts**; and Enfield, Connecticut. They called themselves the **Central Ministry**, a name that was used officially until 1918, but is still in popular use today. After 1921, the Ministry was exclusively called the **Parent Ministry** until its dissolution in 1957. When the Ministry was revived later that year, the name Parent Ministry was resurrected and used until the Ministry ended in 1988. *See also* BISHOPRIC.

MOTHER ANN (1736–1784). This is how **Ann Lee** is usually referred to by Shakers and those who study them. Shakers and those who have a special affection for Shakerism often just use the word "Mother" when giving testimony or speaking of her. *See also* LEE, MOTHER ANN.

MOTHER'S FIRST BORN. This designation refers to those who were grown up when the communities were gathered in the 1790s, had received the faith from **Mother Ann** or one of her companions, and retained a fervor for Shakerism that time did not seem to diminish. These men and women were the mainstays of the various Shaker communities until well into the 19th century. Most often related by blood, they formed a strong and united basis for community life. All of the first Shaker societies were on lands owned by some of these First Born. One of the last of these to die was Elizabeth Wood of **Enfield, Connecticut.** She was 95 years old at the time of her death in 1864.

MOTION SONG. This is a Shaker **song** that is sung with hand and body movements. Examples of these are "Let Me Have Mother's Gospel" and "As the Waves of the Mighty Ocean." Both songs are still used in Shaker worship. Gesturing was introduced by Mother **Lucy Wright** to help keep the tempo of the songs.

MOUNT LEBANON, NEW YORK. In 1861, the Shaker village in New Lebanon got its own post office. The **North Family** had charge of this until 1898 when it moved to the **Office** of the **Church Family.** Sister **Sarah "Sadie" Neale** was postmistress until the post office closed on 30 January 1930. After 1861 Mount Lebanon was used by Shakers to refer to their parent village. *See also* NEW LEBANON, NEW YORK.

MOUNT LEBANON MINISTRY. This was the name of the Ministry of New Lebanon from 1861 until 1893.

MOUNT MORRIS, NEW YORK. *See* GROVELAND, NEW YORK.

– N –

NARCOOSSEE, FLORIDA (1896–1924). SPIRITUAL NAME: Olive Branch, this name was given years after the **Era of Manifestations** and is more properly a nickname. FEAST GROUND: none. BISHOPRIC: **Mount Lebanon.** FAMILIES: one settlement. MAXIMUM POPULATION AND YEAR: 12 in 1915. INDUSTRIES: pineapples, lumber, sugar cane, bananas, turpentine, oranges. NOTABLE SHAKERS: **Ezra Stewart,**

Sadie Marchant, Egbert Gillett, Benjamin DeRoo. UNIQUE FEATURES: This was the last fairly long-lived Shaker community to be founded. It was the only one in Florida.

BRIEF HISTORY: By the 1890s Shaker **trustees** Isaac Anstatt of **Watervliet** and Benjamin Gates of Mount Lebanon began to suggest that it might be beneficial for the Shakers to move to the South. Taxes were high in the North and little profit could be made because the extensive farms there were largely maintained by hired labor. The only way ends could be met was to sell off land. In the South, the growing season was much longer, there was no need for winter fuel or to overwinter stock, land was cheap, and hired help also relatively inexpensive. The Shakers could consolidate and leave behind the large farms and settle in new buildings built for their convenience. A meeting of the entire **Church Family** of Mount Lebanon was held at the **First Order** on 1 December 1894 to discuss these matters. That November land in Florida had been examined by Ministry **elder Joseph Holden** and trustees Anstatt and Gates. They were impressed and wished to share their findings at this open meeting. All had a chance to speak and there was little dissent, except from Mary Ann Hazard, a trustee.

The Shakers decided to pay $94,500 for over 7,000 acres at Narcoossee in Osceola County, near **Ashton**, south of Orlando. Isaac Anstatt's name was on the deed. In February 1895, Andrew Barrett and Minerva Reynolds from Mount Lebanon's Church Family led four other Shakers to their new home. By 1904 they had erected a steam powered sawmill and were catching abundant fish from the lakes. In 1909 the new town of **St. Cloud** was formed. From 1895 until 1919, 39 people signed the **probationary covenant**. Of these, just two would die as Shakers, but the death of the first one from an overdose of chloroform would plunge the Florida Shakers into the national spotlight. Sadie Marchant passed away after having received a fatal dose of chloroform from Elder Egbert Gillett on 22 August 1911. Almost immediately a charge of murder was brought against Gillett and the proceedings went on into 1912 before he was exonerated.

It is interesting that, although there was little voiced dissent against the Florida purchase, almost none of the Church Family Shakers of **New Lebanon** moved there. As it turned out, most did have reservations about leaving their home, but these were not voiced at the meeting. Even had they been, however, the Florida property might still have been purchased. Shaker trustees had often operated independently, most with dire results. This proved true with Florida. The Church Family took on a very heavy debt, and it fell to the few able-bodied **sisters**, organized by trustee **Emma Neale**, to pay it. The cloak industry and the fancy goods trade gradually lifted the family out of a crushing debt.

Rumors that the Shakers were leaving Florida had been frequent as early as 1915, but by 1923 they must have been serious enough for Ezra Stewart to leave. In addition, Egbert Gillett and Mabel Marston left and got married in March 1924. Amanda Tiffany and Benjamin DeRoo were the last to leave when they moved to the Church Family at Mount Lebanon in May 1924, and William Tyson, a non-Shaker, was hired to look after the property. Gradually the holdings were sold off, the last piece passing out of Shaker hands in the late 1930s.

LAST SHAKER: Benjamin DeRoo (1876–1933). Born in Holland, Michigan, he signed the probationary covenant in Florida on 25 March 1913. When the Florida community closed he moved to the Church Family, Mount Lebanon, where he died.

NEALE FAMILY. Emma and **Sarah Neale** are well-known Shakers. Those writing about the Neales, however, almost always confuse the various members of the Neale family to include incorrect information about them. It is helpful to list all of them and sort out their individual histories. Six Neale children joined the East Family of **New Lebanon** on 3 December 1855. They were Eliza Ann, Henry, Emma, Sarah, Anna, and Joel. The youngest child, Cornelia Charlotte, was not born until 1856.

Eliza Ann, born in 1842, lived at the East Family until 1862 when she was admitted to the **Church Family**. She left the Shakers in 1864. She has been incorrectly listed as going to **Watervliet**. Henry, born in 1843, left the Shakers from the East Family between 1860 and 1865. Emma, born in 1847, died a Shaker in 1943. She lived her entire life at **Mount Lebanon**. Sarah, born in 1849, lived at the East Family until 1863 when she was sent to Watervliet. She returned to Mount Lebanon in 1896. She died a Shaker at **Hancock** in 1948. Anna, born in 1851, left the Shakers from the East Family between

1865 and 1870. Joel, born in 1853, was admitted to the Church Family in 1861 and left the Shakers in 1870. Cornelia Charlotte never lived at the East Family. In 1861, when she was five years old, she was admitted directly to the Church Family. In 1865 she was sent to Watervliet and lived at the **North Family** with her sister Sarah. She left the Shakers in 1883 from Watervliet. Since her nickname was "Ann" she is confused with her sisters Anna and Eliza Ann. In addition, she died at Mount Lebanon in 1902, but was not a Shaker. She lived in Boston and was visiting her sisters Emma and Sarah when her death occurred. Pictures taken at Watervliet show Sarah and Cornelia Charlotte ("Ann") Neale. These are often mislabeled as Sarah and Emma Neale.

NEALE, EMMA JANE (1847–1943). For those writing about **Mount Lebanon** in the 20th century, a knowledge of the life and work of Emma Neale is essential. She was born on 10 June 1847 in Hinsdale, New Hampshire. Her father was a London-born wool merchant. She had four sisters and two brothers. On 3 December 1855, she and five of her siblings were admitted to the East Family of **New Lebanon**. This family was actually right over the state line in the town **of Hancock, Massachusetts**. She was sent to live at the **First Order of the Church** on 15 May 1861. Here she attended school and in 1866 began helping out as a teaching assistant. In 1872, due to the lack of men, she began teaching the boys' school. In October 1886 she was appointed one of the **Office deaconesses**. By 1897 she was first Office deaconess and in 1901 became one of the five **trustees** of the entire Mount Lebanon community.

When the Florida property was purchased in 1895, the **Church Family** at Mount Lebanon Shakers took on an enormous debt that they could not easily pay off. It fell entirely on trustee Emma Neale to find a way to save her **family** from financial ruin. She organized the few able-bodied **sisters**, and they worked on a wide variety of fancy goods. A catalog, "Products of Intelligence and Diligence," advertised their products. In addition, after Clarissa Jacobs of the Second Family gave up the cloak industry in 1899, Sister Emma took it up and formed "E. J. Neale & Co." in 1901. This business proved to be very lucrative. After this time, she was the principal trustee for the entire society. It fell to her to keep things going for as long as possible. She was an expert manager, but as resources dwindled, it became difficult to operate at a deficit. By 1920, there were fewer than 20 in the family and the herb industry was almost gone. As early as World War I, proposals to sell the Church Family property had been advanced, but nothing had come of it. In 1921, the younger members of the Church Family were sent to live at Hancock, in preparation for vacating the place. Still no buyers followed through, and if it had not been for the income from the sale of the Florida community in 1924, the Church Family would have been in serious debt. Finally, in October 1930, Emma was able to sell the property for $75,000 to an organization that intended to found a school for boys. Along with the remaining Church Family Shakers—**Sarah Neale**, Charles Gannebin, Martin Jones, and Benjamin DeRoo—she moved into **Ann Lee Cottage**. Here they sold fancy goods, cloaks, and greeted visitors.

One of these visitors was John S. Williams of Old Chatham, New York. He nicknamed her the "eldress" because she was so alert and sharp even in her old age. Unfortunately later writers incorrectly use his good-natured bantering to conclude that she actually was an **eldress**, and she has often been incorrectly depicted as such. Due to failing health, she moved to the **North Family** around 1940 and died there 28 November 1943. She had been a Mount Lebanon Shaker for almost 88 years and a trustee for 58 years.

NEALE, SARAH (1849–1948). Also known as Sally or Sadie Neale, she was born on 8 July 1849 in Williamstown, Massachusetts. Along with five of her siblings, she joined the East Family of **New Lebanon** on 3 December 1855. In 1863, she was sent to live at the North Family, **Watervliet**. There she taught school for 20 years. Pictures of her at the time show her with her natural sister Cornelia Charlotte (also known as "Ann") who had also been sent to live at Watervliet. In 1871, she helped **Elder George Lomas** start the newspaper the *Shaker*. She read proof and performed duties connected with the running of the paper, including figuring out the assessment rolls for the individual communities. She also wrote articles.

In 1895, when the **Mount Lebanon** Shakers sent some of their number to Florida, the resources of the **Church Family** became strained. To fill the vacancies, she was sent there to live in 1895. In 1898, the post office was transferred from the North Family to the

Office at the Church Family. She moved to the Office to take care of the post office and had this job until the post office closed in 1930. She was also made orchard **deaconess** and supervised the gardens and feed. In 1923, she became a **trustee** of the society.

Sarah enjoyed company, and early collectors such as Edward and Faith Andrews formed a deep friendship with her. Many of their pieces from New Lebanon came through her. When the Church Family was sold in 1930, she moved to **Ann Lee Cottage**. In the 1940s she went to live at **Hancock**, where she died 17 February 1948.

NEW CANAAN, CONNECTICUT (1810–1812). For a brief time, a small group of **New Lebanon** Shakers lived on 130 acres of land purchased from Stephen Fitch, who had recently joined the **North Family**. Perhaps the Shakers were desirous of having a community so near New York City and the ocean. In 1811, Fitch left the Shakers and made efforts to get his three sons back from the community. He also made trouble over the land. Since the soil was not fertile, and the surrounding population seemed indifferent to Shakerism, it was decided to sell the place after just two years.

NEW ENFIELD. Refers to the **Enfield, New Hampshire**, society, which was founded after the one at **Enfield, Connecticut**.

NEW GLOUCESTER, MAINE. This is the town that contains the **Sabbathday Lake** Shaker society. The was incorporated in 1774, but did not include Sabbathday Lake until 1816 when the plantation was annexed to the town.

NEW LEBANON, NEW YORK (1787–1947). SPIRITUAL NAME: Holy Mount. FEAST GROUND: Holy Mount. BISHOPRIC: New Lebanon. FAMILIES: **First Order of the Church (Church Family)**, **Second Order of the Church (Center Family)**, **Second Family**, East Family, South Family, **North Family (Gathering Order)**, **Upper** and **Lower Canaan** Families (Gathering Orders). MAXIMUM POPULATION AND YEAR: 615 in 1842. INDUSTRIES: brooms, dried sweet corn, garden seeds, medicinal extracts, herbs, mops, baskets, chairs, fancy goods, cloaks, dairy products. NOTABLE SHAKERS: Father **Joseph Meacham**, David Meacham, **Calvin Green**, **Isaac Newton Youngs**, **Daniel Boler**, **Orren Haskins**, **Richard Bushnell**, **Frederick Evans**,

Alonzo Hollister, Giles Avery, Joseph Holden, Robert Valentine, Benjamin Gates, **Ernest Pick,** William Perkins, **Ruth Landon, Harriet Bullard, M. Antoinette Doolittle, Anna White, Sarah Collins, Lillian Barlow, Emma Neale, Sarah Neale,** Amelia Calver. UNIQUE FEATURES: New Lebanon was the **center of union** for all of the Shaker societies from 1787 until 1946. Although for a short time around 1820, **Union Village** may have been slightly larger, New Lebanon was consistently the largest society until 1902. It had three Gathering Orders, and the home farms of the society were in two states and three towns. Moreover, it had a **chair industry** and manufactured medicinal extracts on a large scale. While not every **family** there could boast of spectacular buildings, the North Family had one of the largest barns in the United States, and the First Order of the Church included a beautiful brick **dwelling house** and the immense boiler roofed **Meeting House.** Finally, much of Shaker history is written from the New Lebanon perspective.

BRIEF HISTORY: In 1779, a revival of religion broke out along the New York-Massachusetts border. The center for this enthusiasm was the northern section of the town of **Canaan, New York,** called New Lebanon. The Baptist minister Joseph Meacham and the Presbyterian minister Samuel Johnson and other preachers led this **New Light** "stir." When the revival had waned, a few participants visited **Niskeyuna** near Albany. They had heard about **Mother Ann.** They were so impressed with her that they returned to New Lebanon filled with a fervor that they shared with others. Soon, hundreds were making the trip to see Mother Ann. Almost all of Joseph Meacham's large congregation converted. When the last of the English leaders, Father **James Whittaker,** died in 1787, Father Joseph Meacham became the head of the Shaker church. Since his home base was at New Lebanon, and the location was closer to New England where so many Shakers lived, Meacham made that place the center of union instead of **Watervliet.**

Father Joseph and the other leaders gathered the scattered Shakers together in a plan known as **gospel order.** At the Meeting House, new leadership was formed and these **First Parents** were sent out to the various places where Shakers were concentrating. Preaching to the **world** ceased with the death of Mother Ann, and it did not begin again until the death of Father Joseph. From 1787 until 1792, New Lebanon was carefully gathered into three **orders** or families of the church. All of the other small, individual families, most often bearing the last name of the leader, were collectively known as the **Order of Families**. In 1799, Mother **Lucy Wright**, who succeeded Father Joseph, had a Gathering Order put into place to receive new members. In 1811, the entire society was reorganized. The First Order (**First Family**) was retained. The Second Order (Second Family) was disbanded and its members divided between the First and the Third families. The Third Family then became the Second Order of the Church. What had been three families was now the First Family of the Church, split into two orders, the first and the second. All other families at New Lebanon were gathered as the Second Family of the Church, and the title Order of Families suppressed. Besides living at the actual Second Family site, there were branches of this family on the mountain at the East House and further down the main road at the South House. The East Family gained its own set of **elders** and **trustees** and became a separate family in 1826. The South House did not become fully independent until 1863. Meanwhile, the North Family developed two branch Gathering Orders in the nearby town of Canaan, New York. Since the East Family of New Lebanon was actually in **Hancock, Massachusetts**, the society at New Lebanon was in three towns and two states. Allegorically, this arrangement represents the virgin, the married, and the novices.

Due to missionary work and a high interest in those days in the Shakers, New Lebanon grew rapidly. In 1803, the society had 351 members. By 1835 there were 587. As late as 1860, there were 550 Shakers, but a high percentage of them were children. This became a serious problem as the young continued to leave and few adults converted. After the Civil War this crisis became clear and the population dropped steadily. By 1885 there were 261 and in 1895 only 188.

In 1873, the North Family took charge of the Shaker newspaper, but doctrinal disputes forced them to give it up in just two years. After that it was published at **Canterbury**, and that place became the public face of Shakerism. In the midst of the crisis over the newspaper, the First Order of the Church suffered a devastating fire set by a hired man. The dwelling house known as the "Great House" and its contents as well as seven other buildings were destroyed. A few days later another fire set by the same person destroyed the herb house. This business was the major source of income for the family. Earlier in that decade, the East Family closed due to a tremendous debt caused by a dishonest trustee.

On the positive side, the new chair business at the South Family was continuing to grow under the capable direction of Elder **Robert Wagan**, and the North Family was making major efforts to reach out to the **world** in the areas of various reform movements. Still, the numbers were diminishing and the Lower Canaan Family closed in 1884. The Second Order of the Church or Center Family merged into the First Order in 1896, not long after that family bought land in Florida to start a new colony. The next year, the Upper Family was moved to the North Family at **Enfield, Connecticut**. In this way, **Mount Lebanon** (New Lebanon's name since 1861) had only four families in 1900 and was barely the largest society. That distinction passed to Canterbury in 1902 and thereafter.

The decline was especially severe in the Church Family, which had 39 members in 1903—an 82 percent decline in 40 years! The remaining handful of able-bodied sisters had the onerous task of lifting the society out of a crushing debt caused by the purchase of land in Florida. Meanwhile, the North Family hosted a national peace conference in 1905 and continued its efforts in reform. At the other end of the village, the South and Second Families concentrated on the chair business. All four families still had large home farms, but these were managed by hired help. In 1930 there were 28 elderly Shakers and the Church Family property was sold to become the site of the Lebanon School for Boys, later Darrow School. In 1947, the **Ministry** decided to move the last group of Shakers from North Family to Hancock. This was accomplished in October 1947.

LAST SHAKER: Curtis White (1888–1951) grew up at the Second Family where he worked on the farm. In 1940, when that family was sold, he moved to the North Family where he continued to garden and be involved in the dairy. In 1947 the North Family closed and, with the rest of the community, he joined the Church Family at Hancock. He died of pneumonia on 21 February 1951. Mary Dahm (1885–1865) lived at Mount Lebanon from 1938 until 1947, but she is more properly the last Watervliet, New York, Shaker.

NEW LIGHTS. The Standing Order of Congregationalism dominated the religious life of Massachusetts during the colonial period. After the Great Awakening there was a growing uneasiness with the state of religious matters and many groups of religious dissenters called New Lights emerged. They were seeking a new or greater light. These New Lights, often Baptists, resented the state-supported, "Old Light" Congregational churches. The Shakers had a wide appeal to New Lights and hundreds of them joined the Shakers at the **opening of the gospel**. *See also* CLOUGH, HENRY; GOODRICH, CASSANDANA; MEACHAM, JOHN; MEACHAM, JOSEPH; WRIGHT, LUCY.

NISKEYUNA (NISKAYUNA, NISQUEUNIA). This was the Indian name of the first property owned by the Shakers in America. On 6 August 1774, the Shakers landed in New York City from England. Hearing of inexpensive land, Father **William Lee** and Father **James Whittaker** accompanied **John Hocknell** to the Manor Rensselaerwyck. A two-hundred-acre plot, seven miles northwest of Albany, was leased by John Hocknell in 1775 before he returned to England to bring over other Shakers, including his family. John Partington, one of the original English Shakers, also purchased a tract of land and had his own house on it. The Shaker society that would grow from this place was later known as **Watervliet, New York**.

NORTH FAMILY (1799–1947). Except for **Groveland** and **North Union**, all of the other 16 long-term Shaker societies had a North Family; yet only one, the North Family of **New Lebanon**, is remembered today. That particular **family** attained such a prominence that for most people just saying the name conjures up pictures of **Eldress Anna White**, Elder **Frederick Evans**, and a host of other famous Shakers.

It is no exaggeration to say that many volumes could be written about the various Shakers and notable events that are connected with the North Family of New Lebanon. Moreover, this fame did not just happen over time; the family was in the forefront of Shakerism at its very inception in 1799. By then, it had become clear to Shaker leaders that there had to be an **order** set up to accommodate people seeking admission into the society. In addition, many young adults had left the community. Clearly there was a need to modify the Shaker family system as devised by Father **Joseph Meacham**. His system left no way for new members to join. The Shakers needed new members and individuals, but mostly families with children were seeking admission. As a result it was decided by Mother **Lucy Wright** that a new **Gathering** or **Novitiate Order** should be put into place. The result was the creation of the North Family on the property once owned by early convert Amos Hammond. Exceptional leaders such as **Calvin Green** and **Ebenezer Bishop** were put in charge. At first it was thought that such Gathering Orders to train new converts could be regional. It was the intent, for example, that the North Family serve the Shaker societies at **Hancock, Watervliet**, and **Tyringham.** Soon it became clear that the best way was for each Shaker community to have its own Gathering Order. By 1810, every Shaker village reorganized itself to do this. All new Shaker societies formed Gathering Orders as they were founded.

The duties of the elders of the North Family at New Lebanon included missionary work and preaching at the **public meeting** held in the **Meeting House.** First-time visitors to the village encountered these leaders first. This took on more importance when, by 1830, the formal missionary work had ended and the developing tourist industry helped lead thousands to attend Shaker meeting on the Sabbath. So many joined the North Family that branches in the nearby town of **Canaan, New York,** had to be set up.

The original function of the North Family and its branches was to gather candidates that after a suitable time could be sent to the other families at New Lebanon. In time, however, a core group of "progressive" or "liberal" Shakers dominated the North Family. Although it was a Gathering Family, these Shakers stayed there for life. They included Elder Frederick Evans (the most famous Shaker of the 19th century), Eldress Anna White, Martha Anderson, **M. Catherine Allen, Daniel Offord**, Cecilia DeVere, Eldress **M. Antoinette Doolittle**, and Elder **Richard Bushnell.**

Starting in 1860 and continuing until 1910, the North Family gained a reputation for involvement in various movements: for example, pacifism, women's rights, vegetarianism and diet reform, hygiene, animal protection, scientific farming. Members wrote newspaper articles, tracts, books, and even edited the Shaker newspaper for a short while. At the same time they began to go out on missionary tours to cities and nearby churches. They involved themselves with Spiritualism, Christian Science, and the Koreshan Unity. The crowning achievement of their efforts occurred in 1905 when they hosted a national peace conference.

Using the money that had been prudently put aside by trustee Charles Bushnell, the North Family built the largest Shaker barn ever constructed and transformed their property into a model farm with new buildings and the purchase of every latest piece of equipment. Large orchards were planted and new kitchen gardens laid out to help support the vegetarian meals they served. Furthermore, their immense dwelling used a ventilation system and had central heat by 1870.

In spite of these efforts, the North Family could not escape the changes brought to Shakerism by a decline in membership, yet they held on the longest of the eight families at New Lebanon. After 1910, they began to receive Shakers from other communities that had closed. These included **believers** from **South Union**; **White Water**; **Harvard**; **Shirley**; **Enfield, Connecticut**; **Enfield, New Hampshire**; and Watervliet, New York.

After 1940, Shakers from the rest of Mount Lebanon also consolidated at the North. The North Family finally closed in October 1947, when it was merged with the **Church Family** at nearby **Hancock, Massachusetts**. The last North Family Shaker was Mary Dahm (1885–1965), who lived at the North Family from 1938 until 1947.

NORTH UNION, OHIO (1822–1889). SPIRITUAL NAME: The Valley of God's Pleasure. FEAST GROUND: Jehovah's Beautiful Square. BISHOPRIC: North Union until 1862, thereafter Union Village. FAMILIES: Center (Middle), East (**Gathering Order**), Mill. MAXIMUM POPULATION AND YEAR: 159 in 1852. INDUSTRIES: brooms, broom handles, stocking yarn, firewood, lumber, fine stock, the sale of milk and vegetables, maple sugar, flour. NOTABLE SHAKERS: **Richard Pelham**, James Prescott, **Clymena Miner**. UNIQUE FEATURES: North Union was the only Shaker society located so near a major city. The boundary of Cleveland borders Shaker land. This opened up direct urban markets for dairy and garden products, but it also prevented the Shakers from having any privacy. Also, North Union did not own land apart from the home property. The society had a five-story gristmill, which was quite a landmark before it was blown up by its new owner in 1886. Finally, North Union was the first Shaker site to be completely obliterated. No buildings remain. With the exception of some gateposts and two lakes, it is difficult to visualize that the Shakers ever were there.

BRIEF HISTORY: In 1812 Ralph Russell moved to Ohio from Windsor Locks, Connecticut. In 1820, he met James Darrow and became interested in joining the Shakers. When he attempted to join at **Union Village**, he was encouraged to use his family land to begin a separate Shaker society. Though he and his immediate family left the Shakers, his property formed the nucleus of North Union. On 31 March 1822 a public meeting was held and the community was fully organized during the next few years. The **Center Family** dwelling was erected in 1826. The Mill Family had a gristmill five stories high as well as a sawmill. The Center Family had a woolen mill. The Shakers dammed Doan Brook to create two lakes to power the mills.

North Union was prosperous and did not ever suffer from dishonest **trustees**, but the encroachment of Cleveland and the diminishing number of Shakers made the continuation of the community doubtful. Nordhoff enumerated 102 Shakers in 1874. By 1889, there were just 27 believers on over 1,300 acres of land. All of them lived at the Center Family, and the other two families were rented to outsiders. The village was suffering from neglect, and this caught the attention of the **Ministry** visiting from **Mount Lebanon** in 1889. They recommended that the property be sold in spite of the objections of the surviving Shakers. Twenty-one of the last North Union Shakers moved to the North Family at **Watervliet, Ohio**. The rest moved to Union Village. On 24 October 1889, the society was dissolved. In 1892, the Shakers were paid $316,000 for the property by T. A. and Lawrence Lamb. The Lambs were part of the Shaker Heights Land Company, a group of developers.

LAST SHAKER: Harriett Snyder (1837–1924). When North Union dissolved, she moved to the North Family, Watervliet, Ohio. When that society closed in 1900, she joined the Center Family at Union Village. In 1920 the Shakers left Union Village, and she went to the **Church Family** at **Canterbury, New Hampshire**. She is buried in that place.

NOVITIATE. This refers to an adult who has just joined the Shakers and is trying the life. Unlike Roman Catholic usage, it does not mean the building that houses the candidate. The Shakers of today also use the term novice to designate new members who are adults. Persons of any age may join the Shakers, but those over 18 years of age must sign a **probationary covenant** upon entering the society. This guarantees the novice all the rights and privileges of Shaker membership, including food, clothing, lodging, and health care. Moreover, the novitiate member is expected to participate fully in Shaker meeting, help lead prayers at meals, and have the title "**brother**" or "**sister**" used before his/her first name. In addition, every member, including novices, must work to the extent that each is able. This may be housework, cooking, laundry, gardening, care of livestock, farming, building repair and maintenance, or office work. The probationary covenant protects the Shaker Society from subsequent lawsuits for back wages should a candidate decide to leave the community and seek remuneration for labor performed while a member. No Shaker is paid for work done while a member, although the society is generous to those who decide to leave.

NOVITIATE ORDER. *See* GATHERING ORDER.

NOYES, MARY ELIZABETH (1845–1926). Elizabeth "Lizzie" Noyes joined the community at **Sabbathday Lake** a dozen years after her father Josiah and his brother Thomas did. In the meantime, she graduated from Hebron Academy and was going to teach school in Missouri. After a visit to her father in 1872, she decided to become a Shaker and was admitted in November 1873. Her high energy level and dominant personality allowed her to become a respected and highly valued member almost at once. **Trustee Aurelia Mace** had a list of "nine gems," girls of great promise that had been raised at Sabbathday Lake. She added Lizzie Noyes as the "tenth gem." Besides every variety of domestic work, she was the teamster for the **sisters** and did any job that needed to be done. This included picking fruit, working on fancy goods, making soap, and repairing buildings. Yet it was in the manufacturing of fancy good that she excelled. By this time the fancy goods trade had become the mainstay of the community's income.

In 1880, Lizzie was made **eldress** at the same time that **William Dumont** was appointed first elder. Together they led the community through its golden age of prosperity, 1880–1926. Perhaps no pair of elders ever worked so closely and harmoniously as they did. This was in great contrast to the conditions existing in most other Shaker societies. They are the reason the Sabbathday Lake was able to survive so long. For example, the population of the community in 1920 was the same as it had been in 1900. Every other Shaker society was declining or had closed during that time. In 1903, Eldress Elizabeth became first in the Maine **Ministry**, another task added to the many she already performed: eldress, trustee, and postmaster.

As eldress she had a strong influence on the young girls in the community. Her strong work ethic was passed on to them, and she expected them to measure up. These exacting standards kept the sisters at a high rate of productivity. Visitors to the community would not have guessed that the Shakers were actually dying out in most places. Life at Sabbathday Lake seemed to just get better. This powerhouse of a Shaker led the community right up until the time of her death in 1926. The void in leadership after her death was never filled. *See also* TEN GEMS OF PRICELESS WORTH.

NURSE SHOP. Although Shakers had a reputation for longevity and good health, inevitably in a community of any size, a few people would need nursing on either a short- or long-term basis. A building set aside for this purpose was known as the Nurse Shop or Infirmary. Many of the sisters who worked in these shops were highly skilled. Some had a real aptitude for the work and did it for years. In some communities there were also physicians who were Shakers. If not, outside doctors were employed. All Nurse Shops that are part of contemporary museums show an array of herbs and herbal extracts that the Shakers may or may not have used. As the communities aged, those societies surviving into the 20th century hired trained nurses and doctors to care for their sick. At least one Shaker sister, Mary Dahm of the South Family at **Watervliet, New York**, was a trained nurse. By the 1940s, when there were no longer young people to care for the aged, Shakers began to enter rest homes or nursing homes.

– O –

OFFICE. The Shakers lived a routine and orderly existence. This would not have been possible if outsiders were allowed to roam freely. People who had business to transact with the Shakers stopped at a building set up for this purpose called the Office or **Trustees' Office**. All fully organized Shaker **families** had an Office and that is where the **Office deacons (trustees)** and **Office deaconesses** lived. The first floor of this building had a store where Shaker and non-Shaker goods were sold. There were also dining facilities for visitors who were staying overnight. Guest bedrooms and the apartments of the trustees and Office deaconesses made up much of the rest of the building. In addition, the Office had a business office and parlor to entertain guests and relatives of community members. In several communities the post office was also located in this building.

OFFICE DEACON AND OFFICE DEACONESS. This is another name for a Shaker **trustee**. It was not until the 1890s that women who served as Office deaconesses became trustees.

OFFORD, DANIEL (1845–1911). He was born 16 November 1845 in Richmond, Surrey, England. His father William Offord came under the influence of a renegade Shaker from the United States named Evans (no relation to **Elder Frederick Evans**). He decided to join the community at **New Lebanon**. His wife had no interest in the Shakers and eventually moved to Australia to live with her married daughter Betsey. In September 1850, William Offord and his sons William Jr. and Nathaniel arrived at the **North Family**. They were sent to live at **Canaan**. Meanwhile, Ann, Rhoda, and Miriam Offord, more of William's children, came in 1851. Finally in 1856, William's last children, Daniel and Emily, arrived at the North Family.

Daniel was only five years old when his father left for America, and he lived with his mother. When he was eight, he joined a small community formed by Evans, the itinerant preacher. He worked at grinding and preparing charcoal for medicinal purposes. His father visited him in 1856 and easily persuaded him to come to New Lebanon. Daniel enrolled at the Shaker district school for boys that met only in the winter. During the summers he helped cut wood. He was characterized as polite and obedient.

Daniel had unusual mechanical ability and did almost all of the plumbing, steam fitting, and machine work at the North Family. He also had charge of the teams. In addition, he was against hiring outside help and took on more duties as the ranks of the **brethren** thinned. His interests in diet reform led him to become a vegetarian, and he experimented with the milk diet. In January 1883, he became second elder in association with Elder Frederick Evans. In this capacity he had the care of boys and young brethren. After Evans was released in 1892, Elder Daniel took his place as the head of the **family**. If anyone seemed to be the perfect Shaker brother, it was Elder Daniel Offord. That is why the community was shocked when he ran off with a young **sister**. During the morning of 5 December 1895, when he did not seem to be around, an alarm was raised. Knowing that he was very industrious, it was at first feared that he may have fallen into one of the ponds while working after hours at the mills. Gradually, as the pieces were fit together, it was discovered that he had eloped with Sister Mabel Franklin, age 27.

Mabel Franklin had joined the North Family in 1894. She had been a stenographer at the nearby Tilden chemical works and previous to joining had visited the family often. Very intelligent and stylish, she developed a strong influence over the young sisters. They hung pictures according to her directions, and she taught them to ride her bicycle. She also encouraged them to lay aside wearing the lace cap and to start wearing artistic fashions instead of the Shaker uniform.

Sister Mabel's presence also affected Elder Daniel. For many years he had been discouraged with the failure of Shakerism to attract enough members. He spoke to other elders, visited other cooperative societies and even contacted the Salvation Army in New York City. While the **Mount Lebanon** and **Watervliet** Shakers were planning to start a colony in Florida, Elder Daniel thought about leaving the Shakers for an adventure of a different kind. He may have believed in "Social Shakerism." This scheme, supposedly advanced by him in the 1890s, would have the more progressive members move to California and form a large cooperative commune. Celibacy would not be required and anyone could join without regard to beliefs. It was thought that all of the North Family and Canaan Shakers, at least 50 in all, would go along with this, and that another 50 would come from the other societies. To cover the cost of their move to California, the North Family property would be sold or leased.

Considering the presence at the North Family of such stalwarts as Eldress **Anna White**, Martha Anderson, **Catherine Allen**, and many others, not to mention the very devout Shakers at **Upper Canaan**, this idea of Social Shakerism catching on at the **novitiate** families was at best extremely optimistic. Whether this was a true statement of his frame of mind or not, Elder Daniel did leave the family in the company of Sister Mabel Franklin. When **trustees** examined the books he kept, they discovered that he had been taking a little from the accounts and putting it aside under his own name in a bank in New York. Before he left he had decided to take a certain amount for each year he had been a Shaker. Immediately after this discovery, the Shaker trustees used their connections to track him down. Rumor had it that he got as far as Colorado before being totally fleeced out of everything except his clothes. In this pitiful condition he returned and begged to be readmitted on 29 October 1898. No record of what happened to Mabel Franklin has survived.

Due to the charity—some have said credulity—of Eldress Anna White, he was allowed to rejoin. He had given years of faithful service and his father William and his sisters Rhoda and Emily had died faithful Shakers. Moreover his sisters Ann and Miriam were still in the community. As the chronicler of his life put it, Daniel Offord never had to be punished. Throughout his entire life he punished himself. To make up for his actions, he exhausted himself trying to do everything. Since there were hardly any men, he was reinstated as elder in 1903. His final years were literally filled with hard work. He did become an advocate of Christian Science and welcomed the Salvation Army to the North Family on more than one occasion. When he did not show up for breakfast on 25 February 1911, it was not because he had run off. He was discovered dead from a heart attack while doing early morning work at the sawmill.

OLD ENFIELD. This refers to the society at **Enfield, Connecticut**, which was founded before the one at **Enfield, New Hampshire**.

OPENING OF THE GOSPEL. Shaker leaders opened the testimony of Christ's second appearing at **Niskeyuna (Watervliet), New York** on 19 May 1780. This was coincidentally known as the "Dark Day" throughout New England and New York because the sun did not seem to rise that day and even at noon there was darkness. This phenomenon was caused by large forest fires that had darkened the sky.

OPENING THE MIND. This is another name for the Shaker practice of **confession** of sins.

ORDER. This term has many meanings in relation to the Shakers. In the most generic sense, order refers to the Shaker way of life as a whole. In this context, it is similar to a Catholic nun saying that she belongs to the Benedictine or Dominican order. Eldress **Anna White** used the term order in this way in her writings and influential book *Shakerism: Its Meaning and Message.*

Also in the larger sense, the term order was used to mean any systematic organizational plan based on a set of rules, such as **gospel order**.

When used in relation to Shaker **family** organization, order meant the ranks or divisions within the **Church Family**. In societies that were large enough, the Church Family had a **First** and **Second Order**. These orders did not worship with the other Shakers and in the early years held themselves apart.

All Shakers belonged to one of two orders, depending upon the nature of the family where they resided and the **covenant** they signed. Most adult Shakers belonged to the **Church Order**. They did *not*, however, have to live in the Church Family to be Church Order. The covenant they signed was one of the Church as a whole. All other Shakers belonged to the **Gathering Order** or **novitiate**. Terms such as **Junior Order** refer to the Gathering Order and its ranks. An illustration using the Shaker community at **Enfield, Connecticut**, will make this clear.

Enfield had five families. The Church Family was also known as the **First Family**. The **Second Family of the Church** was actually called the North Family for most of its existence. The North Family had a branch called the East Family. The Church Order at Enfield, therefore, was made up of the Church, North, and East Families. The South Family was the principal Gathering Order. It had a branch at the West Family, where new converts went to live with their families. Within the Gathering Order there were rankings depending upon how far along a person was in the process of becoming a Shaker. For example, someone who was still married to someone who actively opposed the Shakers or someone who owned property in the **world** or had business with outsiders might live at a branch of the Gathering

Order. In contrast, a person coming into the Shakers without encumbrances might steadily move through the Gathering Order.

Finally, from a Shaker point of view, the true meaning of order was to follow the rules and regulations of the community. Individual Shakers were judged as either orderly or disorderly to the extent that they followed the dictum "To keep to one's order." This was epitomized by Elder **Amos Stewart** of **New Lebanon's** Second Family. Whenever he left the Mill where he worked to return home he stopped and closed each gate and fence to keep order. Each sex living and socializing with each other separately is another example of keeping to one's order.

ORDER OF FAMILIES. When Shaker communities were first organized, many individual converts who lived near the newly gathered **Church Family** were able to stay on their property and form their own Shaker **families**. These small units were designated by the last name of the prominent convert who owned the land. At **New Lebanon**, for example, these included the Walker Family, the Spier Family, and the Talcott Family. All of these small families, not part of the Church Family, were called the Order of Families. This loose confederation left too much room for individualism and a tight control of property was not possible in such a scattered arrangement. As oral **covenants** gave way to the first written covenants, and then revisions made of these, it became clear that something also had to be done with so many small, vulnerable families. Starting in 1811, these small families were united in a common interest under one set of **trustees** and **elders** as the **Second Family of the Church**. This arrangement replaced the Order of Families.

OUT FAMILY. People who were seriously interested in the Shaker life but had not gathered to one of the established Shaker societies lived in what was an out **family**. The goal was that these people either form a distinct Shaker society themselves or eventually gather at one of the already organized communities. In addition, since all Shaker societies except **North Union** had large tracts of land, there were often individual farms on distant sections of Shaker land. These buildings were sometimes used for families who wished to join the Shakers but were not ready to give up their independence. These out families were near the communities and not expected to be permanent arrangements. In essence they were a part of the **Gathering Order**. Toward the end of the 19th century, some Shakers began to use the term out family to designate people who lived in the **world** and for whom they had deep friendship. These people were not Shakers even though they were sometimes referred to using the title **brother** or **sister** before their names. *See also* FRIENDS OF THE HOLY SPIRIT.

– P –

PARENT MINISTRY. This is the last commonly used name for the **Ministry**. This term replaced the designation **Central Ministry**. Its first recorded usage for ministerial appointments was on 16 April 1921 when Eldress Caroline Tate, former **Church Family eldress** of **Enfield, Connecticut**, was made **trustee** at **Watervliet, New York**. Thereafter all appointments and official documents use the term. *See also* MINISTRY OF NEW LEBANON.

PARKER, DAVID (1807–1867). The Shakers at **Canterbury** were a prosperous community because of good, stable leadership, spiritual and temporal. Perhaps Canterbury's finest **trustee** was David Parker. He was born in Boston, Massachusetts, on 12 May 1807. In 1827 he was brought into the society. His talents were recognized while he was still a young man, and on 8 May 1837 he was appointed to be second in the **Ministry** of New Hampshire. He held this position until 13 October 1846 when he became associate trustee. Two years later he was made first trustee and held that important role until his untimely death in 1867. Under his leadership Canterbury reached its highest point of prosperity. He bought land near **Groveland** to expand the home farm, managed the extensive mill system, and beautified the property by having sugar maple trees set out. So successful was he that he earned a reputation that spread to other Shaker communities. Whenever serious consultation was needed, his help was enlisted. For example, David Parker was one of the trustees who went to **Shirley** to see what could be done about lifting that society out of debt due to unwise involvement with a factory. His service to the

Shakers was excellent, and had he not died at the age of 59 in 1867, he might have been able to assist in the many economic scandals that plagued the society after the Civil War.

PELHAM, RICHARD (1797–1873). Much of the history of western Shakerism has been ignored or forgotten. The life of Richard Pelham certainly is an example of this. He has the unique distinction of having founded three Shaker communities. In addition, for his entire life he seems to have been obedient and such a stalwart **believer** that no matter what was asked of him, it did not make him waver.

Richard was born 8 May 1797 on the frontier in what would later be Indiana. He was the youngest of eight children. His mother died after he was born and his father moved the family back home to Talbot County, Maryland. Here he was placed with an uncle, E. L. Pelham, who was a physician. He and his wife had no children. In 1808, he moved with his uncle to Lyons, New York. His uncle was a strong Methodist, but this did not satisfy Richard, so he set out to find his fortune in Ohio. Before settling down in the new city of Cincinnati, he decided to visit his relatives. He learned that his cousin Phoebe Lockwood and her husband had joined the Shakers and decided to visit her at **Union Village** where she lived. On his way there he heard terrible things about the Shakers. He thought that he would just leave a quick message for her. Instead he was warmly greeted by **Elder** Matthew Houston. He not only met Phoebe Lockwood, she asked him to stay a few days. This hospitality made a deep impression on him. After closing up his business affairs in Cincinnati, he became a Shaker at Union Village. He was a tailor, a horticulturalist, a teacher, and a woodsman. Most of all, however, he had the **gift** of preaching. This skill caused him to be sent to evangelize the area around what would later be **North Union**. He also founded **White Water, Ohio**, and **Sodus, New York**.

In 1834 Richard Pelham became second in the **Ministry** at North Union. He stood in association with Elder David Spining. After six years he was released and came back to Union Village where he lived in the **Church Family**. Two years after this, in 1842, he was sent to the **Second Family** where he had started a large medicinal herb business. From the beginning of 1847 until the end of 1856 he was second elder at **Watervliet, Ohio**. One of the first things he did was to reopen **public meeting**. The woolen factory and sawmill were also started while he was there. In September 1856, Watervliet was completely reorganized when 20 Shakers came to live there from White Water. They brought their own elders with them and took over the **Center Family**. By the end of the year, he was back at Union Village as an assistant **trustee** and bookkeeper. His expertise was soon needed at North Union where he was sent to be first trustee in 1859. That society was in debt $2,500 and spiritual conditions were deteriorating. Within five and a half years, he had paid off the debt.

When he had been released from the Ministry of North Union in 1840, Richard Pelham thought that his days of leadership were over. His health had not been good, and he was content to be a regular member until his death, which he believed was near. His years of service as elder at Watervliet and trustee at both Union Village and North Union, as well as his organization of the medicinal herb industry, all occurred after 1840. In fact, he lived until 10 January 1873 when he died at the Second Family, Union Village. By the time of his death there was no leadership position he had not held.

PENNEBAKER, FRANCIS (1840–1902). Born in Kentucky in 1840, he and his three siblings, Sarah, **William**, and Thomas, were brought to the **Pleasant Hill** Shakers in 1849 after their parents died in a cholera epidemic. They lived at the West Family. As a young man, he worked in the gardens, but during the 1860s he went to Cincinnati, Ohio, to become a dentist. He returned to Pleasant Hill by 1870 and spent the remainder of his life at the West Family. When he came back, he refused to wear the traditional Shaker garb. That he was allowed to do this shows how soft the leadership had become. In fact, it was not only relaxed; it was incompetent.

By the 1870s Pleasant Hill had accumulated a large debt. **Elder** Benjamin Dunlavy did not have the ability to cope with the management of such a large operation. Since the beginning, Pleasant Hill's **Church Order** had been located at three **families** that fronted the main road. These were the Center, the West, and the East Families. Though each of these families had a separate set of elders, they were united in temporal interest by one set of **trustees** who lived at the **Trustees' Office**. In 1878, Francis and William Pennebaker led the West Family out of joint interest. Less than two weeks later, the East

Family followed their lead. From this point, each of the three parts of the Church Order at Pleasant Hill was independent. The Pennebakers hoped that individual management of the families would bring greater prosperity. It would also free them from the control of those whom they deemed incapable. Since Francis Pennebaker was inventive and mechanically inclined, he invented an "Improved Dumping Wagon." He and his brother William received a patent for this wagon in 1882. They hoped that this would bring in revenue. Though the design was attractive, the cost of manufacturing them was prohibitive and few were ever made.

The division of the village and the consequent hard feelings worsened in 1886 when the society realized that the late Elder Benjamin had involved them in a needless debt of $14,000. The Pennebakers, already isolated at the West Family, looked on as the community had to mortgage more land. Also since the separation of the families, the population had plummeted from over 200 to just 34 in 1900.

When the **Ministry of Mount Lebanon** visited Pleasant Hill in 1889, they were dismayed at what they found going on, especially at the West Family. For example, that family raised horses and had a racetrack. Also, due to hay fever, Elder Francis had to leave for the mountains or lakes every summer while the ragweed bloomed. The **Ministry** felt the family just did as they pleased about everything. No doubt they reflected the attitude of their elder, Francis Pennebaker.

PENNEBAKER, WILLIAM (1844–1922). He was the younger brother of **Francis** and Sarah **Pennebaker** of **Pleasant Hill**. With his siblings he came to Pleasant Hill in 1849. He lived at the West Family where he was a cabinetmaker. During the 1870s he went for training at Cincinnati, Ohio, and became a physician. From this point, his life parallels that of his brother Francis. He did not wear Shaker garb, and he helped lead the rebellion in 1878 against a united interest in the **Church Order**. In addition to receiving a patent for an "Improved Dumping Wagon," he had charge of the West Family business affairs in land leases and cattle and farming operations. When Pleasant Hill was dissolved in 1910, he lived on the property and was cared for by the new owner by condition of the sale agreement. He was the last Pleasant Hill Shaker **brother** to die and its second-to-last Shaker.

PERKINS, ABRAHAM (1807–1900). He was born in Sanbornton, New Hampshire, on 13 October 1807. When he was 17, he started to study law in the office of one of his older brothers. He did not find these studies very appealing. After the death of this brother in 1826, Abraham opened a school in Andover, New Hampshire. One of his associates was Hendrick Robinson who had recently become a Shaker at **Enfield, New Hampshire.** Robinson encouraged him to join the Shakers, and in spite of many reservations, he decided to give it a try. Accordingly, he entered the North or **novitiate family** on 27 March 1827. After a year he moved to the **Church Family.** He became the teacher in the boys' school for 14 years. In addition he became **caretaker** of the boys. On 3 September 1845 he was appointed to be second **elder** of the Church. His associate as first was Elder Orville Dyer. Just over a year later, he became second in the New Hampshire **Ministry.** In 1852 he became first with **Henry C. Blinn** of **Canterbury** as second. It seems that the Church at Enfield beckoned him no matter what else he might do. He was back at Enfield as first elder in 1863, but returned to the Ministry in 1867 before returning as a first elder for a final time in 1877. He chose to retire to Canterbury in 1894. During the decades of his leadership, he was noted for his **songs.** Many of these are still sung today.

PHILADELPHIA, PENNSYLVANIA (1858–1896). This community of Shakers was unique. Unlike all of the other Shaker societies, the Philadelphia Shakers were urban and had no connection with agriculture. Also, though many of the communities had African American members, whites made up the vast majority in these places. The racial composition of the Philadelphia Shakers was the opposite of this. Finally, the Philadelphia Shakers are largely forgotten. Few maps showing Shaker settlements have a notation for the Philadelphia community, though it lasted 38 years. This is 14 years longer than the well-known Florida Shaker society and over two-thirds as long as **Groveland.**

The origin of the Philadelphia Shakers is intertwined with the life of religious visionary Mother **Rebecca Cox Jackson.** She first visited **Watervliet, New York,** in 1836, but it was not until 1843, while staying with some Perfectionists in Albany, that she decided to become a Shaker. Though she did not actually join until 1847, she and her constant companion Rebecca Perot visited occasionally. In 1851, they left Watervliet and went back into the **world** to preach. They returned to the South Family in 1857 where they were commissioned to return to Philadelphia with the blessing of the **Ministry** and **elders**. Eldress Paulina Bates informed Jackson that **Mother Ann** approved of this mission and that she (Eldress Paulina) was speaking for her on these matters. Accordingly, Mother Rebecca and her companions went to Philadelphia, where they began a Shaker **family**. The first meeting was held on 30 April 1859.

There is little evidence of this community that has survived. In 1873, when Elder **Henry C. Blinn** made his long journey to Kentucky, he visited the Philadelphia community. He describes a small group of women living in a townhouse at 522 South 10th Street. This integrated community also included a Jewish woman. They did domestic work and laundry. The next year, Nordhoff, while visiting Watervliet, learned about the community and commented that it was composed of 12 colored women.

There are a few references in Shaker journals to the Philadelphia Shakers. As late as 1889, a visitor found 12 in the community. Also there is a strong likelihood that not all of the Shakers lived in one location. Officially, the last of the Philadelphia Shakers—Rebecca Jackson Perot, Harriet Ann Jones, Leah Collins, and one other—moved to the West Family at Watervliet on 25 May 1896. Perot died in 1901. In 1908, however, **Mount Lebanon** scribe **Alonzo Hollister** noted that there were still Shakers there. Their ultimate fate is not known. Mary Ann Gillespie of the Maine Ministry died while visiting the Philadelphia Shakers in 1887.

PICK, ERNEST (1859–1940). He was born in Libie, Bohemia, on 9 June 1859. His family had means, and he was well educated, going to grammar school for eight years and completing four years of college. In 1884, he immigrated to the United States and went to California. He was admitted to the **North Family, Mount Lebanon**, in 1886. The next year he moved to the **Second Family** briefly before coming back to the North Family in 1890. At the end of 1894, he moved a final time to the Second Family. His early work at the Second Family was as a farmer, and he managed the sweet corn business started by **Elder** Dewitt Clinton Brainard. Between 1900 and 1903, his mother Bertha Pick joined the family. He may also have been responsible in part for the large influx of members of eastern European descent at the South and Second Families at Mount Lebanon and at **Hancock**.

Records for the Second Family are scarce and no date has been found for his appointment as elder, but he is referred to as Elder Ernest by contemporary Mount Lebanon Shakers. From all accounts he was well liked by the members of the Second Family and its close allies, those living at the South Family. These two small families were heavily involved with the **chair industry** and down-to-earth in their lifestyle. In contrast, at the other end of the village the North Family was agricultural and lived according to a set of "principles." The tension between the two styles of living came to a crisis in 1909 when Eldress **Catherine Allen** of the **Central Ministry** expelled Elder Ernest for supposedly holding the hand of Sister **Lillian Barlow**. They were observed while they were in the sitting room of the family. Eldress **Sarah Collins** of the South Family believed that Elder Ernest and Sister Lillian were innocent victims of North Family self-righteousness since Eldress Catherine had once been a member of that family. This is interesting because at the time Eldress Catherine was in the Central Ministry and did not live at the North Family, yet she is labeled as a meddling North Family Shaker. The result of the scandal was that Lillian remained at the Second Family and was chastised. Elder Ernest was sent away. One account has it that he returned to Bohemia where he inherited $15,000 from his mother. This may be true, but when he returned he lived for at least a few months at the Shaker society at **Enfield, Connecticut**. He came back to the Second Family in 1910. Apparently his transgressions were forgiven.

When Margaret Eggleston became the eldress of the Second Family in 1908, she decided to revive the chair industry. Chair production, which had become sporadic at best, was moved from the South Family to the stone workshop at the Second Family, and here Elder Ernest and Sister Lillian made chairs. They shipped them up to the South Family to be finished and sold by Eldress Sarah Collins and her crew. In 1915, they received tremendous help when William Perkins, a skilled woodworker, joined the family. Eight years later, Elder Ernest accidentally caused a fire that totally destroyed the stone workshop. He had been filling an automobile with gasoline when it ignited. He and Sister Lillian traveled to **Watervliet** to secure replacement parts for the lost machinery. They set up a new factory in an adjacent building at the Second Family. This was the final home of the chair business. While Brother William and Sister Lillian worked on chairs, Elder Ernest managed the farm and orchards. A young brother named Curtis White helped him.

By the mid-1930s, it was long past the time when the tiny Second and South Families should have closed. The catalyst for this may have been the death of William Perkins in 1934. Since it is unlikely that he wished to go back to the North Family, and he could not live alone with Lillian Barlow at the Second Family, Elder Ernest left for Bohemia, now part of Czechoslovakia. He visited his relatives. He also traveled to Palestine. His religious roots were in Judaism, and he was obsessed with the idea of a Jewish homeland. When he returned, he made his home in Pittsfield, at the home of Mrs. Karl E. Termohlen. He spent his time farming and died in 1940 of a sudden heart attack. His remains were cremated. It is of note that the Reverend John Gratten of the Congregational Church officiated at his funeral. By this time, this non-Shaker minister conducted the funerals at both Mount Lebanon and Hancock. In his will Ernest left $500 to the Berkshire Athenaeum and $8,000 to Geulath Ha-aretz, the redemption of the land fund of the Jewish National Fund. *See also* FURNITURE.

PLEASANT HILL, KENTUCKY (1806–1910). SPIRITUAL NAME: Pleasant Hill. FEAST GROUND: Holy Sinai's Plain. BISHOPRIC: Pleasant Hill until 1868 when it came under the jurisdiction of **South Union**. In 1889, along with South Union, it was placed under **Union Village**. FAMILIES: Center, East, West (all part of the **Church Order**), West Lot, North Lot (**Gathering Order**). MAXIMUM POPULATION AND YEAR: 490 in the early 1820s. INDUSTRIES: agriculture, especially broom corn, garden seeds, fruit preserves, raising fine stock. NOTABLE SHAKERS: **Micajah Burnett, John Dunlavy, Francis Pennebaker, William Pennebaker, Jane Sutton.** UNIQUE FEATURES: Pleasant Hill is an architectural gem. The buildings are magnificent. Eastern villages such as **Enfield, Connecticut**, and **Mount Lebanon, New York**, had some buildings on the same scale, but these are mostly gone. The monumental buildings of stone and brick at Pleasant Hill survive. Although epitomized by the **Trustees' Office, Center Family** dwelling, and the **Meeting House**, every place at Pleasant Hill has beautiful buildings. In fact, a high percentage of the major buildings built by the Shakers still exist. This is especially true of the **dwelling houses**. Ironically, these external reminders of the Shakers are in great contrast to the lack of in-depth research on the site. Even *Shakerism: Its Meaning and Message,* the last major Shaker history written by the Shakers, does not mention Pleasant Hill, though there is a photo of the Center Family dwelling.

BRIEF HISTORY: Elisha Thomas, Samuel Bonta, and Henry Bonta, farmers along Shawnee Run in Mercer County, Kentucky, desired to hear more of Shakerism from the first missionaries. Accordingly, in June 1806, a large meeting was held in Elisha Thomas' barn. Eastern Shaker **Benjamin Seth Youngs** addressed them, and a large number of listeners converted. In 1808 the name of the community was changed from Shawnee Run to Pleasant Hill. By 1810, there were 34 believers and 100 more not yet gathered. The organization of the society at Pleasant Hill proceeded rapidly. Elisha Thomas' farm was the nucleus that eventually encompassed 4,000 acres of land. This farmland was very fertile and close to the Kentucky River. In this way, the Pleasant Hill Shakers could market their products as far away as New Orleans.

Although the population peaked early, Pleasant Hill enjoyed a large population for many decades. For example, in 1863, the village still had 350 members. The addition of scores of converts from Sweden in 1868 and 1869 helped keep figures high and as late as 1880, there were 203 Pleasant Hill Shakers. A severe collapse after this caused the population to plummet to a mere 34 in 1900. This spectacular decline of 83 percent is unprecedented in Shaker history. The reasons for this collapse are many. As early as the 1820s, there were severe problems in governance, especially among the younger Shakers. The membership wanted to be consulted about decisions, and to some Shaker leaders, this was a dangerous situation. Consequently, Shakers there got a reputation for being troublesome.

Other western communities, such as **Watervliet, Ohio**, were influenced by what was happening at Pleasant Hill. The result of this discontent was that western Shakerism lost a good portion of the second generation. In addition, the Pleasant Hill Shakers emerged from

the Civil War in a weakened economic state. The railroad and westward expansion challenged the society to transform its markets at the
exact same time the old leadership was unable to do so. Complicat-
ing matters, in 1878, Shaker leaders William and Francis Pennebaker
led the East and West families out of joint interest with the Center
Family. These three Shaker families had been united in temporal interest since the beginning. Benjamin Dunlavy, **trustee** of the Center
Family, proved to be an incapable trustee who had accumulated a
debt of $40,000 by 1880. Shaker lands were mortgaged to help clear
this debt. Further mistakes by Dunlavy cost the society an additional
$20,000 which was paid for by mortgaging more land. In 1896, over
700 acres in the central part of the society were sold, including the
Trustees' Office. (Clark and Ham, *Pleasant Hill and Its Shakers*,
73–79).

All of this time, the religious spirit at Pleasant Hill was very low.
Members visited nearby camp meetings or attended other Protestant
churches. A few faith-filled members such as the Rupe sisters and
Jane Sutton with her hotel business at the East Family did try their
best to keep Pleasant Hill going, but it was impossible. By 1910, the
remaining 12 Shakers deeded the final 1800 acres of land to George
Bohon, who agreed to care for them for the rest of their lives. This
action did not go unchallenged by the **Central Ministry**, who
brought the Pleasant Hill Shakers to court to sue them in an attempt
to prevent them from giving away their lands. The **Ministry** was not
successful.

LAST SHAKER: Mary Settles (1836–1923). Born in Louisville, Kentucky, she joined the Pleasant Hill Shakers in 1859 with her two children, Edward K. and Fannie Settles. When the community was dissolved, she stayed on and was cared for by George Bohon as part of
the agreement made at the time of the sale of the property.

POLAND HILL, MAINE (1819–1887). This is where the North Family of the **New Gloucester (Sabbathday Lake)** Shakers was located.
The site is in the town of Poland, Androscoggin County, 1.2 miles
north of the **Church Family** (Sabbathday Lake), which is in the town
of New Gloucester, Cumberland County. In 1819, the family of Shakers that had been at Gorham was moved to Poland Hill. From that
point, Poland Hill became the **Gathering Order**. The family never

really prospered and suffered from the lack of sufficient men and from bad leadership. A large granite **dwelling house**, smaller in size but similar in scale to the **Great Stone Dwelling** at **Enfield, New Hampshire**, was begun in 1853. Due to the various problems, it took 26 years to complete, and was used just eight years before the family was closed in 1887. Notable Shakers include Joseph Brackett, author of "Simple Gifts," Otis Sawyer, Sophia Mace, Nehemiah Trull, **Philemon Stewart**, and Isaiah Wentworth. The last Poland Hill Shaker was Elizabeth Haskell (1852–1920). Following the closure of Poland Hill, she moved to Sabbathday Lake. She eventually became a member of the Maine **Ministry**.

PRIVILEGE. Being a Shaker is voluntary. So great are the spiritual benefits that the Shakers see a person's desire to be a Shaker as a privilege. The word privilege, however, is also often used in reference to someone who left the Shakers and then came back. If accepted into the community again, the person was said to have received a second privilege. Most of those who returned to the Shakers left again. Some were given a third or even a fourth privilege, but this was not the norm. Two privileges, if that, were the most people generally received.

In addition, the term was used to admonish if it was thought an individual's behavior was contrary to Shaker practices. The dictum "Prize your precious privilege in Zion," for instance, is an example of the word used in this context. In **Mother Ann's** day, the word privilege was used in reference to **confession** or **opening the mind**. During the **Era of Manifestations**, the word privilege is frequently found in inspired messages.

PROBATIONARY COVENANT. Also known the Novitiate or Conditional Covenant, this is a legal document signed by a person who wishes to become a Shaker. This legal agreement states that being given temporary residence in the community is to be considered full compensation for any labor that may be performed or services given. It also outlines that the signer is obliged to live by the rules of the community as well as to be obedient to its leaders.

Probationary covenants make fascinating reading because they belie the myth that no one was joining the Shakers. Hundreds and hundreds of people joined the Shakers right until the end of the 19th century. The Shakers did not lack converts, but lacked suitable converts who persevered. Almost everyone who joined had a short stay in the community. This was the problem that always plagued the Shakers.

PUBLIC MEETING. Shaker meeting or worship was open to the **world** from 1780. From 1784 until 1796, however, no external missionary work was carried out. All energy had to be expended in gathering the communities into **gospel order**. In time, however, the Shakers found that the system as set up by Father **Joseph Meacham** did not accommodate adults who might join. To remedy this, the Shakers started a **Gathering Order** in 1800. The first of these was the **North Family** at **New Lebanon**. One function of the leading **elder** at the Gathering Order was to preach at the public meeting on the Sabbath.

It was only natural that the elder in charge of the **novitiate** class should preach to the world on Sunday. In the early years these elders did a lot more missionary work outside than preaching inside. Those to whom they preached would then come to a community to experience the life. After 1830, however, the great crowds gathering at public meeting were very much a part of the tourist market, and this became a fundamental part of Shaker outreach to the world. It was not unusual for hundreds of visitors to attend Shaker meeting on Sunday.

The Shakers held public meeting Sunday morning during the warmer months of the year, usually from May until October, at their **Meeting Houses**. In the smaller societies, everyone attended the public meeting. At larger places such as **Watervliet** and New Lebanon, the **Church Family** held its own service in the afternoon while all of the other Shaker families attended the public meeting.

By the 1880s as the number of Shakers diminished, many of the communities began to stop the tradition of public meeting. The testimony was withdrawn and private services continued in the meeting room of the **family** dwelling. By 1900, few, if any, of the Meeting Houses were used for worship.

In 1963, under the influence of Sister **Mildred Barker** and Brother **Theodore Johnson**, the Shaker society at **Sabbathday Lake** once again opened public meeting. This practice continues to this day. Up until that time visitors known to the family could attend the meeting that was held each Sunday in the meeting room of the **dwelling house**. Though visitors may join the community for worship any Sunday of the year, the Meeting House is only used in the warmer months.

– Q –

QUI VIVE TRIO. This was the singing trio at Canterbury from about 1910 until about 1930. It was directed by **Elder Arthur Bruce**. **Sisters Helena Sarle** (1867–1956), Jessie Evans (1867–1937), and Lillian Phelps (1876–1973) made up the trio. *See also* SONGS.

– R –

ROUND STONE BARN. Shakerism has always been closely tied to the agrarian. Consequently the Shakers needed various types of farm buildings. Certainly the most well known of the Shaker barns was the round stone barn at the Shaker village in **Hancock, Massachusetts**.

After the original communities were settled, a building phase started that would transform Shaker communities into showplaces of innovation and convenience. The construction of this barn in 1826 is typical of the energy and prosperity of the societies in those times. An earlier barn had burned in 1825, and the Shakers were anxious to have a suitable replacement. It is not known who first thought to have a round barn at Hancock, although, according to tradition, **Elder** William Deming and **trustee** Daniel Goodrich designed it. They hired masons and commenced constructing a round stone barn with walls between two and a half and three and a half feet thick. Measuring 270 feet around and 21 feet high, the barn could accommodate 70 head of cattle. Since it was built on a hill, wagons could enter on the upper level of the barn and pitch hay down into the central manger. Manure pits under the first floor made for easy cleanup. The price of the barn was $10,000, an enormous sum for the time.

The original barn had a conical roof, but this was struck by lightening in 1864. The interior was gutted and had to be rebuilt. This time the Shakers chose a flat roof and cupola. Eventually a monitor was added to provide air circulation.

Time and neglect caused severe cracking of the walls and, in 1968, the barn was completely rebuilt. Today it is a symbol of Hancock Shaker Village, a museum restoration of the former **Church Family**.

ROYAL FAMILY OF SHAKERISM. This refers to the large and extended branches of the Goodrich family of Pittsfield and **Hancock**, Massachusetts. So many members from this clan became **elders**, **trustees**, or **deacons** that the term royal was sometimes used to describe them.

– S –

SABBATHDAY LAKE, MAINE (1794–PRESENT). SPIRITUAL NAME: Chosen Land. FEAST GROUND: Mount Hermon. BISHOPRIC: **Alfred**. FAMILIES: Church, North (also called Poland Hill, the **Gathering Order**), Square House (Gathering Order). MAXIMUM POPULATION AND YEAR: 187 in 1784. INDUSTRIES: seeds, herbs, brooms, dry measures, sieves, oak staves for molasses, fancy goods, spinning wheels, churns, woodenware, oval boxes. NOTABLE SHAKERS: **Otis Sawyer,** Joseph Bracket, **William Dumont, Delmer Wilson, Theodore Johnson, Arnold Hadd, Aurelia Mace, Elizabeth Noyes, Prudence Stickney, Frances Carr.** UNIQUE FEATURES: Sabbathday Lake continues as a Shaker village. It is the only place in the world where a visitor may attend a Shaker service or speak to living Shakers. In addition to the spiritual aspects of Shaker life, at Sabbathday Lake, a rich oral tradition has been preserved. Also, traditional music, community-tested foods, and a working farm are parts of the way of life that have survived there. The remaining believers still offer their **testimony** to the **world**, and they seek interested inquirers who may feel that they are called to live the Shaker life.

BRIEF HISTORY: In November 1782, a group from Gorham consisting of Elisha Pote, Nathan Freeman, and Joseph Stone came on a missionary tour to an area known as Thompson's Pond Plantation in the town of New Gloucester. At Gowen Wilson's farmhouse, they opened their testimony. As a result of their efforts, a number of families embraced Shakerism. These included the Wilson, Merrill, Holmes, Briggs, and Pote families. On 19 April 1794, the society was organized, and the process of gathering and organizing a community began. The **Meeting House** was raised on 19 April 1794. The next year, a **dwelling house** was built across the road. In 1800, over 140 Shakers lived in the society, and the number of Shakers remained just under this figure until the 1840s. Starting in 1823, however, an increasing portion of the membership was made up of children.

After long and unsuccessful efforts, primarily at Alfred, the **Ministry of New Lebanon** sought out the **Canterbury Ministry** to take over direct control of the Maine communities in 1830. This action virtually isolated Alfred and Sabbathday Lake from the greater Shaker world. The Canterbury Ministry was initially received favorably, but following the death of Father **Job Bishop**, their authority began to erode. By the 1850s, the Canterbury Ministry petitioned the Lebanon Ministry to be released as the Maine Shakers had rejected their authority. In 1859, the Lebanon Ministry relented and restored the Maine Ministry as autonomous. As part of the deal, the Canterbury Ministry provided the resource most needed—committed and capable **believers**. Nearly a dozen members, mostly from Canterbury, were transferred to fill leadership positions in Maine. They occupied everything from deaconships to the Ministry.

The Lebanon Ministry replaced most of the officeholders but not key **trustees**. This oversight was almost fatal, because almost immediately, a series of dishonest trustees put Sabbathday Lake under a crushing debt. In 1860, the Ministry appealed to all of the other Shaker villages to send financial help to the community at **New Gloucester**. Each Shaker society was assessed based on population. This money relieved the immediate debt, but the community still struggled.

Sabbathday Lake was known among the other Shakers as "The least of Mother's children in the East." The society's remoteness, its location in an area that was not as prosperous as many other places where the Shakers lived, the lack of membership, and the financial instability all made this description an apt one.

Following the lead of Alfred, in 1870 there was a proposal to sell the property and move to Kansas. This did not materialize, and when Nordhoff visited in 1874, he noted that the buildings were not in good repair. The dwelling house at the Church was especially in need of major improvements or had to be replaced. It had been the dream of the community to be able to erect a new structure. Due to the financial troubles, this had been postponed. Slowly, money was saved so that a new house could be built. In 1883, construction began on a large brick dwelling that was completed by the end of 1884.

Nothing symbolizes the turnaround in fortunes more than building of the central brick dwelling. This was accomplished through the hard work of a core of dedicated Shakers. From 1860 onward, trustee Aurelia Mace noted that the faithful young **sisters** she dubbed the "nine gems" had been added to the community. In 1873, a tenth gem, in the person of Elizabeth Noyes, joined. While the others had come into the society as children, Lizzie Noyes was 28 years old. Originally from Maine, she had been a schoolteacher. Her intelligence, boundless energy, and competence caused her to become the first **eldress** in 1880. A young man, only 19 years old, named William Dumont joined the community in 1870. He was a skilled farm manager and had a deep concern for the boys being brought up in the village. At the time Lizzie Noyes was appointed eldress, William Dumont was made first elder. Together they presided over the golden age of the community from 1880 to 1926. On 1 April 1890, the postal address of the community changed from West Gloucester to Sabbathday Lake. During this time, in contrast to what was happening in other Shaker villages, Sabbathday Lake was a stable, prosperous community. From the 1890s until the 1920s, the village population stayed virtually the same. Except for Alfred, all other Shaker communities were either closing or declining rapidly.

Eldress Lizzie Noyes died in 1926. The following year, the Maine Ministry was dissolved, and Elder William resigned from being trustee. He died in 1930. By then, the effect of the Great Depression made it advisable to consolidate the two Maine Shaker communities. As a result, Alfred was closed, and its 21 Shakers moved to Sabbathday Lake in May 1931. The group from Alfred was young, but most importantly, religious. They had been raised under the tutelage of Eldress **Harriett Coolbroth**, who had instilled traditional Shakerism in her charges. This inner strength helped the society last through the economic tensions of the Depression and the privations of World War II. While those Shakers who had always been at Sabbathday Lake had the highest leadership positions, it was Sister **R. Mildred Barker**, formerly of Alfred, who kept the Shaker spirit alive. In 1960,

Theodore Johnson, a Harvard-educated scholar, joined the community. In a manner reminiscent of the Noyes-Dumont partnership, Sister Mildred and Brother Ted were able to revitalize the community. A new Shaker publication, the *Shaker Quarterly*, was commenced in 1961. **Public meeting** opened after a 76-year hiatus in 1963. A general outreach to the world brought in a few new converts. Though Brother Ted died unexpectedly in 1986 and in 1990 Sister Mildred passed away, the community survives today because of their efforts.

ST. CLOUD, FLORIDA. *See* NARCOOSSEE, FLORIDA.

SARLE, CORA HELENA (1867–1956). The 1880s saw the largest number of people join the Shaker society at **Canterbury, New Hampshire**. "Helena" Sarle was part of this influx. Born in North Scituate, Massachusetts, in 1867, she entered the **Church Family** at Canterbury in 1882. Since her health was poor, **Elder Henry Blinn** asked her to use her artistic talents to illustrate a book of drawings of native plants. He intended for this to be used in the Shaker school. This task necessitated that she spend many hours out in the fields and woods. This helped her gain her health and resulted in a book of over 180 botanic drawings. In time, her love of art led her to become a folk artist. She painted on many surfaces including glass. Her illustrations of nature can be found on parts of some of the poplar ware made by the community. These works are highly prized by collectors.

Cora signed the **covenant** in 1888 and became a great burden-bearer at Canterbury. In addition to her many artistic works, which were sold to provide income, she cooked and did needlework. She was also a part of the **Shaker Quartette** and the **Qui Vive Trio**. To the many girls who joined the community, she was known as "Grammy."

SAVOY, MASSACHUSETTS (1817–1821). In 1810, a notorious preacher named Joseph Smith started a church in the remote, mountainous town of Savoy. His enthusiasm diminished, however, after his first wife showed up, much to the consternation of the woman he had just married. He left the congregation in haste and it was left to flounder without a leader until Shaker missionaries Morrell Baker and **Calvin Green** came to the area in 1817. There are two accounts of how the Shakers came to send missionaries to this wild region. One is that a spirit dressed as an old woman called at the **Office** of the **Second Family** at **New Lebanon**. While the **sisters** fed her, she spoke of a religious revival that was taking place in Savoy and that the people needed assistance. Soon after, the Shakers at New Lebanon received a letter from Elisha Smith, a member of New Lebanon's **Back Order**. He said that while on business, he stopped at the home of a Baptist leader in Savoy who told him a revival was going on in the town, and that he did not seem to be able to help them. He figured the Shakers could do some good for them.

When the Shaker missionaries arrived, they found a ready audience. By 1819 there were 48 Shakers and the property had grown to 1,500 acres. A **Meeting House** had been built against the side of Shaker James Cornell's house, and all seemed well. A two-year drought (1820–1821) and a plague of grasshoppers, however, reduced the community to complete dependence upon other Shaker villages for food for themselves and their animals. The new **Ministry of New Lebanon** that took office in 1821 decided that the community at Savoy should be dissolved, and that its members move either to **Watervliet** or New Lebanon. A high percentage of the 80 Savoy Shakers remained faithful. The Lewis, Haskins, Rice, and Cornell families, to name a few, greatly enriched New Lebanon by their presence for most of the 19th century.

SAWYER, OTIS (1815–1884). He was born on 2 May 1815 in Portland, Maine. In 1822 he was brought to live with the Shakers at **Poland Hill**, the **Gathering Order** for the **New Gloucester** society. Joseph Brackett was the second **elder** of the **family** and had a big influence on young Otis. The lack of a sufficient number of men in Shaker ranks to hold leadership positions is clear when it is considered how many appointments Brother Otis had during his life. When he was 21 years old he became second elder of the family, and in 1840 he was made a **trustee**. Due to changes in the Maine **Ministry** in 1842, the second elder's position became vacant. This was in the midst of the **Era of Manifestations** and, through the inspiration of **Holy Mother Wisdom**, Brother Otis was chosen (Hadd, "The Burden I Will Never Shun: Elder Otis Sawyer," 95). He also taught school, and then was removed from the Ministry to become trustee at

New Gloucester. Not long after, he became first elder of the Church, a job he did not wish. Much to his relief he was again appointed to the Maine Ministry in 1859, this time as first elder. His companions for the next 25 years were Eldress Hester Ann Adams and Eldress Mary Ann Gillespie. These exemplary leaders led the Maine Shakers through times of terrible financial scandals at New Gloucester and a continuing decline in membership at both societies.

Elder Otis left many accomplishments. He compiled **songs**, wrote the histories of the Maine communities, compiled lists of the dead, organized ministerial correspondence, and started Shaker libraries at **Alfred** and **Sabbathday Lake**. The greatest trials of his life, however, were in dealing with recalcitrant and often scandalous members, especially **Philemon Stewart**, John Kaime, Isaiah Wentworth, Lois Wentworth, and Hewitt Chandler. In addition to these tasks, he had to find a way to complete the large granite dwelling that had been begun at Poland Hill and collect money so that a new dwelling could be built at the **Church Family** in New Gloucester. These efforts were undermined by Elder **John Vance** at Alfred.

In the end, the house at Poland was completed and New Gloucester was able to build its dwelling. That large brick building, home to the Shakers of today, is a lasting memorial to Elder Otis. Yet his greatest accomplishment was the great love the Maine Shakers had for him. His death was something that some of them never got over. His fatherly presence and the confidence he inspired helped shape a whole generation of Maine believers.

SECOND FAMILY OF THE CHURCH. When Shaker communities were first organized, this term was used interchangeably with the term **Second Order of the Church**. Starting in 1811, the larger societies that had second orders no longer used the designation second family to mean the same thing. Instead a Second Family of the Church was created to unite all of the small, individual Shaker **families** that had once been part of the **Order of Families**. For example, at **New Lebanon**, the families that were not part of the **Gathering Order** or part of the **Church** or **First Family** (First and Second Orders), were united under the umbrella of the Second Family of the Church. The small families were gathered into three sites. The principal place was the actual Second Family itself. Branches were organized known as the South House and the East House. Eventually, these would become separate, independent families. **Alfred, Canterbury, Union Village,** and **Hancock** also had second families. At **Tyringham,** both **Enfields, Shirley,** and **Harvard,** the Second Family was also called the North Family. At **Watervliet, New York,** it was the West Family. **Groveland** and **Sabbathday Lake** did not have Second Families, and, except at Union Village, this designation was not used in the western Shaker communities. *See also* FIRST ORDER OF THE CHURCH.

SECOND ORDER OF THE CHURCH. At first, this name was synonymous with the term **Second Family of the Church.** They were both used to denote the same part of the **Church Family** at **Hancock, Watervliet,** and **New Lebanon.** In 1811, the Shakers at New Lebanon broke up their Second Family and out of their Third Family formed the Second Order of the Church. Their **First Family** or **First Order** remained intact. From this point onward, the Second Order of the Church was no longer the Second Family. In essence, the Church Family was one **family** divided into two sites, the First Order and the Second Order. A new Second Family of the Church was created at New Lebanon in 1814. This family had nothing to do with the Second Order. It was the unification of all of the former small individual non-gathering families under a united interest.

SEXTON, DOLLY (1776–1884). She has a triple distinction. First, she is the Shaker who has lived the longest so far. She was five days short of being 108 at the time of her death. Although Malinda Welch of the **Canaan** Shakers was said to be 119 when she died in 1827, this cannot be verified. Second, Sexton was the last survivor from the second generation of Shakers. This was the group whose parents had received the faith from **Mother Ann** or one of her companions. Third, and most importantly, she is the last person to die who saw Mother Ann. When Sexton was a small child, Mother is said to have held her in her arms.

Sexton was born in Stephentown, New York, on 6 May 1776. She gathered to the Shakers at **New Lebanon** with her two sisters and lived, except for a brief period, at the East Family from 1781 until 1872—91 years. After the East Family closed due to a dishonest

trustee, Sexton moved to the **First Order of the Church** at **Mount Lebanon**, where she died on 1 May 1884.

SHAKER BIRTHDAY. This is the day commemorated by a Shaker of the day he/she first joined the society. As opposed to having a birthday party, Catholic monks and nuns often mark their feast (name) day as a date to celebrate. So too among the Shakers, the day that a person "came among **believers**" was a noteworthy day, far eclipsing an individual's birthday. So important was this to Shakers that when believers visited other Shaker societies, they often wrote down the day they "came among Believers." Surviving guest books show this information, and it is often the only source of biographical information on some Shakers.

SHAKER BRIDGE. This is the bridge that Shaker **trustee Caleb Dyer** of **Enfield, New Hampshire**, had constructed at the narrow point of Lake Mascoma. It allowed the Shakers access to the railroad that passed through North Enfield. "Boston John" Clark designed this causeway, and it lasted until the hurricane of 1938. A new bridge replaced it and some of the original timber was used in the modern construction.

SHAKER CENTRAL TRUST FUND. This refers to the irrevocable trust fund that was set up in 1959 to provide for the remaining Shakers. The money for this fund came from the accumulated wealth of the **Hancock** community and any money and investments that came under the management of the Hancock **trustees** as the various communities were closed and sold. Should there be no more Shakers, the fund provides money for educational programs. The specific details of the trust are available for those who wish to know them. It is sufficient to remark that one of the most overlooked aspects of the trust is that it allows for new Shakers. Access to funds is allowed after a person has been a Shaker for five years. This in no way determines the status of a Shaker, something that is reserved for the **covenant**, yet it shows that even as late as 1959, provision was made for the admission of new members. The present-day Shakers, in keeping with the trust, only allow a person to sign the Church covenant after five years of living with the community, though anyone entering the Shakers is required to sign a **probationary covenant**.

SHAKER HEIGHTS, OHIO. This near suburb of Cleveland is where the former Shaker society of **North Union** was located. No Shaker buildings remain. The site was rebuilt by the Van Sweringen brothers' company early in the 20th century.

SHAKER LANDING DAY. 6 August 1774 is the day that **Mother Ann** and her companions landed in New York City from England. This day continues to be commemorated with a special worship service at **Sabbathday Lake**. This day is also known as Arrival Day or simply the Glorious Sixth.

SHAKER QUARTETTE. During the late 19th century and early 20th century, **Canterbury** not only became the largest society, but also led in the development of Shaker music. Under the guidance of sympathetic elders, vocal and instrumental musical groups formed to entertain visitors. The best known of these was the "Shaker Quartette." They performed not only in the community but at local venues as well. They had a standard repertoire of 100 **songs** which they had memorized and sang without accompaniment. Sisters **Helena Sarle** (1867–1956), Jennie Fish (1857–1920), Josephine Wilson (1866–1946), and Jessie Evans (1867–1937) made up the quartette. *See also* QUI VIVE TRIO.

SHAKER SEMINAR. Every July a group of 65 to 90 people gather to attend a week-long seminar on the Shakers. Originally sponsored by Elmira College and directed by Dr. Herb Wiseby, the program began in 1975. When Berkshire Community College took over the sponsorship and Gustave Nelson became the director, events expanded and more traditions were added. Since 2000, Hancock Shaker Village has sponsored the seminar. There have been 36 seminars held the past 33 years, and in 2008 Hamilton College will assume cosponsorship.

SHAKER STATION. This was the postal address of the **Enfield, Connecticut**, Shakers from 24 May 1876 until 31 July 1911.

SHAKERS, NEW YORK. This was the postal address for the **Watervliet, New York**, community.

SHAKERTOWN. This is the popular name for various Shaker communities in the West: **South Union** and **Pleasant Hill, Kentucky**; **West Union, Indiana**; and **Union Village,** Ohio.

SHAWNEE RUN, KENTUCKY. This is the original name for **Pleasant Hill.** It was changed in 1808.

SHEPHERD, WALTER SIGLEY (1852–1933). Elder **Frederick Evans** made two missionary trips to England. The latter yielded a number of adults who came to the United States and joined the **North Family** at **Mount Lebanon.** One of these was Walter S. Shepherd. He was born in Guide Bridge, Lancashire, England, on 15 December 1852. In 1887 he immigrated to the United States and spent one year in New Mexico. On 18 January 1888 he was admitted to the North Family. Those that lived with him while he was still a **young believer** recall that he was thin and very tall, several inches more than six feet, and that he possessed quiet mannerisms. In fact, he was not much of a conversationalist because he seemed to dwell in the other world. In addition, his ideas of reform fit those in vogue at the North Family. He was also polite and well liked. He signed the **probationary covenant** on 28 February 1888. In 1892 he was appointed second **elder** of the North Family.

The Shakers at **Enfield, Connecticut,** possessed fine land and beautiful buildings. However, they did not have sufficient membership by the 1890s, and their future was doubtful. The **Central Ministry** was very interested in trying to save the place if they could. Since 1893, they had assumed control of the **Hancock bishopric,** of which Enfield was a part. They decided to send Shakers from Mount Lebanon to Enfield to fill jobs and hold places rapidly being vacated by death and departure. In January 1895, Sister Fanny Tyson from the **Church Family,** Mount Lebanon, was sent to be an **Office sister** at the Church Family, Enfield. Walter Shepherd moved from the North Family, Mount Lebanon, to the South Family, Enfield. The real intention of the Central Ministry was to have him replace 75-year-old Elder **George Wilcox** of the Church Family. Since Elder George did not believe in sharing any power, the Central Ministry moved cautiously. Enfield's South Family was a **Gathering Order,** so Elder

Walter could feel at home since the North Family, his former home, was one as well. The intention was for him to observe what was happening in the whole community. No doubt both he and Sister Fanny informed the **Ministry** of what they saw.

A year and a half later, he moved to the Church Family and signed the **covenant**. At this point, if things had gone according to the plan, Elder George would have voluntarily stepped down and let younger leadership try to salvage what they could. This did not happen. Elder George would not give up his position and remained elder until his death in 1910. Moreover, the Ministry did not press him unduly on this. Perhaps they felt they had done enough since in 1897, they sent the entire **Upper Canaan Family** to Enfield to take over the North Family. Changing the elders at the Church Family may have seemed too drastic a takeover. In the meantime, Elder Walter gained an ally from his old home when Sister Lucy Bowers joined the Church Family, Enfield, in January 1896. In 1901, his situation improved even more when Sister Ann Offord of the North Family, Mount Lebanon, replaced Sister Fanny Tyson in the Office.

Though he may have been withdrawn and retiring when a young man, as he advanced in years and the condition of Shakerism worsened, he became more outspoken. His correspondence shows quite a degree of frankness as he describes events in the larger world of Shakerdom. His dislike of the machinations of Elder George is clear. When Elder George finally died in 1910 during his 91st year, immediately Elder Walter became both first elder and **trustee** of the Church Family. In 1911, he was appointed second in the Central Ministry, standing with Elder **Joseph Holden**. In this capacity he was able to ready Enfield for sale. In November 1914, the former Church, North, and East Families were sold to a tobacco conglomerate. By provision of the sale, the remaining Church Family Shakers were allowed to stay as long as they liked. The building that had been Elder George's shop was moved and fixed up for them. In 1917, however, they decided to leave Enfield. On 15 October 1917, Elder Walter returned to the North Family, where he took charge, though he was never appointed its elder. After the death of Joseph Holden in 1919 he became first in the Central Ministry. He died at the North Family on 11 January 1933. The last years of his life were spent helping to close out communities.

Brother **Ted Johnson** of **Sabbathday Lake** referred to Elder Walter as one of the "suicide Shakers." Certainly from statements he supposedly made in interviews, this would be true. Sometime during his life he came to the firm belief that Shakerism was not going to continue, and there was no reason to try to keep it going. This change in his thinking most likely took place when he lived at Enfield in the early 20th century and was kept at a distance by Elder George. All around, he could see the collapse, and the Central Ministry did not seem strong enough to cope with getting a handle on matters. Once the leadership of the Shakers decided to end the religion, it was going to be extremely difficult for those who were in the community and wanted to see it survive. The history of Shakerism since 1960 shows this quite vividly.

SHIRLEY, MASSACHUSETTS (1793–1908). SPIRITUAL NAME: Pleasant Garden. FEAST GROUND: Holy Hill of Peace. BISHOPRIC: **Harvard**. FAMILIES: Church (**First Family**), North (**Second Family** and at times the **Gathering Order**), South (Gathering Order). MAXIMUM POPULATION AND YEAR: 118 in 1820. INDUSTRIES: brooms, mops, applesauce, fancy goods. NOTABLE SHAKERS: Elijah Wilds, Jonas Nutting, **John Whiteley**, Josephine Jilson. UNIQUE FEATURES: Shirley was always a small community that existed in the shadow of the nearby and larger Harvard society. In fact, those doing Shaker research often make the error of not distinguishing between them when reading surviving diaries and journals. The house of Elijah Wilds had a closet where **Mother Ann** hid to escape persecution. This hiding space was later the subject of a Shaker song.

BRIEF HISTORY: When Mother Ann first visited Harvard, Massachusetts, in June 1781, she found many men and women anxious for a new way of living the **Christlife**. This interest went far beyond the **Square House** or the home of Isaac Willard, the earliest places Mother stayed in Harvard. A sizable group came from the nearby town of Shirley and the neighboring town of Lancaster. Most notable among this group were the brothers Elijah and Ivory Wilds. They lived in the extreme southern part of Shirley, along the Lancaster town line. So great was their faith that Father **Joseph Meacham** allowed them to erect a **Meeting House** in 1792. The next year the scattered families were gathered into full **gospel order**. Elijah Wilds' property became the First or **Church Family** while Ivory Wilds' lands formed the North or Second Family. Over the line in Lancaster a South Family was started in 1797. This family was the Gathering Order until 1827 when it was broken up. In 1849, it was opened again when John Whiteley and his family joined. It closed a final time in 1873.

Shirley and **Tyringham** were the smallest of the original 11 Shaker societies. Historians have wondered why it was ever founded, given that Harvard was so close by and neither society was ever very large. In 1790 there were 43 Shakers at Shirley. By 1803, this had grown to 92. Gradually this increased until 1820 when 118 people lived there. After this date, the community averaged 75 Shakers until 1860. By that time, children made up a high percentage of the membership. In the meantime, the society had contracted a huge debt due to the construction of a factory in 1848. For a small society with limited resources, the factory venture was too optimistic. The lack of converts and the financial troubles caused a severe downturn in the fortunes of the community. **Elder** and **trustee** John Whiteley did a fine job at management, but the talent to assist him was limited, as were the cash resources. When the society celebrated its centennial in 1893, hope was expressed that they could continue if they only got some new members. The lands and the buildings were in good condition, but by 1900 there were just 12 Shakers remaining. Elder John's health gave way that winter and he was so incapacitated that he had to be relieved of his duties in 1904. Since there was no Shaker man available to replace him, Elder **Joseph Holden** of the **Central Ministry** was appointed a trustee of the society, and Henry Hollister was sent from **Hancock** to run the farm. This was in preparation of closing the community and selling the land. From 1905 until 1908, Holden lived at Shirley and conducted the general business of the **Ministry** from there. In October 1908, the Commonwealth of Massachusetts bought the holdings for an industrial school for boys. On 6 January 1909, the last Shakers left Shirley for Harvard.

LAST SHAKER: Annie Belle Tuttle (1868–1945). Born in New Hampshire, she joined the Church Family at Shirley in 1876. When Shirley closed in 1909, she moved to Harvard with the rest of the community. Ten years later when Harvard was dissolved, she moved to the **North Family** at **Mount Lebanon**, where she died in 1945. In fact, she is the last Shaker to die at Mount Lebanon while Shakers still lived there.

SISTER. This is the proper title that precedes the name of every Shaker female of legal age. The exception is the title of **eldress**, which is used for those of that rank. The word sister shows the equality of all Shakers and recognizes the religious significance of their lives. Worldly journalists have sometimes substituted the title Miss when writing about certain Shakers. During the middle years of the 20th century, some Shaker sisters seem to have encouraged this usage.

SLINGERLAND, (JOHN) JOSEPH RAMSEY (1844–1920). There are people who become infamous. Among those who study the Shakers, no one would deny that Joseph Slingerland is universally acknowledged to be a "bad" Shaker. Not only did he waste hundreds of thousands of dollars of community funds, he also tried to use money rightly belonging to others for his own personal use. Unlike one of the **trustees** of **Sabbathday Lake** who did this, he never ended up serving a prison sentence. Nonetheless, his story is an interesting one and offers a clear glimpse into the climate of late 19th-century Shakerism.

John Ramsey Slingerland was born in New York City on 9 August 1844. On 31 January 1854, he and his younger brother, Aaron Shields Slingerland (1846–left 1859), were taken to the **New Lebanon** Shakers by their mother. Her husband had recently committed suicide and she could not raise her two boys. She did not join the community herself but left her sons, who were admitted to the **First Order of the Church**. In those days, Shaker boys went to school only during the winter terms. On 3 February 1854, the Slingerland boys joined the class, which was taught by **Calvin Reed** and Henry G. Hollister. Almost at once, John started using the name Joseph. In fact, since all legal documents and journal entries that refer to him use the name Joseph, many do not even know that his birth name was John.

His time as a student in the Shaker school ended on 11 March 1859 when he was 14. The census of 1860 lists him as a shoemaker at the First Order, and for the four-month winter term starting in 1867, he assisted William Calver as a teacher in the school. In 1868 he signed the **covenant**. Very little else is known about his early adult years. Census enumerations list him as a farmer. The only position he held within the family was that of farm deacon. It is not even certain when or where he obtained a medical degree. Yet there is a hint to indicate the type of life for which he would later be remembered. While at **Mount Lebanon**, he misused money to purchase a farm for his mother in Agawam, Massachusetts. No lasting repercussions of this action, however, seem to have been taken against him.

Individual Shakers should always be studied in the context of the larger community. Although Brother Joseph had been a First Order of the Church Shaker at Mount Lebanon since childhood, he was part of a network of societies that existed in many states. As members living in the **center of union**, the Mount Lebanon Shakers had a responsibility to help other communities, and they did. For example, in 1883, Andrew Barrett was sent from the Church at Mount Lebanon to be **elder** of the Church at **Harvard**. Many Shakers, especially after the **Lower Canaan Family** closed, were also sent to Harvard during the 1880s. Starting in the mid-1890s, almost 40 Mount Lebanon Shakers, mostly from **Upper Canaan**, were sent to **Enfield, Connecticut**. That Joseph Slingerland should go to **South Union, Kentucky**, was not an unusual event, as some have claimed. In addition, it has been said that the **Ministry** was trying to transfer one of their problems. It is true that he had taken community funds to purchase the farm in Agawam, Massachusetts, for his mother. Those familiar with the Ministry of that time (**Daniel Boler**, **Giles Avery**, Eliza Ann Taylor, and **Harriet Bullard**), however, know that they were leaders of impeccable character. They desired what was good and would not have placed someone where that person could do wrong. Such a person would be much easier to supervise nearer to home. The most likely reason for Slingerland's move is that the western Shakers needed help. Brother Joseph was one of the few relatively young men. He was confident and made a good appearance. In spite of his minor past offense, it is highly doubtful that anyone envisioned the trouble he would cause.

Whatever may be the reason he was sent to the West, the Ministry had confidence in him. He arrived at South Union in 1888, where he seems to have proved himself by trying to force those who were not following community rules to leave. The Ministry visited South Union in 1889 and praised him for his perseverance in these efforts in spite of opposition from some members. On 19 April 1889, he moved to **Union Village** since he was to be made second in the Ministry of the West. On 12 May, he was officially appointed to a newly formed Union Village Ministry that had control over **Pleasant Hill** and South Union, Kentucky, in addition to the Ohio communities. This gave him a good deal of power, which he was already using in advising the Ministry of Mount Lebanon to close **North Union** and **Watervliet, Ohio**. Also working to his advantage, Elder Matthew Carter, first in the western Ministry, suddenly died of a heart attack 24 July 1890. This left Elder Joseph in the highest leadership position and, in theory, in charge of all the Shakers in Ohio and Kentucky. Just two years earlier he had been a Mount Lebanon Shaker who had never even been to the West.

Elder Joseph wasted no time in coming up with many ideas to spend the money that had been realized from the sale of North Union. In cooperation with the **trustees** of Union Village, he remodeled and repaired many buildings, planted new fruit trees, renewed the gardens, put in miles of expensive fencing, and even started a wine business. His most memorable achievement, however, was the extravagant renovation of the old **Office** at the **Center Family**. The result was a building that had ornate decorations, porches, towers, and many kinds of marble. It eventually received the nickname **Marble Hall**.

When the Shaker communities at **Watervliet** and Mount Lebanon, New York, became interested in buying land in Florida to start a new colony, Elder Joseph helped them look at suitable sites. Inspired by their initiative, he decided that perhaps the Ohio and Kentucky Shakers might found a new colony as well. After examining various places he purchased two former plantations on the Georgia coast in 1898. Later that year, after the first location did not work out, he bought additional land in **White Oak**. Here a longer lasting community was founded. Lands were sold or remortgaged to pay for White Oak. To finance some of his speculations, Elder Joseph closed the community at Watervliet, Ohio, and attempted to sell the property. He had been trying to accomplish this since 1889 when North Union closed. The extent of his machinations started to be revealed in 1901, when Union Village trustee **James Fennessey** filed a lawsuit to prevent Elder Joseph and first Ministry Eldress Elizabeth Downing from using community funds for their own purposes. As his record was examined, it was discovered that about $400,000 had been recklessly spent in speculative ventures that had no hope of ever making a positive return. The acquisition of a building in Chicago, a cemetery in Memphis, and a hotel in St. Paul, Minnesota, were just a few of his reckless acts.

When White Oak had to be abandoned along with the magnificent buildings the Shakers had just built, the **Central Ministry** removed both Elder Joseph and Eldress Elizabeth. Rather than live under supervision at Union Village and where his mistakes would be constantly recalled, he moved to the Florida Shakers at **Narcoossee**. That next year he tried to move to South Union. Perhaps he had the intention of somehow taking over one of their abandoned dwellings. The community protested so much, however, that he was forced to leave. He had some hopes of taking over the community at **Shirley**, which was closing and up for sale. Elder **Joseph Holden** of the **Central Ministry** actually lived at Shirley for a number of years in preparation of its liquidation. He had no intention of allowing that valuable property to be squandered, and Joseph Slingerland moved to Union Village before joining the **Church Family** at **Hancock, Massachusetts**, on 15 April 1907. A few girls who grew up at Hancock have left oral histories and some contain reminiscences about him. They recall being cautioned about having anything to do with him and that he was very strange acting. On 30 September 1910, he left Hancock for South Union, where he died of a stroke on 24 September 1920.

Joseph Slingerland's legacy is as an example of someone given ultimate power yet totally incapable of managing anything. He wasted hundreds of thousands of dollars on ridiculous schemes by mortgaging property and spending the proceeds from the sale of former Shaker communities. He forced the society at Watervliet, Ohio, to close and almost bankrupted Union Village, one of the most valuable of all Shaker communities. After he was removed from the Ministry, he roamed from community to community seeking out a new place of which to take advantage. In the earliest years of this quest he was in the company of a young sister named Frances Cary from South Union. The supreme irony is that he was first in the Ministry of the West. His primary duties should have been spiritual. It could be asked if he ever performed this side of his duties or if he actually even believed in Shakerism as he grew older. This is a sad indictment against someone who grew up in the highest echelon of the Shakers, the First Order of the Church at Mount Lebanon.

SODUS, NEW YORK (1826–1836). In 1815, Abijah Pelham and his family moved to Ohio from Lyons, Wayne County, New York. Not long after this they joined the Shakers at Union Village. This caused great excitement in Wayne County. When Pelham returned there in 1820 on business, he stayed at his son Joseph's house in Galen. Many people became curious to know more about the Shakers, and after he got back to Union Village, Abijah sent his son *The Testimony of Christ's Second Appearing*. This book was read by anyone interested. In 1825, **Richard Pelham** of the Shaker society at North Union, Joseph's brother, visited Wayne County on business and also as a missionary. He preached anywhere he was allowed. Throughout 1825, more and more people became Shakers, some journeying to **Watervliet** and **New Lebanon** to unite there.

The large number of converts and the prospect for many more prompted the Shakers to make a permanent society in the area. In 1826, the Shaker paid $12,600 for 1,300 acres of land at Sodus from Robert C. Nichols. On 1 March 1826, the Shakers took possession and began to gather. **Elder** Jeremiah Talcott and Eldress **Polly Lawrence** from New Lebanon were appointed leaders. They were assisted by John Lockwood and Lucy Brown. In spite of the unexpected death of Eldress Polly that next July, the Sodus community flourished. At once, 200 acres were under cultivation and there was a gristmill, two **dwelling houses**, stables, barns, and other small buildings. That year there were 72 Sodus Shakers. By 1835, the community had grown to almost 150. That next year, however, the Shakers learned a canal had been proposed that would go through their property. By New York state law, the Sodus Canal Company would have the right to seize any land it wished. As a result, the Shakers decided to move to another location. In November they sold their land and 23 buildings to the canal company and purchased almost 1,700 acres further inland at **Groveland** in Livingston County. Ironically, the canal was never built and, within two years, the Shakers were asked to take their property back. This they declined to do and the continued history after 1836 of what once was the Sodus Shakers more properly belongs to that of Groveland.

SONGS. For many **believers** and for those outside the community as well, Shaker songs are what first touched their hearts in the search for the divine. It has been estimated that there are between 8,000 and

10,000 Shaker songs in various variations in surviving hymnals. When it is considered that at any one time there were not more than 4,500 Shakers, including children, this is a remarkable number of extant songs.

There are 50 early tunes attributed to **Mother Ann Lee**, Father **William Lee**, Father **James Whittaker**, and **John Hocknell**. Many of these are for the **dance**, though some were meant to be sung. They reflect the free and fairly unorganized worship of the first Shakers. By the 1780s, however, Father **Joseph Meacham** sought to have more order in worship and the use of solemn songs became widespread. These were **laboring songs**, sung in connection with worship **exercises** also known as dances. These songs did not have words, and many were derived from popular ballads. They used vocables, words composed from various sounds and letters without regard to meaning. In 1805, the Shakers opened their missionary efforts in Ohio and Kentucky. At the time, there was a great need to state Shaker beliefs in verses so that all could understand. As a result, the solemn songs quickly gave way to long, doctrinally worded hymns with recognizable folk-tune settings. In 1813, 140 of these were published as *Millennial Praises*. This is the first published Shaker songbook. During this time, Mother **Lucy Wright** introduced motions into songs to help keep the tempo.

In time various types of Shaker songs developed. The anthem, for example, was introduced at **New Lebanon** in 1812. Derived from New England singing schools, the anthem is a long song with a prose text. These were prevalent in Shaker music from 1812 until 1822 and then later between 1837 and 1847 during the **Era of Manifestations**. They recorded the long songs received by the **instruments**. Also there were special songs used as funerals or to welcome visitors. Songs that used more detailed motions than just the raising and lowering of the arms were called **motion songs**.

From the time of Father Joseph, Shaker song was closely allied to the exercises that were done in worship. Exercises created from the 1780s—for example, the Holy Order and the Regular Step—influenced the solemn laboring of the songs. As the Quick Dance, the Round Dance, and **marches** were developed, short songs were sung at worship to give the participants a rest. Songs used during exercises began to have words in 1811. By the 1820s worded laboring songs were common and accompanied the Round, the Hollow Square exercises, and the Circular and Compound marches. More exercises were developed as a result of the Era of Manifestations. Thousands of **gift songs** from the Spirit world also entered the Shaker repertoire.

After the Civil War, the New Hampshire Shakers became interested in changing Shaker singing by introducing methods used by non-Shakers, including organ accompaniment and four-part harmonies. Nicholas A. Briggs (1841–left 1895) of **Canterbury** and James G. Russell (1843–1888) of **Enfield, New Hampshire**, traveled to various communities to advocate music improvements. Since singing and the exercises used in worship were connected, a change in singing style had wide-ranging consequences. When organ music and harmonies came into worship, the exercises and marches faded out. Since Shaker membership had aged and was so diminished, this was a natural adaptation to changing times. Some Shaker societies ended exercising at worship in the 1870s. Other used it less and less, until by 1900 it was almost nonexistent. The last marches were done at **Sabbathday Lake** in 1903 and the last dances at Canterbury in 1913. The final holdout seems, as in many other aspects, to have been **Alfred**, where young people continued to march until 1930.

Sister **R. Mildred Barker**, who grew up at Alfred, made it a point to learn as many songs as possible. She and her contemporaries learned from elderly **sisters** songs that had not been current for decades. Since public meeting was reopened in 1963, visitors have heard some songs from an early period of Shaker music history.

Most of the information for this entry is from the landmark work *The Shaker Spiritual* by Daniel W. Patterson. *See also* LETTERAL NOTATION.

SONYEA, NEW YORK. See GROVELAND, NEW YORK.

SOULE, GERTRUDE MAY (1894–1988). She was born on 19 August 1894 in Topsham, Maine. In 1906 she joined the **Sabbathday Lake** Shakers. As a young **sister**, she contributed to the fancy goods trade.

In 1925, she left the community to live with the woman who had been Elder William's nurse. Together they ran a gas station on the Maine coast. Although no longer a part of the community at Sabbathday Lake, she kept in contact with a number of the sisters, especially **Eldress Prudence Stickney**, who had been her **caretaker** and mentor. After her companion died in a car accident in 1937, her thoughts turned to coming back to the Shakers. Eldress Prudence encouraged her in this. On 9 December 1940 she returned to the community but left again on 20 September 1942. Finally, she rejoined for the last time in January 1943.

Eldress Prudence had been sick for many years, and by the mid-1940s it was apparent that she could no longer lead the community. The **Parent Ministry**, however, delayed replacing her for many years, and Eldress Prudence died in 1950. At that time the Parent Ministry chose Gertrude Soule to be the eldress. After this appointment, she signed the **covenant** and donned the cap, which she wore until her death. Her appointment was the first one done at Pittsfield, where the Ministry had moved in 1946.

When Eldress **Emma B. King** reconstituted the Parent Ministry in 1957, it was her intention to have two other **Canterbury** sisters, Ida Crook and Aida Elam, serve with her. Only reluctantly did she include a Sabbathday Lake sister, Eldress Gertrude Soule, in place of Aida Elam. Eldress Gertrude's appointment to the reconstituted **Ministry** in 1957 was the last one done at Pittsfield since Eldress Emma had her attorney draft an amendment to the covenant moving the seat of the Ministry to Canterbury.

Sister **R. Mildred Barker** had been the spiritual leader of the Sabbathday Lake Shakers since the late 1940s when the community had petitioned for her to become the eldress. Instead she had been made a **trustee** in 1950. Nonetheless, her deep Shaker spirituality influenced the community. When new members began joining, her guidance was essential. All of this made Eldress Gertrude very uncomfortable. She paid one of her periodic visits to Canterbury on 15 September 1971 and decided not to come back to Sabbathday Lake. For months, the Sabbathday Lake Shakers did not know of her intention to stay at Canterbury and looked for her return. Her desire to live out the rest of her life at Canterbury became clear in December 1971 when the reconstituted Ministry, of which Eldress Gertrude was the lead, appointed Sister Mildred Barker as second eldress of Sabbathday Lake.

Eldress Gertrude's remaining life at Canterbury is fondly recalled by those who knew her during those years. She loved to greet visitors and was often seen around the entrance to the **Trustees' Office** where she lived. She died in her sleep on 11 June 1988. Since the remaining Ministry sister, Eldress **Bertha Lindsay**, did not appoint a replacement, the reconstituted Ministry ended with Eldress Gertrude's death. The Shaker covenant, amended in the 1940s, states that the Ministry may have no more than three, but cannot have fewer than two, members.

SOUTH UNION, KENTUCKY (1807–1922). SPIRITUAL NAME: Jasper Valley. FEAST GROUND: Holy Ground. BISHOPRIC: South Union until 1889 when it came under the jurisdiction of **Union Village**. FAMILIES: Center, North, East, West. MAXIMUM POPULATION AND YEAR: 350 in 1827. INDUSTRIES: brooms, garden seeds, canned and preserved fruit, raising breeds of cattle, hogs, sheep, and chickens. NOTABLE SHAKERS: **Harvey Eades**, Logan Johns, Jane Cowan, Nancy Moore. UNIQUE FEATURES: The post office once run by the Shakers still exists. It is the last remaining Shaker post office and is housed in the 1917 structure built by the Shakers. Across the street from this is a large tavern and inn also once run by the Shakers. Today the museum at South Union runs the inn. Finally, South Union was the last of the western Shaker communities to close.

BRIEF HISTORY: When the first Shaker missionaries came to the West in 1805, the first state they visited was Kentucky. They arrived at the church at Paint Lick where Matthew Houston was the pastor. After visiting a church at Cane Ridge, the missionaries went into Ohio where they met **Malcolm Worley** at **Turtle Creek**. As a result of their efforts at Turtle Creek, the Shaker societies at Union Village and **Watervliet, Ohio**, were founded in 1805 and 1806. This success, however, did not cause them to forget about Kentucky. In October 1807, Matthew Houston, eastern Shaker missionary **Issachar Bates**, and **Richard McNemar** from Turtle Creek went on an extensive preaching tour in Logan County around the Gasper River. Among the first converts were John and Jesse McComb, Charles and Sally Eades, Neal Patterson, and John Rankin. During the next few years many people joined the Shakers around the Gasper area, and in 1808 the name of the Shaker settlement became South Union. By 1810 membership rose to 165 and, in 1811, **Benjamin Youngs**, Joseph Allen, Molly Goodrich, and Mercy Pickett became the first members of the South Union **Ministry**.

There were over 300 Shakers at South Union in the late 1820s, but numbers generally averaged about 250 until after the Civil War. In 1813, a **family** was formed at Black Lick, four miles west of South Union. Eventually this became the home of South Union's children. Though sometimes referred to as the School Family, in 1822 this site was renamed Watervliet in honor of the place in New York where Ministry **elder** Benjamin Youngs was from. It closed in 1837. From 1817 until 1829, the South Union Shakers also had a mill family at Drake's Creek, 16 miles away. This was to increase their milling power in addition to the fulling, grist, and sawmills they already operated. They venture did not prove to be a success. (Boice, Covington, Spence, *Maps of the Shaker West*, 51–58).

The most important event that affected life at South Union was the Civil War. In addition to having a devastating impact on their economic life, the conduct of the war resulted in a constant ebb and flow of armies from both sides across their land and, consequently, a severe disruption of community life. Ministry eldress Nancy Moore kept a diary that has been published and details these long war years.

In 1852, 237 Shakers lived at South Union. Right after the Civil War, membership spiked again at over 300, but this was short lived, and a serious decline set in that diminished the number to 99 in 1880 and 55 by 1900. With the large farm, scores of buildings, and aging membership, it was inevitable that the society would have to close. In preparation for this, furniture auctions began in 1920 and continued until April 1922. In 1921, the **Central Ministry** made preparation to sell the property. The nine surviving community members, two men and seven women, were given the choice to accept a $10,000 stipend or be provided for at the Shaker society at **Mount Lebanon, New York**. Seven accepted the money and began to leave immediately. The last of them was gone by the end of April 1922. Josie Bridges moved to Mount Lebanon that month, followed by Logan Johns that December. On 15 March 1922, South Union was sold to two men interested in cutting lumber on the land. When this was accomplished, the land was resold at auction on 22 September 1922. The 4,000 acres were divided into 60-acre parcels, and 5,000 people turned out to go through the Shaker buildings. In all, $229,000 was realized from the sale of land. Oscar S. Bond of Louisville bought the part of the property that contained most of the Shaker buildings, and he operated a large farm on the site for many years. With the sale of South Union, 117 years of western Shakerism ended.

LAST SHAKER: Although Annie Farmer did not die until 1942, she was not a Shaker at the time of her death. In 1922 she chose to receive the $10,000 stipend and leave the community. In contrast, Logan Johns (1840–1924) after South Union closed joined the **North Family** at Mount Lebanon. He died there in 1924.

SPIRITUAL MARRIAGE. This concept seems to have found its way into Shaker communities after so many **Adventists** joined them between 1845 and 1846. By that time, the Shakers were having many difficulties attracting sufficient numbers of capable adults, and most of the children they raised were leaving. The idea of spiritual marriage or spiritual wives was to allow worthy young members to pair off and have children. These couples were to be carefully chosen and the only purposes of their unions would be to have and raise offspring. As a consequence, the children would be pure and could help fill up the ranks.

The North Family at **Canterbury** and the **Church Family** at **Harvard** seem to be the places where a few members were the most enthusiastic for spiritual marriage. Never was this concept given any credence by the **Ministry at New Lebanon**. Members who insisted on this change in Shaker policy were forced to leave. *See also* GROSVENOR, ROXALANA.

SPIRITUAL NAMES OF THE COMMUNITIES. In 1842, during the **Era of Manifestations**, also known as the Era of Mother's Work, Shaker communities received spiritual or mystical names. For a few years some Shakers used these names in journals, diaries, or letters, but the practice died out until recent times. Today the **Sabbathday Lake** Shakers often refer to their home as "Chosen Land." In some Shaker **bishoprics** the names follow a pattern. Studying the spiritual names gives insight into Shaker topology and theology. Here is a list of the communities and their spiritual names by the bishoprics as they existed in 1842:

Bishopric	Community	Spiritual Name
Maine	Alfred, Maine	Holy Land
	Sabbathday Lake, Maine	Chosen Land
New Hampshire	Canterbury, New Hampshire	Holy Ground
	Enfield, New Hampshire	Chosen Vale
Harvard	Harvard, Massachusetts	Lovely Vineyard
	Shirley, Massachusetts	Pleasant Garden
Hancock	Hancock, Massachusetts	City of Peace
	Tyringham, Massachusetts	City of Love
	Enfield, Connecticut	City of Union
New Lebanon	New Lebanon, New York	Holy Mount
	Watervliet, New York	Wisdom's Valley
Union Village	Union Village, Ohio	Wisdom's Paradise
	Watervliet, Ohio	Vale of Peace
	White Water, Ohio	Lonely Plain of Tribulation
North Union	North Union, Ohio	Valley of God's Pleasure
South Union	South Union, Kentucky	Jasper Valley
Pleasant Hill	Pleasant Hill, Kentucky	Pleasant Hill
Groveland	Groveland, New York	Union Branch

Narcoossee, Florida, was founded in 1896 and had the name Olive Branch. This name had nothing to do with the Era of Manifestations and referred to Shaker efforts to revive their fortunes by new ventures in places with warmer climates. This was late for the use of such names. Several Shaker communities did not have spiritual names: **West Union, Indiana**, dissolved before spiritual names were used; **Philadelphia, Pennsylvania**, was founded after the Era of Manifestations; and **White Oak, Georgia**, was very short-lived and founded after the Era of Manifestations. The community at **Gorham, Maine**, was closed in 1819, but received a spiritual name in 1850. **Elder Abraham Perkins** of the New Hampshire **Ministry** called it Union Branch.

SPRINGFIELD PRESBYTERY. On 10 September 1803 five Presbyterian ministers who had been suspected of having unorthodox views
decided to leave the Presbytery of Kentucky and form their own presbytery, the Presbytery of Springfield. This group continued to drift
out of Calvinism, and on 28 June 1804 they dissolved the Presbytery
of Springfield. Henceforth they were called **New Lights**, revivalists,
schismatics, or Christians. Eventually Robert Marshall and John
Thompson went back to Presbyterianism in 1810. Barton W. Stone
stayed a New Light. **Richard McNemar** and **John Dunlavy** became
Shakers in 1805. The dissolution of the Springfield Presbytery and
the conversion of so many to Shakerism permanently weakened the
Presbyterian church in that part of the country.

SQUARE HOUSE. This is the name of the large square house built in
1769 for **Shadrack Ireland** in **Harvard, Massachusetts**. In 1781,
this house was bought for **Mother Ann** for $536.74, and it became
the base of operations for her missionary tours in eastern Massachusetts. The Square House was always called Mother's House as she
paid for more than half of it herself. This is how strongly she felt
about the place. This house was extensively remodeled by the Shakers, and it was always a point of interest for visiting Shakers to see
the room where Mother Ann slept. The house remained a part of Harvard Shaker village until the property was sold in 1918.

STEWART, AMOS (1802–1884). After 1800, Shakerism attracted
many families that were not related by blood to **Mother's First
Born**. Of the many families that joined at **New Lebanon**, one of the
most influential was the Stewarts. In those days very few children
were taken into the Shakers without at least one parent. The arrival of
the Stewarts is of note because neither of the parents joined the community. Siblings Amos, Charles, Mary, and **Philemon Stewart** were
brought to the **Second Order of the Church** at New Lebanon by
Nathan Kendal, one of the **family's trustees**, on 5 March 1811. Over
time, few children stayed who did not come in with a parent. Once
again, the Stewarts were the exception. Except for Charles, who left
in 1836 when he was 37 years old, the others remained stalwart believers. In fact, both Amos and Philemon Stewart were well-known
and important Shakers.

Amos Stewart was born on 9 May 1802 in Mason, New Hampshire. Stewart grew up at the Second Order of the Church. This family seems to have produced more than its share of excellent leaders. Many of the men who would later have positions of leadership at New Lebanon and in the **Ministry** came from the Second Order. The number of boys who stayed was related to the capability and interest of the **elders**. Inspiring leadership of this type was Amos Stewart's greatest gift. He also was a cabinetmaker and had a great interest in anything mechanical. In 1826, when only 23, he became second elder of the Second Order. He was in a position to influence such boys and young men as **Giles Avery**, **Orren Haskins**, **Alonzo Hollister**, and Calvin Reed.

On 31 December 1840, he became first elder of the Second Order with one of his boys, Giles Avery, as second elder. Both of these men shared their deep Shaker faith and a love of woodworking. Stewart continued in this capacity until 1849 when he was appointed to the Ministry to fill the place left vacant by the death of **Ebenezer Bishop**. This appointment was quite an honor. Stewart was the first person to fill a place in the **Ministry of New Lebanon** who had not been selected by one of the original leaders of the Shakers. He was a symbol of the evolution of Shakerism beyond the first believers.

Stewart was the leading force in the Ministry during the difficult decade of the 1850s. This was a time of great instability. The children of Mother's First Born were dying and many young and middle-aged people were leaving. In addition, few adults of quality were seeking admission. This left Stewart and other members of the third generation to cope. What the ultimate fate of Shakerism would have been under his pastoral care will never be known because as an act of goodwill he resigned from the Ministry to be the first elder of the **Second Family** at New Lebanon in 1858. This large family was desperate for stable leadership and Stewart was asked to help them. Thus he willingly gave up being the most powerful man in Shakerdom to help a troubled family.

Going to the Second Family brought them tremendous relief. His stay with them was intended to be brief, but his energy and wisdom guided them for over 25 years until his death on 7 March 1884.

One final story gives insight into his character. For many decades Stewart made **furniture** and helped wherever woodworking needed to be done. In November 1865, he caught his left hand in a planing machine and it was severed. Within a few months, he was back at cabinetmaking using an artificial hand. He even signed pieces of furniture noting that it was made by him using one hand. He epitomized the best type of leader that Shakers had.

STEWART, EZRA (1869–?). He was born in Canada in 1869. His first contact with the Shakers was on 9 July 1898 when he arrived at **Shirley** for a visit for a couple of days. **Elder John Whiteley** gained a favorable impression of him and encouraged him to come back. They met again in Boston on 20 July and the next day returned to Shirley, where **Brother** Ezra was taken on trial. Right away he proved himself an industrious worker and started sewing mops for sale. In so many ways, Brother Ezra seemed the perfect candidate for Shirley. He was only 29 years old, he was a hard worker, and he was a male. By then Shirley only had a handful of members and Elder John, the only man, was 79 years old. The presence of Brother Ezra gave him hope that all might not be lost. In 1900 his hopes were increased when 25-year-old John Pine joined the community. That year Brother Ezra had a very disagreeable confrontation with one of the older **sisters** at Shirley. It has been speculated that she had been unjustly criticizing him for a long while. Whatever the reason, their argument was so severe that Brother Ezra left the community on 23 June 1900. His departure ensured that Shirley would not survive.

He believed he had been treated unfairly and appealed to Elders **Joseph Holden** and **Ira Lawson** of the **Central Ministry**. Since they lived at **Hancock**, they invited him to join them there. Accordingly he was admitted to the **Church Family** at Hancock on 26 June 1900. He signed the **novitiate** covenant on 4 January 1901. His abilities and dedication while at Hancock impressed the **Ministry**, and they sent him to be the leader of the Florida Shakers at **Narcoossee** on 2 February 1903.

His work in Florida was the third and final phase of his life as a Shaker. He took charge of the farm and extended operations as much as possible. In 1908, the county commissioners hired him to go to Tampa and represent the county with an exhibit at the state fair. Not only did he show off the bounty of the land, he discussed the Shaker religion with anyone who would listen. He also had the distinction of escorting the infamous Carrie Nation about the fair. The well-known and feared temperance advocate reminded him of **Mother Ann**. In spite of what may have seemed like a promising venture, the Florida Shaker colony languished. Optimistic reports and postcards depicting the beautiful scenery (and perhaps Ezra Stewart as well) belied the fact that the colony was not gaining any new permanent members. It simply never got over the notoriety caused by the scandal after the mercy-killing of member Sadie Marchant in 1911. In addition, by that time, the **Mount Lebanon** and **Watervliet** societies could not send any helpers to them. When the West was evangelized in 1805, many capable leaders were sent to help them. The greatly depleted populations of all the communities made this impossible in the case of Florida.

Accustomed as he was to the warm climate, Elder Ezra declined to return to Mount Lebanon when the Florida colony closed in 1924. As early as 1910, he had speculated by buying up house lots. After he left the Shakers he continued to buy and sell property in Tampa from 1924 until 1931. In 1934, he was 65 and managed an apartment house there. After this, no knowledge of him is available. When his name is mentioned, it is easy to think of the phrase "unrealized potential" in regard to his life with the Shakers.

STEWART, PHILEMON (1804–1875). Philemon was born on 20 April 1804 in Mason, New Hampshire. His father brought him, along with his three older siblings, to the Shakers at **New Lebanon** on 5 March 1811. He was placed at the **Second Order of the Church** where he grew up. In 1826, he was made an associate of the two **Office deacons**. This would seem to indicate that he was being groomed for future leadership positions. When the **Trustees' Office** at the Church was reorganized in 1828, however, Philemon was sent to become **caretaker** of the boys, a job he held for 10 years. Being in charge of the boys was a disagreeable job for most Shakers, and the task was generally given to young men in the hope that they would have the energy and patience to deal with the boys. This pattern of promotion and then demotion would follow him the rest of his life.

He was a great enthusiast for the latest and best agricultural practices and also became a tireless advocate for "progressive reform" of the Shaker diet. His fervor for causes such as the Graham diet and his inability to appreciate opinions other than his own set him on a collision course with those in charge. His big chance for power came when the **Era of Manifestations** opened in 1837. It was the perfect vehicle for him to assert himself. Immediately he became the principal male medium of the Church at New Lebanon. The messages he received were lengthy and highly critical. Since the **Ministry** supported the manifestations, Philemon's influence grew to such an extent that he was able to attack with impunity those who did not have much faith in the visions, especially the deeply religious Shaker theologian **Calvin Green**. He moved to the **First Order of the Church** in September 1838, and in March 1841 was elevated to the position of second **elder** of the First Order. The following year, by inspiration, he received *A Holy, Sacred and Divine Roll and Book*. This work was in two parts and over 400 pages in length. Specific directions had been received regarding its publication and distribution. In November 1842, he was released as an elder. No doubt this freed him to work on getting his book published in 1843 and sending out 500 copies of part one to rulers in the **world**.

By 1850, most of the enthusiasm for the Era of Manifestations had passed and, in 1854, he was sent to be first elder of the **Second Family** at New Lebanon. It was hoped that he could use his zeal for good in this large family. Almost at once he clashed with the strong female leadership since they would not acquiesce to everything he wanted. The situation worsened until 1858, when he was removed and replaced by his brother **Amos Stewart**. He was sent back to the Church to live, but at the Second Order rather than the First Order.

In May 1860, he was transferred to be second **trustee** of the small Shaker family at **Poland Hill, Maine**. Though he saw it as exile, this assignment was his last chance to prove himself as a capable leader. Elder John Kaime was ineffectual, and trustee Isaiah Wentworth was dishonest. Had Philemon desired to do good and really be a leader, his place in Shaker history might have turned out differently. Too preoccupied with his own ideas, however, he clashed with the female leadership of the family, was frequently absent, and developed an inappropriate friendship with a young **sister**. He issued an ultimatum that demanded the removal of the eldresses at Poland Hill and his elevation to first in the Maine Ministry or he would return to **Mount Lebanon**. The leaders of the Maine Shakers requested he be withdrawn to New Lebanon. He went back to the Second Order in April 1863 and devoted the remainder of his life to writing critical reports on the condition of Shaker life. This did not mean, however, that he cut himself off from the community. For example, during the great fire of February 1875, he helped care for Elder **Daniel Boler** who had been injured fighting the conflagration. The turmoil of the fire no doubt hastened his own demise on 20 February 1875.

STICKNEY, PRUDENCE (1860–1950). Even before she was born, Prudence Stickney was promised to the Shakers. She was the 13th child of William and Charlotte Stickney. Her father knew **Elder Otis Sawyer** and he told him that he would someday bring the child to the Shakers. Accordingly, she was given to Elder Otis in 1865. He took her to live at **Poland Hill**. When she later joined the **Church Family**, she first came under the influence of Sophia Mace, who was her teacher in the Shaker school. Later, as a young **sister**, she was nurtured by Sister **Aurelia Mace**. "Little Prudie," as she was called, was one of Sister Aurelia's "nine gems." These were girls who joined the Shakers after the Civil War and, except for one, stayed faithful til death. Taken as a group, they were hardworking and devout. Because of them and the excellent leadership of Elder **William Dumont** and Eldress **Lizzie Noyes**, **Sabbathday Lake** was able to retain a position of strength well into the 20th century.

Having grown up so loved, Sister Prudie got the opportunity to serve as a mother to others when she was appointed assistant **caretaker** of girls in 1882. She helped Sister Ada Cummings, who was in charge. In addition, she worked in the fancy goods trade, at cloakmaking, and in the kitchen. In 1890, she replaced Sister Serena Douglas as second eldress. Though this appointment lasted but a year, it was a prelude to the decades she would soon serve in the elders' lot. By 1892, she was once again the second eldress, a position she held until 1926 when she became first eldress. During this time, she was dominated by the larger-than-life energy and spirit of Eldress Elizabeth Noyes, first eldress. Eldress Lizzie had successfully pulled the community out of debt and no aspect of life at Sabbathday Lake escaped her notice. Eldress Prudence, by contrast, was frail, gentle, and easy to manipulate. Throughout Sabbathday Lake's golden age, 1880 to 1926, Eldress Lizzie led the sisters in every way. This does not imply that Eldress Prudence was discontent and wished it to be otherwise. She was willing to be subordinate and spent her energy on the young sisters, though ultimately none of these persevered as Shakers. In 1915, she took on the added burden of being second **Ministry** eldress, again under Eldress Lizzie.

One of the most interesting facets of Eldress Prudence's life was that she was a firm supporter of Herbert Hoover. Before, during, and after his presidency, she carried on a correspondence with him. It has been suggested that, since she really did not follow politics, she was attracted to him because he was a Quaker. In 1939, he came to Sabbathday Lake to visit her. School was closed for the occasion so that the children might attend the reception.

Every Shaker leader since 1850 has faced the sad situation of diminishing numbers. The bright optimism of the 1890s and early 20th century dimmed at Sabbathday Lake as the "gems" died and those on whom much hope had been placed left the community. Among these were Laura and Lizzie Bailey, **Gertrude Soule**, Ada Frost, Ethel and Irene Corcoran, Emma Freeman, and Ruth Miller. When Eldress Lizzie died in 1926, Eldress Prudence was made trustee and first eldress. For the first time in her life, she stood alone as the one in charge of everything. Her counterpart, Elder William, was 75 years old and in failing health. The decisions she made were not always in the ultimate best interest of the community, but made to appease or help someone who had sought her favor. She worked tirelessly to build up the home, especially during the years of the Great Depression and World War II. Never having had the chance to develop real leadership skills, however, she relied heavily upon Sisters Jennie Mathers and Iona Sedgeley to help her manage. Their untimely deaths in the 1940s and her own failing health left Sabbathday Lake without an official leader. Sister **R. Mildred Barker** fulfilled this role until 1950. That year Eldress Prudence died and Sister Gertrude Soule replaced her, not as the choice of the community, but as the wish of the **Parent Ministry** and Eldress Prudence. *See also* TEN GEMS OF PRICELESS WORTH.

SUTTON, (MARY) JANE (1832–1920). She was born in Kentucky and brought to live at the **Pleasant Hill** Shakers in 1834 when she was two years old. During the **Era of Manifestations** she received at least one **song**. She worked at housekeeping and was a seamstress. By 1880 she was also a **trustee** of the **Center Family**. In 1896, a businessman named A. M. Barkley from Lexington, Kentucky, opened a hotel at the East Family. Jane Sutton managed this "Shakertown Inn." Her involvement with the hotel brought her a rebuke from the **Central Ministry**, but she continued nonetheless. When Pleasant Hill was sold, she continued to live there and was cared for by the new owner, according to the agreement made in the terms of sale. She died in 1920.

– T –

TAYLOR, LEILA SARAH (1854–1923). Leila Taylor did not join the Shakers until she was middle aged. Indeed, two-thirds of her life was spent outside the community. She was born on 11 December 1854 in Westfield, Massachusetts. Her father Wesley Taylor was a homeopathic physician; her mother was Sarah Moore. During the 1870s she graduated from Boston University and began teaching in various schools throughout the Connecticut Valley of Massachusetts. In 1897, she became the principal of Wayland Center School, outside of Boston. She also helped teach in the high school and upper grammar school grades.

For many years she had been a member of the Grange, since that organization valued female members and treated them equally. In 1900, while traveling with her friend Mary Alice Simpson, she visited **Mount Lebanon**. Both of them were impressed with the peacefulness of the scene and decided to join. They resigned their jobs and were admitted to the **North Family** that July.

Since she had been an English teacher, Leila was given the task to write Home Notes about the North Family for the local newspaper the *Chatham Courier*. Just seven months before, the Shaker newspaper the *Manifesto* had been discontinued. "Home Notes" had been a regular feature of the paper. In addition, since journals from the period do not survive, her columns provide a detailed look into what was going on at the North Family during the first dozen years of the 20th century. She also wrote the obituary notices when family members died. These often included a poem she had composed for the occasion.

Sister Leila is more familiar to people studying the Shakers today than she was to those of her own time. Her fame was immortalized because she typed and edited *Shakerism: Its Meaning and Message.* When **Eldress Anna White** set out to write this history of the Shakers, she needed someone who could help her put it in publishable form. Sister Leila had been a member only a couple of years when Eldress Anna began to dictate the work to her. Many assume that, since her name appears as a coauthor, she was an eldress. In fact, she had only just signed the **covenant** in 1903, less than a year before the work was published. In 1910, after Eldress Anna died, she became second eldress of the North Family. She stood in association with Eldress Sarah Burger. In 1914 Eldress Sarah went into the **Central Ministry**, but she also retained her place as first at the North Family. This left the actual running of the family to Eldress Leila. Her burdens increased in 1918 when she became a society **trustee**. All during this time, she tried to gather souls to the Shakers. As the virtual leader of the North Family, it was her job to greet inquirers and encourage those who might have an interest in joining the community. She died unexpectedly of a stroke in June 1923. After her death, little, if anything, was done to encourage people to join the Shakers at Mount Lebanon. Eldress Leila was the last leader at the North to be solely in the elders' lot. With her death, the North Family ceased to be a **Gathering Order**, although it was not closed until 1947.

TEN GEMS OF PRICELESS WORTH. When **Sabbathday Lake trustee Aurelia Mace** published her book *The Alethia* in 1897, she dedicated it to "'My Ten,' Gems of Priceless Worth." These were nine girls brought up at Sabbathday Lake between 1861 and 1886, a period of 25 years. When 28-year-old **Lizzie Noyes** joined the society in 1873, she became the tenth gem. All except one of these women remained faithful. Even the one who did leave did not do so until she was almost 44 years old, and she stayed very close to the community. Thus these women gave Sabbathday Lake a strong impetus and assured its continuance well into the 20th century.

The original nine gems were as follows: Clara Blanchard (1852–1910), Lillie Dale Bubier (1852–1910), Sirena Douglas (1853–1924), Sarah Fletcher (1853–1923), Amanda Stickney (1854–1927), Mary Ella Douglas (1855–1893), Nellie O. Whitney

(1857– left 1901), **Prudence Stickney** (1860–1950), and Ada Cummings (1862–1926). The tenth gem was Lizzie Noyes (1845–1926).

TESTIMONY. In the early days this term was used in a general sense to mean the gospel. In this way, the testimony could be opened by a person to an individual or to the **world**. During the 19th century various Shakers wrote down how they came to be Shakers. These were called testimonies and were used for didactic purposes. Individual testimonies may be found in collections of Shaker manuscripts, but the most important and well-known testimonies were collected and published in 1816. These *Testimonies of the Life, Character, Revelations and Doctrines of Mother Ann Lee and the Elders with Her* provide a detailed account of **Mother Ann** and her first followers. In addition, the word testimony is used in the title of the first major treatise on Shaker theology, *The Testimony of Christ's Second Appearing*.

Testimony also refers to a person's contribution to the worship service. During Shaker worship, an individual who has something to contribute normally stands and offers a reflection on the readings, **songs**, or previous testimonies. This is all part of the work of the meeting and everyone is encouraged to offer a testimony.

THEOLOGY. In 1968, Brother **Theodore Johnson** of **Sabbathday Lake** wrote, "The Shaker way never produced a theology, if by theology we mean a formal, organized body of thought in regard to the godhead, his relation to man, and man's place in His scheme of history" (Johnson, *Life in the Christ Spirit: Observations on Shaker Theology*, 3). Realizing this, it is nonetheless possible to examine fundamental theological topics.

For the Shaker, God is the all-knowing, all-present, all-loving, all-powerful Great First Cause. Being pure Spirit, God has no sex as we understand it. When Shakers refer to God as "Father-Mother," it means they are attributing to the godhead the traditionally male characteristics of strength and power and the traditionally female characteristics of compassion and mercy.

Shakerism did not have a long time to develop a complete system of Christology. Before the finer points could be detailed, the declension of numbers had set in. The main currents, however, point to the idea that **Jesus** was not the Christ or the anointed one from his birth, but from the time of his baptism by John in the Jordan. The virgin birth and miracles of Jesus' early life are accepted as proof that he was chosen. Moreover, Jesus taught a life of holiness and purity that entailed self-denial and taking up the daily cross against sin. His death on the cross did not gain redemption or take away sins for humanity because the blood of one person cannot do this for another. It is only by living a life of repentance and giving up sin that an individual person can accomplish this. After his death, the followers of Jesus looked for him to come again. This was realized by a return of the Christ Spirit in **Mother Ann Lee**. "Mother Ann was not Christ, nor did she claim to be. She was simply the first of many Believers wholly embued by His Spirit, wholly consumed by His love" (Johnson, 7). When Mother Ann spoke, it was Christ in her that did so. This quiet and unobtrusive second coming, moreover, is available to all who want to live the Shaker life.

Though Shakerism does not have specific sacraments, it is suprasacramental. For example, rather than have bread at worship as Holy Communion, for the Shakers every meal they share together is a Eucharist. In the same way the water of Baptism does no good if a person has not first received the baptism of the Holy Spirit.

Shakers believe that there has always been a continuing revelation of God's truth. It is therefore futile to cling to a creed or dogma since the soul travels in spirituality and the work of God is progressive and increasing. One dispensation has prepared the world for the next. God spoke to the first Shakers and still speaks today to all who would listen. The Scriptures of the Bible, "while a guide to God's laws and to His acts in history are in no sense either a summation of His Law or the final expression of his role as the God of History" (Johnson, 11).

After death, Heaven is a state attained by those whose life on Earth has made them ready to unite eternally with God in fullness of love. Hell is the state of those who by their own free will have separated themselves from God. Heaven and Hell are not physical places, but are spiritual and those who are there are incorporeal. For those spirits not yet able to attain Heaven, an intermediate place akin to the concept of Purgatory exists, where a soul can work out its salvation. Shakers in this world are closely associated with all those who have died and offer prayers for the dead.

Shaker worship centers on living the **Christlife** to the fullest extent possible. If a person keeps the commandments of God, that person is worshipping. Formalized worship services have taken various forms over the years as the circumstances of the church have evolved. In summary, Shakerism is a way of life that expresses itself in a life of **celibacy** and community. Spiritual travel is possible because periodic confession of sin helps a soul leave behind the old and embrace the possibility of a higher life. By giving all talents and time to a greater good, the soul travels on the path of regeneration. This life values all persons equally, making no distinctions between the sexes. Violence, injustice, and lawlessness have no place in this Christlife.

TRINITY. The Shakers do not believe in this concept. They see the trinity as a man-made way to explain God that reflects the bias of a male-dominated church at the time of the Council of Nicaea. The Shakers address God as Father-Mother. For them, this is the proper way to acknowledge God in all power and greatness. Though masculine pronouns are often used to describe God, the Shakers believe that a reliance on the maleness of God fails to take note of God's feminine attributes. The strongest manifestation of this is the Shaker belief in the Holy Spirit or **Holy Mother Wisdom**. This Holy Spirit is with the Shakers constantly and guides the **believer**. In this context, **Jesus of Nazareth** and **Ann Lee** were humans chosen by God to show the world what living the divine life entailed. In Ann Lee this reached its final form because it was God reaching out through the female, thus completing the work done by Jesus, a man.

TRUSTEE. No organization can survive unless it has a firm financial base. When Father **Joseph Meacham** organized the first Shaker communities into **gospel order**, he set up **deacons**, later called trustees, to have charge of temporal matters. This he adopted from his former Baptist upbringing. Another name for a trustee is **Office deacon**. In **families** of sufficient size, there were two men who filled the role of Office deacon or trustee. These men lived in a separate building called the **Office**. This is where visitors who had business to transact were expected to go since outsiders were not allowed to wander around Shaker property. Trustees also had the legal authority to transact business in the name of the Shakers. Besides assisting those with business at the Office, trustees served as peddlers of Shaker goods and traveled on business trips to various places, some quite distant from the community. In addition, all the property of the community was held in trust in the names of the trustees. This legal authority also extended into children's **indentures** and the Shaker **covenant**. So important was the role of trustee that a Shaker family was not considered to be truly independent and "set off" until it had its own set of trustees. For example, the **North Family** at **New Lebanon** was created in 1800, but came under the jurisdiction of the **Church Family** trustees. In 1814, the North Family got its own trustees, and its history as a separate family dates from then.

Another important aspect of the power of the trustees was their ability to do great harm if they were not honest. Various communities suffered grave financial hardship due to bad trustees such as **Joseph Slingerland** and Isaiah Wentworth, who either stole money or ran up huge debts that could not be paid without large loans from other Shaker societies. Other trustees were not capable or too infirm to carry out their tasks successfully. Each of these situations hurt the Shakers, and some societies never recovered from the loss.

The prosperity of a community was directly linked to the capability of its trustees. By far the most successful and best Shaker trustee was **Ira Lawson** of **Hancock**. **David Parker** of **Canterbury** and Edward Fowler of New Lebanon were also among the greatest Shaker trustees.

Until the 1890s women did not do the traditional jobs associated with the trustees. Nothing in Shaker belief prevented this, but while there were sufficient men, the concept of women trustees was not fully realized. Women had been appointed since the earliest times to work in the Office as **Office deaconesses**. Theoretically they had all of the financial powers men had, but their roles were mostly running the store set up in the Office and providing meals for visitors who may have been staying overnight there. They also did the housekeeping chores.

As the number of men declined, women took on more of the work of the trustees and their names are found on legal documents. In addition, as whole societies shrank in number, various men and women from the different families were appointed society trustees to run all of the financial affairs that once were done in smaller family units.

TRUSTEES' OFFICE. *See* OFFICE.

TURTLE CREEK, OHIO. This was the early name for **Union Village, Ohio.**

TYRINGHAM, MASSACHUSETTS (1792–1875). SPIRITUAL NAME: City of Love. FEAST GROUND: Mount Horeb. BISHOPRIC: **Hancock.** FAMILIES: Church (**First Family**) and North (**Second Family** and **Gathering Order**). MAXIMUM POPULATION AND YEAR: 101 in 1830. INDUSTRIES: seeds, herbs, rakes, maple syrup. NOTABLE SHAKERS: **Grove Wright**, Albert Battles, Richard Van Deusen, Michael McCue, Harriet Storer, Wealthy Storer, Julia Johnson. UNIQUE FEATURES: Tyringham was always a very small community, never numbering more than 70 adults. Few Shakers visited and, as a result, the community retains an air of mystery. This has been fueled by an oral tradition that says that 23 members left on a day in January 1858. All types of myths and stories have grown around this event. In reality the average age of those who left was 14 so the event was most likely a correction to the high numbers of children the community had. Though all Shaker societies had a high percentage of children, Tyringham had the highest percentage of any. In 1855, 52 percent of the 77 Shakers there were under 21 years old. In particular, the **Church Family** had very few adult women. This condition existed nowhere else in Shakerdom at the time. It is not surprising that in 1875, Tyringham became the first long-lived Shaker society to close.

BRIEF HISTORY: After the first converts received the faith from **Mother Ann** in 1780, they returned to their homes. Among those who had been involved in the **New Light** revival at **New Lebanon** in 1779 were three brothers living in Tyringham: Joshua, Abel, and William Allen. The Allens had a link with Father **Joseph Meacham** that predated his involvement as one of the leaders of the New Light revival at New Lebanon. An older relative of Meacham's, also named Joseph Meacham, was the founding minister of the Congregational Church at Coventry, Connecticut, the town where the Allens were born. Through marriage and association, the Allens were connected to the Fay, Herrick, Clark, and Culver families at Tyringham. It was in this way that Shakerism came to be planted there and among those families.

In April 1782, Shaker meetings were held in various homes, and Father **William Lee** and Father **James Whittaker** visited to lend encouragement. By 1784, the large Stanley family, as well as the Pratt and Patten families, had joined the Shakers. The Stanleys, Pratts, and Pattens were from Belchertown, Massachusetts, a place where the three Allen brothers and the Fays had lived prior to moving to Tyringham. Mother Ann, though never coming to Tyringham herself, visited Belchertown during her missionary tour of 1783 to see Jonathan Bridges, a convert who deserted during the Revolutionary War due to his beliefs. As a result of this interconnectedness, over half of the 99 Shakers buried in the Shaker cemetery at Tyringham are from these first families.

In 1792, under the guidance of the **Ministry** of Hancock, Tyringham was gathered into full **gospel order**. William Clark's farm formed the nucleus of the First or **Church Family**. The farms of the Allen brothers formed the property of the Second or North Family. In time a cluster of buildings was erected along a stream south of the Church Family. This South House was adjacent to the mills there. A few Shakers lived at the site, but it was never a Shaker **family**. Had the society grown sufficiently in time, no doubt the South House would have developed into another family. Actually, even Tyringham's two small families were so connected that they shared one covenant. When a Gathering Order was established, it was at the North Family. Unlike other places, however, the original Shaker family members stayed on, and no central **dwelling house** was ever built at the North.

These arrangements reveal how small the community was. Though some excellent adult converts were attracted, during the 1820s the leaders at Tyringham decided to increase their community by the wholesale adoption of children. Poorhouses in Connecticut, most notably at Norwalk, were the source of some of these. Others came from contacts the Shakers made during their seed and peddling routes. Already by 1830, those under 16 years of age numbered over 30 percent of the community. This steadily climbed until over half were preadults by 1855. Since these children came and went with great frequency, the society was always in flux. After the departure of 23 children in 1858, numbers became more manageable, but the lack of adults became clear as well. In 1865 there were only 26 adults in the one remaining family. Since Tyringham was financially sound, it continued on until two of the most prominent men, Michael McCue, age 49, and Hasting Storer, 51, died in the early 1870s. This prompted the Ministry to break up the community. In April 1875, three of the survivors left: two to Hancock and 12 to **Enfield, Connecticut**. Tyringham's closing was a serious psychological blow to Shakers, who had hoped that the numerical decline could be halted.

LAST SHAKER: Elizabeth Thornber (1837–1920). When the society closed in 1875, she moved to the Hancock Shakers.

– U –

UNION. This means the lifelong struggle to maintain a strong connection with fellow **believers**, the Church, and God. This is one of the virtues every Shaker strives to practice. Since living in community is essential to the **Christlife**, every person who would be a Shaker must shed any selfish trait that may prevent a full union of self. Union has also meant the act of uniting with the community upon joining. So important was this ideal that, when the communities of the Shaker West were gathered, the word union was used in the names of four of the seven societies: **West Union, Indiana**; **North Union** and **Union Village**, Ohio; and **South Union, Kentucky**. Moreover, during the **Era of Manifestations**, the Shaker society at **Enfield, Connecticut**, was given the name "City of Union" and **Groveland, New York**, and **Gorham, Maine**, became "Union Branch."

UNION MEETING. These were scheduled meetings between a small number of Shaker **brothers** and **sisters** to socialize and sing hymns. Since Shaker brothers and sisters did not usually have informal times together, leaders thought that having union meetings periodically would strengthen community life and allow brothers and sisters to get to know each other out of the context of the work and worship environment. Certain evenings were set aside for such meetings, and a half-dozen Shakers would sit in chairs facing each other in a line. These meetings took place in a retiring room. Union meetings are referred to in Shaker manuscripts from the early years until the 1860s.

After that time, changing demographics and a more relaxed community life allowed Shakers to associate more freely, although brothers and sisters did not enjoy casual association until recent times.

UNION VILLAGE, OHIO (1805–1912). SPIRITUAL NAME: Wisdom's Paradise. FEAST GROUND: Jehovah's Chosen Square. BISHOPRIC: Union Village. FAMILIES: **Church Order** (Center, Brick, North, and South), **Square House** and Grist Mill (two mill families under the care of the Church), North Lot and West Lot (**Gathering Order**), East, West Brick, and West Frame. MAXIMUM POPULATION AND YEAR: 634 in 1818. INDUSTRIES: brooms, garden seeds, medicinal herbs and extracts, fancy goods, baskets, raising of fine stock, farming, and gardening. NOTABLE SHAKERS: George Baxter, **David Darrow**, **Ruth Farrington**, **James Fennessey**, **Oliver Hampton**, **Richard McNemar**, Moore Mason, **Clymena Miner**, **Joseph Slingerland**, **Malcolm Worley**. UNIQUE FEATURES: Union Village played a major role in Shaker history. It was the oldest and the leading community in the Shaker West. At one early point in its history, it briefly surpassed **New Lebanon** in membership. In addition, it also had the largest number of **families**—11 in all, though many were very short lived. During its final 20 years, imprudent **trustee** Joseph Slingerland ran the society into tremendous debt due to his extravagance. Reminders of this can be seen today in the ornate **Trustees' Office** now called **Marble Hall**.

BRIEF HISTORY: Mother **Lucy Wright**, having heard of a large religious revival in what was then the western part of the United States, decided to send Shaker missionaries into the area. Accordingly, **John Meacham**, **Issachar Bates**, and **Benjamin S. Youngs** left New Lebanon and arrived at Turtle Creek, Ohio, on 22 March 1805. The "Great Kentucky Revival" had spread into Ohio, and in 1802, a Presbyterian preacher named Richard McNemar had come from Kentucky to **Turtle Creek, Ohio**, to be the pastor of the church there. The Shaker missionaries wanted the chance to preach at McNemar's church. First they stopped at the house of church member Malcolm Worley. They received hospitality and encouragement. Worley became a Shaker and was the first convert in the West. Soon McNemar received the faith and almost all of his church followed him into the Shakers. On 25 May 1805, the society at Turtle Creek was organized as Union Village. David Darrow and Ruth Farrington were sent from the East to be the **First Parents** and head the **Ministry**. There was such growth that the next year, a society was formed at **Beaver Creek**. This became known later as **Watervliet, Ohio**. Eventually scattered Shakers would be brought together into two more Ohio communities, **North Union** and **White Water**.

The high-water mark of membership in 1818 was never surpassed and the remainder of Union Village's history shows a decline. Some decades were worse than others, but sufficient converts never came in after the earliest years to sustain the membership at such an initially high level. As a result, the families were reorganized periodically to better use remaining resources. This fluctuation was reflected in the financial status of the society as well. Flooding, dishonest trustees, fire, and pestilence all diminished Shaker wealth. In spite of this, however, the society was fairly prosperous until Joseph Slingerland was sent from **Mount Lebanon** to "help" Union Village. Slingerland had no business sense, but this did not prevent him from spending money on favorite projects and schemes. These losing propositions included a hotel, a cemetery, and extensive improvements to the Trustees' Office at the **Center Family**. So palatial was the transformation that the building eventually became known as Marble Hall. Slingerland used all of the money that had been realized from the sale of North Union in 1889, and kept spending. His most fantastic waste of funds was the purchase of thousands of acres of land in Georgia in 1897 for a new colony. It has been surmised that he dreamed that this settlement called **White Oak** would attract Shakers from Ohio and Kentucky who might wish to consolidate their societies there. He may have thought that he was only doing what the Mount Lebanon and **Watervliet** Shakers had done in 1896 when they bought land in Florida for a new society.

The diminished numbers and the large debt helped bring a discouragement to Union Village that never lifted. Trustee James Fennessey did get them out of debt, but the religious fervor of the remaining Shakers was low. The entire property was put up for sale and bought by the Church of the United Brethren in Christ. The sale was completed on 15 October 1912 for $325,000 and the property passed out of Shaker hands on 5 March 1913. The 16 remaining Shakers were almost all very old, and young **sisters** from the **Canterbury**

Shakers arrived in December 1912 to care for them. Terms of the sale allowed the Shakers to remain in Marble Hall for up to 10 years beginning 1 March 1913. This arrangement continued until 3 July 1920 when the Canterbury sisters released Marble Hall. This was earlier than they were obliged to, but the new owners needed new space and the Shakers were glad to help. The Canterbury Shakers had had the building painted and put in a heating system, new toilets, and baths as gifts. The three surviving Union Village Shakers—all women—decided to return to Canterbury as well. They are buried at that village.

LAST SHAKER: Ellen Ross (1836–1927). When the Shakers vacated Union Village in 1920, she moved to the Shaker society at Canterbury, where she is buried.

UNITED SOCIETY OF BELIEVERS (CALLED SHAKERS). This is the official name of the Shakers. It appears on the prototype 1830 **covenant** revision that still serves the Shakers today. Moreover, legal documents use this title universally. In essence it tells the whole of what the Shakers are all about. The name shows that, though the Shakers are a community formed of very diverse individuals, it is united. This unity manifests itself in a **believer's** willingness to live communally in a Shaker society gathered for that purpose. All goods and services produced by the Shaker go into a common fund used by all. No one is paid wages, but all may take as they need.

Technically speaking, the true official name is actually **Alethian Believers**. In 1896, **Elder Alonzo Hollister** of the **Church Family** at **Mount Lebanon, New York**, petitioned the **Ministry** for the change as the name was not of Shaker origin and so negative. This was right after he published his tract "The Mission of Alethian Believers." They acquiesced, but no one has ever taken to the name except **Sister Aurelia Mace** of **Sabbathday Lake**. In 1899, she published a book entitled *The Alethia*.

UNITED SOCIETY OF BELIEVERS IN CHRIST'S FIRST AND SECOND APPEARING. It is not known when this name for the Shakers began to be used. It can be found in many 19th-century articles and books on the society. For example, it appears in the introduction to the "first" or 1883 edition of the hymnal published by the

North Family of **Mount Lebanon.** This name is often said to be the official name of the Shakers, but it is not. *See* THE UNITED SOCIETY OF BELIEVERS (CALLED SHAKERS).

UPPER CANAAN SHAKERS (1813–1897). This **family** was first organized in 1813 in the Powder Mill House located below the **North Family's** sawmill. It was set up as a branch of the North Family, where converts who were not ready to make a full commitment to Shakerism would have a place to try their **union** and at the same time have the necessary contact with their families. In 1814, they removed to the old farmstead known as the Walker or West House. This was located below the new gathering family organizing near the **Second Family's** carding machine. Hence they were known as the **Lower Family.** In 1819, the Peabody Farm was bought in the nearby town of Canaan, and they became the Upper Family of Canaan, since the family by the carding machine eventually bought the Madison Farm in Canaan, and this was below them.

Unlike the Lower Canaan Shakers, the Upper Family seems to have been prosperous for most of its history. Its population peaked in 1840 when it had 39 members, and its average population was around 35 members. Much of its prosperity was due to good leadership. One of the latter leaders, second **Eldress** Margaret Turner, was especially gifted at gathering young **sisters.** As a result, by the 1880s the family had an enviable number of young women. Among these were: Mariette Estey, Alice Braisted, and M. Angeline Brown. These young women would live into the middle years of the 20th century and be great burden-bearers.

Although Upper Canaan was financially sound and had young members, it was closed in March 1897. The **Central Ministry** urged them to remove to the splendid farm at the North Family of Shakers at **Enfield, Connecticut.** This place not only had truly magnificent buildings, it had very rich land. In addition, it was the **Ministry's** way of outmaneuvering the takeover of the property by a non-Shaker farm manager. The bad feeling that this move caused ruined any chance of their success at Enfield. A remnant of the family returned to **Mount Lebanon** in 1913, this time to the **Church Family.** They eventually moved to **Hancock** in 1921.

– V –

VANCE, JOHN BELL (1833–1896). He was born in Baileyville, Maine, on 9 May 1833, and his parents were Shubal and Elizabeth Moshier Vance. He was descendant of an old Maine family. His grandfather William Vance had been a member of the convention forming the first constitution of Maine following its separation from Massachusetts. His father ran a hotel and later worked at lumbering. While the family was living in Lebanon, Maine, his father heard about the Shakers and decided he would someday join. In the meantime, he placed his son John with the **Alfred** Shakers in 1838. He himself did not join until 1864 when he entered Alfred with his daughter Mary.

Though the Shaker school was simple, John read everything he could. In addition he excelled at mathematics and explored algebra and geometry. This love of learning made him a natural teacher and he commenced his career in the Shaker school as a teacher when he was 16 years old. Even when he was an **elder** and **trustee**, he continued to teach in the school. To improve the level of education, he abolished half-year terms for boys and girls. Henceforth they all attended a full year together. He also had his salary from the town used to buy equipment and make improvements in the school.

Given his abilities, it is not surprising that he would rise in the ranks of Shaker leadership. When he was 19 he was made elder of the **Gathering Order**. This meant that he became the preacher at **public meeting**. His excellent sermons and talents as a speaker led him to lecture in cities of Maine, Massachusetts, and New York. In 1872, he was made elder of the **Church Family** and its senior trustee. In most Shaker societies the combination of these two jobs proved to be disastrous. In contrast, at Alfred, Elder John did all things well. In fact, along with being elder, trustee, and teacher, he also did tailoring and preparation work for the poplar trade.

In the 1870s, after it was clear that the society was not moving to Kansas, he reorganized the village. At the same time, he familiarized himself with music so that he might improve the quality of singing in the society. His knowledge of herbs was used many times in his role as community physician. After Elder **Otis Sawyer** died in 1884, Elder John became first in the Maine **Ministry** and senior trustee at both Alfred and **Sabbathday Lake**. He died unexpectedly on 13 March 1896 at the age of 62. His loss was immeasurable to the Maine Shaker communities. Despite the bad weather his funeral was attended by representatives from almost all of the eastern communities.

– W –

WAGAN, ROBERT M. (1833–1883). He was born in New York City on 24 May 1833 and taken in at the South House of the **Second Family** of **New Lebanon** in October 1839. Not only was he among the very few young men brought up by the Shakers who stayed faithful, he possessed a real talent for business management. This ability first became apparent when he was made a **family deacon** at the South House, which was part of the Second Family. In 1863, when the South Family was set off as a separate family, he was made second **elder** under Elder Joseph Hawkins. This gave him the opportunity by 1870 to completely reorganize the **chair industry**. Slowly the business grew under his guidance. Catalogs were issued, and a new factory was built. Since he was a **trustee** at the South Family, the name R. M. Wagan and Co. became the official name of the company, and this title was used for decades after he died. To make the marketing of the chairs more successful, he opened a show room at the South Family. Chairs were moved up into a room on the second floor of the shop and the room was paneled in clapboards. Cushioned chairs were placed all around as seating. In addition to the chair industry, Elder Robert also took a great interest in the farm. He and Brother William Potter of the South Family patented an improved green-corn cutter. Along with Shakers chairs, this corncutter was exhibited at Philadelphia for the Centennial Exposition in 1876.

On Christmas 1879, he became the elder of the South Family. In spite of the turmoil affecting life at **Mount Lebanon**, the South Family was busy expanding its chair business under Elder Robert's expertise. This happy state of affairs ended abruptly on Thanksgiving, 29 November 1883, when Elder Robert died from pneumonia. Benjamin Gates, a trustee of the **Church Family**, took over the financial side of the business until William Anderson was send to have charge of the business in January 1884. (Note: Robert Wagan's last name rhymes with "ray gun.") *See also* FURNITURE.

WATERVLIET, NEW YORK (1775–1938). SPIRITUAL NAME: Wisdom's Valley. FEAST GROUND: Center Square. BISHOPRIC: **New Lebanon.** FAMILIES: Church (**First Order**), North (**Second Order**), West (**Second Family**), South (**Gathering Order**). MAXIMUM POPULATION AND YEAR: 304 in 1840. INDUSTRIES: broom corn, sweet corn, canned fruit and vegetables, garden seeds. NOTABLE SHAKERS: **Mother Ann Lee**, Father **William Lee**, **John Hocknell**, **Abiather Babbit**, **Issachar Bates**, **Freegift Wells**, Chauncey Miller, **George Albert Lomas**, Anna Case, Isaac Anstatt, Hamilton De Graw. UNIQUE FEATURES: Watervliet was the first Shaker home in America. Furthermore, Watervliet was the place where the **Era of Manifestations** formally commenced, and the society's cemetery still has individual grave stones, making it one of a handful of such Shaker cemeteries today even though it was the norm at one time.

BRIEF HISTORY: The first year the Shakers were in America, they had no permanent home. In 1775, John Hocknell, a member with means, leased 200 acres of land seven miles northwest of Albany. This wilderness tract, called **Niskeyuna**, had been part of the Manor Rensselaerwyck. In the summer of 1776, **Mother Ann** moved there, and the **believers** began to make a home for themselves. They anticipated that others would join them, and they were right. In 1780, large numbers of revivalists from the border country of New York and Massachusetts made their way to Niskeyuna and received Mother's **testimony**. These returned to their homes, and pockets of Shakerism were scattered throughout New England and New York. Mother Ann and the first **elders** made numerous missionary trips. Though they faced violent persecution, the church continued to grow. After Mother Ann died, leadership passed to Father **James Whittaker**, who did not seem to favor one **"center of union"** over another. It was his successor in 1787, Father **Joseph Meacham**, who concentrated leadership at New Lebanon. Niskeyuna, by now called Watervliet, was no longer the administrative center, but it remained an important society nonetheless.

In 1803 there were 61 Shakers in community. After the establishment of a Gathering Order at the South Family, growth was explosive. Many families with large numbers of children joined. Among these were the Youngs, Buckingham, and Wells families. By the early 1820s, there were 200 Shakers and in 1834 the number had climbed to 302. It was just as the community was reaching the highpoint of membership that it was plunged into a very important phase of its history. In 1837, a revival began among the young girls of the society that spread to all other Shaker communities. **Songs**, visions, inspired art, and messages were received by scores of **instruments** during the next dozen years. This period is known as the Era of Manifestations or the **Era of Mother's Work**.

Membership may have peaked at close to 350 during the 1840s, but it remained just under 300 until 1860. During this time, a group of mostly black Shakers led by Watervliet Shaker **Rebecca Jackson** founded Shakerism's only urban community in **Philadelphia**. After the Civil War years, however, it was clear that few capable members were joining. For a time, the **Mount Lebanon** Shakers were in a position to send some of their members to help out at Watervliet, especially at the South Family. In 1892, the society also got a boost when the 34 **Groveland** Shakers took over the North Family. In addition, a Shaker newspaper was founded at Watervliet in 1871. This venture was intended to spread the Shaker message and attract more converts. Begun with great enthusiasm, the paper was so adversely affected by conditions at Watervliet, including a fire and lack of enough people to manage it, that the paper's publication after two years had to move to the **North Family** at Mount Lebanon.

By 1900 only 90 lived at Watervliet in the four **families**. The North Family closed in 1919, and the surviving Groveland Shakers had to move once again. This time it was to the South Family. It is curious that in every Shaker village, except those in the **New Lebanon bishopric**, the Church or Center families were the last to be vacated. Membership usually consolidated into them. At Watervliet, as at New Lebanon, the last stand was made at the Gathering Orders. The **Church Family** was sold for $60,000 to Thomas B. Bergan in 1924. In 1926, Albany County bought it from him for $160,000 as the site of a home for tuberculosis patients. It was called the Ann Lee Home. In 1938, the **Parent Ministry** closed the South Family after the death of Eldress Anna Case. Two of the three remaining **sisters** Grave Dahm and Mary Dahm moved to the North Family at Mount Lebanon. Freida Sipple joined the Church Family at **Hancock**. LAST SHAKER: Mary Frances Dahm (1885–1965) was born in Kinderhook, New York. When she was three years old, her father placed her and her older sister Grace at the South Family, Watervliet. By the time she came of age, there were so many elderly people that she decided to receive nurse's training. She went to school in Albany and became a registered nurse. She survived the closing of Watervliet in 1938. She moved to the North Family at Mount Lebanon and lived there until that family closed in 1947. She then moved to the Church Family at Hancock, and again survived the closing of that community. In 1959, although she remained a Shaker, rather than move to another community, she took an apartment in Pittsfield. She died 25 August 1965 and was buried in her family's plot in Kinderhook, New York.

WATERVLIET, OHIO (1806–1900). SPIRITUAL NAME: Vale of Peace. FEAST GROUND: Holy Circle. BISHOPRIC: **Union Village**. FAMILIES: First (former South Family), North (the **Office**), West Family (also called the West Lot—it was the **Gathering Order**). The Mill Family and the School Family were two short-lived **families** that were gathered in 1811 and broken up in 1820. MAXIMUM POPULATION AND YEAR: about 100 in 1823. INDUSTRIES: woolen products, gardening, and farming. NOTABLE SHAKERS: none, though **Richard McNemar**, **Richard Pelham, Issachar Bates**, and **Clymena Miner** lived there for a time. UNIQUE FEATURES: Although it was fully independent, in reality, this society functioned more as an **out family** of Union Village, located just 22 miles south. It was the second Shaker society formed in the West. In spite of being a small society, many Shaker publications bear the name. That is because, in 1832, Richard Mc-Nemar, the most important of the early Ohio converts, moved from Union Village to Watervliet where he continued his large publication efforts. Also, a strong oral tradition holds that the Shakers at Watervliet marched in worship right until the end of their community in 1900.

BRIEF HISTORY: In 1805, a camp meeting organized at **Turtle Creek** by Shaker missionaries from the East attracted much attention. Most of the members of Beulah Church at **Beaver Creek** were in attendance and invited the Shakers to visit. After two meetings in May and June 1805, John Huston became the first convert. Less than a year later, in April 1806, there were about 12 Shakers at Beaver Creek, including John Patterson. His property formed the base for the subsequent development of the Shaker community. They gathered and worshiped on 26 April 1806 led by Shaker missionaries Issachar Bates and **Benjamin Seth Youngs** (Boice, Covington, and Spence, *Maps of the Shaker West*, 41–43). Though this is considered the founding of the community, the society was not organized into **order** until 12 September 1812. In 1813, the Beaver Creek community began to be referred to as Watervliet in honor of the first Watervliet in New York State. Around 1816, a Gathering Order was started at the West Lot (West Family). In 1820 the large brick dwelling was finished at the South Family and this family changed its name to be the First or **Center Family**. After 1830, the North Family became the Office and its members removed to the Center Family.

Watervliet never grew significantly. In 1810 it had 56 members. Although Shaker historians Green and Wells note that the society had "almost 100" members in 1823, it is likely that the number was much smaller (Green and Wells, *A Summary View of the Millennial Church*, 83). In 1852, there were just 52. This was apparently so low that the **Ministry** had 20 Shakers from the **White Water** society transferred to Watervliet to augment the population. Though small, Watervliet did not escape the problems that affected the larger societies. For example, in 1827, at the time that some members were being influenced by the independent spirit shown by the **Pleasant Hill** Shakers, Elder Issachar Bates of the Center Family was attempting to run the community autocratically. This caused a very bad feeling as the community split along party lines (Johnson, *The Struggle for Watervliet, Ohio*, 11–21). By 1874, Nordhoff records 55 members, including seven minors (Nordhoff, *The Communistic Societies of the United States*, 206). It is interesting that this was one of the few Shaker societies that he did not visit. In 1889, when **North Union** closed, 21 Shakers—12 men and 9 women—were sent to live at the North Family at Watervliet.

The "Home Notes" section of the Shaker newspaper, the *Manifesto*, records optimistic reports on the farming activities at Watervliet starting in 1889. In spite of this and the added membership gained from the breakup of North Union, **Joseph Slingerland** of the Union Village Ministry decided to close the community. The money that would be realized from the sale was needed to help pay the immense debt Slingerland had accumulated. On 11 October 1900, the 12 remaining Shakers were split between the North Family and the Center Family at Union Village. It was anticipated that the Shakers would receive $47,000 from the sale to Dennison University. The final sale took place on 14 August 1906. Mr. Seymour B. Kelley paid $27, 683 and took out three promissory notes for $10,000 each. The Shakers paid a commission of $7,683 for the sale of the property.

LAST SHAKER: Sarah Ann Kripe (1836–1913). She joined at Watervliet in 1841 with her mother and sister. When Watervliet closed she moved to the Center Family, Union Village, where she died 22 February 1913.

WELLS, FREEGIFT (1785–1871). He was the youngest of the 14 children of Thomas Wells and Abigail Youngs Wells. This large family lived at Southold, Long Island, and was converted to Shakerism by the testimony of **Seth Youngs Wells**, an older brother of Freegift Wells. Freegift was admitted to the Shaker society at **Watervliet, New York**, on 20 May 1803 when he was 18 years old. Although he held positions of authority at Watervliet, schoolteacher and **elder**, he is perhaps best known for his work as a craftsman. His work journal, which commences in December 1812, documents his lifetime of making tools, **furniture**, and chairs. Both his furniture and the smaller objects he made are highly collectible.

Had he remained his whole life at Watervliet, **Brother** Freegift might have been remembered as a well-known woodworker and cabinetmaker. In 1836, however, he was sent to be first in the **Ministry** at **Union Village**. This portion of his life remains controversial. When he arrived at Union Village on 27 April 1836, he was confronted with a large Shaker village that still had not recovered from the death of Father **David Darrow** in 1825. Father David's successor, Solomon King, was not strong enough to be in charge of such a large enterprise. During his term in the Ministry, scores of highly skilled young people had left. These included some children of the children of founders. In addition, there was tremendous agitation by some members to be allowed to have more of a say in the governance of the village. Under Elder Solomon, things had slipped badly. The population was down considerably, and many troublemakers still lived there. Although he did not officially resign until February 1836, Elder Solomon placed his associate David Meacham in charge for the interim until the **Ministry of New Lebanon** could appoint a successor. David Meacham was the son of Father **Joseph Meacham's** brother David. Solomon King was the son of Father Joseph's sister Ruth. Thus Elder Solomon placed his first cousin in his place. Although Elder David Meacham had made progress in the months he was in charge, with the arrival of Elder Freegift as first minister, Union Village once again had a strong man of action, yet he took measures to the opposite extreme. He believed that he was to be in charge of all aspects of Shaker life and was envious of anyone whom he perceived as even the slightest threat.

Almost at once he changed the diet of the Shakers and restricted reading materials. He then started to persecute the founders and oldest Shakers. A natural target for his jealousy was Elder **Richard McNemar**, who had just returned from being first elder at **Watervliet, Ohio**. McNemar had been a faithful Shaker for over 30 years and acted in various capacities as a troubleshooter for the Ministry. Elder Freegift made it clear that McNemar was now an ordinary member and had no place other than being a humble brother in the ranks. When the **Era of Manifestations** came to Union Village in 1838, Elder Freegift used the spurious testimony of an **instrument** named Margaret O'Brien to publicly rebuke and humiliate McNemar at meeting. After the attack in June 1839, Richard McNemar and **Malcolm Worley** were expelled from the Shakers. The total injustice of this action upset many sincere Shakers. They had been so conditioned to trust the elders, however, that they did not prevent the expulsions. Soon after, the Ministry of New Lebanon stepped in at the request of McNemar and the instrument was discredited. Nonetheless, the incident contributed to McNemar's death and was a heavy blow to morale.

Elder Freegift was not successful in halting the loss of membership. When he took charge in 1836 there had been 330 Shakers at Union Village. This was down from the 500 who were there when Father David died in 1825. When Elder Freegift resigned on 19 April

1843, there were no more than 275 in all. In spite of his reforms and the religious enthusiasm generated by the Era of Manifestations, the village continued to diminish.

When Elder Freegift returned to Watervliet in 1843, it was to be elder of the **Church Family**. He held this position until 1857. For many of these years, he also taught school. While elder and afterwards, he used his considerable mechanical skills to make improvements in the buildings and make furniture and tools. He was always working right up until his death at some project to improve the home.

WELLS, JENNIE (1878–1956). Few Shakers ever lived in so many different Shaker communities as did Jennie Wells. Her long life as a Shaker follows the dissolution of one society after another, each forcing Jennie to move.

Jennie was born in Buffalo, New York, in 1878 and was placed at the West Family of the **Groveland** Shakers when she was only four years old. In 1884, when that family dissolved, she went to live at the East Family until 1892, when the entire Groveland society closed. At that time she moved with the community to the North Family at **Watervliet, New York**. Here she signed the **covenant** and was **caretaker** of the children. She was also involved in the usual domestic work of the sisterhood. In 1919, the North Family closed and its survivors were moved to the South Family at Watervliet.

In 1931, she was sent to live at the **North Family** at **Mount Lebanon** to help care for the aged and infirm. At age 53, she was one of the youngest **sisters**, and her whole personality seemed to blossom with this work. She became "in charge" as much as she was able. Moreover, she still loved to greet visitors and kept up a spirited correspondence with some. These letters provide great insight into what was happening at Mount Lebanon, for family journals were no longer being kept. She is actually the one who caused the events that precipitated the closure of Mount Lebanon. In 1947, she gave an interview that found its way into the *New Yorker* magazine. Ministry **Eldress Frances Hall** was not pleased that visitors had such easy access to the North Family. This incident and pressing economic reasons helped seal the fate of the North Family.

In October 1947, the North Family, the last of the Mount Lebanon community, moved to **Hancock**. Under the much more restrictive rule of Eldress Fannie Estabrook, Jennie's best entertaining days were over. She still kept up her letter writing and did manage to have visitors on occasion. To be different, and no doubt aggravate Eldress Fannie and the others, she wore the Shaker dress. Pictures of her show her in this outfit in contrast to the rest of the sisters. She died at Hancock in 1956. Her residence in six different Shaker families charts the decline of the **New Lebanon bishopric**.

Since Sister Jennie was so gregarious, she was also involved in the sale and distribution of many Shaker objects. While at Watervliet, she helped Eldresses **Ella Winship** and Anna Case gather material for the New York State Shaker Museum collection.

WELLS, SETH YOUNGS (1767–1847). From 1785 until almost 1800, the Shaker testimony was withdrawn from the world. So much energy was needed to organize scattered believers into communities that no effort was spent in missionary work. Nonetheless, many outsiders began petitioning for admittance. The result was the formation of **Gathering Orders**, starting at **New Lebanon** late in 1799 and spreading to all Shaker communities by 1810.

The opening up of the society for new members occurred at an auspicious time for Seth Youngs Wells. He was a schoolteacher and principal of a high school in Albany and had also taught at Hudson Academy in Hudson, New York. The nearby Shaker community at **Watervliet** attracted him, and he was admitted in 1798. His skill as a preacher was noted and he eventually returned to his native Southold, Long Island, and converted most of his large family. Of his 13 siblings, 9 joined the Shakers. In addition his father, Thomas Wells, and his mother, Abigail Youngs Wells, also joined. Her brothers were **Isaac Newton Youngs** and **Benjamin Seth Youngs**. Seth Youngs Wells' youngest brother was **Freegift Wells**.

In all, 19 members of his family became Shakers in 1803. Four years later, Seth was appointed **elder** at the South Family, which was the Gathering Order at Watervliet. It was the duty of the elder of this family to speak at **public meeting** on the Sabbath. His preaching ability, educational background, and deep faith made him a perfect elder for the South Family, and he held this position until 1844. In the meantime, he became superintendent of schools for the **New Lebanon bishopric** in 1821. Through his efforts schools were organized and the Lancastrian system of education employed. Eventually, he visited and supervised Shaker schools in all of the communities of the East.

Although most of the first Shaker theological works were written by western Shakers, Seth Wells helped edit the second edition of the *Testimony of Christ's Second Appearing* in 1810. He also compiled *Millennial Praises* in 1812, and under the pseudonym "Philanthropos" he wrote *A Brief Illustration of the Principles of War and Peace.* With Elder **Calvin Green** he coauthored in 1823 *A Summary View of the Millennial Church*, and in 1827 co-edited with him *Testimonies Concerning the Character and Ministry of Mother Ann Lee and the First Witnesses of the Gospel of Christ's Second Appearing.*

The decade before he died, he became involved with the **Era of Manifestations**. He cautioned against excess, however. Had the **Ministry** heeded this warning, perhaps some of the divisiveness caused by the messages received by the **instruments** could have been avoided.

WEST GLOUCESTER, MAINE. This was the postal address of the **Sabbathday Lake** Shakers until 1 April 1890, when it changed to Sabbathday Lake. The Shaker post office was located in the **Trustees' Office**. The date of its establishment is not known, but the first postmaster on record was Brother Samuel Kendrick, who retired in 1887.

WEST UNION, INDIANA (1807–1827). Spritual Name: None. FEAST GROUND: None. BISHOPRIC: **Union Village**. FAMILIES: Center, North, South, West. MAXIMUM POPULATION AND YEAR: 300 in 1812. INDUSTRIES: saw, grist, and fulling mills, agriculture. NOTABLE SHAKERS: **Issachar Bates**. UNIQUE FEATURES: West Union was the only Shaker society ever formed in Indiana, and it was the first major community to close. In addition, it was abandoned between 1812 and 1814. No buildings remain.

BRIEF HISTORY: As early as 1807, converts to Shakerism were living along the Wabash River near Vincennes. That next year, Issachar Bates, one of the three original Shaker missionaries from the East, was sent by Union Village to see whether the place should be gathered into a society. In 1809, Bates was made the **elder** at **Busro**, as this place was called until 1816. As the gathering continued, 30 Shakers from Red Banks, Kentucky, joined so that by 1810, there were 199 in all. More Shakers were added when the small Shaker settlements at Eagle Creek and Straight Creek, Ohio, were closed. In such a short while, Busro had grown to 300 believers and over 1,300 acres, yet this prosperity was deceptive. Malaria continued to be a major killer, and in 1811 and 1812, the tremendous New Madrid earthquake occurred. Not long after this, major trouble with the Indians threatened and then the War of 1812 broke out. It was felt prudent that the entire society move to Union Village for safety. This process took two months. In 1814 members returned to find a destroyed village. They rebuilt and had a stable society of about 200 members until 1827. That year it was decided to close the society to avoid the punitive fines that were levied on those who refused militia duty. West Union Shakers were divided among Union Village, **White Water**, **South Union**, and **Pleasant Hill** societies.

LAST SHAKER: Marguerite Fellows Melcher erroneously reports in her book *The Shaker Adventure* that Sarah Pennebaker (1840–1916) of Pleasant Hill was the last Shaker from West Union. This is not true, since Sister Sarah was born over a dozen years after West Union closed! In fact she was the sister of **Francis and William Pennebaker**. It is not known at this time who the last West Union Shaker was.

WHIPPING STONE. A white marble marker surrounded by a cairn commemorates the spot where Father **James Whittaker** was brutally whipped by a mob in 1783 at **Harvard, Massachusetts**. Shakers to this day bring a stone when visiting the spot. In some circles of Shaker enthusiasts, this place is wryly referred to as the "whiping stone" since the actual lettering on the marker misspells the word whipped as "whiped."

WHITCHER, MARY (1815–1890). Mary Whitcher's image is one of the most familiar to those who collect Shaker paper. In 1882, *Mary Whitcher's Shaker-House-Keeper* was published and her portrait is on the front cover.

The Whitcher name goes directly back to the origin of the **Canterbury** Shaker society. Her grandfather was Benjamin Whitcher, an early convert whose farm was the nucleus for the **Church Family**. Other members of her family held positions of trust and care at Canterbury. Mary Whitcher was born in 1815 in Laurens, New York. She joined the Shakers at Canterbury in 1826. Eventually she became a **trustee, family eldress,** schoolteacher, and a member of the **Ministry.** No doubt it is her role as trustee from 1876 to 1880 that caused the drawing of her to be used in the 1882 "cookbook."

WHITE, ANNA (1831–1910). She was born on 21 January 1831 in Brooklyn, New York. Her parents, Robert and Hannah Gibbs White, were Quakers. She was educated at Mansion Square Seminary in Poughkeepsie. While a teenager, her father converted to Shakerism and lived on and off until his death with the **Hancock** Shakers. His example led her to investigate the Shakers for herself. Her family was firmly opposed to this and one of her uncles offered her an estate of $40,000 if she would give up the idea of becoming a Shaker.

Anna joined the **North Family** at **New Lebanon** on 16 October 1849. For the rest of her life she kept this day as her real birthday. Her enthusiasm never wavered. Under the wise tutelage of **Eldress Antoinette Doolittle, Sister** Anna was formed into a young Shaker of great promise. Around the time she entered, Elder **Frederick Evans** had decided to become a vegetarian. She joined him in this practice, which was at first unpopular at the North Family. Gradually the entire North Family became vegetarian. In addition, almost as soon as she arrived, she was favored with inspired **songs.** Over the next 60 years she wrote hundreds of songs. Many of these have been published and are still sung today. In 1850, when she had been a member only six months, she was permitted to sign the **covenant.** Her first major duty was to care for visitors and inquirers. In addition she helped with the various housekeeping tasks. She also knit and did palm leaf work. In 1865, she became second eldress, standing with Eldress Antoinette Doolittle. After Doolittle died, Eldress Anna became first eldress in 1887.

Since the 1850s, the North Family had become the most liberal and progressive Shaker **family.** Sharing the elders' lot with Elder Frederick for so many years influenced her to take a strong interest in reform movements. She contributed articles to the Shaker *Manifesto* and compiled two books of Shaker music. Her published material consists of a series of memorial books to recently deceased Shakers and essays on reform and religion. She supported all efforts to improve physical and spiritual conditions in the world.

As the 20th century approached she became interested in trying to change political policies. Besides writing on behalf of Alfred Dreyfus in France, she became a strong advocate of pacifism and disarmament. She was vice president of the New York branch of Women's International League of Peace and Arbitration. The crowning achievement of this work was an international peace conference held at **Mount Lebanon** on 31 August 1905. She was one of the speakers and later traveled to Washington, D.C., to present the resolutions to President Theodore Roosevelt.

The opening years of the new century saw Eldress Anna at the forefront of activities at home and on the national front. She encouraged Sister Ada Grace Brown of the North Family to open a private school for girls. She helped set up **Ann Lee Cottage**, a place where visitors of the more refined class could spent the summer and perhaps join the Shakers after seeing how wonderful the life was at Mount Lebanon. Along with Sister **Leila S. Taylor** of the North Family, she coauthored the last general history of the Shakers written by Shakers, *Shakerism: Its Meaning and Message*. She was a member of the National American Woman Suffrage Association and vice president of the National Council of Women. Toward the end of her life she became an advocate of Christian Science. She died in December 1910, deeply mourned by the members of the North Family.

Though her obituary was in *The New York Times* and the peace conference of 1905 had attracted national attention, Eldress Anna's impact among her fellow Shakers outside of the North Family was limited. For example, very few Shakers attended the peace conference and some of the Shakers from the other families at Mount Lebanon purposely made life difficult for her. In *Shakerism: Its Meaning and Message*, she concludes with a stirring call to action addressed to fellow Shakers. She asks them to really start living the life and not be so concerned with the accumulation of wealth. She saw no value in wearing the Shaker habit if internally the person did not wish to live the life seriously. Her ideas, as worthy as they may have been, came too late. By 1904 there were only about 700 Shakers. Almost all of these were older women and young girls. The few men who were able to work were stretched thin doing many jobs at once. At that point in time nothing could have saved at least half of the communities. They had diminished beyond hope and were just hanging on. As in her work on behalf of peace, Eldress Anna was practically a lone voice in her plea to fellow Shakers. Finally, since she was an idealist, she did not see that those from the outside sometimes used her to accomplish their own pet projects. She also trusted some who were not capable, and listened to bad advice. In truth she did manage to bring the North Family into modern times, but after her death the momentum was lost. *See also* NORTH FAMILY.

WHITE OAK, GEORGIA (1898–1902). Spritual Name: None. FEAST GROUND: None. BISHOPRIC: **Union Village.** FAMILIES: one settlement. MAXIMUM POPULATION AND YEAR: 10 in 1900. INDUSTRIES: grape cultivation, livestock, farming. NOTABLE SHAKERS: none. UNIQUE FEATURES: White Oak was the last Shaker **family** ever founded. It also was the society that had the briefest history.

BRIEF HISTORY: By the 1890s, there was certain agitation among some of the trustees of **Mount Lebanon** and **Watervliet** to explore lands in warmer climates so that Shakers might resettle there. High taxes, a short growing season, and a rapidly aging population were the reasons advanced for thinking about moving Shaker societies to the South. These ideas appealed to **Joseph Slingerland**, a **trustee** at Union Village. While other Shaker communities purchased land in 1896 in Florida, his attention turned to Georgia. It has been said that his vision included moving all of the Shakers remaining in Ohio and Kentucky into one large place in coastal Georgia.

On 1 February 1898, **Elder** Joseph Slingerland, Samuel Goodwin, William Ayer, Eugene Columbain, Eldress Elizabeth Downing, Laura Fudger, and Julia Foley left Union Village for their new home near Brunswick, Georgia. The next day transactions were closed on 10,500 acres of land the Shakers had purchased for $26,000 in Glynn County. This property consisted of two plantations called Altama and Hopeton. Supplies of all kinds, including livestock, were shipped there from Union Village. Things never went well, and two of the Shakers, William Ayer and Julia Foley, left and got married in Savannah on 12 April. Elder Joseph and Eldress Elizabeth returned to Union Village on 15 April. The Shaker property was then managed by a non-Shaker named R. T. Clark.

Since Elder Joseph's thirst for speculation was limitless, the following October the Shakers bought 6,995 acres of land from L. T.

McKennon for $16,500. This property was located 20 miles south of Brunswick in White Oak. He spent an additional $20,000 building a large house with extravagant appointments, including floors covered with linoleum, large tables with marble tops, a large artesian well, four bathrooms, and a dining room that could seat 24 people. To help pay for this land and magnificent house, the Shakers borrowed $30,000 using the Altama and Hopeton plantations as collateral.

Visiting Shakers from Florida praised the beautiful surroundings and the fertility of the land, yet they remarked that the climate was not healthy. This certainly was true for Elder **Oliver Hampton** of Union Village who died there not long after visiting in 1901. He was buried on the property and an oral tradition states that there is another unnamed Shaker buried there as well.

By this time, Elder Joseph Slingerland's dishonest activities had caught the attention of the **Central Ministry** and it fell to **James H. Fennessey**, a trustee of Union Village, to pull the community out of debt. One of the first things was to sell off the White Oak property before any more loss could occur. The large house built by the Shakers was torn down in 1957.

LAST SHAKER: The last person to die a Shaker who lived at White Oak was Joseph Slingerland (1844–1920).

WHITE WATER, OHIO (1824–1916). SPIRITUAL NAME: Lonely Plain of Tribulation. FEAST GROUND: Chosen Square. BISHOPRIC: **Union Village**. FAMILIES: Center, North, South. MAXIMUM POPULATION AND YEAR: 200 in 1846. INDUSTRIES: seeds, brooms, sorghum molasses, fruit, farm produce. NOTABLE SHAKERS: Mary Green Gass, Stephen Ball, Henry Bear, Charles Sturr. UNIQUE FEATURES: Due to subsequent purchases of land and an increase in population, in 1845 the **Center Family** was moved to what was the Middle Family. The former Center Family became the North Family. The new Center Family, however, did not build a new **Meeting House** but continued to use the one at the North Family. Thus at White Water, the Meeting House was not located at the Center Family but at the North Family. In addition, in 1852, **Rufus Bishop** of the **Ministry of New Lebanon** died at White Water while on a visit. He was the only member of the **Ministry** to die in the Shaker West and the only one to die while on a visitation.

BRIEF HISTORY: During the early years of the 1820s the fervor for Shakerism had not dimmed for the people of Ohio, and Miriam Agnew, who lived near the Dry Fork of the Whitewater River, asked the Shakers to open their testimony near her farm. The Agnew, Boggett, and McKee families were the first to gather to the Shakers. Within a year, the Ministry at Union Village decided to close the small Shaker society at Darby Plains near Columbus and consolidate the members with those at White Water. The new community numbered a little less than 90. In 1824, land was purchased and the White Water Shaker society began. In 1825, Calvin Morrell, Stephen Williams, Phoebe Lockwood, and Mary Bedle were chosen by Union Village to replace the earlier leaders who had come from Darby Plains.

Similar to all other Shaker villages, a period of growth and expansion followed the first settlement and eventually three major families were established: the Center, the North, and the South. In 1845, the original First or Center Family moved to the Middle Family and the old Center became the Second or North Family. In 1855 the former Walker farm was established as the South Family and became the **Gathering Order** until 1862. That year the Gathering Order was moved back to the North and the South for a time was used to house the boys from the Center Family. The South Family was dissolved in 1889 and sold in 1914.

By 1830, defections from the ranks had weakened Shaker life and the Shakers tried to fill up the vacancies with children. In 1840, the society numbered 79, but almost one-third, or 24, were children under 15 years of age. In 1846, after the **Adventist** disappointment, 120 Millerites swelled the ranks at White Water and brought the total population to the artificially high number of 200. While some of the Millerites did stay faithful Shakers, many left; by 1850, only 138, including former Adventists, lived at White Water. Membership leveled off and with the help of large numbers of children, Shaker numbers stayed between 120 and 140 for 20 years. By 1870, the society owned 1,400 acres of land, but there were only 22 men older than 15.

The seed business was ended in 1874 and the fading of the village can be seen in the population figures. By 1880 there were 65 and in 1900 48, again, one-third of them children under 15. Unlike other places in the Shaker West, however, the White Water Shakers seem to have retained a high degree of religious faith. If the devastating fire of 1907 had not occurred, it is interesting to speculate whether the society would have lasted much longer than it did. That fire destroyed the dwelling of the Center Family as well as two other buildings and claimed the lives of three elderly Shaker **sisters**. This tragedy prompted the Ministry to call for the dissolution of the community. In 1912, the North Family closed, and in 1916, the Center Family closed. Parts of the property are now privately owned and a large portion is controlled by the Hamilton County Park District.

LAST SHAKER: Mary Green Gass (1848–1933). After White Water closed in 1916, **Eldress** Mary Gass made her way to the Shaker community at **Hancock, Massachusetts**. She arrived there on 17 December and lived in the Church Family **Office** until 6 July 1917 when she moved to **Mount Lebanon**. She died there in 1933, age 85.

WHITELEY, JOHN HENRY HORSEFAL (1819–1905). John Whiteley did not even hear of the Shakers until he was an adult man with a family. He was working in the wool room of the Ballardville Mill in Andover, Massachusetts, when a coworker told him that his religious views seemed to be like those held by the Shakers. He visited the society at **Shirley** and joined almost at once. Though he was 29 years old when he joined, he still lived a long life with the Shakers. He was with them 56 more years.

Born in Huddersfield, Yorkshire, England, he came to the United States in the summer of 1842. He first settled in Newburgh, New York. His daughter Sarah E. Whiteley was born there in 1843. Later that year he took up 80 acres of land near Elgin, Illinois. In 1845, his son John Whiteley Jr. was born in the township of Wayne, Dupage County, Illinois. Besides his farm, he worked as a wool sorter in nearby Dayton and Elgin. The climate proved to be harmful to him, and he was advised by a doctor to move back East. In 1847 he took a job in the wool room of the Middlesex Company in Lowell. The next year he went to the Ballardville Mill in Andover where he learned of the Shakers. His youngest child, Joseph S. Whiteley, was born there in 1848.

He first visited Shirley on 27 January 1849. So favorable was the impression made by the Shakers that he brought his family with him to join on 5 March 1849. When they were admitted, the society at Shirley was already in decline. The South Family had been broken up a number of years. Since the Whiteleys and a couple of others decided to try the life at Shirley, the South House was again reopened and the Whiteley family moved in. For four years, John and his family distinguished themselves by their fervor and hard work. In 1853, he was made **elder** and **trustee** at the North Family. This was the **Gathering Order** at Shirley, and it was hoped that Elder John would be able to attract others. In the late 1850s his mother Elizabeth Whiteley, a widow, came from England and settled at Shirley. She lived with her son at the North Family. In 1865 his daughter Sarah E. Whiteley left and married a young Shaker from Shirley named Samuel Burns. Later that same year his youngest son, Joseph, left to go to Colorado with his uncle. The last of his children, John Jr., left between 1865 and 1870. Their departures saddened him, but did not lessen his determination to persevere as a Shaker.

In 1871, he was released from the North Family to become first in the **Ministry** of **Harvard** and Shirley. From this point until he was relieved of this office in 1904, he split his time between the two villages. In 1884, he was also made trustee and first elder of the Church at Shirley. Since by then Shirley had fewer than 30 members, his duties in the Ministry did not hinder him from taking on the burden of the spiritual and temporal care of the **Church Family**. While at Shirley he lived at the **Trustees' Office**.

After he was appointed to the Ministry, Elder John kept a personal diary that provides detailed information about life at Harvard and Shirley. In spite of holding many positions at once, his great energy allowed him to carry on without difficulty. In 1890 he visited England for two months. When Shirley celebrated its 100th anniversary in 1893, he wrote an eloquent piece on Shirley history for the *Manifesto*. In spite of all signs to the contrary, he held on to hope that somehow new people would join the community. He boasted of the well-cultivated land, superb buildings, and faithful members. All they lacked were new recruits. Though some people did join, they did not stay. In 1901 his health had deteriorated so much that he could no longer keep his diary. A series of strokes incapacitated him. On 16 August 1904 he was removed from the Ministry. Elder **Joseph Holden** of the **Central Ministry** made plans to live at Shirley and begin the process of selling off the entire place. **Brother** Henry Hollister was also transferred there to carry on the farm. Elder John died 12 August 1905.

WHITTAKER, JAMES (1751–1787). **Mother Ann Lee**, Father **William Lee**, and Father James constituted the core group of early Shaker leaders known as the **First Parents**. They had a bond of kinship that went back to the first days in **Manchester, England**. Father James was born in Oldham, England, on February 1751. Ann Lee was one of his relatives and she brought him up. He became a weaver and a member of the artisan/merchant class. When **Mother Ann** decided to come to America, he came with her as her strongest supporter outside of her brother William Lee. After the Shaker testimony was publicly opened in May 1780, his **gifts** as an orator were used to gather souls. Many came to be Shakers because of him. Children were particularly drawn to him. By all accounts he was the most approachable of the First Parents.

When Mother Ann died in September 1784, Father James succeeded her as head of the Shaker Church. His time in office is well documented in terms of telling about the many places he visited, but nothing is said about what may have been a power struggle between him and **Joseph Meacham**. At that time no "**center of union**" as yet existed, and Father James moved from place to place. His missionary exhortations and the physical abuse he suffered contributed to his early death. He had a premonition of his demise, and he decided to die at the **Enfield, Connecticut**, Shaker society. This may have shown his support for David Meacham. Father James died on 20 July 1787. With his death, the leadership of the Shakers passed entirely into American hands. *See also* "J. W." STONE; MINISTRY OF NEW LEBANON.

WILCOX, GEORGE (1819–1910). George Wilcox was a part of that strong third generation of Shakers in the East. These were the last to join the Shakers in large numbers and remain faithful. He was born 14 March 1819 in Foster, Rhode Island. His parents, David Wilcox and Betsey Fry Wilcox, belonged to a group of "Christian" believers. The Shakers from **Enfield, Connecticut**, heard about them and sent missionaries into the area of rural Rhode Island where this group lived. Many were converted, and these families, named Damon, Burlingame, Fry, Wilcox, and others, would contribute a great deal to Enfield's prosperity for most of the 19th century. In March 1827, the Wilcox family moved to Enfield and joined the community. Young

George was sent to live at the **Church Family**, where he would reside for the next 83 years.

Brother George signed the **covenant** in 1841. Since he showed a great deal of promise, in 1844 he became second **elder** of the Church. He was not quite 25 years old. In this capacity he guided the young brethren and worked doing gardening and farming. In 1851 he was made first elder of the Church. In this role as elder he had found his niche. He remained elder until his death in 1910. No other Shaker served as elder as long as he did: 66 years. Elder George was in office for such a lengthy period for two reasons: He enjoyed being in charge; and there were few other men available to do the job. As men either left or died, Elder George took on their responsibilities as well. For example, in 1864, after Nathan Damon's departure, Elder George became a **trustee** of the Church Family. He also held this job for the rest of his long life.

At the North Family, trustee Omar Pease built a very large and modern shop for the **sisters**. This immense white clapboard structure dominated the landscape. Elder George did not wish to be outdone, so in 1876 he built an even bigger structure in brick to be the new **dwelling house** of the Church Family. Enfield actually did not need these buildings since its population had declined dramatically. No doubt Elder George used the arrival of the **Tyringham** Shakers who moved to Enfield after their village closed as a good reason to expand.

The **Ministry** wanted to relieve Elder George of the many burdens of office. In 1895, they sent **Walter Shepherd** from **Mount Lebanon** to Enfield as a possible leader. Elder George did not resign, however, and Walter Shepherd had to wait 15 years until Elder George died to succeed him. Enfield was a prosperous society with excellent farmland and magnificent buildings. Perhaps its ultimate fate might have been different if younger leadership could have been successfully introduced during the 1890s. As it was, Elder George lingered on, presiding each year over fewer and fewer Shakers, but never missing an opportunity to make money and keep himself in charge of almost everything. He died from old age, close to his 91st birthday, in 1910.

WILSON, CHARLES DELMER (1873–1961). He was born on 8 July 1873 in Topsham, Maine. In 1882, he and his brother Harris were brought to the Shakers at **Sabbathday Lake** by their mother. As a child, "Dellie" came under the influence of **Sister Aurelia Mace** and Sister Ada S. Cummings, who were his teachers. His Sunday School teacher was Sister Sarah Fletcher, who was responsible for first teaching him about Shakerism.

Dedicated young men were few in most Shaker communities, but at Sabbathday Lake, **Elder William Dumont** had succeeded in attracting scores of men. Nonetheless, many responsibilities were given to young Delmer. When he was 14 he had the care of the large dairy herd. Also that year, his mother came back to get him from the Shakers, and he refused to leave. In time, every aspect of the farm came under his management. In the meantime, he developed skills as an excellent woodworker, and throughout his life he made **furniture**, all either for his personal use or as gifts to members of his community.

In 1894, two of the sisters who were in charge of fancy goods sales at the Poland Spring House sold the two oval carriers that had been given them by the **Mount Lebanon** Shakers. Demand for them became so high that all available oval boxes were modified for sale. At first **Brother** Delmer added handles to existing carriers and refinished them. To satisfy demand, they also purchased oval boxes from **Alfred** and carriers from Mount Lebanon. In 1896, Brother Delmer began making his first carriers. He refined his techniques by designing equipment so that in a few years he increased output from 30 in 1896 to over 1000 by 1908. During the winter of 1922–1923 he made 1,083. Since he made many thousands of these carriers, he earned the title "dean of the Carrier Makers."

In 1896, he and Brother Chellis Wing built the greenhouse so that the sisters might grow flowers to sell. In addition, his interest in photography was great, and he started a postcard industry from pictures he had taken of the buildings and grounds at Sabbathday Lake. He also did oil paintings. As the number of brethren diminished, he filled in wherever he was needed. He also managed the extensive apple orchards and the great mill. Even today, many of the structures and the property show the marks of Brother Delmer.

On 23 February 1927 he was appointed a **trustee**, and on 14 May 1931, he was made **elder** of the **Church Family**. He never used the title of elder, however, and was always called Brother Delmer.

Though toward the end of his life hired labor worked the farm or it was leased out, Brother Delmer kept an active interest in the operations. He died of lung cancer on 15 December 1961.

WINSHIP, ELLA E. (1857–1941). She was born in Bristol, Rhode Island, on 11 July 1857. In 1870 she joined the Shaker community at **Groveland, New York**, and eventually became the second **eldress** under Polly Lee. When Groveland closed in 1892, its members were sent to live at the North Family at **Watervliet, New York**. In 1919 the North Family closed, and Eldress Ella moved to the South Family at Watervliet, but her tenure at the South Family was short. In 1923, she was appointed to the **Parent Ministry** and moved to the **North Family** at **Mount Lebanon**. Ten years later she appointed herself eldress of the North Family while becoming first in the Ministry. In order to help close out Watervliet, she was made a **trustee** of that community in 1937. She died at Mount Lebanon in 1941.

WINTER SHAKER. Through all of Shaker history, people have always been joining or leaving the communities. The name of "winter Shaker" has been given to a person who joined in the fall after the harvest was in and then left in the spring before planting started. In a community based on agriculture, as all Shaker villages were, this could be a serious problem. An examination of journals, diaries, and **probationary covenants**, however, shows that there was not one particular time of year when people left in large numbers. Apostasy often came in connection with other circumstances. If, for example, a young person of promise decided to leave, he/she was often followed by friends. This was especially true among young adults. In addition, since many children were sought after by the Shakers themselves and brought to the communities, it can hardly be said that these youth were joining to escape the winter.

Again, the concept of winter Shakers is not clearly mentioned in Shaker journals and seems to be a rather late development. Frustrated leaders spoke of it to visitors such as Charles Nordhoff when he made a tour of the communities in 1874. "Winter Shaker" is as good a description as any to attempt to characterize what must have been an unsettling occurrence, but it does not stand the scrutiny of close examination.

WORLD. Shakers saw their communities as **Zion**. Everything else was the world. Use of the phrase "the world" was common among the Shakers.

WORLD'S PEOPLE. Anyone who was not a Shaker belonged to this category. This term was often used to categorize a visitor or some outsider who was particularly flashy or ostentatious, though it does not necessarily have a negative connotation. *See also* WORLD.

WORLEY, MALCOLM (1762–1844). He has the distinction of being the first Shaker convert in the West. He joined 27 March 1805, just five days after the arrival of the three Shaker missionaries at **Turtle Creek**. He was born 19 July 1762. At the time of the opening of the Shaker testimony, he was living at Turtle Creek, Ohio, with his wife Peggy and their children. He was a farmer and a member of **Richard McNemar's** church. His life had been deeply influenced by the Kentucky Revival. As time passed, however, his confidence had been shaken, and he received divine assurance that soon he would receive help. When Shaker missionaries **John Meacham**, **Issachar Bates**, and **Benjamin S. Youngs** came to Turtle Creek, he offered them hospitality. They were the answer to his prayers and he joined the Shakers. His home became the base of operations for a while, until 5 June 1806 when Father **David Darrow** moved into a new house built on the land recently purchased from Timothy Sewall. The Worley farm became part of the **Center Family**. The site of his house was later the place where the brick **Office** stood from 1826 to 1892.

In 1839, along with Richard McNemar and Garner McNemar, he was directed to leave the Shakers by **instrument** Margaret O'Brien. This was a complete shock to the aged **Brother** Malcolm. He had been totally faithful and given up everything he had for the establishment of the community. **Elder Freegift Wells**, however, was extremely jealous of the high esteem that the community had for the McNemars and Malcolm Worley. Since the society was caught up in the **Era of Manifestations**, he had Margaret O'Brien declare that the men had become idols and must leave. Worley was taken to Brown County, Ohio, by one of the brethren, Ithamar Johnson. Brother Ithamar reluctantly agreed to do this, though it was a great trial for him since he knew Worley was blameless. While Richard McNemar traveled to **New Lebanon** to appeal to the **Ministry** there, Malcolm Worley boarded out. When McNemar, completely exonerated, returned in triumph, Worley was able to come back to his home. He remained faithful until his death on 3 August 1844, but three of his children, Rebecca, Joseph, and Joshua, left the Shakers after he died. They initiated legal proceedings to recover land that their father had so generously given to the Shakers when **Union Village** was gathered. The case was decided in favor of the Shakers in 1848, though it cost them $1,200 in legal fees.

WRIGHT, ELEAZAR. *See* MCNEMAR, RICHARD.

WRIGHT, GROVE (1789–1861). The principal strength of early Shakerism was the network of family connections that held communities together. For example, Mother **Lucy Wright**, the head of the Shakers until 1821, had numerous siblings and half-siblings who became and remained fervent Shakers. More importantly, they had children, the majority of whom stayed faithful. This gave the Shakers quite a boost and helped ensure a continuity in leadership.

Mother Lucy's brother John had a son, Grove, born in Pittsfield, Massachusetts, on 17 January 1789. In 1792 when **Hancock** was gathered into **gospel order**, he joined with his family. Since Hancock had too many boys and **Tyringham** needed some, nine-year-old Grove was sent there to live in 1797. Transfers among communities in a **bishopric** were common. Amid the shadowy, steep hills of Tyringham, Grove grew into manhood as a farmer helping to work the large Shaker holdings. He was also under the care of Thomas Paten, who was a carpenter. Young Grove learned woodworking skills from Paten, and eventually he became a noteworthy craftsman of Shaker **furniture**. He signed the **covenant** at Tyringham, and it appeared that he would be settling down for a quiet life in the smallest Shaker society in the East.

Fate had other plans. Actually, fate expressed itself in the wishes of Mother Lucy, who had another career earmarked for her nephew. While simply being related would have been enough to notice him, he must have shown other talents for her to choose him to become second in the bishopric **Ministry** in 1818. In this capacity, he stood in association with **Elder** Nathaniel Deming. They visited Tyringham and **Enfield**, but lived mostly at Hancock. In addition to his spiritual duties as minister to hundreds of people, he used his cabinetmaking skills to produce furniture, pails, and table swifts. His pieces are highly collectible and his fame as a craftsman is well known.

Just as important, however, were his considerable **gifts** as a spiritual leader. His gentle approach and calm influence did a great deal to foster community life in all its aspects. In November 1845 he was elevated to be first in the Ministry and held this position until he resigned in 1860 due to ill health. In fact, he suffered from a bad skin disease and as early as 1855 had asked to be released. These were crisis years for the Shakers and the unsettled nature of the societies had made it unwise to release him until his health was so bad that his request had to be granted.

Life after 42 years in the Ministry may have seemed like an anticlimax. Curiously, after being released as minister, he moved to Enfield, Connecticut, to live. Thus his youth and early manhood were spent at Tyringham, his adult years and old age at Hancock, and his final six months at Enfield, where he is buried. While there, he did not retire from work. He used his time to make cupboards and fix furniture. In every way he was truly a man of the Hancock bishopric, and stands as a symbol of the excellent type of member the Shakers had from the second generation.

WRIGHT, LUCY (1760–1821). One of the great strengths of early Shakerism is that it attracted converts of high quality. Lucy Wright was born in Pittsfield on 5 February 1760. At the time of her birth, Pittsfield was little more than an outpost in the last part of Massachusetts to be settled. Her family, however, was one of the most prominent families. Her early life was not one of privation or struggle. In 1779 she married Elizur Goodrich, a young man from a large and prosperous family. Their marriage took place at an ironic time. Just as they were married, the **New Light** Revival was winding down. Dissatisfied revivalists were soon to come upon **Mother Ann** and her companions. Elizur met Mother Ann and immediately converted. His wife, however, was not enthusiastic. Eventually she came around and became a close companion of Mother Ann's. In fact, she nursed Mother Ann during her final illness. Mother Ann's fondness for her and her own abilities made her the perfect person to assume the dominant role in the female leadership.

While Father **James Whittaker** and Father **Joseph Meacham** lived, Mother Lucy was not able to come into her own as a leader. After their deaths, she became in effect the sole leader of the Shakers. This did not happen without challenges, but she prevailed due to **Elder Henry Clough**. During the 25 years of her leadership, the Shakers expanded into the West and all but two of the long-lived Shaker societies had been founded by the time of her death on 7 February 1821. Wright's energies were boundless and her presence seemed to be everywhere. She introduced the concept of having a **Gathering Order** and greatly expanded this type of order at **New Lebanon**. Though cautious about the codification of Shakerism, the first major works on Shaker history and theology were published while she lived. She also cautioned about accepting children without their parents. Later Shakers chose to ignore her warnings, with dire consequences.

Her influence continued after her death since she named her successors. These men and women, **Ebenezer Bishop**, **Rufus Bishop**, **Ruth Landon**, and **Asenath Clark**, served without interruption for almost 30 years. Many Shakers and non-Shakers have seen her as the greatest leader the Shakers ever had after **Ann Lee**.

– Y –

YOUNG BELIEVER. When the first **gathering** or **novitiate families** were set up, the people who joined them were called young believers. This was in contrast to those who had joined at the beginning when the communities were first organized. The first Shakers were **Mother's First Born** and their families. In time, the term young believer had no relevance since in this context all subsequent Shakers could be called young believers.

YOUNGS, BENJAMIN SETH (1774–1855). Watervliet, New York, was organized into full **gospel order** not long after **New Lebanon** in 1788. The process of consolidating scattered **believers** into **families** took many years, and in 1794, when Benjamin Seth Youngs joined the Shakers at Watervliet, it was still a new community. His **gifts** as an effective preacher were recognized by Mother **Lucy Wright**, and she sent him with **Issachar Bates** on missionary tours throughout

New England and New York. This was in preparation for the great work that lay ahead for him as one of the three Shakers who carried the gospel west in 1805. That year, along with **John Meacham** and Issachar Bates, he was sent as a missionary to Ohio and Kentucky. Joining forces with able western ministers such as **Richard McNemar**, Youngs evangelized the region. On one memorable occasion in 1806 at Matthew Houston's church in Paint Lick, Kentucky, he stood on a log and preached before 600–800 people for three hours.

Though Youngs was a preacher, his lasting fame as a Shaker came from the fact that he was the principal author of *The Testimony of Christ's Second Appearing*. This was the first major work of Shaker theology. Youngs began it in July 1806 and finished it on 10 April 1808. In the meantime, he wrote back and forth to New Lebanon for approval. He spent the wintertime writing and resumed his preaching and missionary work during the spring and summer. After the book was published, he then turned his attention to full-time missionary activity once again.

In 1809 he went to **Busro, Indiana**, and then in May 1809 to **South Union**, or Gasper as it was called. The Gasper believers were fervent and held to their beliefs with fortitude in spite of persecution. From this home base, he traveled throughout the area. In 1811, the Gasper Shakers were organized into full gospel order with Benjamin S. Youngs and Molly Goodrich as first ministers. In 1812, they received the parental titles of Father and Mother. Until the summer of 1836, Father Benjamin, or **Elder** Benjamin as he was commonly called, was first in the **Lead** at South Union. His boundless energy and knowledge of what was happening even at the **out families** was taken for granted. This gave confidence to **young believers**. His leadership, however, was not without its challenges. Over and over he admonished believers not to become involved with the **world**. He roundly condemned what he considered to be the loose ways that seemed to be the norm at **Pleasant Hill**. He also spoke out against using slaves.

What had been accepted leadership in 1809, however, by the 1830s caused much tension. By then, almost all of the eastern Shakers who had come to the West as missionaries were either dead or had returned home. For decades, Elder Benjamin had made frequent trips east so the **Ministry of New Lebanon** was aware of conditions at South Union. It was clearly time for westerners to take charge. Elder

Benjamin's presence just inspired more rebellion and tension. In May 1836, while Elder Samuel Turner was visiting the Ministry at New Lebanon, they asked him not to return to the West where he had been a missionary since 1806. That summer, Elder Benjamin was recalled home to Watervliet, New York. He died there in 1855. His grave is in the center row, where **Mother Ann**, **Giles Avery**, **Ruth Landon**, **John Hocknell**, and other famous Shakers are buried.

YOUNGS, ISAAC NEWTON (1793–1865). He was born 4 July 1793 in Johnstown, New York. His parents were Seth Youngs and Martha Farley Youngs. Although the family was Methodist, Seth Youngs became interested in Shakerism. Several members of the Wells and Youngs families were Shakers at **Watervliet**, and Seth Wells visited them in 1793. He joined the Shakers at Watervliet a year later. His wife chose not to join, and the care of Isaac, who was an infant, passed on to his uncle and aunt, Benjamin and Molly Youngs. They were not actual Shakers, but had some measure of faith. In 1800, he was admitted to the South Family at Watervliet. By 1803, he was part of the **Children's Order** at the **Church Family**.

His opportunities for formal schooling were limited, and when he was 10 he began to receive instruction in tailoring. This began a lifelong and reluctant career in this trade. His childhood and earliest life as a Shaker at Watervliet ended when he was transferred to the **First Order of the Church** at **New Lebanon**. This was the most elite **family** in all of Shakerdom, and he would live here for the rest of his life. As he grew into manhood, the exacting standards set for the First Order members created a good deal of tension for him. His natural impulses, which were strong, had to be restrained if he were to live the life required of him. His work, but above all his prayer life, kept him faithful.

One of the most interesting aspects of his life is that he was a prolific writer. He kept a diary and wrote many unpublished works. From these materials, it is possible to know a great deal more of him than of most other Shakers of that time. Glendyne R. Wergland's book *One Shaker Life: Isaac Newton Youngs* is the definitive work on his life. Wergland provides detailed information about his struggles, hopes, and reflections. In addition, the story of his occupation as an important clockmaker and tailor are carefully told. So many facts are skillfully woven into such an engaging story that a good sense of what it must have been like to live in the community can be glimpsed. In 1815, Isaac's father Seth Youngs killed himself by cutting his throat. It can be assumed that some sort of mental disorder was present in the family because, as he aged, Brother Isaac himself became troubled by anxiety and mental problems. He eventually had to be confined and, after distracting his **caretaker**, on 7 August 1865 he committed suicide by jumping from the fourth floor of his room in the First Order **dwelling house**. His death spared him further sufferings and living long enough to see the further decline of the society and the destruction of most of his home by fire 10 years later.

– Z –

ZION. This term means any place where Shakers live. Collectively it referred to all of the Shaker Villages. These were the physical places, but they only had significance because **believers** lived there.

Appendix A
List of Those Who Served in the Gospel Ministry

BEFORE THE GATHERING OF NEW LEBANON, 1774–1787

1774–1784

Mother Ann Lee

Father William Lee
Father James Whittaker

1784–1787

Father James Whittaker

THE MINISTRY OF NEW LEBANON, 1787–1946

In 1861, the postal address of the Shakers in New Lebanon was changed to Mount Lebanon. After this, the name "Mount Lebanon Ministry" was commonly used. In 1893, the Mount Lebanon Ministry took direct control of the dissolved Hancock bishopric. As a result, the title "Central Ministry" came into use, and it is still employed by many today in reference to the Ministry during any part of Shaker history. Starting in 1918, the Ministry began to call itself the "Parent Ministry." From 1921 until the dissolution of the Ministry in 1957, "Parent Ministry" was the exclusive title they used for themselves.

1787: Those Who Lived in the Meeting House at New Lebanon

Mother Lucy Wright
Sarah Harrison
Thankful Hamlin
Desire Turner

Father Joseph Meacham
Childs Hamlin
Henry Clough
Jethro Turner

255

1790

Mother Lucy Wright
Sarah Harrison
Desire Turner
Thankful Hamlin

Father Joseph Meacham
Henry Clough
Jethro Turner

1792

Mother Lucy Wright
Thankful Hamlin

Father Joseph Meacham
Henry Clough

1793

Mother Lucy Wright
Rebecca Kendall

Father Joseph Meacham
Henry Clough

1796

Mother Lucy Wright
Rebecca Kendall

Henry Clough

1798

Mother Lucy Wright
Rebecca Kendall
Ruth Hammond

Abiather Babbit

1800

Mother Lucy Wright
Ruth Hammond

Abiather Babbit

1804

Mother Lucy Wright
(Polly) Ruth Landon

Abiather Babbit

1805

Mother Lucy Wright   Abiather Babbit
Ruth Landon   Ebenezer Bishop

1807

Mother Lucy Wright   Abiather Babbit
Ruth Landon

1821

Ruth Landon   Ebenezer Bishop
Asenath Clark   Rufus Bishop

1849

Ruth Landon   Rufus Bishop
Asenath Clark   Amos Stewart

1850

Asenath Clark   Rufus Bishop
Samantha Fairbanks   Amos Stewart

1852

Asenath Clark   Rufus Bishop
Betsey Bates   Amos Stewart

1856

Betsey Bates   Amos Stewart
Eliza Ann Taylor   Daniel Boler

1858

Betsey Bates   Richard Bushnell
Eliza Ann Taylor   Daniel Boler

1859

| Betsey Bates | Daniel Boler |
| Eliza Ann Taylor | Giles B. Avery |

1869

| Eliza Ann Taylor | Daniel Boler |
| Polly Reed | Giles B. Avery |

1881

| Eliza Ann Taylor | Daniel Boler |
| Harriet Bullard | Giles B. Avery |

1891

| Harriet Bullard | Daniel Boler |
| (Helen) Augusta Stone | Joseph Holden |

1892

| Harriet Bullard | Joseph Holden |
| Augusta Stone | |

1899

| Harriet Bullard | Joseph Holden |
| Augusta Stone | Ira R. Lawson |

1905

| Harriet Bullard | Joseph Holden |
| Augusta Stone | |

1908

| Harriet Bullard | Joseph Holden |
| M(innie) Catherine Allen | Walter Shepherd |

1914

| M. Catherine Allen | Joseph Holden |
| Sarah Burger | Walter Shepherd |

1919

| M. Catherine Allen | Walter Shepherd |
| Sarah Burger | Arthur Bruce |

1922

| Sarah Burger | Walter Shepherd |
| Ella E. Winship | Arthur Bruce |

1933

| Ella E. Winship | Irving Greenwood |
| (Annie) Rosetta Stephens | |

1938

| Ella E. Winship | Irving Greenwood |
| Rosetta Stephens | |

1939

Ella E. Winship
Rosetta Stephens
(Mary) Frances Hall
Josephine Wilson

1941

Rosetta Stephens
Frances Hall
Josephine Wilson

1946

Frances Hall
Josephine Wilson
Emma B. King

THE POST-NEW LEBANON MINISTRY, 1946–1957

After Rosetta Stephens was released from the Ministry on 12 February 1946, the place of parental authority was changed from New Lebanon to Pittsfield, Massachusetts. The latter is where Eldress Frances Hall lived. Though a member of the Hancock community, she lived in the Trustees' Office, which was actually located over the city line in Pittsfield.

1946

Frances Hall
Emma B. King

1957

Emma B. King

On 31 March 1957, Eldress Emma announced that the Ministry was dissolved, and the two remaining societies, Canterbury and Sabbathday Lake, were on their own and were to look after their own affairs.

THE RECONSTITUTED MINISTRY, 1957–1988

Eldress Emma reconstituted the "Parent Ministry" a few months after making the decision to dissolve it. No doubt her immediate concern was to be allowed to appoint herself a trustee at Hancock so that village could be closed and the property disposed of.

1957

Emma B. King
Ida Crook
Gertrude M. Soule

1965

Emma B. King
Gertrude M. Soule
(Lily) Marguerite Frost

1966

Gertrude M. Soule
Marguerite Frost

1967

Gertrude M. Soule
Marguerite Frost
(Goldie) Bertha Lindsay

1971

Gertrude M. Soule
Bertha Lindsay

Gertrude M. Soule died at Canterbury on 11 June 1988. Since Eldress Bertha did not name a successor, the Ministry was automatically dissolved according to the *Amendments to the Shaker Church Covenant* made in the 1940s.

Appendix B
Covenant or Constitution of the Church of the United Society in the Town of New Gloucester, 3 December 1832

General revisions were made to the Church Order covenants in 1801, 1807, 1814, and 1832. In 1877 Elder Giles B. Avery (1815–1890) proposed a large number of revisions, but these were never enacted. In 1929 the covenant was amended regarding the handling of communal funds, and around 1946 it was amended again, this time to move the seat of parental authority from New Lebanon, New York, to Pittsfield, Massachusetts, and to state that the Ministry must have no more than three and no fewer than two members. On 7 September 1957 the covenant was amended a final time to move the seat of parental authority to Canterbury, New Hampshire, and to state the conditions under which the Parent Ministry could discontinue a society or family and provide for the survivors. Since these amendments are very minor, the covenant has remained virtually unchanged for 175 years. The 1832 covenant printed below is similar to other Church Order covenants that were used in all the communities from this date until they closed. *Since this is the covenant still used by the sole remaining Shaker community, it is the one signed by new Shakers who have lived in the society a sufficient time (five years) and are deemed ready to do so by the members. Following the long-established custom of Maine Shakerism, this covenant is read to the community the first Sunday in January each year.*

THE SHAKER CHURCH COVENANT: PREAMBLE

We, the Brethren and Sisters of the United Society of Believers (called Shakers) residing at New Gloucester in the county of Cumberland and State of Maine being connected together as a religious and social community, distinguished by the name and title of the Church of the United Society, in the town of New Gloucester, which for many years has been established and in successful operation, under the charge of the Ministry and Eldership thereof, and feeling the importance not only of renewing and confirming our spiritual covenant with God and each other, but also of renewing and improving our social compact, and amending the written form thereof, do make, ordain, and declare the following articles of agreement as a summary of the principles, rules and regulations established in the Church of the said United Society, which are to be kept and maintained by us, both in our collective and individual capacities, as a covenant or constitution, which shall stand as a lawful testimony of our religious and social compact, before all men, and in all cases of question and law relating to the possession and improvement of our united and consecrated interest, property and estate:

ARTICLE I: THE GOSPEL MINISTRY

Section 1: Their Origin, Call and Institution

We solemnly declare to each other and to all whom it may concern, that we have received, and do hereby acknowledge as the foundation of our faith, order and government, the testimony or Gospel of Christ, in his first and second appearing, and we do hereby solemnly agree to support and maintain the true primitive faith and Christian principles, the morals, rules and manners pertaining to the said Gospel, as ministered by the founders of this Society, and kept and conveyed through a regular order of ministration, down to the present day.

And, although, as a religious society, we are variously associated, with respect to the local situations of our respective communities, yet we are known and distinguished as a peculiar people, and consider and acknowledge ourselves as members of one general community, possessing one faith, and subject to one united, parental and MINISTER-IAL administration, which has been regularly supported from the first foundation pillars of the Institution, and which continues to operate for the support, protection and strength of every part of said community.

Section 2: Their Order and Office

We further acknowledge and declare that for the purpose of promoting and maintaining union, order and harmony throughout the various branches of this community, the primary administration of parental authority has been settled in the first established Ministry at New Lebanon, NY, there to rest and remain as the center of union to all who are in Gospel relation and communion with the Society. The established order of this Ministry includes four persons; two of each sex.

Section 3: Perpetuity of Their Office and How Supplied

We further acknowledge and declare that the said primary administration of parental authority has been and is perpetuated as follows: Namely, that the first in the office and calling possesses the right given by the sanction of divine authority, through the first founders of this Society, to prescribe or direct any regulation or appointment which they may judge most proper and necessary respecting the Ministry or any other important matter which may concern the welfare of the Church, subsequent to their decease. But in case no such regulation or appointment is so prescribed or directed, then the right to direct and authorize such regulation and appointment devolves upon the surviving members of the Ministry, in council with the Elders of the Church, or others, as the nature of the case in their judgment may require. Such appointments being officially communicated to all concerned, and receiving the general approbation of the Church, are confirmed and supported in the Society.

This is agreeable to the example recorded in the Scriptures, and continued by the founders of this Society, and is in the order and manner which has been regularly practiced, acknowledged, and maintained in the Community from the beginning.

Section 4: Of the Ministerial Office
in the Several Societies or Communities

We further acknowledge and declare, covenant and agree that the Ministerial office and authority in any Society or Community of our faith, which has emanated, or which may emanate, in a regular line of *order from* the center of union aforesaid, is, and shall be acknowledged, owned and respected, as the spiritual and primary authority of such Society and Community, in all matters pertaining to the Ministerial office. And in case of the decease or removal of any individual of said Ministry, in any such Society, his or her lot and place shall be filled by agreement of the surviving Ministers, in council with the Elders and others, as the nature of the case may require, together with the knowledge and approbation of the primary Ministerial authority at New Lebanon, NY, aforesaid, to which they are responsible.

Section 5: Powers and Duties of the Ministry

The Ministry being appointed and established as aforesaid are vested with the primary authority of the Church and its various branches.

Hence, it becomes their special duty to guide and superintend the spiritual concerns of the Society as a body of people under their care and government, and in connection with the Elders in their respective families and departments, who shall act in union with them, to give and establish such orders, rules and regulations as may be found necessary for the government and protection of the Church and Society within the limits of their jurisdiction, and also to counsel, advise and judge in all matters of importance, whether spiritual or temporal. The said Ministry are also invested with authority in connection with the Elders, Deacons, and Trustees, and to assign offices of care and trust to such brethren and sisters as they, the said Ministers and Elders, shall judge to be best qualified for the several offices to which they may be appointed; and we do hereby covenant and agree that such nominations and appointments being made and officially communicated to those concerned, and receiving the general approbation of the Church, or of the families concerned, shall thenceforth be confirmed and supported, until altered or revoked by the authority aforesaid.

ARTICLE II: INSTITUTION OF THE CHURCH

Section 1: The Object and Design of Church Relation

We further acknowledge and declare that the great object, purpose and design of our uniting ourselves together as a church or body of people, in social and religious compact, is faithfully and honestly to occupy, improve and diffuse the various gifts and talents, both of a spiritual and temporal nature, with which Divine Wisdom has blest us, for the service of God, for the honor of the Gospel, and for the mutual protection, support, comfort and happiness of each other as brethren and sisters in the

Gospel, and for such other pious and charitable purposes as the Gospel may require.

Section 2: Who Are Not Admissible into Church Relation

As the unity, stability and purity of the Church essentially depend on the character and qualifications of its members, and as it is a matter of importance that it should not be encumbered with persons who are under any involvement or incapacity, natural or moral: Therefore, no member of any company or association in business or civil concern, no co-partner in trade, no person under any legal embarrassment or obligation of service, no minor, no slave or bond servant, no insane person, no profane person, nor any person who lives in willful violation of the known and acknowledged principle of moral conduct, shall be deemed qualified for admission into the covenant relation and communion of the Church.

Section 3: Preparation for Admission into Church Relation

In order the Believers may be prepared for entering into the sacred privilege of Church relation, it is of primary importance that sufficient opportunity and privilege should be afforded under the Ministry of the Gospel for them to acquire suitable instruction in the genuine principles of righteousness, honesty, justice and true holiness, and also that they should prove their faith and Christian morality by their practical obedience to the precepts of the Gospel according to their instructions. It is also indispensably necessary for them to receive the one united spirit of Christ, and to become so far of one heart and mind, that they are willing to sacrifice all other relations for this sacred *one*. Another essential step is to settle all just and equitable claims of creditors and *filial* heirs, so that whatever property they may possess shall be justly their own. When this is done, and they feel themselves sufficiently prepared to make a deliberate and final choice, to devote themselves, with all they possess, wholly to the service of God, without reserve, and it shall be deemed proper by the leading authority of the Church, after examination and due consideration, to allow them to associate together in the capacity of a Church, or a branch thereof of Gospel order, they may then consecrate themselves and all they possess to the service of God forever, and confirm the same by signing and sealing a written covenant predicated upon the principle herein contained, and fulfilling on their part, all its obligations.

Section 4: Admission of New Members

As the door must be kept open for the admission of new members into the Church, when duly prepared, it is agreed that each and every person who shall at any time after the date and execution of the Church Covenant, in any branch of the Community, be admitted into the Church as a member thereof, shall previously have a fair opportunity to obtain a full, clear and explicit understanding of the object and design of the Church Covenant, and of the obligations it enjoins upon the members. For this purpose, he or she shall, in the presence of two of the Deacons or acting Trustees of the Church, read, so as to be able freely to acknowledge his or her full approbation and acceptance thereof, in all its parts. Then he, she or they (as the case may be), shall be at liberty to sign the same; having signed and sealed it, and being subject to all the obligations required of the original signers, shall thenceforth be entitled to all the benefits and privileges thereunto appertaining; and the signature or signatures thus added shall be certified by the said Deacons or Trustees, together with the date thereof.

Section 5: Concerning Youth and Children

Youth and children, being minors, cannot be received as members of the Church possessing a concentrated interest in a united capacity, yet it is agreed that they may be received under the immediate care and government of the Church, at the desire or consent of such person or persons as have a lawful right to or control of such minors, together with their own desire or consent. But no minor under the care of the Church can be employed therein for wages of any kind.

ARTICLE III: OF THE TRUSTEESHIP

Section 1: Appointment, Qualifications and Powers of Trustees

It has been found necessary for the establishment of order in the Society in its various branches, that superintending Deacons and Deaconesses should be appointed and authorized to act as Trustees or agents of the temporalities of the Church. They must be recommended by honesty and integrity, their fidelity in trust and their capacity for the transaction of business; of these qualifications the Ministry and Elders must be the judges. The official Trustees of the Church are generally known among us by the title of Office Deacons, *of which there must be two or more*; and being appointed by the authority aforesaid, they are invested with power to take the general charge and oversight of all the property, estate and interest, dedicated, devoted, consecrated and given up for the benefit of the Church; to hold in trust the fee of all the lands belonging to the Church; also all gifts, grants and donations which have been or may hereafter be dedicated, devoted, consecrated and given up aforesaid; and the said property, estate, interest, gifts, grants and donations shall constitute the united and consecrated interest of the Church, and shall be held in trust by the said Deacons, as acting Trustees, in their official capacity, and by their successors in said office and trust forever.

Section 2: Duties of the Trustees

It is and shall be the duty of the said Deacons or acting Trustees to improve, use and appropriate the said united interest for the benefit of the Church in all its departments; and for such other religious and charitable purposes as the Gospel may require; and also to make all just and equitable defense in law for the protection and security of the consecrated and united interest, rights and privileges of the Church and Society, jointly and severally as an associated community, as far as circumstances and the nature of the case may require; *Provided, nevertheless,* that all the transactions of the said Deacons or acting Trustees, in the use, management, protections, defense and disposal of the aforesaid interest, *shall be for the benefit and privilege and in behalf of the Church or Society as aforesaid; and not for any private interest, object or purpose whatever.*

Section 3: Trustees to Give Information and Be Responsible to the Ministry and Elders

It shall also be the duty of the Trustees to give information to the Ministry and Elders of the Church of the general state of the temporal concerns of the Church and Society committed to their charge; and also to report to the said authority all losses sustained in the united interest thereof, which shall come under their cognizance. And no disposal of any real estate of the Church, nor any important contract shall be considered valid without the previous approbation of the authority aforesaid, to whom the said *Deacons and Trustees are and shall, at all times, be held responsible in all their transactions.*

Section 4: Books of Account and Record to Be Kept

It shall also be the duty of the Deacons or acting Trustees to keep, or cause to be kept, regular books of account, in which shall be entered the debt and credit accounts of all mercantile operations and business transactions between the Church and others; all receipts and expenditures, bonds, notes and bills of account, and all other matters that concern the united interest of the Church; and also a book, or books, of records, in which shall be recorded a true and correct copy of this Covenant; also all appointments, removals and changes in office of Ministry, Elders, Deacons and Trustees; all admissions, removals, departure and decease of members, together with all other matters and transactions of a public nature which are necessary to be recorded for the benefit of the Church, and for the preservation and security of the documents, papers and written instruments pertaining to the united interest and concerns of the Church, who, together with the Trustees, shall be the official auditors of the same; and the signature of one or more of said auditors, with the date of inspection and approval, shall be deemed sufficient authority for the correctness and validity of the facts and matters so recorded.

Section 5: Trustees to Execute a Declaration of Trust

For the better security of the united and consecrated interest of the Church to the proper uses and purposes stipulated in this covenant, it shall be the duty of the Trustee, or Trustees, who may be vested with the lawful title or claim to the real estate of the Church, to make and execute a declaration of trust, in due form of law, embracing all and singular the lands, tenements and hereditaments, with every matter of interest pertaining to the Church which at the time being may be vested in him or them, or that may in future come under his or their charge of office, during his or their said Trusteeship. The said declaration shall state expressly that the said Trustee, or Trustees, hold all such lands, tenements or hereditaments, and all the personal property of every description belonging to the Church or Society, in trust for the uses and purposes expressed in and subject to the rules, conditions and regulations prescribed by the covenant and constitution of the said Church or Society, or any amendments thereto which shall hereafter be adopted by the general approbation of the Church, and in conformity with the primitive faith and acknowledged principles of the Society. And the said declaration shall be in writing, duly executed under his or their hands and seals, and shall be recorded in the Book of Records provided for in the previous section.

Section 6: Vacancies in Certain Case; How Supplied

We further covenant and agree that in case it should at any time happen, in the course of Divine Providence, that the office of Trustees should become wholly vacant, by the death or defection of all the Trustees in whom may be vested the fee of the lands or real estate belonging to said Church or Society, then, and in that case, one or more successors shall be appointed by the constitutional authority recognized in this Covenant, according to the rules and regulations prescribed by the same. And the said appointment, being duly recorded in the Book of Records, provided for in this article, shall be deemed, and is hereby declared to vest in such successor or successors, all the rights, interest and authority of their predecessors, in respect to all such lands, property or estate belonging to the Church or Society as aforesaid.

ARTICLE IV: OF THE ELDERSHIP

Section 1: Choice and Appointment of Elders

The united interest and objects of Believers established in Gospel order, require that Elders should be chosen and appointed for the spiritual protection of families, whose business it is to take the lead in their several departments in the care and government of the concerns of the Church and of the different families established in and pertaining to the Society. Their number and order should correspond with that of the

Ministry. They are required to be persons of good understanding, of approved faithfulness and integrity, and gifted in spiritual administration. They must be selected and appointed by the Ministry, who are to judge of their qualifications.

Section 2: Duties of the Elders

As faithful watchmen upon the walls of Zion, it becomes the duty of the Elders to watch over their respective families; to instruct the members in their respective duties; to counsel, encourage, admonish, exhort and reprove as occasion may require; to lead the worship; to be examples to the members of obedience to the principles and orders of the Gospel, and to see that the order, rules and regulations pertaining to their respective families or departments are properly kept.

ARTICLE V: OF FAMILY DEACONS AND DEACONESSES

Section 1: Their Qualifications and Appointments

The office of family Deacons and Deaconesses has long been established in the Church, and is essentially necessary for the care, management and direction of the domestic concerns in each family, order or branch of the Church. They are required to be persons of correct and well-grounded faith in the established principles of the Gospel, faithful in duty, closely united to their Elders, and of sufficient capacity in business. Of their qualifications, the Ministry and Elders by whom they are chosen and appointed must be the judges. Their number in each family is generally two of each sex, but may be more or less, according to the size of the family and the extent of their various duties.

Section 2: Their Duties and Obligations

The Deacons and Deaconesses of families are entrusted with the care and oversight of the domestic concerns of their respective families. It is their duty to make proper arrangements in business; to maintain good order; watch over, counsel and direct the members in their various occupations, as occasion may require; to make application to the office

Deacons or Trustees for whatever supplies are needed in the several departments of the family; to maintain union, harmony and good understanding with the said office Deacons; and to report to their Elders the state of matters which fall under their cognizance and observation. But their power is restricted to the domestic concerns of their respective families and departments, and does not extend to any immediate or direct correspondence with those without the boundaries of the Church. They have no immediate concern with trade or commerce, therefore it is not their business to buy and sell, nor in any way to dispose of the property under their care, except with the counsel and approbation of the Trustees.

ARTICLE VI: PRIVILEGES AND OBLIGATIONS OF MEMBERS

Section 1: Benefits and Privileges of Members in Church Relation

The united interest of the Church having been formed and established by the free-will offerings and pious donations of the members, respectively, from the commencement of the institution, for the object and purposes already stated, it cannot be considered either as a joint tenancy or a tenancy in common, but as a *consecrated whole*, designed for and devoted to the uses and purposes of the Gospel forever, agreeable to the established principles of the Church: Therefore it shall be held, possessed and enjoyed by the Church, in their united capacity, as a sacred and covenant right: That is to say, all and every member thereof, while standing in Gospel union and maintaining the principles of this covenant, *shall enjoy equal rights, benefits and privileges, in the use of all things pertaining to the Church, according to their several needs and circumstances*; and no difference shall be made on account of what anyone has contributed and devoted, or may hereafter contribute and devote to the support and benefit of the institution.

Section 2: Proviso

It is nevertheless stipulated and agreed that the benefits, privileges and enjoyments secured by the Covenant to the members of the Church, shall not be considered as extending to any person who shall refuse to comply with the conditions of this association; or who shall refuse to submit to the admonition and discipline of the constituted authority of the Church; or who shall willfully depart from the principles and practice of those religious and moral obligations which have been established in the Church, agreeable to the primitive faith and distinguished principles of this institution: of which refusal or non-compliance the leading authority acknowledged in the first articles of this Covenant shall be the proper and constitutional judges.

Section 3: Obligations of the Members

As subordination and obedience is the life and soul of every well-regulated community, so our strength and protection, our happiness and prosperity, in our capacity of Church members, must depend on our faithful obedience to the rules and orders established in the Church, and to the instruction, counsel and advice of its leaders. Therefore, we do hereby covenant and agree that we will receive and acknowledge, as our Elders in the Gospel, those members in the Church who are or may be chosen and appointed for the time being to that office and calling by the authority aforesaid; and also that we will, as faithful brethren and sisters in Christ, conform and subject ourselves to the known and established faith and principles of our community, and to the counsels and directions of the Elders, who shall act in union, as aforesaid, and also to all the orders, rules and regulations which are or may be given and established in the Church, according to the principles and by the authority aforesaid.

Section 4: Duties of the Members

The faithful improvement of our time and talents in doing good, is a duty which God requires of man, as a rational, social and accountable being, and this duty is indispensable in the members of the Church of Christ. Therefore it is and shall be required of all and every member of this institution unitedly and individually, to occupy and improve their time and talents to support and maintain the interest of the Society, to promote the objects of this Covenant, and discharge their duty to God and each other according to their several abilities and callings, as members in union with one common lead; so that the various gifts and talents of all may be improved for the mutual benefit of each other and all concerned.

Section 5: Concerning Wages and Removals

As we esteem the mutual possession and enjoyment of the consecrated interest and privileges of the Church a valuable consideration, fully adequate to any amount of personal interest, labor or service, devoted or consecrated by any individual; we, therefore, covenant and agree, in conformity with an established and well-known principle of the Church, that no person whatever under its care and protection, can be employed for wages of any kind, on his or her individual account, and that no ground is or can be afforded for the recovery of any property or service devoted or consecrated as aforesaid; and it is also agreed that in case of the removal of any member or members from one family, society or branch of the Church to another, his, her or their previous signature or signatures to the Church or Family Covenant from whence such member or members shall be removed, shall forever bar all claims which are incompatible with the true intent and meaning of this Covenant, in the same manner as if such removal had not taken place. Yet all who shall so remove, in union with the authority aforesaid, shall be entitled to all the benefits and privileges of the Order in which they shall then be placed, so long as they shall conform to the rules and regulations of the same.

ARTICLE VII: DEDICATION AND RELEASE

Section 1: Dedication and Consecration of Persons, Property and Service

According to the faith of the Gospel which we have received and agreeable to the uniform practice of the Church of Christ from its first establishment in this Society, we covenant and agree to dedicate, devote, consecrate and give up, and by this Covenant we do solemnly and conscientiously dedicate, devote, consecrate and give up ourselves and services together with all our temporal interest to the service of God and the support and benefit of the Church of this community, and to such other pious and charitable purposes as the Gospel may require, to be under the care and direction of such Elders, Deacons and Trustees as are or may be appointed and established in the Church by the authority aforesaid.

Section 2: Dedication and Release of Private Claim

Whereas, in pursuance of the requirement of the Gospel, and in the full exercise of our faith, reason and understanding, we have freely and voluntarily sacrificed all self-interest, and consecrated and devoted our persons, services and property, as aforesaid, to the pious and benevolent purposes of the Gospel: Therefore, we do hereby solemnly and conscientiously, unitedly and individually for ourselves and our heirs, release and quit claim to the Deacons, or acting Trustees of the Church for the time being, for the uses and purposes aforesaid, all our private personal right, title, interest, claim and demand of, in and to the estate, interest, property, and appurtenances so consecrated, devoted and given up; and we hereby jointly and severally promise and declare in the presence of God and before these witnesses that we will never hereafter, neither directly nor indirectly, under any circumstances whatever, contrary to the stipulations of this Covenant, make nor require any account of any interest, property, labor or service, nor any division thereof which is, has been, or may be devoted by us, or any of us, to the uses and purposes aforesaid, nor bring any charge of debt or damage, or hold any claim nor demand whatever against the said Deacons or Trustees, nor against the Church or Society, nor against any member thereof, on account of any property or service given, rendered, devoted or consecrated to the aforesaid sacred and charitable purposes.

In confirmation of all the aforesaid statements, covenants, promises and articles of agreement, we have hereunto subscribed our names and affixed our seals, commencing on the third day of December 1832.

Appendix C
Conditional, Probationary, or Novitiate Covenant

The following is the novitiate covenant that is currently signed by anyone seeking to become a Shaker today:

Whereas_____ Lately of_____
Has applied for admission into the United Society of Shakers, in New Gloucester, County of Cumberland, and State of Maine and as it is desirable for said_____to more fully investigate the faith and principles of the Society, and also to demonstrate his sincerity, competency and eligibility to membership:

    Now, therefore, it is agreed on the part of the said_____ and said Society, its officers and members, that said_____ may be permitted a temporary residence in said Society for the purposes aforesaid; provided that the privilege of such residence shall be considered as full compensation for any labor that said_____ may perform, or any service that he may render said Society, its officers or members, while residing therein. And this agreement will forever debar him from any claim, action, or cause of action for wages or compensation of any kind against the said society, its officers or any member thereof, during h__ said residence.

    Said_____ agrees to conform to the rules and regulations of said Society, and to refrain from acts, conduct or speech that would be prejudicial to its interests, and that he will present no claim for compensation for labor or any services while residing in said Society, as aforesaid.

    The connection of said_____ with said Society may be terminated at the option of himself, or of said Society or its officers at any time.

Witness my hand and seal this_____day of _____
two thousand_____.
  Witness:

_____

Appendix D
Current Rules Governing How the Shakers Live

There have been four general codifications of the rules governing Shaker life and custom:

Millennial Laws of 1821, Millennial Laws of 1845, Rules and Orders of 1860 and the *Orders* of 1887. Unfortunately, the only ones generally quoted are the *Millennial Laws of 1845*. Ironically, these were the ones least adhered to and the ones in effect for the shortest time. Presented below are the *Orders* of 1887. *They still govern Shaker life today* and have been in effect the longest. Following the tradition of Maine Shakers, *these are read to the community the second Sunday of January each year.* They may be revised as necessary, and the last changes made were in the 1940s. The *Orders* below reflect these changes that have been made over time so that *this is the most current version of the Shaker rules and shows the deletions that have been made.*

ORDERS FOR THE CHURCH OF CHRIST'S SECOND APPEARING, ESTABLISHED BY MINISTRY AND ELDERS OF THE CHURCH, MT. LEBANON, NOVEMBER 1887

Preface

Believers in Christ's Second Appearing must be led and governed by one and the same spirit which is the spirit and law of Christ.

The first and great command enjoined upon Believers is, that we love the Lord with all our whole souls. Secondly that we love the Brethren & Sisters as ourselves.

This appendix is based on the following: Hadd, "Orders for the Church of Christ's Second Appearing," *Shaker Quarterly*, vol. 24, 31–48.

Under the influence of the first, we shall always be obedient to our Elders & Parents in the Gospel. Under the second we shall do unto others as we would they should do unto us.

It may not be improper to remark that the laws and orders of Zion, relative to the confessing of sin, separation from the spirit of the world, within & without, a proper intercourse between the sexes, reconciliation between contentious parties, regard of, and respect for anointing of God, for the leading and governing of the Church of God, and the transmission of the same to successors &c. are unchangeable.

But rules, attendant upon local circumstances and the social relations and duties of Society, are subject to such modifications, amendments, or repeals, as circumstances require for the union and protection of the various branches and families of Society throughout.

It is, consequently the privilege and duty of the Ministry and Elders of each Society and family to add to, or diminish the number of such as their situation and circumstances may require for the safety and protection of the people under their charge; that Zion may be the abode of heaven born souls, passing and repassing each other like angels on errands of love.

Part 1

Section 1: Orders Concerning duties of Trustees, Family Deacons & Deaconesses, & Members Thereunto

1. Believers must not run in debt to the World.
2. Trustees should counsel with the Ministry & Elders before making any heavy purchases or sales.
3. Believers should not require interest of each other for money borrowed to purchase the necessaries & comforts of life.
4. Members should not purchase articles of considerable value for themselves, without the union of Elders & Deacons, each sex in its own order.
5. No new fashions, concerning clothing, or important wares of any kind, may be introduced into the Society of Believers without the union of the Ministry of the Society.
6. When members need spending money, they should apply to those in order for keeping the same & to them all returns should be rendered.

Section 2: Orders Concerning Physicians

1. Brethren should not apply medical aid to Sisters, who are sick, without the knowledge of the female Physicians and nurses of the family.
2. The Physicians should, at all times, hold themselves responsible to the Elders.

Part 2

Section 1: Concerning Confession of Sin and Opening of the Mind

1. Any member having sin unconfessed, should confess it to God before the Elders, before attending Meeting for worship.
2. Breaking the sacred Orders of the Gospel should be confessed as sin.
3. All trials, if opened at all, should be opened to the Elders, and to them only.
4. A member admonished for a fault or reproved by the Elders, should not make inquiry of the Elders or others, to find out who made their faults known to the Elders.
5. [DELETED] Members should not go to the Ministry to open their minds without the knowledge of their Elders, unless the Ministry call upon them for that purpose in which case it is their duty to be free.
6. If a person should discover a sin committed by any common member, or any official person, low or high, either in temporal or spiritual care, & have reason to believe it has not been confessed, it is the duty of such discoverer to reveal the fact to the Ministry, Elders or to someone appointed to hear openings.
7. If any Brother or Sister have ought to open concerning a person of the opposite sex, such member should open it to their own Elders.

Section 2: Order Concerning the Worship of God, Attending Meeting, &c.

1. All persons who are at home and able, are required to attend Meetings at the appointed times, unless detained by very important business. If not able information should be given by themselves, or others, to the Elders.

2. Believers gathered into family order and communal relation, should not neglect to attend their home Meetings to attend Meetings abroad.

Section 3: Orders Concerning Sabbath,
Christmas, Fasting & Prayer Days &c.

1. The Sabbath should be sacredly kept for the worship of God.
2. Worldly literature should not be read on the Sabbath.
3. Riding or walking out, for mere recreation, should not be done on the Sabbath.
4. Christmas should be kept analogous to the Sabbath, and in conformity to Christ's mission of peace. Believers if not in union with other members of the family, or Society, should now make reconciliation with the disaffected.
5. Days appointed by the government for Fasting and Prayer, should be sacredly kept by Meeting for Prayer &c.
6. Appointed days for Thanksgiving should be kept by attending one Meeting and the remainder of the day should be appropriated to cleaning and putting in order places often neglected.

Part 3

Section 1: Orders Concerning the Social Intercourse of the Sexes

1. The Gospel strictly forbids all private union between the sexes, in any place or under any circumstances.
2. One Brother with one Sister should not be together by themselves when consistent to avoid it, longer than to do short errands and necessary duty.
3. Brethren and Sisters should not make presents to each other in a private manner.
4. Brethren and Sisters should not touch each other unnecessarily.
5. When Brethren or Sisters go to rooms occupied by the opposite sex, they should knock before entering.
6. Brethren and Sisters should not dress in garments belonging to the opposite sex.

Section 2: Orders Concerning Language of Believers

1. No filthy stories should be told by Believers.
2. Evil speaking to one another and back biting are forbidden by the Gospel.
3. Gossiping that would make discord and mischief and bringing up faults of past experience that have been confessed is contrary to the Gospel and forbidden.
4. Worldly titles should not be applied to Brethren & Sisters.

Section 3: Concerning Literature of Believers

1. [DELETED] Elders should have knowledge of the character of all books brought into the family.
2. [DELETED] All letters sent out, or received, by members not sent to transact business with Believers or the world, should be shown to the Elders.
3. [DELETED] But the Office Deacons are allowed to write, or receive, letters on temporal business only without showing them to the Elders.

Section 4: Orders Concerning Going Abroad
and Intercourse with the World

1. [DELETED] When Believers need to go abroad, out of the line of their ordinary business, they should obtain union of the Elders.
2. [DELETED] When Brethren or Sisters go from home for a ride, for a visit, or on business, they should give the Elders an account of their proceedings and circumstances attending their journey, when they return home.
3. [DELETED] It is not good order for Believers to attend theaters, or shows, to gratify an idle curiosity.
4. One Brother, with one Sister, should not walk out into the fields, nor ride out away from home, without a third person, nor take with them for company only a small child.
5. [DELETED] In families, and with members in covenant relation, no members, but those appointed for that purpose, should keep the money.

Section 5: Orders Concerning the Dead

1. When a person is dying those present should kneel in prayer.
2. The corpse should not be dressed in costly garments.
3. Coffins, for burial, should be cheap and plain, unembellished with needless ornaments.

Section 6: Orders to Prevent Loss by Fire

1. [DELETED] No persons should carry fire about the dooryard or among the buildings, unless safely secured in a lantern, firebox, or other safe vessel.
2. [DELETED] No one should enter a clothes room, closet, or other place, not frequented, with an open light.
3. [DELETED] Lighted lamps, lanterns or candles, should not be carried on to hay or straw mows.
4. [DELETED] No open lights should ever be taken to barns, and lanterns should not be opened in the barns at all.
5. [DELETED] Lighted lamps, candles or lanterns, should not be held over, nor hung upon shaving boxes or baskets, or places where there would be a liability of fire.
6. [DELETED] It is not allowable on any occasion, to boil oil or varnish, in any building, anywhere.
7. No ashes should be taken up in a wooden vessel, nor should they be emptied in their place of deposit, it made of wood, in the after part of the day.
8. [DELETED] Ash vessels should not be set on shaving baskets, nor hung on wood boxes and places liable to fire.
9. [DELETED] The snuff of burning lamps or candles should not be thrown into spit boxes containing saw dust or combustible matter nor should matches be thrown therein.
10. [DELETED] Spittoons containing combustible matter should not be set or left near the stove or fireplace.
11. [DELETED] Chimneys should be burned out once a year, and this should be done when the roofs are wet, or covered with snow.
12. All members occupying a room having a stove with fire in it, should see that the stove door is closed and the room secured from fire before leaving it for the night, or longer at any time.

[This is the halfway mark. Until 1938, reading the *Orders* was done on two successive Sundays.]

Section 7: Miscellaneous Orders

1. Wrestling, scuffling, beating, striking or fighting are entirely forbidden by the Gospel.
2. It is an established order for Believers to kneel in prayer on retiring to rest at night, & at table before eating; and in thanksgiving on rising in the morning [DELETED] and on rising from meals.
3. Liquid that would deface buildings, should not be thrown out of the windows.
4. The refuse of fruits should not be thrown out on to the door yards or paths, and no rubbish should be left to cumber the door yard.
5. [DELETED] Brethren and Sisters should not throw away their old shoes or garments, but they should be delivered to those having the charge of such things.

Section 8: Conditional Orders

1. The family Deacons and Deaconesses are responsible to the Elders, in all matters of importance that come under their charge, concerning the temporal business of the family.
2. Members employed by the Trustees to do business in their line, at home or a broad, must render to them a full account of their business transactions, with their use of money, when their business is performed.
3. [DELETED] In families, where the full order of officials is established, members should apply to family Deacons & Deaconesses for needful articles of convenience, or use, and for money for contingent expenses.
4. [DELETED] Brethren or Sisters should not go into dwelling rooms, of the opposite sex, after Meetings in the evening except on important or needful occasions.
5. [DELETED] Brethren or Sisters should not make for themselves or others, important or costly articles, without the union of Deacons or Deaconesses, each sex in their own order.

6. [DELETED] Brethren and Sister when at home should not write to those of the opposite sex, without the knowledge and union of their Elders.
7. [DELETED] Brethren should not occupy their rooms, while the Sisters doing the needful chores therein, unless necessitated to do so by sickness or infirmity.
8. One Sister alone should not walk out into the fields or barns &c, but should have a female companion.
9. Gates should be closed on Saturday nights and Sabbath days.
10. [DELETED] Shop rooms should be cleaned up and tools put in order on Saturday nights.
11. When panes of window glass get broken in windows fronting the street, they should be mended before Sabbath.
12. Believers should not play with dumb beasts, as cats, dogs, rabbits &c. nor in any case make room companions of them.

BOOK 2: COUNSELS TO BE OBSERVED

1. Trustees and all others desiring any member to do business for them, at home or abroad, should apply to the Elders for the same.
2. Those who go out on business for the Trustees have no right to buy or sell or to do business for themselves in a private manner.
3. As Trustees are called to be examples to the members in godliness, gospel plainness, prudence and good economy, they should not purchase for themselves, or receive as a present, to be kept by them, articles that are superfluous, or unnecessary.
4. All Believers gathered into family or Community order should attend to meals with the family as far as circumstances will admit.
5. [DELETED] When an individual is so unwell as to be necessary to be moved to the infirmary, the physician or nurse should inform the Elders.
6. [DELETED] When Brethren or Sisters need medicinal aid they should apply to the Elders and nurses of their own family if there be such, if not to those who are appointed.
7. If any member should be overcome with anger and charge a Brother or Sister with lying, or wound the feelings of others, such person is not justified until restored by confession & reconciliation.

8. In retiring time, members should resort to their rooms and observe the time in silence, and labor for a gift of God, before attending Meetings.
9. [DELETED] When Brethren and Sisters place themselves in ranks they should keep their ranks straight, both to the right and left and front and rear.
10. When any person is kneeling in prayer whether in Meeting or elsewhere, all who are present should respectfully attend.
11. Brethren and Sisters should avoid leaving Meetings until they close, unless it be really needful.
12. Where there is dwelling house room provided, shops should not be occupied or frequented on the Sabbath day, but when duty renders it necessary to visit them, the errands should be short as consistent.
13. Shop windows should be closed on the Sabbath, unless need require them open.
14. Work should not be done on the Sabbath that can be consistently be avoided.
15. Boisterous talking & laughing conversation on war, politics & worldy subjects in general are improper on the Sabbath.
16. [DELETED] Believers should not call nicknames nor use by words or vulgar expressions.
17. [DELETED] Believers should never use or repeat profane language in their conversation.
18. [DELETED] It is ungodly for Believers to talk of rejecting their privilege in the way of God and among Believers.
19. [DELETED] Members unfortunately breaking or seriously damaging furniture of the dwelling rooms should report the same to the Elders.
20. [DELETED] The furniture of dwelling rooms should be plain in style.
21. [DELETED] Boys and youth should not use guns for sporting, hunting for sport is a dissipating and demoralizing pursuit.
22. [DELETED] Visiting between the world and Believers should be done at the Office, as far as is possibly consistent.
23. [DELETED] Public stores should be secured by locks.
24. [DELETED] When Brethren and Sisters wish to make presents of much magnitude to their friends or acquaintances they should obtain union of their Elders and those in temporal care.

25. [DELETED] Believers should not company with hired servants except duty require.
26. [DELETED] Brethren and Sisters should avoid thronging the Office late in the evening to visit guests.
27. Buildings out of repair should be repaired or taken down.
28. Doors or gates should not be left swinging but either closed or fastened open.
29. [DELETED] It is unsafe to shoot near buildings unless the wadding be of leather shavings or something not liable to catch fire.
30. [DELETED] It is uncleanly to allow cattle, horses, or sheep to run the door yards.
31. Door yards should be mown twice a year or oftener.
32. It is not nice to cut up the door yards into little cross paths or by ways.
33. When members are about the farm and pass through bar or gateways they should leave them closed, unless they find them evidently open on purpose.
34. All farm tools, machines, carts, carriages &c. should be stored indoors when not in use, and in their seasons of use, put away on Saturday night if at home.
35. [DELETED] No kinds of beasts should be kept for mere curiosity or show.
36. Believers should avoid lounging in the window openings of the dwelling house or shops and especially on the Sabbath.
37. Slamming doors & gates is not good practice. It is rough and uncultived behavior.
38. When Believers enter the dwelling house, it is good culture to walk softly.

CONCLUSION

The Elders of each and every family should keep a copy of the book of orders, and counsels adapted to the family in which they are called to preside, and the Orders and Counsels should frequently be read and spoken to the family. A few, and those on one and same subject at a time.

It is important for the prosperity and protection of a family, every member should know the orders and Rules of Believers' Society.

WITNESSING TESTIMONIES

We, the present Ministry and Elders of Mt. Lebanon, do conscientiously acknowledge our full approbation of the foregoing Orders, Rules and Counsels, which have been established in the Church for the Union and Protection thereof.

As we do solemnly promise, in presence of God Our Heavenly Parents faithfully to maintain and support the same as far as wisdom may direct.

Daniel Boler
Giles Avery
Eliza Ann Taylor
Harriet Bullard

Copy

The following suggestions were made by Brother Delmer Wilson and inserted into the *Orders* book. It is dated 24 January 1932.

The life of a good believer teaches us it is a good practice to clean out our plates before leaving the table.
It is good practice to eat our meals at the tables instead of depending so much upon lunches.
Let us shun the appearance of ingratitude.

Appendix E
Daily Schedule of a Shaker

This is the horarium followed today in the community at Sabbathday Lake, Maine. The bell referred to is the large bell that is at the top of the dwelling house.

7:30 a.m. One of those preparing breakfast rings the warning bell, and the brethren and sisters and their guests gather in their respective waiting rooms.

7:40 a.m. A signal calls the community into the dining room. Once assembled, the community stands for a silent grace. Conversation is allowed at meals, but men and women sit at separate tables. When the meal is finished, the tables are cleared and psalms books distributed. Each Shaker takes a turn leading prayers. Two psalms are said out loud with the leader and the community alternating the verses. A passage is read from the Bible, followed by a series of intercessory prayers. Morning prayers end with a Shaker song.

8:15–11:30 a.m. This time is reserved for work, shopping, chores, etc.

11:30 a.m. The community gathers in the kitchen for prayers.

11:50 a.m. The bell is rung and the community gathers the same as at breakfast.

12:00 p.m. The Shakers have their principal meal at noon. When dinner is finished, the afternoon is spent much like the morning.

5:00–5:30 p.m. The community gathers in the dining room for informal conversation and socializing. Tables are joined so that all may sit together. A light supper follows this time of fellowship.

After supper there is free time. Some gather in the community room to read or watch TV. Generally, the Shakers have retired to their rooms by 9:00 p.m.

By Saturday evening, the Scripture readings that will be used at meeting on Sunday are written on a small chalkboard that hangs in the foyer of the dwelling house. Members prepare themselves for the Sabbath by reading these. On Sundays, there is no formal breakfast. After a pick-up breakfast, members spend quiet time in anticipation of meeting, which is at 10:00 a.m. In the warmer months public meeting is held in the 1794 Meeting House. Otherwise, public meeting is held in the dwelling house chapel. The Sabbath is observed by attendance at meeting and private time. After dinner at noon, members have time to spend as they wish, until the informal gathering in the evening.

On Wednesday evenings, a reading meeting is held at 5:00 p.m. Shaker writings are read aloud with the various people present each taking a turn. A discussion accompanies the readings.

The community gathers at other times as needed, for example, to practice a song from one of the hymnals.

Appendix F
Format of a Shaker Worship Service

Meeting is held every Sunday morning at 10:00, either in the 1794 Meeting House (in the summer) or in the chapel of the dwelling house. At other times meeting is held in the evening to commemorate a special event such as Mother Ann's birthday.

The retiring bell is rung 15 minutes before meeting. The Shakers and their guests begin to gather in the meeting room and sit in silence. At the appointed time the bell is rung and the community leaders file into the room and take their places. Men and women sit in rows of benches facing each other. A wooden lectern is placed perpendicular to the benches so that the space between them is not obstructed. A small table with flowers is the only decoration.

One of the Shakers recites a psalm, there is silence, and the leader stands and directs that the first set song be sung. This is from one of the Mount Lebanon hymnals used in worship. An Old Testament reading and a New Testament reading and the second set song complete the formal part of the service. A brief welcome is given, and all are told that they should feel free to participate in testimony or song as they feel moved. After this, the community members stand and give personal testimony. Generally the first one to speak is the eldress who gives a short sermon on the readings. This delineates the theme and participants may take this idea and develop it or they may introduce other thoughts that have come to mind from the readings and previous testimonies. Songs are sung between testimonies, and meeting continues until all who wish to share their thoughts have done so. Intercessory prayers and the recitation of the Lord's Prayer close the meeting.

Bibliography

CONTENTS

INTRODUCTION

This bibliography was put together for maximum use as a resource guide. The carefully chosen titles of the bibliography sections allow easy access to locate desired books. The first part of the bibliography is on general works and histories, which treat the Shakers as a whole. Information on site-specific locations is next, conveniently divided into "eastern" and "western" communities. The following section on periodicals gives the essential facts about these publications, and it completes the parts of the bibliography that treat the Shakers as a group. The heart of the bibliography is "People," including those who died in the faith as well as apostates. Before turning to the final sections on the various aspects of Shaker material culture, "Theological Works" offers examples of the religious motivation that made these physical objects possible.

For someone just starting out in Shaker studies, the "General Works" section provides comprehensive works that no serious researcher can do without. For example, Richmond's two-volume bibliography *Shaker Literature* contains information about almost every work by or about the Shakers that was published before the early 1970s, and Pike's *A Guide to Shaker Manuscripts* catalogs the world's largest collection of Shaker manuscripts. Equally helpful, *Maps of the Shaker West; A Journey of Discovery* untangles the scores of Shaker landholdings once scattered throughout the Midwest, while Murray's *Shaker Heritage Guidebook* covers every major Shaker site.

The section of the bibliography that follows next contains general histories or works that place the entire Shaker movement in a particular context. The best known of the general Shaker histories are White and Taylor's *Shakerism; Its Meaning and Message*, Melcher's *The Shaker Adventure*, Andrews' *The People Called Shakers*, and Stein's *The Shaker Experience in America*.

One of the three basic tenets of Shakerism is community. Individual Shakers have always lived out their lives in close association with others. The next two parts of the bibliography place the Shakers in the context of their homes. For all of Shaker history, there has been a great emphasis on the eastern communities, especially New Lebanon. To restore a balance, items dealing with the various Shaker communities have been divided into "eastern" and "western."

Every one of the 12 eastern societies has at least one work that details its history. Although each of the works listed offers important information, a few are exemplary. For example, Eastman's *Alfred, Maine; The Shakers and the Village* is especially evocative and useful due to the quality of the pictures and the fact that the people in them were identified by surviving Alfred Shakers living at Sabbathday Lake. *Simply Shaker; Groveland and the New York Communities* by Kramer fills the niche so long left vacant for a history of a community that was both "eastern" and "western." Finally, Langeveld's *Report on the History and Present State of the West Family Site at Hancock Shaker Village* is a fine example of how a little known Shaker family can be brought to life by serious research.

For most readers, any work on the Shaker West will be new information, although Neal's *The Journal of Eldress Nancy*, Piercy's *The Valley of God's Pleasure*, and Clark and Ham's *Pleasant Hill and Its Shakers* have been available for decades. Besides these, the even older series of six works by MacLean has never been surpassed in its scope. Since the last of these was written in 1904, this shows how much research still needs to be done on the western Shakers. Some smaller works, such as Hunt's *Summers at Watervliet* and Johnson's *The Struggle for Watervliet, Ohio*, provide valuable information but deal with small periods of time. The need is especially great for in-depth scholarly treatment of the largest western communities, Union Village and Pleasant Hill.

Since Shakerism is a way of life, the primary focus of this bibliography is on people. Whenever they joined, whether in childhood or as mature adults, some persevered in their commitment until death. A few of these left us testimonies of their lives in the form of biographies. In addition, the most well-known Shakers have been remembered in poems, stories, and songs. These biographies and memorial books begin the "People" section. They range from works on the first Shakers, such as *Testimonies of the Life, Character, Revelations, and Doctrines of Our Ever Blessed Mother Ann Lee, and the Elders with Her* and *The Life and Gospel Experience of Mother Ann Lee* to *Growing Up Shaker* by Sister Frances A. Carr, a present-day believer. Moreover, they provide useful information for writers and collectors. For example, for those interested in well-known Shakers, the *Autobiography of Elder Giles B. Avery* and Wergland's *One Shaker Life: Isaac Newton Youngs, 1793–1865* offer insights that are important for understanding how 19th-century Shakerism unfolded. For the collector, *Making His Mark: The Work of Shaker Craftsman Orren Haskins* and *Shaker Furniture Makers* are essential starting points. Since material on individual Shakers is often hard to locate, some of the mini-biographies that have appeared in the *Shaker Quarterly* on recent Shakers are included. For the same reason, the all-but-forgotten western Shakers are adequately represented by such works as *Mother's First-Born Daughters*, *In Memoriam Elder William Reynolds*, and *A Brief Memorial of Mother Ruth Farrington*. Taken all together, the biographies and memorials serve as a supplement to the *Shaker Image* revised by Magda Gabor-Hotchkiss. This outstanding volume provides scores of detailed and accurate biographies. Because every attempt was made to identify all of the people in the photographs that make up the *Shaker Image*, for the first time, in many cases, names can be matched with faces.

Most people who joined the Shakers eventually left. A small number of them wrote about their experiences, most often negatively. These apostates form the basis for the next part of the bibliography. Only material from those who had actually been Shakers at one time in their lives is included.

The most famous work of apostate literature is *A Portraiture of Shakerism* by Mary Marshall Dyer. Her half-century campaign against the Shakers is the subject of DeWolfe's balanced and thorough study *Shaking the Faith: Women, Family and Mary Marshall Dyer's Anti-Shaker Campaign, 1815–1867* and a rebuttal of her charges was made by her husband Joseph Dyer in *A Compendious Narrative*. Since apostate literature is often quoted by writers, the classic works by Brown, Chapman, Elkins, Lamson, and Rathbun will be familiar to many readers.

Above all else, Shakerism is a religion. The purpose of "Theological Works" is to list writings that explain the faith. All of the major Shaker theological works are listed: Meacham's *A Concise Statement*, Youngs' *The Testimony of Christ's Second Appearing*, Dunlavy's *Manifesto*, and Green and Wells' *A Summary View of the Millennial Church*. Exposition on the Shaker religion, however, did not cease after the publication of the early volumes. In particular, Avery's *Sketches*, Blinn's *Advent of Christ in Man and Woman*, and Eads' *Shaker Sermons* show that Shakers in every corner of Shakerdom were writing on their faith. Yet two individuals, Alonzo Hollister and Frederick Evans, both of Mount Lebanon, were particularly prolific in this regard. What is remarkable is that Hollister's three-part *Pearly Gate* series was written as a Shaker catechism at the exact time when most societies were closing, no longer taking children, or no longer holding public meeting. That is perhaps why so much of his work is so little read. It had little impact at the time, and people writing on the Shakers in later years were more interested in the material objects of Shakerism.

No treatment of Shaker theology would be complete without the inclusion of Brother Theodore Johnson's *Life in the Christ Spirit* and "Shakerism for Today." These contemporary works show how Shakerism is understood now and why it is still relevant.

Once the people, places, and religion of the Shakers have been given their rightful places, the culture generated by Shakerism can be explored in its proper context.

Music has always been a major part of Shaker worship, and efforts were made early on to collect some of the vast amount of songs. Wells' *Millennial Praises. . . .* stands at the head of these efforts. Blinn's *A Collection of Hymns and Anthems* and McNemar's *A Selection of Hymns and Poems* are examples of eastern and western efforts in this regard. As important as the many efforts were, however, the Shakers of today and their guests use the two volumes of Shaker music compiled by Mount Lebanon's North Family, *Shaker Music, Original Inspirational Hymns and Songs* and *Original Shaker Music*. Finally, the Shakers' study of music as a science finds ample evidence in Haskell's *A Musical Expositer. . . .* and Youngs' *A Short Abridgement of the Rules of Music*. The discussion of Shaker music by outsiders begins with Andrews' *The Gift to Be Simple*. Later works have been written by learned music scholars, most notably Roger Hall and Daniel Patterson. Indeed, Patterson's *The Shaker Spiritual* is an exhaustive study of the music that inspired the believers, past and present.

Patterson has also produced another classic work on the Shaker Spirit drawings, *Gift Drawing and Gift Song: A Study of Two Forms of Shaker Inspiration*. This greatly enhances knowledge of these drawings, which first were studied by the Andrewses in *Visions of the Heavenly Sphere: A Study in Shaker Religious Art*.

The beauty of Shaker buildings and the material objects made by the Shakers have been the subject of many books of photography. Butler and Sprigg's *Inner Light: The Shaker Legacy,* and the two works by Williams, *Chosen Land* and *A Place in Time* are among the best of this genre.

Sister R. Mildred Barker of the Sabbathday Lake Shakers once remarked that she did not want to be remembered as a Shaker chair. This is indicative of the volume of works that have been produced on the material culture of the Shakers. Again, beginning with the works of the Andrewses, *The Community Industries of the Shakers* and *Shaker Furniture: The Craftsmanship of an American Communal Sect,* the popularity of this type of work has continued unabated. The length of this section of the bibliography reflects this. A wide selection of Shaker studies in this area has been included. The furniture books of Rieman and Burks dominate the field. Muller and Rieman's *The Shaker Chair* deals with perhaps the most identifiable Shaker object. Much smaller pieces also have been the subject of study. The three field guides go into exacting detail on all aspects of Shaker woodenware, baskets, and poplarware, and Miller's *From Shaker Land and Shaker Hands: A Survey of the Industries* is so thorough that it is doubtful it can ever be surpassed.

This section of the bibliography also offers a list of some of the catalogs from major exhibits of Shaker objects. Goodwillie and Miller's *Handled with Care: The Function of Form in Shaker Craft* is a fine example of this.

The Shaker museums at Canterbury, Hancock, and Pleasant Hill have restaurants. Enfield, New Hampshire, Hancock, Canterbury, and Pleasant Hill also have large herb gardens. Many of the titles in the culinary section are books written by cooks and gardeners from these villages. Works by contemporary Shaker cooks, Eldress Bertha Lindsay and Sister Frances A. Carr, help recall that Shaker hospitality and community life are not just in the distant past.

GENERAL WORKS

Boice, Martha, Dale Covington, and Richard Spence. *Maps of the Shaker West; A Journey of Discovery.* Dayton, Ohio: Knot Garden Press, 1997.

Canterbury Shaker Village Guide to the Collection. Canterbury, N.H.: Shaker Village, 1983.

Cottrell, Rachel W. B., ed. "Shaker Death Records." *New England Historical and Geneological Register* 115 (January/April 1961): 32–45, 118–35.

Emlen, Robert. *Shaker Village Views.* Hanover, N.H.: University Press of New England, 1987.

Gabor-Hotchkiss, Dr. Magda, comp. *Volume 1 Guide to Bound Shaker Manuscripts in the Library Collection of Hancock Shaker Village.* Pittsfield, Mass.: Hancock Shaker Village, 2001.

———, comp. *Volume II Guide to Unbound Shaker Manuscripts in the Library Collection of Hancock Shaker Village.* Pittsfield, Mass.: Shaker Community, 2001.

———, comp. *Volume III Guide to Printed Work in the Library Collection of Hancock Shaker Village.* Pittsfield, Mass.: 2001.

———, comp. *Volume IV Shaker Community Industries: Guide to Printed Shaker Ephemera in the Library Collections of Hancock Shaker Village.* Pittsfield, Mass.: Hancock Shaker Village, 2003.

Hartgen Frances C., comp. *Shaker Quarterly: Index Vol. 1–14. 1961–Summer 1974.* Orono: Fogler Library, University of Maine, 1977.

Hatcher, Kenneth, and Anne Gilbert, comps. *Shaker Articles and References in the Magazine ANTIQUES: Shaker Index 1928–2000.* United Society of Shakers, Sabbathday Lake, 2003.

Kirk, John T. *The Shaker World; Art, Life, Belief.* New York: Harry N. Abrams, 1997.

McKinstry, E. Richard, comp. *The Edward Deming Andrews Memorial Shaker Collection.* New York: Garland Publishing, 1987.

Meader, Robert F. W., comp. *Catalogue of the Emma B. King Library of the Shaker Museum.* Old Chatham, N.Y.: Shaker Museum Foundation, 1970.

Mooney, William T. *A List of Shaker Names from the Official Church Record of Watervliet, Ohio 1800–1882.* Dayton, Ohio: Knot Garden Press, 2003.

Murray, Stuart. *Shaker Heritage Guidebook.* Spencertown, N.Y.: Golden Hill Press, 1994.

Paterwic, Stephen. "Helpful Sources for Researching Your Shaker Ancestors." *New England Ancestors* 7 (Holiday 2006): 28–29.

Pike, Kermit J., comp. *A Guide to Shaker Manuscripts in the Library of the Western Reserve Historical Society; With an Inventory of Its Photographs.* Cleveland: Western Reserve Historical Society, 1974.

Richmond, Mary L., comp. *Shaker Literature: A Bibliography in Two Volumes.* Hancock, Mass.: Shaker Community, 1977.

Shaker Heritage: An Annotated Pictorial Guide to the Collection of the Shaker Historical Museum. Shaker Heights, Ohio: Shaker Historical Society, 1980.

Winter, Esther C., and Joanna S. Ellett, comps. *Shaker Literature in the Rare Book Room of the Buffalo and Erie County Public Library.* Buffalo, N.Y.: Buffalo and Erie County Public Library, 1967.

HISTORIES

Andrews, Edward Deming. *The People Called Shakers; A Search for the Perfect Society.* New York: Oxford University Press, 1953.

———, and Faith Andrews. *Fruits of the Shaker Tree of Life; Memoirs of Fifty Years of Collecting and Research*. Stockbridge, Mass.: Berkshire Traveller Press, 1975.

———. *Work and Worship; The Economic Order of the Shakers*. Greenwich, Conn.: New York Graphic Society, 1974.

Brewer, Priscilla J. *Shaker Communities, Shaker Lives*. Hanover, N.H.: University Press of New England, 1986.

Chmielewski, Wendy E., Louis J. Kern, and Marilyn Klee-Hartzwell, eds. *Women in Spiritual and Communitarian Societies in the United States*. Syracuse, N.Y.: Syracuse University Press, 1993.

Coleman, Wim, ed. *The Shakers*. Carlisle, Mass.: Discovery Enterprises, 1997.

Desroche, Henri. *The American Shakers; From Neo-Christianity to Presocialism*. Amherst: University of Massachusetts Press, 1971.

Evans, Jessie. *The Story of Shakerism, by One Who Knows* [pseud.]. East Canterbury, N.H.: Shakers, 1907.

Foster, Lawrence. *Religion and Sexuality*. New York: Oxford University Press, 1981.

———. *Women, Family, and Utopia*. Syracuse, N.Y.: Syracuse University Press, 1991.

Fried, Albert, ed. *Socialism in America; From the Shakers to the Third International*. Garden City, N.Y.: Doubleday & Company, 1970.

Frost, Marguerite. *About the Shakers*. Canterbury, N.H.: [Canterbury Shakers, n.d.].

———, Sister Marguerite. *The Shaker Story*. Canterbury, N.H.: Canterbury Shakers, [n.d].

Garrett, Clarke. *Spirit Possession and Popular Religion*. Baltimore: Johns Hopkins University Press, 1987.

Hinds, William Alfred. *American Communities: Brief Sketches of Economy, Zoar, Bethel, Aurora, Amana, Icaria, the Shakers, Oneida, Wallingford, and the Brotherhood of the New Life*. Oneida, N.Y.: Office of the *American Socialist*, 1878.

Hollway, Mark. *Heavens on Earth: Utopian Communities in America, 1680–1880*. 2nd ed. New York: Dover Publications, 1966.

Kern, Louis J. *An Ordered Love; Sex Roles and Sexuality in Victorian Utopias—the Shakers, the Mormons, and the Oneida Community*. Chapel Hill: University of North Carolina Press, 1981.

Kitch, Sally L. *Chaste Liberation; Celibacy and Female Cultural Status*. Urbana: University of Illinois Press, 1989.

Marini, Stephen A. *Radical Sects of Revolutionary New England*. Cambridge, Mass.: Harvard University Press, 1982.

Melcher, Marguerite Fellows. *The Shaker Adventure*. Princeton: Princeton University Press, 1941.

Morse, Flo. *The Shakers and the World's People*. New York: Dodd, and Mead, 1980.

———. *The Story of the Shakers*. Woodstock, Vt.: The Countryman Press, 1986.

———. *Yankee Communes: Another American Way*. New York: Harcourt, Brace Jovanovich, 1971.

Nordhoff, Charles. *The Communistic Societies of the United States*. New York: Harper & Brothers, 1875.

Noyes, John Humphrey. *History of American Socialisms*. Philadephia: J. B. Lippincott, 1870.

Pitzer, Donald E., ed. *America's Communal Utopias*. Chapel Hill: University of North Carolina Press, 1997.

Promey, Sally M. *Spiritual Spectacles; Vision and Image in Mid-Nineteenth-Century Shakersism*. Bloomington: Indiana University Press, 1993.

Robinson, Charles Edson. *A Concise History of the United Society of Believers Called Shakers*. East Canterbury, N.H.: Canterbury Shakers, 1893.

Sasson, Diane. *The Shaker Spiritual Narrative*. Knoxville: University of Tennessee Press, 1983.

Shi, David E., ed. *In Search of the Simple Life: American Voices, Past and Present*. Layton, Utah: Gibbs M. Smith, 1986.

Stein, Stephen J. *The Shaker Experience in America*. New Haven: Yale University Press, 1992.

Tyler, Alice Felt. *Freedom's Ferment: Phases of American Social History from the Colonial Period to 1860*. Minneapolis: University of Minnesota Press, 1944.

Van Kolken, Diana. *Introducing the Shakers*. Bowling Green, Ohio: Gabriel's Horn Publishing Company, 1985.

Weisbrod, Carol. *The Boundaries of Utopia*. New York: Pantheon Books, 1980.

White, Anna, and Leila S. Taylor. *Shakerism; Its Meaning and Message*. Columbus, Ohio: Press of Fred J. Heer, 1904.

Williams, John S. *The Shakers; A Brief Summary*. Old Chatham, N.Y.: Shaker Museum Foundation, 1956.

SHAKER COMMUNITIES

Eastern Societies

Allen, Francis Olcott, ed. *The History of Enfield, Connecticut*. 3 Vols. Lancaster, Pa.: Wickersham Printing, 1900.

Anderson, Russell H. "The Shaker Community in Florida." *Florida Historical Quarterly* 37 (July 1959): 29–44.

———. "The Shaker Communities in Southeast Georgia." *Georgia Historical Quarterly* 50 (June 1966): 162–72.

Andrews, Edward Deming. *The Hancock Shakers; The Shaker Community at Hancock, Massachusetts, 1790–1960.* Hancock, Mass.: Shaker Community, 1961.

Barker, Sister R. Mildred. *Holy Land: A History of the Alfred Shakers.* Sabbathday Lake, Maine: Shaker Press, 1983.

———. *The Sabbathday Lake Shakers: An Introduction to the Shaker Heritage.* Sabbathday Lake, Maine: Shaker Press, 1978.

Brainard, Jesse Miriam. "Mother Ann's Children in Connecticut." *Connecticut Quarterly* 3 (December 1897): 460–74.

Bridge, Ruth. *The Challenge of Change; Three Centuries of Enfield, Connecticut History.* Canaan, N.H.: Phoenix Publishing, 1977.

Bridges, Madeline S. "A Wonderful Little World of People." *Ladies Home Journal* 15 (June 1898): 6–7.

Burns, Deborah E. *Shaker Cities of Peace, Love, and Union; A History of the Hancock Bishopric.* Hanover, N.H.: University Press of New England, 1993.

Cameron, Nellie L. *Hancock Through the Years.* Pittsfield, Mass.: Pittsfield Printing, 1976.

Chandler, Lloyd H. "The New Hampshire Shakers." *Historical New Hampshire* (8 March 1952): 1–18.

———, Seth. *History of the Town of Shirley, Massachusetts, from its Early Settlement to A.D. 1882.* Published by the Author, 1883.

Columbia County at the End of the Century; A Historical Record. . . . Hudson, N.Y.: Record Printing and Publishing, 1900, 678–90.

[Dwight, John Sullivan]. "The Shakers at Lebanon." *The Harbinger* 5 (August 14, 21, 1847): 156–58, 174–76.

Eastman, Harland H. *Alfred, Maine; The Shakers and the Village.* Sanford, Maine: Wilson's Printers, 1986.

[Ellis, Franklin]. *History of Columbia County, New York.* Philadelphia: Everts & Ensign, 1878, 307–10.

Emerich, A. Donald, ed. *Mount Lebanon Shaker Village; Self-Guided Walking Tour.* Mount Lebanon Shaker Village, 1991.

Filley, Dorothy M. *Recapturing Wisdom's Valley; The Watervliet Shaker Heritage.* Albany: Albany Institute of History and Art, 1975.

Gilder, Cornelia Brooke. *Views of the Valley; Tyringham 1739–1989.* Hop Brook Community Club, 1989.

Hess, Wendell. *The Enfield (N.H.) Shakers; A Brief History.* [n.p.], 1988.

Horgan, Edward R. *The Shaker Holy Land; A Community Portrait.* Harvard, Mass.: Harvard Common Press, 1982.

Hulings, Martha A. *Shaker Days Remembered.* Albany: Shaker Heritage Society, 1983.

Johnson, Clifton. "The Passing of the Shakers." *Old-Time New England* 25 (July, October, 1934): 2–19, 40–66.

——, Theodore E. *Hands to Work and Hearts to God: The Shaker Tradition in Maine.* Brunswick, Maine: Bowdoin College Museum of Art, 1969.

Kramer, Fran. *Simply Shaker; Groveland and the New York Communities.* Rochester, N.Y.: Rochester Museum & Science Center, 1991.

Langeveld, Dirk. *Report on the History and Present State of the West Family Site at Hancock Shaker Village.* [n.p.], 2006.

Lockerby, Jenny, comp. *'Very Pleasant Reading': Hancock Shakers Write to the Manifesto, 1889–1899.* Hancock Shaker Village, 2004.

[Lossing, Benson John]. "The Shakers." *Harper's New Monthly Magazine* 15 (July 1857): 164–77.

Lyford, James Otis. *History of the Town of Canterbury, New Hampshire, 1727–1912.* Concord, N.H.: Rumford Press, 1912.

[Mace,] Aurelia. *The Aletheia: Spirit of Truth.* Farmington, Maine: Press of Knowlton, McLeary, 1899.

Miller, Amy Bess. *Hancock Shaker Village/The City of Peace; An Effort to Restore a Vision 1960–1985.* Hancock, Mass.: Hancock Shaker Village, 1984.

——, Michael K. *Images of America: Enfield, Connecticut.* Arcadia Publishing, 1998.

Myers, Eloise. *Tyringham: A Hinterland Settlement.* Tyringham Historical Commission, 1989.

Olton, Jean Z., comp. *The Town of Colonie: A Pictorial History.* Town of Colonie, N.Y., 1990.

Ott, John Harlow. *Hancock Shaker Village; A Guidebook and History.* Revised Edition. Hancock, Mass.: Shaker Community, 1976.

Parsons, Usher. *A Centennial History of Alfred, York County, Maine.* Philadelphia: Sanford & Evert, 1872.

Patchett, *Anna E. Historically Speaking; Selected Subjects Pertaining to Livingston County, New York.* Genesco, N.Y.: Livingston County Historical Society, 1978.

Paterwic, Stephen. "Mysteries of the Tyringham Shakers Unmasked: A New Examination of People, Facts, and Figures." *Historical Journal of Massachusetts* 31 (Winter 2003): 1–20.

Phinney, Jane Benedict. *Taking the High Road; A Two Hundred Year History of a Hilltown; Savoy, Massachusetts, 1797–1997.* [n.p.], 1997.

Roueche, Berton. "A Small Family of Seven." *New Yorker* 23 (23 August 1947): 42–51.

Sears, Clara Endicott, comp. *Gleanings from Old Shaker Journals.* Boston: Houghton Mifflin, 1916.

Shaver, Elizabeth, ed. "Fifteen Years a Shakeress." Originally published in 1872 in *Galaxy* Magazine. Albany: Shaker Heritage Society, 1989.

———. *The Watervliet Shaker Cemetery, Albany, New York.* Albany: Shaker Heritage Society, 1992.

———, and Ned Pratt. *The Watervliet Shakers & Their 1848 Shaker Meeting House, Albany, New York.* Albany: Shaker Heritage Society, 1994.

Sherburne, Trudy Reno. *As I Remember It: Being a Detailed Description of the North Family of the Watervliet Shaker Community and Including the District School as Well as the Big Barn at the Church Family.* Holland, Mich.: World of Shaker, 1987.

Skees, Suzanne. *God among the Shakers; A Search for Stillness and Faith at Sabbathday Lake.* New York: Hyperion, 1998.

Sprigg, June. *Simple Gifts; A Memoir of a Shaker Village.* New York: Alfred A. Knopf, 1998.

Starbuck, David R. "Canterbury Shaker Village: Archeology and Landscape." *New Hampshire Archeologist* 31 (1990).

———, and Scott T. Swank. *A Shaker Family Album; Photographs from the Collection of Canterbury Shaker Village.* Hanover, N.H.: University Press of New England, 1998.

Stewart, Watt. "A Mexican and a Spaniard Observe the Shakers, 1830–1835." *New York History* 22 (January 1941): 67–76.

Thurman, Suzanne R. *'O Sisters Ain't You Happy?' Gender, Family, and Community among the Harvard and Shirley Shakers, 1781–1918.* Syracuse University Press, 2002.

Wertkin, Gerard C. *The Four Seasons of Shaker Life; An Intimate Portrait of the Community at Sabbathday Lake.* New York: Simon & Schuster, 1986.

West, Arthur. "Reminiscences of Life in a Shaker Village." [Harvard, Mass.] *New England Quarterly* 9 (June 1938): 343–60.

Wisbey, Herbert A. *The Sodus Shaker Community.* Lyons, N.Y.: Wayne County Historical Society, 1982.

Western Societies

Bauer, Cheryl, and Rob Portman. *Wisdom's Paradise; The Forgotten Shakers of Union Village.* Wilmington, Ohio: Orange Frazer Press, 2004.

Beers, W. H. & Co. *The History of Montgomery County, Ohio, Containing a History of the County; its Townships, Towns, General Local Statistics. . . .* Chicago: W. H. Beers, 1882.

———. *The History of Warren County, Ohio.* Chicago: W. H. Beers, 1882.

Blinn, Henry Clay. "A Journey to Kentucky in the Year 1873." *Shaker Quarterly* 5 (1965): 3–19, 37–55, 69–79, 107–33; 6 (1966): 22–30, 53–72, 93–102, 135–44; 7 (Spring 1967): 13–23.

Boles, John B. *Religion in Antebellum Kentucky.* Lexington: University of Kentucky Press, 1976.

Clark, Thomas D. *Pleasant Hill in the Civil War.* Pleasant Hill Press, 1972.

———, and F. Gerald Ham. *Pleasant Hill and Its Shakers.* Pleasant Hill, Ky.: Shakertown Press, 1968.

Conlin, Mary Lou. *The North Union Story; A Shaker Society, 1822–1889.* Shaker Historical Society, 1961.

Hooper, James W. *Images of America: The Shaker Communities of Kentucky.* Arcadia Publishing, 2006.

Hunt, Melba. *Summers at Watervliet.* Kettering, Ohio: Kettering-Moraine Museum & Historical Society, 1985.

Hutton, Daniel Mac-Hir. *Old Shakertown and the Shakers.* Harrodsburg, Ky.: Harrodsburg Herald Press, 1936.

Janzen, Donald E. *The Shaker Mills on Shawnee Run; Historical Archaeology at Shakertown at Pleasant Hill.* Harrodsbury, Ky.: Pleasant Hill Press, 1981.

Johnson, Lee. *The Struggle for Watervliet, Ohio.* Washington, D.C.: SpiritTree Press, 1999.

MacLean, John Patterson. "The Kentucky Revival and Its Influence on the Miami Valley." *Ohio Archaeological and Historical Quarterly* 12 (July 1903): 242–86.

———. "Mobbing the Shakers of Union Village." *Ohio Archaeological and Historical Quarterly* 11 (July 1903): 103–33.

———. "Origin, Rise, Progress and Decline of the Whitewater Community of Shakers Located in Hamilton County, Ohio." *Ohio Archaeological and Historical Quarterly* 13 (October 1904): 401–43.

———. "The Shaker Community of Warren County. Its Origin, Rise, Progress and Decline." *Ohio Archaeological and Historical Quarterly* 10 (1902): 251–304.

———. "Shaker Mission to the Shawnee Indians." *Ohio Archaeological and Historical Quarterly* 11 (1903): 215–29.

———. "The Society of Shakers. Rise, Progress and Extinction of the Society at Cleveland, Ohio." *Ohio Archaeological and Historical Quarterly* 9 (July 1900): 32–116.

McNemar, Richard. *The Kentucky Revival: Or, A Short History of the Late Extraordinary Out-Pouring of the Spirit of God, in the Western States of America, Agreeably to Scripture-Promises, and Prophecies concerning the Latter Day: With a Brief Account of the Entrance and Progress of What the World Call Shakerism. . . .* Cincinnati, Ohio: John W. Brown, 1807.

[———], comp. *A Review of the Most Important Events Relating to the Rise and Progress of the United Society of Believers in the West; with Sundry other Documents Connected with the History of the Society. Collected from Various Journals. By E. Wright* [pseudo.]. . . . Union Village, Ohio: [Union Press], 1831.

Neal, Mary Julia. *By Their Fruits; The Story of Shakerism in South Union, Kentucky*. Philadelphia: Porcupine Press, 1975.

———. *The Journal of Eldress Nancy Kept at the South Union, Kentucky, Shaker Colony August 15, 1861–September 4, 1864*. Nashville: Parthenon Press, 1963.

Pauly, Fred L. "The Shakers." *Trilobite* 1 (July 1903): 1–4, 9.

Piercy, Caroline B. *The Valley of God's Pleasure; The Thrilling Saga of the North Union Shakers*. New York: Stratford House, 1951.

Thomas, Samuel W., and James C. Thomas. *The Simple Spirit; A Pictorial Study of the Shaker Community at Pleasant Hill, Kentucky*. Harrodsburg, Ky.: Pleasant Hill Press, 1973.

Wallace, Earl D. *The Shakers and the Civil War Battle of Perryville*. Harrodsburg, Ky.: Pleasant Hill Press, 1976.

Whittaker, Thomas. "The Gasper River Meeting House." *Filson Club History Quarterly* 56 (January 1982): 30–61.

———. "History of the United States Post Office, South Union, Logan County, Kentucky 42283." *Filson Club History Quarterly* 47 (April 1973): 145–60.

PERIODICALS

The *Day-Star* began as an Adventist publication, but became Shaker after the failure of William Miller's prophecies of 1843 and 1844. The editor and publisher Enoch Jacobs became a Shaker at Union Village, Ohio. He worked to attract other Adventists to the faith and went on a missionary tour in the East. The paper ceased in July 1847 because of financial troubles and Jacobs' departure from the Shakers.

From 1871 until 1899, the Shakers published a monthly newspaper. Collectively, it is popularly known as the *Manifesto,* though technically that title was only used in the final 17 years. The chronology of the accurate titles is as follows:

Shaker Vols. 1–2 (1871–1872)
Shaker and Shakeress Vols. 3–5 (1873–1874)
Shaker Vols. 6–7 (1876–1877)
Shaker Manifesto Vols. 8–12 (1878–1882)
Manifesto Vols. 13–29 (1883–1899)

In 1961, the Sabbathday Lake Shakers began a quarterly publication devoted to Shaker theological and historical scholarship: *Shaker Quarterly* Vols. 1–14 (1961–1974); Vols. 15–24 (1987–1996).

Starting in 1975, the Sabbathday Lake Shakers printed and published a booklet on herbs: *Shaker Herbalist* Vols. 1–2 (1975) Vol. 3 (1977).

Begun in 1971, this non-Shaker newspaper/messenger eventually had three different names during its 26-year run:

World of Shaker Vols. 1–10 (1971–1980)
Shaker Messenger Vols. 11–24 (1981–1994)
Shakers World Vols. 25–26 (1995–1996)

These scholarly journals have articles and information on the Shakers:

Communal Societies, Journal of the Communal Studies Association (1981–present) *American Communal Societies Quarterly*, A Publication of Hamilton College Library (2006–present)

PEOPLE

Biographies and Memorials

Allen, Minnie Catherine. *Biographical Sketch of Daniel Fraser of the Shaker Community of Mt. Lebanon, Columbia County, N.Y., by Catharine Allen. . . .* Albany: Weed & Parsons, 1890.

———, William B. *History of Kentucky, Embracing Gleanings, Reminiscenses, Antiquities, Natural Curiosities, Statistics, and Biographical Sketches. . . .* Louisville: Bradley & Gilbert, 1872.

Avery, Giles Bushnell. *Autobiography of Elder Giles B. Avery, of Mount Lebanon, N.Y.* East Canterbury, N.H., 1891.

Barker, Sister R. Mildred, "Elder John Vance's 'Dear Brethren and Sisters I Love You.'" *Shaker Quarterly* 13 (Summer 1973): 68–74.

———. "In Memoriam Brother Theodore Elliott Johnson." *Shaker Quarterly* 15 (Spring 1987): 3–9.

———. "In Memoriam Sister Ethel Peacock. Sister Eleanor Philbrook, Sister Elizabeth Dunn." *Shaker Quarterly* 15 (Fall 1987): 83–86.

Bear, Henry B. *Henry B. Bear's Advent Experience.* [Whitewater Village, Harrison Ohio: n.d.]

Biographical Review . . . of the Leading Citizens of Columbia County, New York. Boston: Biographical Review Publishing Company, 1894. [Elder William Anderson 262–65; Elder George W. Clark 286–87; Joseph Holden 111–15; Elder Calvin Reed 522–26]

[Bishop, Rufus, and Seth Youngs Wells, eds.] *Testimonies of the Life, Character, Revelations, and Doctrines of Our Ever Blessed Mother Ann Lee, and the Elders with Her; through Whom the Word of Eternal Life as Opened in This Day of Christ's Second appearing; Collected from Living Witnesses, by Order of the Ministry, in union with the Church.* . . . Hancock, Mass.: J Talcott and J Deming, Junrs., 1816.

Blinn, Henry Clay. *The Life and Gospel Experience of Mother Ann Lee.* Canterbury, N.H., [1882?]

[———, comp.] *A Concise Catechism, Containing the Most Important Events Recorded in the Bible. Also a Short Sketch of the Lives of our First Elders and Parents, Mother Ann, Father William & Father James.* Canterbury, N.H.: Shaker Village, 1850.

Briggs, Nicholas A. "Forty Years a Shaker." Granite Monthly 52 (1920): 463–74; 53 (January/March 1921): 19–32, 56–65, 113–21.

Brooks, Leonard. "Sister Aurelia Mace and Her Influence on the Ever-Growing Nature of Shakerism." *Shaker Quarterly* 16 (Summer 1988): 47–60.

Brown, Grace Ada. *Sister Corrine. Written by Sister Grace Ada Brown. In Memory of Sister Corrine Bishop, Who Passed to Her Spirit Home, Dec. 3, 1929.* [n.p, n.d.].

Budis, Erin M. *Making His Mark: The Work of Shaker Craftsman Orren Haskins.* Old Chatham, N.Y.: Shaker Museum and Library, 1997.

[Bullard], Sister Marcia. "Recollections of My Childhood." *Good Housekeeping* 43 (August 1906): 126–29.

Carpenter, Sister June. "Sister Ada S. Cummings: Caretaker, Teacher, Poet." Shaker Quarterly 22 (Summer 1994): 38–59.

Carr, Sister Frances A. *Growing Up Shaker.* United Society of Shakers, 1995.

———. "In Memoriam: Sister Ethel Mary Hudson 1896–1992." Shaker Quarterly 20 (Fall 1992): 88–91.

———. "Lucy Wright: The First Mother in the Revelation and Order of the First Organized Church." *Shaker Quarterly* 15 (Fall/Winter 1987): 93–100, 128–32.

———. "She Labored for the Gift: Eldress Prudence Stickney." *Shaker Quarterly* 17 (Winter 1989): 135–53.

Collier, Arthur Lake. *A Family Sketch.* [Harvard Shakers] Salem, Mass.: Lavender Printing, 1951.

[Collins, Sarah], comp. *Memorial of Sister Polly C. Lewis.* [Mt. Lebanon, N.Y.: 1899].

Coyle, William, ed. *Ohio Authors and Their Books . . . 1796–1950.* Cleveland: World Book Company, 1962 [John Dunlavy 184; Richard McNemar 420; John Prescott 508; Benjamin S. Youngs 713].

Doolittle, Mary Antoinette. *Autobiography of Mary Antoinette Doolittle Containing a Brief History of Early Life Prior to Becoming a Member of the Shaker Community, Also an Outline of Life & Experience among the Shakers.* Mount Lebanon, N.Y., 1880.

[Enfield, New Hampshire Shakers]. *A Biography of the Life and Tragical Death of Elder Caleb M. Dyer, Together with the Poem and Eulogies at His Funeral, July 21, 1863.* Manchester, N.H.: American Steam Printing Works of Gage & Moore, 1863.

Evans, Frederick W. *Autobiography of a Shaker.* [Albany: Charles Van Benthuysen and Sons], 1869.

———. *Obituary. Death of a Prominent Shaker* [Giles B. Avery] *in the Community at Watervliet, N.Y.* [n.p., 1891].

———. *Obituary. Rufus Crossman, By Elder F. W. Evens* [sic]. *Why I Am a Christian by Walter Shepherd.* Mt. Lebanon, N.Y.: 1891.

Fraser, Daniel. *Witness of Daniel Fraser.* [Mt. Lebanon: 1901].

Grant, Jerry V., and Douglas R. Allen. *Shaker Furniture Makers.* University Press of New England, 1989.

Green, Calvin. "Biographical Account of the Life, Character & Ministry of Father Joseph Meacham . . . 1827." *Shaker Quarterly* 10 (Spring/Summer/Fall 1970): 20–32, 58–68, 92–102.

Hadd, Brother Arnold. "Agreeable to Our Understanding: The Shaker Covenant." *Shaker Quarterly* 24 (1996): 87, 109.

———. "The Burden I Will Never Shun: Elder Otis Sawyer: His Life and Continuing Influence." *Shaker Quarterly* 22 (Winter 1994): 92–121.

———. "And I Shall Make You a Fisher of Men: The Life and Testimony of Elder Elisha Pote." *Shaker Quarterly* 17 (Summer 1989): 55–66.

———. "To the Memory of Our Dear Fathers in the Gospel: Elders John Vance and Elder William Dumont." *Shaker Quarterly* 17 (Winter 1989): 194–213.

———. "A Very Ingenious, Useful Brother: The Life of Elder Henry Green." *Shaker Quarterly* 21 (Summer 1993): 43–51.

[———]. "In Memoriam R. Mildred Barker 1897–1990." *Shaker Quarterly* 18 (Spring 1990): 4–20.

Hampton, Oliver C. *In Memoriam Elder William Reynolds, Departed This Life, at Union Village, Ohio, May 13, 1881, Aged 66 Years, 1 Mo., 9 Days.* [n.p. 1881].

Hess, Wendell. "The 'Simple Gifts' of Elder Joseph Brackett." *Shaker Quarterly* 16 (Fall 1988): 81–91.

Hillenburg, Nancy. "A Shaker Weaver: A Tribute to Sister Elsie McCool." *Shaker Quarterly* 22 (Spring 1994): 19–21.

Hollister, Alonzo Giles, comp. *Prophecy Unsealed [!] by the 'Word of God Reveald [!] out of Whose Mouth Goeth a Sharp Sword'*... *Brief Sketch of Ann Lee the First Anointed, Emancipated, New Woman, as Seen by Those Who Knew Her*. ... Mt. Lebanon, N.Y.: 1905.

Humez, Jean M., ed. *Mother's First-Born Daughters*. Bloomington: Indiana University Press, 1993.

——, McMahon, ed. *Gifts of Power: The Writings of Rebecca Jackson, Black Visionary, Shaker Eldress*. University of Massachusetts Press, 1981.

In Memoriam Elder Henry C. Blinn 1824–1905. Concord, N.H.: Rumford Printing, 1905.

In Memoriam Eldress D. A. Durgin, 1825–1898; Eldress J. J. Kaime, 1826–1898. Concord, N.H.: Rumford Press, 1899.

In Memoriam Mary Hazard. [Mt. Lebanon: 1899].

Johnson, Brother Theodore E., ed. "A Brief Narrative of the Religious Experience of Joseph Pelham." *Shaker Quarterly* 15 (Winter/Fall 1987): 71–82, 103–14; 16 (Spring/Summer/Fall 1988): 3–17, 35–46, 67–72.

——, ed. "A Sketch of the Life and Experience of Issachar Bates." *Shaker Quarterly* 1 (Fall/Winter 1961): 98–118, 145–63; 2 (Spring 1962): 18–35.

——, ed. "A Sketch of the Life and Experience of Richard W. Pelham." *Shaker Quarterly* 9 (Spring, Summer, Fall 1969): 18–32, 53–64, 69–96.

[——]. "In Memoriam Delmer Charles Wilson." *Shaker Quarterly* 1 (Winter 1961): 135–37.

Klyver, Richard D. *Brother James: The Life and Times of Shaker Elder, James Prescott*. Solon, Ohio: Evans Printing, 1992.

Knight, Jane D. *Brief Narrative of Events Touching Various Reforms, by Jane D. Knight, Who Was Reared in the Society of Friends and United with the Shakers at Mount Lebanon, Columbia Co., N.Y., in the Year 1826, in the Twenty-second Year of Her Age*. Albany: Weed and Parsons, 1880.

Lorenz, George. *Service Is Our Life: Excerpts from the Diaries of Sister Jennie Mathers*. Waupaca, Wis.: Carol Press, 1998.

——. *'There Is No Place Like Shirley' Sister Annie Belle Tuttle*. Waupaca, Wis.: Carol Press, 1999.

McNemar, Richard. *A Brief Memorial of Mother Ruth Farrington*. [Watervliet, Ohio: 183?].

——. *The Life and Labors of Father David Darrow*. Watervliet, Ohio: 1834.

——. *Western Review*. [Lives of the First Parent and Ministers of the Shaker West] Watervliet, Ohio: 1834.

Marini, Stephen A. "A New View of Mother Ann Lee and the Rise of American Shakerism." *Shaker Quarterly* 18 (Summer/Fall 1990): 47–52, 56–62, 95–111.

Maynard, Susan. *A Shaker Life: The Diaries of Brother Irving Greenwood 1894–1939.* [n.p], 2006.

Miller, M. Stephen. "The Copley-Lyman Shaker Family of Enfield, Connecticut: An Annotated Genealogy." *American Communal Societies Quarterly* 1 (April 2007): 51–73.

Paterwic, Stephen. "Eldress Doolittle Died 100 Years Ago." *Shaker Messenger* 9 (Fall 1986): 12–13.

Pearson, Elmer R., and Julia Neal. *The Shaker Image.* Annotations, Appendices and Index by Dr. Magda Gabor-Hotchkiss. Pittsfield, Mass.: Hancock Shaker Village, 1994.

Pelham, Richard W. *To the Memory of David Spinning.* North Union: [1841?].

Perkins, Abraham. *Autobiography of Elder Abraham Perkins and In Memoriam.* Concord, N.H.: Rumford Press, 1901.

Phillips, Hazel Spencer. *Richard the Shaker.* Oxford, Ohio: Typoprint Inc., 1972.

Ross, Nan Thayer. *Purple on Silk: A Shaker Eldress and Her Dye Journal.* [Eldress Hester Ann Adams] New Gloucester, Maine: United Society of Shakers, 2003.

[Sabbathday Lake Shakers]. In Memoriam Sister Aurelia G. Mace 1835–1910. [n.p. 1910].

Sampson, Joseph Adam Hall. *Remains of Joseph A. H. Sampson, who Died at New-Lebanon, 12 mo. 14, 1825, Aged 20 Years. Published by the Request of his Friends, for the Benefit of Youth. . . .* Rochester, N.Y.: Printed by E. F. Marshall [also includes an account of the life of Polly Lawrence] 1828.

Sasson, Diane. "Not Such a Simple Life: The Case of William Leonard." *Shaker Quarterly* 20 (Summer 1992): 37–51.

Smith, Brother Wayne. "Brother Stephen Gowen: A Life of Love and Service." *Shaker Quarterly* 19 (Summer 1991): 61–67.

Stein, Stephen J., ed. *Letters from a Young Shaker: William S. Byrd at Pleasant Hill.* Lexington, Ky.: University Press of Kentucky, 1985.

Taylor, Leila S. *A Memorial to Eldress Anna White and Elder Daniel Offord.* Mount Lebanon, N.Y.: North Family of Shakers, 1912.

Thomas, James C. "Micajah Burnett and the Buildings at Pleasant Hill." *Shaker Tradition and Design.* New York: Bonanza Books, 1982, 50–56.

Wells, Seth Youngs, and Calvin Green, eds. *Testimonies Concerning the Character and Appearing Ministry of Mother Ann Lee and the First Witnesses of the Gospel of Christ's Second; Given by Some of the Aged Brethren and Sisters of the United Society, Including a Few Sketches of Their Own Religious Experience: Approved by the Church. . . .* Albany: Packard & Van Benthuysen, 1827.

Wergland, Glendyne R. *One Shaker Life: Isaac Newton Youngs, 1793–1865*. Amherst, Mass.: University of Massachusetts Press, 2006.

[White, Anna, comp.] *Affectionately Inscribed to the Memory of Elder Frederick W. Evans, by His Loving and Devoted Gospel Friends. . . .* Pittsfield, Mass.: Eagle Publishing, 1893.

[———.] *Affectionately Inscribed to the Memory of Eldress Antoinette Doolittle, by her Loving and Devoted Gospel Friends. . . .* Albany: Weed and Parsons, 1887.

[———.] *Dedicated to the Memory of Sister Polly Lewis. The King's Daughter.* [Mount Lebanon, N.Y.: 1899].

[———.] *To Our Well Beloved Mother in Israel. Eldress. Eliza Ann Taylor whose Spirit Passed "within the Vail" November 28, 1897, in the 87th Year of her Age. . . .* Mount Lebanon, N.Y.: 1897.

Wickersham, George M. *How I Came to Be a Shaker*. N.p.: East Canterbury, N.H., 1891.

Williams, Richard E. *Called and Chosen: The Story of Mother Rebecca Jackson and the Philadelphia Shakers*. Metcuchen, N.J.: Scarecrow Press, 1981.

Wilson, Delmer. "The Diary of a Maine Shaker Boy—1887." *Shaker Quarterly* 8 (Spring 1968).

Apostates

Brown, Thomas. *An Account of the People Called Shakers: Their Faith, Doctrines, and Practice, Exempliufied in the Life, Coversations, and Experience of the Author during the Time He Belonged to the Society. To Which Is Affixed a History of their Rise and Progress to the Present Day*. Troy, N.Y.: Parker and Bliss, 1812.

Chapman, Eunice. *An Account of the Conduct of the People Called Shakers: In the Case of Eunice Chapman and Her Children, since Her Husband Became Acquainted with That People, and Joined Their Society. Written by Herself. . . .* Albany: By the author, 1817.

DeWolfe, Elizabeth A. *Shaking the Faith: Women, Family and Mary Marshall Dyer's Anti-Shaker Campaign, 1815–1867*. New York: Palgrave Macmillan, 2004.

Dyer, Joseph. *A Compendious Narrative, Elucidating the Character, Disposition and Conduct of Mary Dyer, from the Time of Her Marriage, in 1799, till she Left the Society called Shakers, in 1815. With a Few Remarks upon Certain Charges Which She Has since Published against the Society. Together with Sundry Depositions. By Her Husband Joseph Dyer. To Which Is An-*

nexed, *A Remonstrance of the Said Mary, for Legislative Interference*. Concord, N.H.: Isaac Hill, 1818.

Dyer, Mary Marshall. *A Portraiture of Shakerism, Exhibiting a General View of Their Character and Conduct, from the First Appearance of Ann Lee in New-England, down to the Present time, and Certified by Many Respectable Authorities. . . .* Haverhill, N.H.: Sylvester T. Gross, 1822.

Elkins, Hervey. *Fifteen Years in the Senior Order of Shakers: A Narration of the Facts, concerning That Singular People. . . .* Hanover, N.H.: Dartmouth Press, 1853.

Haskett, William J. *Shakerism Unmasked: Or, The History of the Shakers; Including a Form Politic or Their Government as Councils, Orders, Gifts, with an Exposition of the Five Orders of Shakerism, Ann Lee's Grand Foundation Vision, in Sealed Pages. With Some Extracts from Their Private Hymns Which Have Never Appeared before the Public*. Pittsfield, Mass.: By the author, 1828.

Lamson, David Rich. *Two Years' Experience among the Shakers: Being a Description of the Manners and Customs of That People, the Nature and Policy of Their Government, Their Marvellous Intercourse with the Spiritual World, the Object and Uses of Confession, Their Inquisition, in Short, a Condensed View of Shakerism as It Is*. West Boyleston, Mass.: By the author, 1848.

Merrill, Althea. *Shaker Girl*. South Portland, Maine: Pilot Press, 1987.

Rathbun, Reuben. *Reasons Offered for Leaving the Shakers*. Pittsfield, Mass.: Chester Smith, 1800.

Rathbun, Valentine Wightman. *An Account of the Matter, Form, and Manner of a New and Strange Religion, Taught and Propagated by a Number of Europeans, Living in a Place called Nisqueunia, in the State of New-York. Written by Valentine Rathbun, Minister of the Gospel*. Providence, R.I.: Bennett Wheeler, 1781.

Woods, John. *Shakerism Unmasked, Or, A Narrative Shewing the Entrance of the Shakers into the Western Country, Their Stratagems and Devices, Discipline and Economy; Together with What May Seem Necessary to Exhibit the True State of That People. By John Woods: Who Lived with Them Seventeen Years. . . .* Paris, Ky.: Office of the *Western Observer*, 1826.

THEOLOGICAL WORKS

Avery, Giles Bushnell. *Sketches of 'Shakers and Shakerism': Synopsis of Theology of United Society of Believers in Christ's Second Appearing*. Albany: Weed and Parsons, 1883.

Barker, R. Mildred. "Revelation: A Shaker Viewpoint." *Shaker Quarterly* 3 (Spring 1963): 7–17.

Basting, Louis. *Christianity*. West Pittsfield, Mass. [Printed at East Canterbury, N.H., 1891].

Bates, Paulina. *The Divine Book of Holy and Eternal Wisdom, Revealing the Work of God; Out of Whose Mouth Goeth a Sharp Sword . . . Written by Paulina Bates . . . Including Other Illustrations and Testimonies. . . .* Canterbury, N.H.: United Society Called "Shakers," 1849.

Bear, Henry B. *A Scientific Demonstration of the Prophecies of Daniel and St. John*. Preston, Ohio: Alexander Smith, Printer, [n.d].

———. Scientific Demonstration of Theology, Prophecy and Revelation. [n.p.] 1896.

Blinn, Henry Clay. *Advent of Christ in Man and Woman*. [East Canterbury, N.H.]: 1896.

———, ed. *The Manifestation of Spiritualism among the Shakers 1837–1847*. East Canterbury, N.H.: 1899.

Briigs, Nicholas A. *God,—Dual*. East Canterbury, N.H.: [United Society of Shakers], [n.d].

Dunlavy, John. *The Manifesto: or, A Declaration of the Doctrines and Practices of the Church of Christ. . . .* Pleasant Hill, Ky.: P. Bertrand, 1818.

———. *Plain Evidences, by which the Nature and Character of the True Church of Christ May Be Known and Distinguished from All Others*. Albany: Hoffman and White, 1834.

[Eads, Harvey Lauderdale]. *Condition of Society: And Its Only Hope, in Obeying the Everlasting Gospel, as Now Developing among Believers in Christ's Second Appearing. . . .* Union Village, Ohio: *Day-Star* Office, 1847.

———. *Discourses on Religion, Science, and Education*. South Union, Ky.: 1884.

———. *Shaker Sermons: Scripto-rational. Containing the Substance of Shaker Theology. Together with Replies and Criticisms Logically and Clearly Set Forth. . . .* Albany: Weed and Parsons, 1879.

Evans, Frederick William. *Celibacy, from the Shaker Standpoint*. New York: Davies & Kent, 1866.

———. *Confession of Sin*. [Mt. Lebanon, N.Y.: n.d.].

———. *God is God*. [Mt. Lebanon, N.Y.: 1892].

———. *Liberalism, Spiritualism and Shakerism*. [Mt. Lebanon, N.Y.: 1880?].

———. *Resurrection*. [Mt. Lebanon, N.Y.: 1890].

———. *Sabbath*. [Mt. Lebanon, N.Y.: 1886].

———. *Shaker Communism; Or Tests of Divine Inspiration. The Second Christian or Gentile Pentecostal Church, as Exemplified by Seventy Communities Of Shakers in America. . . .* London: James Burns, 1871.

———, et al. *Shakers: Compendium of the Origin, History, Principles, Rules and Regulations, Government, and Doctrines of the United Society of Believers in Christ's Second Appearing. With Biographies of Ann Lee, William Lee, Jas. Whittaker, J. Hocknell, J. Meacham, and Lucy Wright.* . . . New York: D. Appleton, 1859.

———. *A Short Treatise on the Second Appearing of Christ, in and through the Order of the Female.* Boston: Bazin & Chandler, 1853.

———. *Tests of Divine Inspiration; Or, The Rudimental Principles by which True and False Revelation, in all Eras of the World, can be Unerringly Determined.* . . . New Lebanon, N.Y.: United Society Called Shakers, 1853.

———. *Treatise on Shaker Theology.* [Mt. Lebanon, N.Y.: 186?].

[Fraser, Daniel]. *The Divine Afflatus: A Force in History.* Shirley, Mass.: United Society, 1875.

[———]. *Shaker Theology. Facts for Christendom.* [New Lebanon, N.Y.: Shakers, n.d.].

[Green, Calvin, and Seth Youngs Wells.] *A Summary View of the Millennial Church, or United Society of Believers (Commonly Called Shakers); Comprising the Rise, Progress, and Practical Order of the Society; Together with the General Principles of Their Faith and Testimony. Published by Order of the Ministry, in Union with the Church.* Albany: Packard and Van Benthuysen, 1823.

[———]. *A Brief Exposition of the Established Principled and Regulations of the United Society Called Shakers.* . . . Albany: Packard and Van Benthuysen, 1830.

Haskell, Della. "What Is Shakerism?" *Shaker Quarterly* 1 (Spring 1961): 21.

Hollister, Alonzo Giles. *Annunciation of the Way and Work of Christ's Manifestation and the New Day of His Visitation.* [Mt. Lebanon, N.Y.: n.d.].

———. *Christ the Harvester.* [Mt. Lebanon, N.Y.: 189?].

———. *The Coming of Christ.* [Mt. Lebanon, N.Y.: 189?]

———, comp. *Divine Judgment, Justice and Mercy. A Revelation of the Great White Throne.* . . . Mt. Lebanon, N.Y., 1895.

———. *Divine Motherhood.* [Mt. Lebanon, N.Y., 1887].

———. *Heaven Anointed Woman.* [Mt. Lebanon, N.Y., 1887].

———. *Interpreting Prophecy and the Appearance of Christ.* Chicago: Guiding Star Publishing House, 1892.

———. *Mission of Alethian Believers, Called Shakers.* . . . Mt. Lebanon, N.Y.: 189?.

———. *The Reapers. The Reapers Are the Messengers—Jesus.* [Mt. Lebanon, N.Y.: 1909.

———. *Shaker Testimony. The Gospel of Eternal (Aionion) Life, Proclaimed in the Season of Judgement.* [Mt. Lebanon, N.Y.: 1891].

——. *Shaker View of Marriage.* [Mt. Lebanon, N.Y.: 188?]

——. *Synopsis of Doctrine Taught by Believers in Christ's Second Appearing.* . . . Mt. Lebanon, N.Y., 1893.

——, and Calvin Green. *Pearly Gate of the True Life and Doctrine for Believers in Christ.* . . . [Part I] Mt. Lebanon, N.Y., 1894.

——. Part II. . . . Compiled by A. G. Hollister. Mt. Lebanon, N.Y., 1900.

——. Pearly Gate. [Part III] Compiled with Notes by A. G. Hollister. Mt. Lebanon, N.Y.: 1904.

Johnson, Theodore E. *Life in the Christ Spirit: Observations on Shaker Theology.* Sabbathday Lake, Maine: United Society of Shakers, 1969.

[——]. "Shakerism for Today." *Shaker Quarterly* 3 (Spring 1963): 3–6.

Leonard, William. *A Disclosure on the Order and Propriety of Divine Inspiration and Revelation, Showing the Necessity Thereof, in All Ages, to Know the Will of God. Also, a Discourse on the Second Appearing of Christ, in and through the Order of the Female. And a Discourse on the Propriety and Necessity of a United Inheritance in All Things, in Order to Support a True Christian Community.* . . . Harvard, Mass.: United Society, 1853.

——. *The Life and Suffering of Jesus Anointed, Our Holy Savior and of Our Blessed Mother Ann . . . In Two Parts. Written by Inspiration, William Leonard, in the Church at Harvard, Mass., October, 1841.* Prepared for publication with notes and appendix by A. G. Hollister. Mount Lebanon, N.Y.: 1904.

Lomas, George Albert. *The Life of Christ Is the End of the World.* Albany: C. Van Bethuysen and Sons, 1869.

——. *Plain Talks upon Practical Religion. Being Candid Answers to Earnest Inquirers.* . . . Albany: Van Benthuysen Printing House, 1873.

Mace, Fayette. *Familiar Dialogues on Shakerism; in which the Principles of the United Society are Illustrated and Defended.* . . . Portland, Maine: Charles Day, 1837.

McNemar, Richard. *A Concise Answer to the General Inquiry, Who, or What are the Shakers.* Union Village, Ohio: 1823.

Meacham, Joseph. *A Concise Statement of the Principles of the Only True Church according to the Gospel of the Present Appearance of Christ.* . . . Bennington, Vt.: Haskell & Russell, 1790.

Offord, Daniel. *Seven Travails of the Shaker Church.* Mt. Lebanon, N.Y.: [1889].

Stewart, Philemon. *A Holy, Sacred and Divine Roll and Book; From the Lord God of Heaven, to the Inhabitants of Earth: Revealed in the United Society at New Lebanon, County of Columbia, State of New York.* . . . Canterbury, N.H.: United Society, 1843.

Youngs, Benjamin Seth. "An Expedition against the Shakers." *Ohio Archaeological and Historical Society Publications* 21 (1912): 403–15.

——. *The Testimony of Christ's Second Appearing Containing a General Statement of All Things Pertaining to the Faith and Practice of the Church of God in This Latter-day.* . . . Lebanon. Ohio: Press of John M'Clean, Office of the Western Star, 1808.

CULTURE

Architecture, Art, and Music

Andrews, Edward Deming. *The Gift to Be Simple; Songs, Dances and Rituals of the American Shakers.* New York: JJ Augustin, 1940.

——, and Faith Andrews. *Visions of the Heavenly Sphere; A Study in Shaker Religious Art.* Charlottesville: University of Virginia Press, 1969.

Blinn, Henry Clay, comp. *A Collection of Hymns and Anthems, for Devotional Worship and Praise.* . . . Canterbury, N.H.: [United Society of Shakers], 1852.

——, comp. *A Collection of Hymns and Anthems Adapted to Public Worship.* East Canterbury, N.H.: Shakers, 1892.

Butler, Linda, and June Sprigg. *Inner Light: The Shaker Legacy.* New York: Alfred A. Knopf, 1985.

A Collection of Millennial Hymns, Adapted to the Present Order of the Church. Canterbury, N.H.: United Society, 1847.

Cook, Harold E. *Shaker Music; A Manifestation of American Folk Culture.* Lewisburg, Pa.: Bucknell University Press, 1973.

[Evans, Frederick William, comp]. *Shaker Music. Inspirational Hymns and Melodies.* Albany: Weed and Parsons, 1875.

Goodwillie, Christian. *Shaker Songs; A Celebration of Peace, Harmony, and Simplicity.* New York: Black Dog and Leventhal, 2002.

Grant, Jerry V. *Noble but Plain: The Meetinghouse at Mount Lebanon.* Old Chatham, N.Y.: Shaker Museum and Library, 1994.

Hall, Roger L. *"Come Life, Shaker Life"; The Life and Music of Elder Issachar Bates.* Stoughton, Mass.: Pinetree Press, 2004.

——. *A Guide to Shaker Music—with Music Supplement.* Stoughton, Mass.: Pinetree Press, 1996.

——, ed. *The Happy Journey; Thirty-five Shaker Spirituals Compiled by Miss Clara Endicott Sears.* Harvard, Mass.: Fruitlands Museums, 1982.

——, comp. *Love Is Little: A Sampling of Shaker Spirituals.* Holland, Mich.: World of Shaker, 1992.

——, comp. *The Story of 'Simple Gifts' Shaker Simplicity in Song.* Holland, Mich.: World of Shaker, 1987.

——, comp. *A Western Music Sampler*. Cleveland, Ohio: Western Reserve Historical Society, 1976.

Haskell, Russell, comp. *A Musical Expositor: Or, A Treatise on the Rules and Elements of Music; Adapted to the Most Approved Method of Musical Writing*. New York: George W. Wood, 1847.

Koomler, Sharon Duane. *Seen and Received: The Shakers' Private Art*. Pittsfield, Mass.: Hancock Shaker Village, 2000.

Lassiter, William Lawrence. *Shaker Architecture*. New York: Bonanza Books, 1966.

[McNemar, Richard]. *A Selection of Hymns and Poems; for the Use of Believers. Collected from Sundry Authors, by Philos Harmonae* [pseudo.]. . . . Watetvliet [*sic*], Ohio: 1833.

Mahoney, Kathleen, and Lilo Raymond. *Simple Wisdom: Shaker Sayings, Poems, and Songs*. New York: Viking Studio Books, 1993.

Nicoletta, Julie, and Bret Morgan. *The Architecture of the Shakers*. Woodstock, Vt.: Countryman Press, 1995.

North Family, Mt. Lebanon, NY. *Shaker Music, Original Inspirational Hymns and Songs*. New York: William A. Pond, 1884.

——. *Original Shaker Music*. New York: William A. Pond, 1893.

Patterson, Daniel W. *Gift Drawing and Gift Song: A Study of Two Forms of Shaker Inspiration*. Sabbathday Lake, Maine: United Society of Shakers, 1983.

——. *Nine Shaker Spirituals with a Brief Account of Early Shaker Song*. Old Chatham, N.Y.: Shaker Museum Foundation, 1964.

——. *The Shaker Spiritual*. Princeton: Princeton University Press, 1979.

Phillips, Hazel Spencer. *Shaker Architecture Warren County, Ohio*. Oxford, Ohio: Typo Print, 1971.

Receiving the Faith: The Shakers of Canterbury, New Hampshire. Stamford, Conn.: Whitney Museum of Art at Campion, 1993.

The Round Stone Barn. Pittsfield, Mass.: Shaker Community, 1968.

Schiffer, Herbert, comp. *Shaker Architecture*. West Chester, Pa.: Schiffer Publishing, 1979.

Schorsch, David A. *The Photographs of William F. Winter, Jr 1899–1939*. New York: David A. Schorsch, 1989.

Shaker Built; A Catalog of Shaker Architectural Records from the Historic American Buildings Survey. US Department of the Interior: National Park Service, 1974.

Shaker Hymnal. East Canterbury, N.H.: Canterbury Shakers, 1908.

A Shaker Sister's Drawings; Wild Plant Illustrated by Cora Helena Sarle. New York: Monacelli Press, 1997.

"Shaker Spirituality and Photographic Documentation." *New Mexico Studies in the Fine Arts* 11 (1987).

Skolnick, Solomon M. *Simple Gifts: The Shaker Song.* New York: Hyperion, 1992.

Sturm, Ann Black, comp. *The Gift of Shaker Song.* Frankfort, Ky.: Stivers Offset Printing, 1981.

Swank, Scott T. *Shaker Life, Art, and Architecture: Hands to Work and Hearts to God.* New York: Abbeville Press, 1999.

Thomason, Jean Healon. *Shaker Manuscript Hymnals from South Union, Kentucky.* Bowling Green, Ky: Kentucky Folklore Society, 1967.

Wells, Seth Youngs, comp. *Millennial Praises, Containing a Collection of Gospel Hymns, in Four Parts; Adapted to the Day of Christ's Second Appearing. Composed for the Use of His People.* Hancock, Mass.: Josiah Talcott, Jr., 1812.

Williams, Stephen Guion. *Chosen Land: The Sabbathday Lake Shakers.* Boston: David R. Godine, 1975.

———. *A Place in Time: The Shakers at Sabbathday Lake, Maine.* Boston: David R. Godine, 2006.

Youngs, Isaac Newton. *A Short Abridgement of the Rules of Music. With Lessons for Exercise, and a Few Observations; for Beginners.* New Lebanon, N.Y., 1843.

Industries and Crafts

Andrews, Edward Deming. *The Community Industries of the Shakers.* Albany: University of the State of New York, 1932.

———, and Faith Andrews. *Shaker Furniture: The Craftsmanship of an American Communal Sect.* Unabridged Republication. New York: Dover Publications, 1950.

Becksvoort, Christian. *The Shaker Legacy: Perspectives on an Enduring Furniture Style.* Newtown, Conn.: Taunton Press, 1998.

Budis, Erin M. *Making His Mark: The Work of Shaker Craftsman Orren Haskins.* Old Chatham, N.Y.: Shaker Museum and Library, 1997.

Close Ties: The Relationship Between Kentucky Shaker Furniture Makers and Their Worldly Contemporaries. South Union, Ky.: Shaker Museum at South Union, 1994.

Community Industries of the Shakers: A New Look: A Catalog of Highlights of an Exhibition at the New York State Museum, 1983–84. Albany: Shaker Heritage Society at Watervliet, 1983.

Flint, Charles L., and Paul Rocheleau. *Mount Lebanon Shaker Collection.* New Lebanon, N.Y.: Mount Lebanon Shaker Village, 1987.

Gibbs, James W., and Robert W. Meader. *Shaker Clock Makers.* Columbia, Pa.: National Association of Watch and Clock Collectors, Inc. [n.d.].

Goodwillie, Christian, and M. Stephen Miller. *Handled with Care: The Function of Form in Shaker Craft*. Pittsfield, Mass.: Hancock Shaker Village, 2006.

Gordon, Beverly. *Shaker Textile Arts*. Hanover, N.H.: University Press of New England, 1980.

In Time & Eternity: Maine Shakers in the Industrial Age 1872–1918. Sabbathday Lake, Maine: United Society of Shakers, 1986.

Jeffrey, Jonathan, and Donna Parker. *A Thread of Evidence: Shaker Textile Industries at South Union, Kentucky*. South Union, Ky.: Shaker Museum at South Union, 1996.

Johnson, Brother Theodore E. *In the Eye of Eternity: Shaker Life and the Work of Shaker Hands*. Gorham, Maine: United Society of Shakers and University of Southern Maine, 1983.

———. *Ingenious & Useful: Shaker Sisters' Communal Industries, 1860–1960*. Sabbathday Lake, Maine: United Society of Shakers, 1986.

Kassay, John. *The Book of Shaker Furniture*. Amherst: University of Massachusetts Press, 1980.

Keig, Susan Jackson. *Trade with the World's People: A Shaker Album*. Hamilton, Ohio: Beckett Paper, 1976.

Kennedy, Gerrie, Galen Beale, and Jim Johnson. *A Field Guide*. Vol. 3, *Shaker Baskets and Poplarware*. Stockbridge, Mass.: Berkshire House, 1992.

Ketchum, Jr., William C. *Simple Beauty: The Shakers in America*. New York: Smithmark Publishers, 1996.

Kindred Spirits: The Eloquence of Function in American Shaker and Japanese Arts of Daily Life. La Jolla, Calif.: Mingei International, 1995.

Koomler, Sharon Duane. *Shaker Style: Form, Function, and Furniture*. London: Courage Books, 2000.

McGuire, John. *Basketry: The Shaker Tradition*. Asheville, N.C.: Lark Books, 1988.

Meader, Robert F. W. *Illustrated Guide to Shaker Furniture*. New York: Dover Publications, 1972.

Milbern, Gwendolyn. *Shaker Clothing*. Lebanon, Ohio: Warren County Historical Society, [n.d.].

Miller, M. Stephen. *A Century of Shaker Ephemera: Marketing Community Industries 1830–1930*. New Britain, Conn.: Dr. M. Stephen Miller, 1988.

———. *From Shaker Lands and Shaker Hands: A Survey of the Industries*. Lebanon, N.H.: University Press of New England, 2007.

Muller, Charles R. *The Shaker Way*. Worthington, Ohio: Ohio Antique Review, 1979.

———, and Timothy D. Rieman. *The Shaker Chair*. Winchester, Ohio: Canal Press, 1984.

Pierce, Kerry. *Pleasant Hill Shaker Furniture.* Cincinnati: Popular Woodworking Books, 2007.

Rieman, Timothy D, and Jean M. Burks. *The Complete Book of Shaker Furniture.* New York: Harry N. Abrams, 1993.

——. *The Encylclopedia of Shaker Furniture.* Atglen, Pa.: Schiffer Publishing, 2003.

——. *The Shaker Furniture Handbook.* Atglen, Pa.: Schiffer Publishing, 2004.

Rose, Milton C., and Emily Mason Rose, eds. *A Shaker Reader.* New York: Universe Books, [1977].

A Sense of Place: Kentucky Shaker Furniture and Regional Influence. South Union, Ky.: Shaker Museum at South Union, 1996.

Serrette, David. *Shaker Smalls.* Sebasco, Maine: Cardigan Press, 1983.

Shaker Design: Hancock Shaker Village Collection. [Tokyo]: Sezon Museum of Art/Hancock Shaker Village, 1992.

Shaker Renderings of Textiles and Costumes from the Index of American Design. Washington, D.C.: Smithsonian Institution Press, 1973.

Shea, John G. *The American Shakers and Their Furniture.* New York: Van Nostrand Reinhold, 1971.

Somer, Margaret Van Alen Frisbee. The Shaker Garden Seed Industry. [Old Chatham, N.Y.:] Shaker Museum Foundation, 1972.

Sprigg, June. *Shaker Design.* New York: Whitney Museum of Art, 1986.

——. and Jim Johnson. *A Field Guide,* Vol. 1, *Shaker Woodenware.* Great Barrington, Mass.: Berkshire House, 1991.

——. *A Field Guide,* Vol. 2, *Shaker Woodenware.* Stockbridge, Mass.: Berkshire House, 1992.

——, *Shaker Original Paints and Patinas.* Allentown, Pa.: Muhlenberg College Center for the Arts, 1987.

——, and David Larkin. *Shaker: Life, Work, and Art.* New York: Stewart, Tabori & Chang, 1987.

Wetherbee, Martha, and Nathan Taylor. *Shaker Baskets.* Sanbornton, N.H.: Martha Wetherbee Basket Shop, 1988.

Williams, John S. *Consecrated Ingenuity: The Shakers and Their Inventions.* Old Chatham, N.Y: Shaker Museum Foundation, 1957.

Culinary

Andrews, Edward Deming, and Faith Andrews. *Shaker Herbs and Herbalists.* Stockbridge, Mass.: Berkshire Garden Center, 1959.

Beale, Galen, and Mary Rose Boswell. *The Earth Shall Blossom: Shaker Herbs and Gardening.* Woodstock, Vt.: Countryman Press, 1991.

Carr, Sister Frances A. *Shaker Your Plate: Of Shaker Cooks and Cooking.* Sabbathday Lake, Maine: United Society of Shakers, 1985.

Haller, James, and Jeffrey Paige. *Cooking in the Shaker Spirit.* Camden, Maine: Yankee Books, 1990.

The Harvard Cook Book. Harvard, Mass.: First Congregational Unitarian Church, 1979.

Lassiter, William Lawrence. *Shaker Recipes for Cooks and Homemakers.* New York: Greenwich Book Publishers, 1959.

Lindsay, Eldress Bertha. *Seasoned with Grace: My Generation of Shaker Cooking.* Edited by Mary Rose Boswell. Woodstock, Vt.: Countryman Press, 1987.

Miller, Amy Bess. *Shaker Herbs: A History and Compendium.* New York: Clarkson N. Potter, 1976.

———. *Shaker Medicinal Herbs: A Compendium of History, Lore, and Uses.* Pownal, Vt.: Storey Books, 1998.

———, and Persis Fuller. *The Best of Shaker Cooking: Revised and Expanded.* New York: Macmillan, 1985.

Paige, Jeffrey S. *The Shaker Kitchen: Over 100 Recipes from Canterbury Shaker Village.* New York: Clarkson/Potter Publishers, 1994.

Tolve, Arthur, and James Bissland III. *Sister Jennie's Shaker Desserts.* Bowling Green, Ohio: Gabriel's Horn Publishing, 1983.

Two Hundred Years of Lebanon Valley Cookery. Lebanon Springs, N.Y.: Ladies' Guild Church of Our Savior, 1966.

WEBSITES

"A place online to find things Shaker": www. Shakertown.net.

Canterbury Shaker Village, Canterbury, New Hampshire: www.shakers.org.

Edward Deming Andrews Memorial Shaker Collection, Winterthur Museum and Library, Winterthur, Delaware: www.winterthur.org.

Enfield Shaker Village, Enfield, New Hampshire: www.shakermuseum.org

Filson Historical Society, Louisville, Kentucky: www.filsonhistorical.org.

Fruitlands Museums, Harvard, Massachusetts, 978–456–3924: www.fruitlands .org. Index of names: www.fruitlands.org/collections/shaker/jSearch.php.

Hamilton College Library (for nonrestricted access to the digitized entire 29 year run of *The Shaker Manifesto, 1871–1899*): http://library.hamilton.edu/ collections/.

Hancock Shaker Village, Pittsfield, Massachusetts: www.hancockshakervillage .org Index of names: www.hancock-shakervillage.org/learn/census_ database.asp.

Library of Congress, Washington, D.C.: www.loc.gov/index.html.

New York Public Library, New York, New York: www.nypl.org.

Ohio Historical Society, Columbus, Ohio: www.ohiohistory.org.

Shaker Heritage Society, Colonie, New York: www.shakerheritage.org.

Shaker Historical Society, 16740 South Park Blvd., Shaker Heights, Ohio 44120, 216-921-1201: shakhist@bright.net.

Shaker Museum and Library, Old Chatham, New York: www.shakermuseum andlibrary.org.

Shaker Village of Pleasant Hill, Harrodsburg, Kentucky: www.shakervillageky .org.

Shaker Workshops: www.shakerworkshops.com.

United Society of Shakers, New Gloucester, Maine: www.maineshakers.com.

Warren County Historical Society, Lebanon, Ohio: wchs@go-concepts.com; www.co.warren.oh.us/genealogy/Research.htm.

Western Kentucky University Libraries, Bowling Green, Ky.: www.wku.edu.

Western Reserve Historical Society, 10825 East Blvd., Cleveland, Ohio 44106, (216) 721-5722: www.wrhs.org (all communities—largest collection of Shaker manuscripts—index nominum has 15,000 names. Collection on 123 reels of microfilm.)

Williams College Libraries, Williamstown, Massachusetts: www.library .williams.edu.

MUSEUMS AND LIBRARIES

Although a number of important items are in private hands, the vast majority of Shaker manuscripts are readily available for research. When visiting Shaker libraries, it is always best to call ahead for an appointment. The Western Reserve Historical Society in Cleveland has the largest collection of Shaker manuscripts. All of it has been microfilmed and is available at many university libraries and all major Shaker libraries. The Library of Congress, the New York Public Library, New York State Museum and Library, the University of Kentucky, and Fruitlands Museums have also microfilmed their Shaker collections. In addition, the Mount Lebanon material at Old Chatham has been microfilmed.

For anyone with a deep interest in the Shakers, a visit to the Shakers themselves is the ultimate way to gain information. The Sabbathday Lake Shakers operate a museum that is open from Memorial Day through Columbus Day.

Guided tours conducted generally by non-Shakers take groups through some of the buildings and property. The dwelling house and other places where the Shakers live and work are private and not part of the tour. To meet the Shakers it is best to call ahead or email the office. The former schoolhouse now houses a modern library with a tremendous collection. As expected, the holdings for the Maine communities are excellent, but material from other Shaker societies is also very strong. The library, moreover, has all of the microfilms that have been made from other Shaker collections.

Canterbury Shaker Village runs guided tours as well, but since Shakers no longer live there, many more buildings are accessible. The site is quite striking in its beauty and there is a nice restaurant. There is also a library, but it has restricted hours. Hancock Shaker Village is larger than Canterbury and visitors can explore the grounds on their own. Guided tours are available at set times throughout the day, but it is not necessary to go on them. What make Hancock quite interesting are its round stone barn and many activities connected to the Shaker farm. In addition, Hancock has a large library that has been fully cataloged. Not far from Hancock is the Shaker Museum and Library in Old Chatham, New York. This place never was a Shaker village, but it has the largest collection of Shaker objects. The library is also one of the very best, with many manuscripts from every community and a number of one-of-a-kind items. The Shaker Museum and library is planning to move to the former North Family site at Mount Lebanon.

At Winterthur in Delaware, the Joseph Downs Collection of Manuscripts and Printed Ephemera contains the Edward Deming Andrews Memorial Shaker Collection. These holdings are extremely strong on Mount Lebanon and Watervliet, New York, as well as on Hancock and Harvard, Massachusetts.

Of all the former Shaker places, Pleasant Hill is the only one that offers excellent accommodations in Shaker buildings and has a fine restaurant. There are self-guided tours through the many exceptionally beautiful buildings where docents are available. Visitors may also go to nearby Shaker landing and take a ride on a small steamboat named the "Dixie Belle" through the palisades of the Kentucky River. The Shakers used this landing to send goods to market.

The best website for those interested in seeing a living community is the one maintained by the Shakers: www.maineshakers.com. Every aspect of Shaker life today is covered, including information on Shaker theology. The power point presentation provides pictures of the Shakers as they go about their activities. The site sponsored by Shaker Workshops (www.shakerworkshops .com) is one of the strongest overall. Some of its many features include: a basic Shaker reading list with links to Amazon.com, a directory of Shaker collections, museums, and libraries, and a connection to a link that has Shaker manuscripts online. Another strong website is www.Shakertown.net, which styles itself as "A place online to find things Shaker." There are many other websites, but the most noteworthy are those maintained by Shaker museums. Canterbury Shaker Village (www.shakers.org), Hancock Shaker Village (www.hancock shakervillage.org), and Pleasant Hill (www.shakervillageky.org) are among the best of these. Fruitlands Museums (www.fruitlands.org) offers online access to its Shaker journals. Finally, Hamilton College, which has a good collection of Shaker manuscripts, has also digitized the complete run of the *Shaker Manifesto*. There is no restriction on access to this website: http//library.hamilton.edu/collections/.

Canterbury Shaker Village, 288 Shaker Road, Canterbury, New Hampshire 03224, 603-783-9511; info@shakers.org; www.shakers.org (library: Canterbury and Enfield, N.H.; Mount Lebanon, N.Y., and the Florida Shakers)

Edward Deming Andrews Memorial Shaker Collection, Winterthur Museum and Library, Winterthur, Delaware 19735, 800-448-3883; www.winterthur.org (library: Watervliet and Mount Lebanon, N.Y., and Harvard and Hancock, Mass.)

Enfield Shaker Village, 447 N.H. Route 4A, Enfield, New Hampshire 03748, 603-632-4346; Chosen.Vale@ShakerMuseum.org; www.shakermuseum.org

Filson Historical Society, 1310 South Third Street, Louisville, Kentucky 40208, 502-635-5083; www.filsonhistorical.org (library: Pleasant Hill, Ky.)

Fruitlands Museums, 102 Prospect Hill Road, Harvard, Massachusetts, 978-456-3924; www.fruitlands.org (library: Harvard and Shirley, Mass. Collection on 21 reels of microfilm) Index of names: www.fruitlands.org/collections/shaker/jSearch.php

Hamilton College Library (for non-restricted access to the digitized entire 29-year run of *The Shaker Manifesto, 1871–1899*), http://library.hamilton.edu/collections/

Hancock Shaker Village, PO Box 927, Pittsfield, Massachusetts 01202, 800-817-1137; info@hancockshakervillage.org; www.hancockshakervillage.org (library: Hancock, Mass., and Mount Lebanon, N.Y.) Index of names: www.hancock-shakervillage.org/learn/census_database.asp

Library of Congress 101 Independence Avenue, SE, Washington, D.C. 20540, 202-707-8000; www.loc.gov/index.html (Library: Union Village, Ohio; Enfield, Conn.; New Lebanon (including Canaan), N.Y.; Pleasant Hill and South Union, Ky. Collection on 32 reels of microfilm)

New York Public Library, Fifth Avenue at 42nd Street, New York, New York 10018-2788, 212-930-0830; www.nypl.org (library: ministerial journals, Mount Lebanon and Watervliet, N.Y. Collection on 9 reels of microfilm)

New York State Museum and Library, Cultural Education Center, Empire State Plaza, Albany, New York 12230, 518-474-5877. (Mount Lebanon, Watervliet, and Groveland, N.Y. Collection on 11 reels of microfilm)

Ohio Historical Society, 1982 Velma Avenue, Columbus, Ohio 43211; 614-297-2300; www.ohiohistory.org (Library: Watervliet, White Water, Union Village and North Union)

Shaker Heritage Society, 875 Watervliet Shaker Road, Suite 2, Colonie, New York 12211, 518-7890; www.shakerheritage.org

Shaker Historical Society, 16740 South Park Blvd, Shaker Heights, Ohio 44120, 216-921-1201; shakhist@bright.net

Shaker Museum and Library, 88 Shaker Museum Road, Old Chatham, New York 12136, 518-794-9100; www.shakermuseumandlibrary.org (all communities but especially Mount Lebanon, N.Y. Mount Lebanon material on microfilm)

Shaker Museum at South Union, PO Box 177, Auburn, Kentucky 42206, 270-542-4167; shakmus@logantele.com

Shaker Village of Pleasant Hill, 3501 Lexington Road, Harrodsburg, Kentucky 40330, 800-734-5611; www.shakervillageky.org

Shaker Workshops' excellent overall website: www.shakerworkshops.com

United Society of Shakers, 707 Shaker Road, New Gloucester, Maine 04260, 207-926-4597; office: www.maineshakers.com; library only: brooksl@shaker.lib.me.us (library: Sabbathday Lake and Alfred, Maine; material on other communities as well; an index nominum and all the microfilms from other Shaker libraries)

University of Kentucky, Margaret I. King Library, Lexington, Ky. 40506, 606-257-3801 (library: Pleasant Hill, Ky. Collection on 5 reels of microfilm)

Warren County Historical Society, 105 South Broadway, Lebanon, Ohio 45036, 513-932-1817; wchs@go-concepts.com; www.co.warren.oh.us/genealogy/Research.htm

Western Kentucky University Libraries, Kentucky Library, Bowling Green, Ky. 42101, 502-745-6258; www.wku.edu (Library: South Union, Ky.)

Western Reserve Historical Society, 10825 East Blvd., Cleveland, Ohio 44106, 216-721-5722; www.wrhs.org; (all communities—largest collection of Shaker manuscripts—index nominum has 15,000 names; collection on 123 reels of microfilm)

Williams College Libraries, 55 Sawyer Library Drive, Williamstown, Massachusetts 01267, 413-597-2501; library.williams.edu (library: Mount Lebanon, N.Y.; Hancock, Mass., and other communities)

About the Author

Stephen J. Paterwic was born in Springfield, Massachusetts, in 1952. After graduating from Iona College (New York) with a B.A. in 1974, he taught in Manhattan and the Bronx while attending New York University, where he earned an M.A. in 1978. He taught briefly in Rhode Island before returning to western Massachusetts in 1983. For 19 years he taught in the Springfield public schools, first at the High School of Commerce and then at the High School of Science and Technology, where he served as chair of the mathematics department. He presently teaches eighth-grade mathematics at West Springfield Middle School. In addition, he reviews mathematics texts for the Great Source division of Houghton-Mifflin Company.

A frequent presenter at Shaker seminars and forums, he is the author of numerous articles on the Shakers. These have appeared in *The Shaker Quarterly, World of Shaker, Shakers World, Communal Societies, The Historical Journal of Massachusetts*, and *New England Ancestors*. He was the keynote speaker at the Annual Communal Studies Association Conference in September 2004 and the Centennial Celebration of the 1905 Mount Lebanon Peace Convention in August of 2005. He currently serves as an overseer of Hancock Shaker Village in Massachusetts and a corporator and trustee of Sabbathday Lake Shaker Village in Maine. The Shakers of Sabbathday Lake have been his lifelong friends and provide inspiration for his spiritual life.